OVERPOPULATED PHILIPPINES

Armando Ang
Copyright 2009 ©

Written and published by Armando Ang © 2009

Anyone interested in the subject matter is free to quote from the book without permission of the author. However, the author request that due credit be given to the author cited in the book.

Printed in the Philippines by

SCR

ISBN No. 971-92688-83

Other books by the same author

Saving the Trees

Saving the Animals

The Dark Side of Catholicism

Tips and Traps When Buying or Building a Home

The Plain Truth About the Unorthodox Protestants

Sonnets from the Bible

Greed & Scams, Inc

The Brutal Holocaust

Child Abuse

Deforestation

The Evil of Gambling

Table of Contents

Dedication and Acknowledgements

I would like to dedicate this book to all the parents and all the mothers-to-be that they may be enlightened to what the future holds for their progeny. We live in a cutthroat society and I hope they are well-prepared for the future for themselves and for their forthcoming children. If worse comes to worst, relatives, friends, and neighbors may not be as reliable as we expected them to be. It is better to rely on oneself and bring up a small family with healthy children and good education than having many children living pathetic lives with little hope of every one of them finishing with a good education.

Armando Ang

This book would not have been possible without the contribution of many authors and researchers with their published works. I want to particularly give thanks to the contributors to Wikipedia, the free encyclopedia and its mother company, Wikipedia Foundation, Inc. for their in depth and updated research on many topics that I find very valuable for this book. More power to them.

I would also like to acknowledge the contributions of *The Philippine Star* and the *Philippine Daily Inquirer* for their daily news regarding the population problems and their collateral articles on the environment and other events. Particular thanks is also due to *Balatbat* newsmagazine that allow me freely to print some of the articles found in their magazine.

My special gratitude goes to the many nameless authors I failed to mention due to lapses on my part who made their articles available on the internet. Without their articles this book would not have been as interesting to read.

PREFACE

The Philippines is under assault, not from outside source but from within. Many are aware of the problem but can do little about it. Even if they wanted to do something about it, it is aggravated but those who do not think it is a problem. The assault is coming from our runaway population explosion. There is more than just the vast number of people in the issue of overpopulation. Many pro-lifers in the country do not seems to grasp the issue of overpopulation in relation to factors such as the quality of life, nutritious food, education, pollution, deforestation population density, traffic problem, crimes, unemployment and poverty, health, etc. Most of them are blind to the suffering of the poor who takes the blunt of the problem because they probably never experienced their kind of hardship and quality of life.

Increasing population naturally entails the need for more of almost everything just to maintain our lifestyle albeit in many low quality for most of the people surviving now. We need more classrooms and teachers for the children and we cannot seem to lick both problems after all these decades because of the exploding population growth. In a stabilized population, there will no longer be need for new classrooms and funds could be channel to improving the education system and getting more children to finish higher education.

. The basic services such as water supply and health services have been inadequate and will continue to plague us in the coming decades. There is not enough clean water to supply even all the inhabitants of the metropolis. Many have to pump up their water need from deep wells that are often contaminated while causing the sinking of the land above in many areas. Public health clinics and hospitals are often crowded with patients and many are dying for lack of medicines. The shelves in the supermarket may be full, but most of the poor do not have the money to buy their basic needs. According to one latest survey, nine millions people are surviving below $1 a day. Even more numbers are surviving below $2 a day. Not only that, they are not getting adequately the basic food necessities, such as protein that would allow them to compete in this world. Protein is essential for children if they want to develop their brains and improve their IQ.

Are we going to continue to export our workers like slaves to other countries? Many of our countrymen are working abroad to earn a decent life for their family back home. Most of these jobs are unwanted by the locals. Some of them could be demeaning and often hard works. There is a serious unemployment and underemployment problems in the country, forcing them to look for jobs elsewhere. There is a need to balance the available jobs against the number of young people joining the workforce every year. Too many people out of work could mean more crimes as they tried to feed themselves and their families. The excessive labor force allows employers to mistreat employees on a hire-fire-hire basis. Many workers have been hired on a contractual work even for simple jobs. The female workers are particularly at a disadvantage. Some have been forced to work on a commission basis selling cigarettes and candies whose commissions do not add up to half the basic salary mandated by law while others are not even given any commission unless they reach a certain quota. This wanton practice is possible only because there are too many unemployed workers in a finite labor market. In fact many of them are willing to work for pittance just to fill their stomachs and that of their loved ones.

Pollution is a problem here to stay. From cradle to grave, we are all polluters of the environment. We need to produce more of the necessities of life to sustain the new generations. Each manufacturing process from food production to manufacturing goods for a better life entails some form of pollutions. More people mean more vehicles, the number one air polluter, to transport the vast number of people from one place to another. There is a need to improve our traffic with more roads except that there is no room for improvement.

We need more landfills to keep our garbage away from sight and they are filling up quicker with more people. We have also become a throwaway society with so many mouths to feed. Soon we will be hauling our garbage to faraway places as most of the nearby garbage dumps are being filled to the brim and at great costs to the needed oil and more air pollution. At garbage dump itself is a source of pollution for groundwater where it sits and a health menace to those who live near it. Toxic fumes are often spew out of the garbage to the detriment of the poor who setup shanties around to the dump to scavenge the garbage for their livelihood.

Overcrowded atmosphere is inevitable with overpopulation. It could only mean more unnecessary contacts and queuing that often lead to antisocial reactions whether in the traffic situation or even in dealing with government offices. More people are getting displaced or harmed whenever disasters struck. A fire in a squatter area could easily displace hundreds of families. The freak accident at the Ultra in Pasig just goes to show how desperate some people are that they are willing to join the crowd in pursuit of a dream house and wealth.

Poverty continues to plague the poor even with a growing economic environment. The poor, where most of the population growths are coming from has to control the growth from their ranks if they are to lick the vicious cycle of poverty. There is a need for breathing space by slowing down their population growth. In trying to uplift the poor, the country is now heavily indebted to the international financial institutions as more funds are being channel to help them. Even while we are indebted, one of the highest taxes imposed on the citizenry cannot seem to put a dent on the budget as the annual shortfall continue to push up the debt. In trying to pay off the huge debt, we have raped our natural resources of forested areas and are now ripping off the earth underneath to mine the gold and other minerals with their deadly pollutions.

Even without the population problem we are already suffering from poverty problems in the past. There is a need to drastically slow down the birth rate, which is almost an impossible task because of the phenomenon of population momentum. It will take decades for the population to stabilize unless some disasters struck to kill off a huge population. The Malthusian catastrophe will come into play in some future date unless we curb our population growth to manageable level. The tsunami of December 27, 2004 in the Indian Ocean that took the lives of about 200,000 people is a strong reminder what nature can do to people in overcrowded situations. All those who died were living in coastal areas as they are swept to the sea or killed outright by drowning.

Last but not least is the issue of the role of the Catholic Church. While the issue on the use of contraceptives by Catholics in developing countries is not an issue, it is a big issue in this country because we have many conservative Catholics remaining faithful to the teaching of the Church on morals and faith. The Church's stand against the use of contraceptive is a doctrine that has no biblical basis. However, through the years, it has become an infallible issue so much so that Pope John Paul I was allegedly murdered when he tried to reverse the Church's teaching against the use of contraceptive. The main reason against the use contraceptive is the so-called "sin of Onan" when Onan refused to impregnate his brother's wife after his death by committing *coitus interruptus*. God had him killed not because of his failure but because of his disobedience to God's command. This is the stand of most of the exegetes who studied this issue. It was only after the Protestant churches came out with a stand allowing the use of contraceptives that the Church took a definitive stand against contraceptives. The Church just wanted to be different from the others without any medical or biblical basis. Most contraceptives per se do not induce abortion since no conception took place in the first place. Any conception is only accidental just as the natural family planning methods.

Two news items prompted me to write this book. The first one is that nine million Filipinos out of around 85 million lived on less than $1 a day. A new threshold has been set by the Asian Development Bank (ADB) setting the Asian Poverty Line at $1.35 a day. That puts 25.4 million Filipinos living below the new benchmark as being poor. (*PS*, August 29, 2008) The new benchmark is a more realistic figure, taking into account inflation, while the $1 has been in use for decades. The other news item is about an eight-year-old girl who committed suicide in a desperate move to end her poverty and that of her family. Underlying the problem of poverty and other problems is that fact that we are an overpopulated country with little room for improvement in the near future. For the sake of millions of unborn children, we need to improve the individual standard of living that will rebound to the improvement of our economy and vice versa.

This book is also an offshoot of the endless debates going on regarding the Reproductive Health Bill. There have been many issues taken up by both sides of the pro-life and pro-choice that I want to put the issue in their proper perspective. The issue should be put to rest once and for all if we are going to move forward and progress rapidly for the benefit of the nation and not for the benefit of a few who think they have the solution to ills of the nation.

The following is a letter I wrote to one columnist in answer to his stand that there is no overpopulating problem in this country. Everyone entitled to his/her opinion and this is my opinion.

I beg to disagree with your assessment that we are not overpopulated. There are many factors that should be considered in taking into account whether a country is overpopulated or not. The standard of living is one good indicator. We may have the resources to feed the population which is doubtful, because not everyone can afford to have a decent meal even if we spread the wealth of the nation equally. Even if there is no corruption, the government does not have the resources to improve the standard of living unless the population explosion is controlled and given a breathing space to solve the perennial problem already in existence and associated with overpopulation.

Our public school students never have enough classrooms to give them a decent education. There are never enough teachers to give them quality education if we go by the reported failure of students to pass the entrance examination to college. Even then, only a small minority ever have the mental capacity to finish a college decree.

The most important natural resources a country ever own are the forest trees. We have practically run out of forest because of greed a few loggers and there is no oil to compensate for this loss. At the rate the forestlands are being converted to commercial and residential use, there may not be enough arable land to sustain our present agricultural needs. Mining may give some relief, but sooner than later that finite resources will run out too.

There is no enough room to accommodate everyone with a decent home. There are so many squatter in all the cities around the country. With most of the workers paid on a daily wage, just enough to hold the body and soul together, the chances of owning a home is a very remote possibility. Only the middle and upper class men can afford to purchase a unit in the high rise buildings.

It used to be that in the 1960s the water reservoir can sustain us even if there is no rain for a year. But today, if the rain does not arrive regularly after six months of drought, we are in big trouble. More reservoirs are needed but we do not have resources to build new impoundments.

We often blamed the local capitalists and foreign investors for the poverty in the country. Yet without them, our situation would even be worse. Most of our compatriots are greedy and we should not expect them to share their wealth. The poor should strive to improve their standard of living by limiting the number of children so as to give the children better food and education so as to compete with others in this world.

As for morality, I do not think it is immoral to try to limit the size of the family. On the other hand, it is the highest form of immorality to bring more children to this world if we cannot give them decent standard of living. Children should not be brought into this world if they are only going to suffer malnutrition, illiterate, more health, envious, or worse lead a life of crime because there is few opportunity to improve their lot.

Experiences have shown that most of the industrialized countries have small or practical zero population growth. In fact, some of them have a "graying" population. We are a long way from this stage because our population momentum is still racing very fast. Demographers are telling us that we have a very young population with more than half below teenage years. We need to put an end to the population momentum to improve the standard of living of a smaller family. By then, most families will opt for a smaller family.

Maxims on Greed and Poverty

Earth provides enough to satisfy every man's need, but not every man's greed...Poverty is the worst form of violence. ~ Mohandas K. 'Mahatma' Gandhi ~

Experience declares that man is the only animal which devours his own kind, for I can think of no milder term to apply to the general prey of the rich on the poor. ~ Thomas Jefferson ~

Much of man's sorrow and suffering stems for his greed for material wealth. His greed does not allow him peace of mind unless the greed is satisfied. Yet, there can be no satisfaction without a change of heart.

When it boils down to love of money, Christians are just as greedy as non-Christians. They are glib with their tongues in getting others to part away their fortunes for their selfish ends.

Men are born with vices and virtues. Greed and the lust for money seem to stand out among them.

There is no fire like passion, there is no shark like hatred, there is no snare like folly, there is no torrent like greed. ~ Buddha ~

Blood is thicker than water, but the thickest of them all is money.

Most of the greediest people are operators of lotteries and other forms of gambling. They thrive on the greediness without any compassion or remorse.

Gambling is one of the greatest scams ever devised by greedy people and it is being copied by same greedy people out to make an easy buck. Gambling should not be operated by the government. If so, who is to protect the welfare of the people from government abuse?

Some of the greediest people on the planet are public servants who hide behind their public service jobs because it is there where public funds are easy for the taking.

Politicians who stole money meant for the education of the poor have one thing in the mind: they want the children to grow up poor so that they can be easily be manipulated come election time.

A greedy person can never be satisfied with what he had. He is always on the lookout for more wealth to accumulate.

Some of the upper classmen do not want the poor to be educated and rise above them. Who would be left to do their dirty jobs?

Greed can make people do things they would not normally do. It can lead people to steal and kill, to plan and execute people, all in the name of material wealth.

Poverty can be found everywhere, in rich as well as poor countries. Most of the problems in the country are caused by the greedy rich and filthy poor in our midst. The greedy rich accumulate their excess wealth while the poor tried their best not to be outdone.

According to George Bernard Shaw, the lack of money is the root of all evil, just as the love of money is the root of all evil, according to St. Paul. The world would be a better place if people are not too greedy to share with those who are less fortunate.

The earth does not have all the resources to satisfy every man's need, and the problem is being compounded by the greed of a few to the detriment of the many.
God's greatest commandment is thou shall have no other gods before me. Man's greatest commandment is thou shall have only gold before me.

Greedy people are always on the lookout for easy money and ways and means to take advantage of the weakness of others such as addiction to certain vices. They are never satisfied with what they have and always want more, making them miserable to the end.

"Avarice and Happiness never saw each other, how then should they become acquainted… Poverty wants some things, Luxury many things, Avarice all things." ~ Benjamin Franklin ~

There is no calamity greater than lavish desires. There is no greater guilt than discontentment. And there is no greater disaster than greed. ~ Lao Tzu ~

'Love' and 'hate' are two of the strongest verb in the English language. But none of them beats the word 'greed' that could turn hating a person into loving his money and vice versa.

Most of us are born with many virtues and a few vices. The vice of greediness seems to stay with most people forever.

The conflicts that are taking place in many parts of the world are due to the concentration of wealth in a few individuals to the detriment of the majority of the poor.

We do not need weapons of mass destruction to kill many people. The greediness of some wealthy people who refused to share their wealth is enough to kill many poor people suffering from illiteracy, unemployment, homelessness, and other ill health conditions.

The planet Earth cannot produce enough to make everyone live a comfortable life. If the wealth were to be distributed equally, we may all end ion poverty.

We must live more simply so that the poor may simply live. ~ F.E. Trainer ~

Chapter 1

OVERVIEW

Overpopulation is a condition where organisms such as the number of human beings living in a confine space and using its resources far exceed the carrying capacity of its environment needed for survival. It is not simply a function of the size or density of the population but include factors such as the available sustainable and non-sustainable resources that made life pleasant and worthwhile. A few examples will suffice to define overpopulation.

The basic needs for survival are clean air and water, safe food, clothing, shelter and health services. Without air, humans can only survive for a few minutes. Without water, humans can survive for only a few days. Without food, humans can survive for a few weeks or months. Without adequate shelter, humans cannot survive the harsh environment for long. Without clothing, we will be living back in the Stone Age. Without medical care for some of the diseases, most people would not survive to old age.

In any given environment, if there are 100 people and there is enough food for 90 there is an overpopulation problem. On the other, if there is enough food, drinking water, shelter to sustain 200 people indefinitely into the future, there is no overpopulation problem. When there are too many people polluting the air, too little water to sustain a decent life or too many people in need of decent homes, there is a serious overpopulation problem.

Another view of overpopulation is the disproportionate consumption of the earth's natural resources. Those who can afford to buy the nonrenewable natural resource products of other producers at the expense of future generations can be said to be overpopulated. Examples are the consumption habits of wealthy nations such as the U.S. with 5% of the world's population consuming 26% of the finite oil produced in the world can be said to be overpopulated.

Still another view is that of arid areas where food production is very limited can be said to be overpopulated when they cannot produced enough for its citizenry or where periodic droughts causing famine leading to starvation. Never mind if they have the resources to buy the needed supplies because of untoward events that are beyond their control. Civil war is one example where civilians have been uprooted and became refugees where they are unwanted. A country that is poor and in perennial disorder can be classified as overpopulated. Poverty has a way in fomenting civil wars. This is borne out statistically where the poorest one sixth of humanity endures four fifths of the world's civil war. Africa is a good example of many ongoing civil wars. In 1999, pone African in five lived in a country racked by civil or cross border war. Ninety percent of the casualties were civilians. Nineteen million Africans were forced to flee their homes. An estimated 20 million landmines lurked beneath African soils. (Guest, 54)

In the context of human societies, overpopulation occurs when the population density is so great as to actually cause impaired quality of life, serious environmental degradation, or long-term shortages of essential goods and services. This is the definition used by popular dictionaries such Merriam-Webster. Overpopulation is not merely an imbalance between the numbers of individuals compared to the resources needed for survival; it is also the quality of life that is experienced by those who inhabit a certain habitat, big or small.

The world is currently increasing at a rate of about 75 million people annually, down from more than annual 90 million a decade ago. It is expected to go even lower by the mid-century to around 34 million annually. This is mostly due to the lower birth rates in the West rather than in the developing countries. Almost all growth will take place in the less developed regions, where the current 5.3 billion people are expected to increase to 7.8 billion in 2050. In contrast, the population of the developed regions will remain mostly unchanged, at 1.2 billion. Some 51 countries such as Germany, Italy, Spain, Japan and most of the eastern European countries are expected to have lower population in 2050 than they at present. Their only remedy to keep the economy robust is accepting immigrants or temporary migrant workers from other countries. That is how some countries were able to prevent the decline of their population. This is no consolation for developing countries with high birth rates because of the limited migrant workers they need. Any financial crisis like the 2008 meltdown will result in their expulsion from the host countries.

There are several causes of overpopulation. It can result from an increase in births of children as is usually the case coupled with the decline in mortality rates due to medical advances, better nutrition and improved sanitation leading to longer life span in most countries. In the rural areas where mortality is high, the parents usually have more children in the hope that some will survive to adulthood and take care of them.

Lack of education often leads to unemployment thereby forcing many to stay at home with nothing better to do than procreate. In poor developing countries, the less educated women mostly stayed at home, bear and care for children. This would account for the high population growth in the least developed countries. Better access to education helps slow down population growth as more women put priority to their careers. A study made by the Ohio State University shows that children whose family sizes were larger did worse in school. It also found that family size increases, parents talk less to each child about school, have lower education expectations, save less for college and have fewer educational materials available.[1]

In mostly developed countries, the increase came mostly from increase in immigration. Most of these immigrants came from areas which are overpopulated in many senses. Many are aspiring to improve their living standard. Within the countries, migration from the rural areas to urban centers is the norm. The increasing number of people can result in overpopulation of cities leading to unsustainable use of basic services and resources.

In many arid areas, there is already overpopulation because there are few resources to sustain life. To be able to sustain life, almost everything have to be imported from distance places. The cost to the environment can be tremendous to supply all the needed basic necessities of life. Whole cities will have to be constructed.

Even renewable resources can have their limitation. Clean water, clean food, clean air, etc. needed to sustain life must be maintained indefinitely to keep the overpopulation problems from arising. Other resources needed to make the quality of life worthwhile must also be taken into consideration. These include basic services and needs such as medical care, employment, education, fuel, electricity, proper sewage treatment, waste management, transportation, recreation, etc. Negative impacts should also be considered such as crowdedness, pollutions of all sorts, squatter problem, garbage disposal, crimes, justice, etc. that could make life miserable.

Some countries have managed to temporarily increase their carrying capacity through advancement in technology such as increasing food production through genetic engineering, irrigation, converting forest or wilderness to agriculture, desert into productive pastures, increasing water supply and reservoir or through

---

[1] http://sixpak.org/vince/overpopulation.html

desalinization of sea water, use of nuclear power, wind power, tidal energy and solar energy to generate power and electricity for the homes or the automobiles. This carrying capacity must be designed to be sustainable and long-lasting to be viable as solution to overpopulation.

There are many books and articles dealing with the problem of overpopulation and their critics. As early as 1729, Jonathan Swift (1667-1745) wrote the satirical essay *A Modest Proposal* where he suggests one solution for both the problem of overpopulation and the growing numbers of undernourished people in Ireland is through cannibalism, particularly the raising of infants as food. He categorically blamed the Catholic Church for its stand on uncontrolled population growth.

Probably the most controversial and talked about book is *An Essay on the Principle of Population* published in 1798 by Thomas Malthus (1766-1834). He theorized that throughout history, societies had experienced at one time or another epidemics, famines, and wars to keep the populations in check.

It was Malthus who proposed his mathematical model the idea that population, if unchecked, increases at a geometric rate (i.e. 1, 2, 4, 8, 16, etc.), whereas the food-supply grows at an arithmetic rate (i.e. 1, 2, 3, 4, 5 etc.). His theory is that human populations will continue to grow until such time that there would not be enough food to go around causing unnecessary starvation and eventually death. That is one way of controlling population growth. He cited several examples in the past. Unfortunately, at the time of his writing, the western world was on the verge of the industrial revolution and revolution in agriculture that derailed his prediction. It was merely a postponement of the inevitable unless human population is kept in check. It was also a time of colonialism that allows the European colonial power to take over the food and essential natural resources from their colonies and exported back to the home country. The result is malnutrition and starvation in the poor colonial countries. The revolutions in agriculture in the 20th century such as the Green Revolution also helped stem widespread starvation around the world. But the cost to the environment of the planet is taking its tolls today. Since his prediction, the human population has exploded to 6.6 billion with no end in sight. It has impacted the earth in such a way that he had not foreseen. The planet Earth today is suffering from all sources of environmental problems such as global warming, ozone depletion, overfishing, pollutions, deforestation, desertification, loss of biodiversity, aquifer depletion, soil degradation, etc. Many of these problems can only aggravate the quality of life for the inhabitants in the future unless drastic measures are undertaken to mitigate the problems. The health and well-being of the planet and its inhabitants are at stake unless something drastic is done to reverse the trend.

Two important books in the 20th century that tried to predict a catastrophe future are *The Limits to Growth* (1972) by the so-called Club of Rome and *The Population Bomb* (1968) by Paul Ehrlich. Both predictions had not yet occurred because of technological advancement and agricultural transformation. However, it is only a question of time when catastrophe will come about unless there is a limit to human population. The earth cannot continue to absorb and feed so many people with its finite resources. There may be times when the world seems to be improving only to collapse sometime in the future. While most predictions of dire consequences of human growth have not come to pass, unprecedented overpopulation will surely destroy us before we realize the truth.

This is the gist of the book by David Pimentel, professor of ecology and agriculture at Cornell University and Mario Giampietro, senior researcher at the National Research Institute on Food and Nutrition (INRAN) in their book, *Food, Land, Population and the U.S. Economy*. They placed the maximum sustainable U.S. population at 200 million to achieve a sustainable economy and avert disaster. The United States must reduce its population by at least one-third while the rest of the world populations have to be reduced by two-thirds. They believe that the agricultural crisis will only begin to impact us after 2020, and will not become critical until 2050. The oncoming peaking of global oil production (and subsequent decline of production), along with the peak of North American natural gas production will very likely precipitate this agricultural crisis much sooner than expected. Geologist Dale Allen Pfeiffer also claims that coming decades could see spiraling food prices without relief and massive starvation on a global level such as never experienced before. The present oil and food crisis is just a harbinger of bad news in the food and energy sectors that we are experiencing.

Beginning in the 1960s, fictional and non-fictional books have been written about overpopulation of the planet and how they are to be dealt with. A little known book *This Crowded Planet* tried to depict some solutions to the overpopulation problem.

The science fiction novel of John Brunner, *Stand on Zanzibar* was published in 1968. The book won a Hugo Award for Best Novel at the 27th World Science Fiction Convention in 1969. The novel's main drive is overpopulation and its projected consequences. Its title refers to an early twentieth century claim that the world's population could fit onto the Isle of Wight (area 381 km²) if they are all standing upright. Brunner remarked that the growing world population now required a larger island—the 3.5 billion people living in 1968 could stand together on the Isle of man (area 572 km²), while the 7 billion people whom he projected would be alive in 2010 would need to stand on Zanzibar with an of area of 1554 km². Throughout the book, the image of the entire human race standing shoulder-to-shoulder on a small island is a metaphor for a crowded world where each person feels hemmed in by a prison made not of metal bars, but of other human beings. By the end of the book, some of that crowd is metaphorically knee deep in the Indian Ocean surrounding the island.[2]

A more definitive novel on overpopulation was Harry Harrison's *Make Room! Make Room!* that became a powerful film, *Soylent Green,* starring Charlton Heston and made in 1973. Set in the year 2022, *Soylent Green* depicts a dystopian future of New York City with a population of forty million living in dilapidated and overcrowded homes with one half of the population unemployed and food in short supply. The air is so polluted to be virtually unhealthy.

Foods have become very rare and expensive. Most people survive on processed rations called Soylent Red and Soylent Yellow. A new product called Soylent Green is a small green wafer which is advertised as "high-energy plankton" is actual made from human flesh.

Logan's Run is a novel by William F. Nolan and George Clayton Johnson (1967), describing another dystopian future society in which the population is kept young by euthanizing everyone who reaches a certain age, thus neatly avoiding the problem of overpopulation. A 1972 film called *Z.P.G* featured an overpopulated and much polluted future Earth, whose world government practices Zero Population Growth, executing persons who violate the 30-year ban on procreation. The film stars Oliver Reed and Geraldine Chaplin as a couple who are unhappy with the laws which govern the world where they live – 21st century Earth. Because of the large population of Earth, a law has been passed disallowing newborn baby for 30 years. Instead, the government provides couples with an alternative horrible looking, walking, and talking dolls!

Reed and Chaplin are unhappy with this state of affairs and decide to have a baby. This is where the movie takes off. Unfortunately, their neighbors found out and demand that the couple

---

[2] http://en.wikipedia.org/wiki/Stand_on_Zanzibar

share the baby with them. The other couple does so, but finds that the neighbors get too attached to the infant. They stop sharing their child, and the neighbors become so angry that they report them to authorities. The couple and their baby are arrested and sentenced to death. Fortunately, the clever husband anticipated this and made a few plans in advance.

Another 1971 film called *The Last Child* was set in the U.S. of 1994. It also took a stab at laws in the future where families are only allowed to have one child even if the first one did not survive childhood. People who are over 65 are forbidden medical care. It was a time when massive overpopulation crisis has resulted in the passage of Draconian laws. It was a story of a married couple who find themselves hounded by the authorities when she refuses to submit to a legally mandated abortion. Chased across country by Population Control agent, they plan to escape to Canada but find the border closed. They receive unexpected help from a retired U.S. Senator who shelters them at great risk to himself, using what political clout and respect he still commands in his own state to block the agent from pursuing the couple. The couple must find a means of escaping the country as the authorities close in on their safe haven.

J. G. Ballard's story *Billennium* pictures a future in which every individual has four, then just three, square meters of living space. Frederick Pohl in *The Space Merchants* described a future in which even public staircases are rented out as living spaces and water and fuel are in short supply. Venus has just been colonized and businesses are advertising people to live in Venus, even though it was still harsh and the climate hot. They will have to wait until the planet has been terraformed.

Robert Silverberg's *The World Inside* imagines a future with mile high towers holding a million people each. The novel is set on Earth in the year 2381, when the population of the planet has reached 75 billion people. Population growth has skyrocketed due to a quasi-religious belief in human reproduction as the highest possible good. Most of the action occurs in a massive three-kilometer high city-tower called *Urban Monad 116*. War, starvation, crime and birth control have been eliminated. Life is now totally fulfilled and sustained within Urban Monads (Urbmons), mammoth thousand-floor skyscrapers arranged in "constellations," where the shadow of one building does not fall upon another. An Urbmon is divided into 25 self-contained "cities" of 40 floors each, in ascending order of status, with administrators occupying the highest level. Each building can hold approximately 800,000 people, with excess population totaling three billion a year transferred to new Urbmons, which are continually under construction.

The modern trend is toward urbanization and overcrowding of metropolitan areas. This is how one author, Pamela Clark view overpopulation in her article *The Real Root of All Evil? Overpopulation!* She wrote: "The harmful psychological effects of overcrowding due to overpopulation were made clear to me in a biology class. I read about an experiment where two rats were put into a cage and allowed to reproduce freely. At first they got along fine. That soon changed. The number of rats multiplied but they remained in the original cage. As their numbers increased, they started to exhibit anti-social behavior. The outcome of overcrowding is the same with humans. The less space people have to live in, the harder it is for them to get along. As people compete, not only for space but also for food, water and air, the more hostile their behavior deteriorates. Crime, and a lack of respect for other people, becomes more common as personal space is reduced. Violence is more prevalent in highly populated areas, as are other forms of criminal behavior. This is probably due to aggression and anxiety brought on by a lack of personal space.

"Overpopulation also leads to poverty, disease and famine as people desperately compete for jobs, food and shelter. As the Earth's population continues to grow, it will be harder to feed people. I was amazed to read about an Indonesian father who blamed the monetary crisis there for his inability to feed his nine children. I felt he should have known how he was going to feed nine children before he got his wife pregnant nine times! I find it pathetic to read about shanty towns of cardboard shacks filled with starving, disease-ridden children. Lack of adequate shelter and clean water leads to the spread of disease, as does overcrowding. Poverty also contributes to a lack of education....

"Overpopulation also contributes to the pollution of our environment. In overcrowded areas such as India and Mexico, the results are truly appalling. In Mexico City, there is a phenomenon known as 'fecal snow' which occurs when the wind picks up the dried excrement lying about and rains it upon the city. Also, global warming seems to be linked to pollution of the air, and the seas are being polluted by oil spills and waste dumping. Fewer people would mean less pollution from cars, factories, planes and trains.

"Man has continued to intrude upon nature's eco-systems. The South American rain forests are being decimated for farming, and the wetlands and forests of North America are being steadily encroached upon by the advance of man's cities and farms. Many species of plants and wildlife have been annihilated by man's trespassing in their habitats.

"Mankind has a responsibility to the planet, our own species and to other life forms to limit reproduction. Much more emphasis needs to be placed on planning family size. More education needs to be made available about the consequences of unchecked population growth. Free birth control and family counseling ought to be made available to everyone. Every child should be planned and every child should be wanted.....

"The population bomb threatening the earth can still be defused. If the population problem were addressed, the rest of the world's woes would be much easier to remedy. Overpopulation underlies most problems facing us today. We can all help by limiting our own family size, encouraging young people to do the same and voting for laws to encourage zero population growth (ZPG). A brighter future will be our reward."[3]

There are also optimistic views of the population problem. In *The Skeptical Environmentalist*, Bjørn Lomborg argues that, because of the falling rate of population growth in most parts of the world and because of new science and technologies, there is little problem with overpopulation. Although science and technologies have come to the rescue in helping alleviate many problems, it is only a question of time the problems will overwhelm their resourcefulness.

Similarly, in his 2007 book *The Improving State of the World*, Indur M. Goklany argues that there is little problem with overpopulation, as humanity's state is rapidly improving overall and environmental problems can be overcome. It proposes that in the early stages of economic and technological development, negative environmental impacts increase because securing access to such necessities as food, shelter, and energy is seen as more important than protecting the environment. As development continues and these supply problems are solved, environmental impact becomes a higher priority, and steps are then taken to reduce it. This pattern can be seen for many environmental indicators, such as air quality, availability of safe water, sanitation, and toxic residues (e.g., DDT and PCBs) in

---

3

http://www.deltacollege.edu/org/deltawinds/DWOnline99/therealrootofallevil

.

html

human tissues, which initially declined with increasing development but have more recently improved.

Those who have an optimistic view of the world's population trends often cite the decreasing fertility rate around the world, deliberately ignoring or deemphasizing the fact that all of them are occurring in developed countries. Dropping fertility rate has the added figure of awarding family with more income for education and better food to improve the living standard which is an important ingredient for lower population growth. Drastic reduction in fertility rate is needed before the Earth is overwhelmed with people. It took the developed countries more than 100 years to attain the goal and will take the some developing countries even less to slow down the population momentum to reach the replacement level with improved education and health care.

The replacement level, also known as ZPG has each family having two children replacing themselves. On a national basis, this is about 2.1 children per family. The additional 5% is to account for premature death and those who for one reason or another never had any child. This is difficult to achieve because of population momentum. China, with its one-child per family adopted in 1979, even legalizing abortion, was able to reduce its fertility rate to between 1.7 and 2.0 children per family for urban dwellers. It was able to prevent at least 250 million births that could put much strain on the environment and the consumption of natural resources. Yet, it is still increasing their population annually. In 2000-2005, fertility at the world level stood at 2.65 children per woman, about half the level it had in 1950-1955 (5 children per woman). In the medium variant, global fertility is projected to decline further to 2.05 children per woman.

Even with the replacement level achieved, the population is expected to grow for another two generations as the present generation started dying off. To compound the problem, there is the growing life expectancy that is also expected to increase the number of people in the world. Global life expectancy at birth, which is estimated to have risen from 46 years in 1950-1955 to 65 years in 2000-2005, is expected to keep rising to reach 75 years in 2045-2050. In the more developed regions, the projected increase is from 75 years today to 82 years by mid-century. Among the least developed countries, where life expectancy today is just under 50 years, it is expected to be 66 years in 2045-2050.[4]

---

[4] http://www.answers.com/topic/overpopulation-1

There is no question that many European countries have achieved depopulation problems due to easy access to abortion and the tendency of the new generations to enjoy their lives and careers. They have such low birth rates that they have difficulties replacing their current populations. During the 1990, a news report from the Organization for Economic Cooperation and Development (OECD) showed that all European nations recorded birth rates of more than 1.3 children per woman. By 2002, 15 countries had rates below 1.3 children per woman while six countries had rates between 1.3 and 1.4 children per woman. The countries with the worst record are from eastern European countries. These countries have fertility rates below the 2.1 needed to maintain the nation's population.[5]

A few countries that prohibit abortion such as Ireland, Portugal and Malta have the highest birth rate. Another factor contributing to the low birth rates is the increasing age of women having their first child. In the last 20 years, the age of women with their first child moved from early 20s to 30s. Many nations no longer offer enough maternity leave in terms of the length of leave and the money women are paid during the leave. That is one reason why some women put off having children until later in their careers.

Underpopulation and depopulation have their own sets of problems. One problem is the shortage of workers to manage the industrial plants and commercial establishments. New immigrants from the Third World countries have to be imported to prevent the plants from being shut down. There will be the problem of graying of the population in these countries. There may not be enough retirement and social security fund to take care of the elderly.

Depopulation may be a problem for some countries, but most countries in the world are suffering from overpopulation. Population growth still outperformed population decline by more than 75 million annually. It is still going to take decades to balance out while the earth continues to suffer from environmental problems. The decline in the West is also good for the planet due to their disproportionate consumption of the world's resources. Their importation of foreign laborers from the developed countries is one way of distributing the wealth of their nations.

The debates on whether there is an overpopulation problem in the world will never end until the harsh reality occurs. It will probably

---

[5] http:www.abortiontv.com/Lies20&%20Myths/underpopulation.htm

take a few more generations to realize whether we are heading toward an unsustainable future or whether technological advances will help us cope in a world teeming with people. Until then, it is necessary to gauge individual countries in relation to their own resources and economic standing and how they survive in an environment of competitiveness and need. It is obvious not every country can attain the high standard of living like those in the developed countries without putting their environment at risk. Likewise, some countries are more blessed with natural resources, more skilled manpower and better business acumen. These disparities are expected to spell the future of each country. Brain drain is a common problem faced by developing countries. Illegal and legal immigration to the developed world on an unprecedented scale has created an unprecedented demographic and political problem in Europe and the United States. Even the controlled and legal migration of talented and well-educated people from the Third World to the developed world denudes it of its limited skills base.

Some critics have advocated that the earth have enough resources to satisfy the needs of more people that those presently inhabiting this planet. In some ways, technological advances were able to defeat some of the problems of overpopulation such as famine and essential services. These problems include uneven distribution of wealth which by itself is already a limiting factor that has kept many people especially children in a state of apathy and poor health. Even the wealthy nations have children suffering some form of malnutrition and ill-health that have been costly in terms of human lives. The problem is more acute in developing countries. Many children never attain their fifth birthday despite government efforts to help them. There are just too many mouths and few resources to help them.

In a bid to increase food production, new farm lands are needed and they are often taken over from forestlands leading to widespread deforestation. As human habitat expands, many farmlands have been converted to residential and industrial uses that led to more encroachment on forestlands. The twin effects of deforestation and agricultural input are loss of species, soil erosion, pollution from the use of pesticides and fertilizer runoff as farming intensifies and new land is brought into production. With the expanding population, the ecosystem that once sustains life is gradually turned into a new chaotic and unsustainable state.

Other issues involving the quality of life would be drastically changed when we lived in a world teeming with people. Everyone has a right to exist in an environment that could produce the best standard for him and his family. This often leads to more social problems as the government often failed to provide all the social services people demand. There is great competition among the people for the meager services when there are too many people competing for a share.

Misdistribution of wealth is constantly reeling its ugly head in underdeveloped countries. According to a 2004 article from the BBC, China, the world's most populous country, is suffering from an obesity epidemic. More recent data indicate China's grain production may have peaked in the mid-1990s, due to over-extraction of groundwater in the North China plain.

Worldwide, the number of people who are overweight has surpassed the numbers who are malnourished. In a 2006 news story, MSNBC reported, "There are an estimated 800 million undernourished people and more than a billion considered overweight worldwide." This misdistribution of the life-saving food is just an indication that many do not have enough income to buy the needed food.

The United Nations indicates that about 850 million people are malnourished or starving, and 1.1 billion people do not have access to safe drinking water. It would be fallacious to suggest that the Earth can support 6 billion people at this point in time. It can only do so on the condition that many live in misery. Others posit that poverty was worse in the past when the population was smaller, and that worldwide poverty is declining as the population grows. Even if the percentage of the world's population living on less than $1 per day has halved in twenty years, there are still too many people living on subsistence to suggest that the Earth is capable of supporting the present population.

A 2007 article from *Investor's Business Daily* suggests that the population explosion has been accompanied by an increase in worldwide living standards. The article suggests that on a per-person basis, real average incomes have more than tripled since 1950 worldwide. Even if true, the fact that several billions of people are living at the edge of poverty does not suggest well for the adding more mouths to people in countries that can hardly keep up with the rising standard of living.

In fact, the UN Human Development Report from 1997 suggests that the last 15-20 years, more than 100 developing countries, and several East European countries, have suffered from disastrous growth failures. The reductions in standard of living have been deeper and long-lasting than what was seen in the industrialized countries during the depression in the 1930s. As a result, the income for more than one billion people has fallen below the level that was reached 10, 20 or 30 years ago. The rosy picture in the developed world does not seem to apply to the Third World. Some demographers even suggested that percentage wise, the standard of living has risen but in real term, it has only grown in absolute term as the population has increased dramatically. To keep the numbers of starving constant, the percentage would have to drop by as much as the population growth.

Overpopulation has had a major impact on the environment of Earth starting at least as early as the 20th century. Many posit that the human population has expanded, enabled by over-exploiting natural resources, with resultant adverse impacts upon biodiversity, aquifer sustainability, climate change and even human health. There are also indirect economic consequences of this environmental degradation in the form of ecosystem services attrition. Beyond the scientifically verifiable harm to the environment, some argue the moral right of other species to simply exist, protected from human exploitation. Says environmental author Jeremy Rifkin, "our burgeoning population and urban way of life have been purchased at the expense of vast ecosystems and habitats.....It's no accident that as we celebrate the urbanization of the world, we are quickly approaching another historic watershed: the disappearance of the wild."

These reflect the comments also of the United States Geological Survey in their paper *The Future of Planet Earth: Scientific Challenges in the Coming Century.* "As the global population continues to grow...people will place greater and greater demands on the resources of our planet, including mineral and energy resources, open space, water, and plant and animal resources.....Clearly, the past half century has been a traumatic one, as the collective impact of human numbers, affluence (consumption per individual) and our choices of technology continue to exploit rapidly an increasing proportion of the world's resources at an unsustainable rate.....During a remarkably short period of time, we have lost a quarter of the world's topsoil and a fifth of its agricultural land, altered the composition of the atmosphere profoundly, and destroyed a major proportion of our forests and other natural habitats without replacing them. Worst of all, we have driven the rate of biological extinction, the permanent loss of species, up several hundred times beyond its historical levels, and are threatened with the loss of a majority of all species by the end of the 21st century."

Some countries like India also have enormous problems with overpopulation. The current population is over a billion, but India does not have as much land mass as China. India is experiencing major problems with declining water tables due to over-extraction beyond sustainable yield. India is building desalinization plants to solve this problem. Because India has the same population density as Japan, some have claimed that India's poverty is caused by underdevelopment, not overpopulation. Whatever the cause, India has one of the poorest standards of living in the world.

The move to industrialize has its own problems. If China and India were to consume as much resources per capita as United States, together they would require two planet Earths just to sustain their two economies. The Worldwatch Institute said the booming economies of China and India are planetary powers that are shaping the global biosphere. The State of the World 2006 report said the two countries' high economic growth hid a reality of severe pollution. The report states that "The world's ecological capacity is simply insufficient to satisfy the ambitions of China, India, Japan, Europe and the United States as well as the aspirations of the rest of the world in a sustainable way."

Nigeria is the most populous country in Africa. The 2006 census gave a population of 140 million and country is projected to have a population of 289 million by 2050. According to the United Nations, Nigeria has been undergoing explosive population growth and one of the highest growth and fertility rates in the world. Health, health care, and general living conditions in Nigeria are poor. Life expectancy for both male and female is 47 years and just over half the population has access to potable water and appropriate sanitation. Nigeria, like many developing countries, suffers from a polio crisis as well as periodic outbreaks of cholera, malaria, and sleeping sickness.

Between 1990 and 2005, Nigeria lost a staggering 79% of its old-growth forests. It is losing 1,355 $mile^2$ of rangeland and cropland to desertification each year. About 35 million people in northern Nigeria are currently suffering from the effects of desertification. While Nigeria's human population was growing from 33 million in 1950 to 140 million in 2006, a fourfold expansion, its livestock population grew from 6 million to 66 million, an 11-fold increase. With the food needs of its people and land and the forage needs of cattle, sheep and goats exceeding the carrying capacity of its grasslands, the country is slowly turning to desert. Nigeria's fast-growing population is being squeezed into an ever-smaller area.

Ethiopia has more fertile land per person than the United Kingdom. In the 1970s, the Ethiopian government seized the farmland from the farmers. This contributed to a 1984 - 1985 famine in Ethiopia. Ethiopia's famine is aggravated by high population growth, bad governance, inefficient agricultural policies, misplaced budgetary priorities, abject poverty, poor infrastructure, lack of access to fertilizers and pesticides, the HIV/AIDS pandemic, and internal conflicts. High population growth is a major factor.

Ethiopia's population has grown from 18 million in 1950 to an estimated 77 million today and is projected to be about 170 million by 2050. Food and Agriculture Organization (FAO) estimated on January 6, 2006, that more than 11 million people in the Horn of Africa countries may be affected by an impending widespread famine, largely attributed to a severe drought, and exacerbated by military conflicts in the region. These conditions of drought, together with other factors including high cereal prices, overpopulation in the region, and conflict, lead to the 2006 Horn of Africa food crisis. Privatization of the farmland is a partial solution to the famine problem. At present the state owns all the land. Limiting the population explosion is a better option.

In Niger, people cutting down trees for firewood contributed to problems of deforestation and desertification. When the country changed its economic policy allowing private ownership of trees, the owners have an incentive to take care of them. People could make more money caring for the trees and selling the fruits, instead of cutting the trees down for firewood. As a result, the deforestation was reversed and the forest grew bigger. This happened, despite the fact that the human population was growing. By adopting property rights, the environment benefitted, and the people became wealthier and better fed. However, this would not prevent natural disasters from happening.

The 2005-06 Niger food crisis was caused by an early end to the 2004 rainfall coupled with the desert locust damage to some pasture lands, high food prices, and chronic poverty. The food shortage impacts some 3.3 million people - including 800,000 children under age five - in some 3,815 villages. On January 16, 2006, the UN directed an appeal for US$ 240 million of food aid for West Africa to feed at least 10 million people affected by the food crisis, with Niger being the worst-affected country.

In 1925, Haiti was a lush tropical paradise, with 60% of its original forest covering the lands and mountainous regions. By 2007, its density is approximately 250 people/km^2 with a fertility rate of 4.86 babies per woman. Since then, the people have cut down all but 2% of its forest cover, and in the process have destroyed fertile farmland soils, while contributing to desertification. Haiti remains one of the least-developed countries in the Western Hemisphere. Haiti now ranks 154th out of 177 countries in the UN's Human Development Index (2006). According to the CIA World Factbook, about 80% of the population lives in poverty. Haiti is the only country in the Americas on the World Health Organization (WHO) list of Least Developed Countries. Unemployment rose sharply in the mid to late 90's peaking at 70% in 1999 before decreasing to the usual rates of around 50% in recent years.

One way at looking at overpopulation is the disproportionate consumption of some people. A person who eats more than his fair share to become obese or spending more than he needs is adding to the environmental problems. Overconsumption contributes to the detriment of the environment and the welfare of other people as long as there are not enough resources to give everyone a decent lifestyle.

Americans have always been the scapegoat it comes to overconsumption. They constitute approximately 5% of the world's population, but produce roughly 25% of the world's carbon dioxide (CO_2), consume about 25% of world's resources, including approximately 26% of the world's energy, although having only around 3% of the world's known oil reserves, and generate approximately 30% of world's waste. The average American's impact on the environment is approximately 250 times greater than the average Sub-Saharan Africans.

The U.S., a multi-culture country cannot be blamed alone for overconsumption. Many of the people contributing to the huge appetite came from other parts of the world. It is the only country that has an open policy for immigrants who helped build up the country and enjoy the benefits of a great nation. Most of the people around the world aspired to immigrate can only lead to further overconsumption.

A state may have large land area and still be overpopulated if it does have the carrying capacity. This is true with many cold and desert regions around the world. One good example is the U.S. State of Arizona. It has enormous land area, but has neither the carrying capacity of arable land or potable water to support its population. While it imports food, using its wealth to offset this shortfall only serves to illustrate that it has insufficient carrying capacity. The only way that Arizona (and Southern California) obtains sufficient water is by extraction of water from the Colorado River beyond its fair share (and beyond its own carrying capacity of innate water resources), based on international standards of fair use per lineal mile of river. Recently Arizona has considered expensive desalinization as a way to eliminate water shortages.

Another example is the city of Los Angeles. According to the California Department of Water Resources, if more supplies aren't found by 2020, residents will face a shortfall nearly as great as the amount consumed today. Los Angeles is a coastal desert able to support at most 1 million people with its own water. The population of California continues to grow by more than a half million a year and is expected to reach 48 million in 2030. Water shortage issues are likely to arise well before then. California is considering using energy-intensive desalinization to solve this problem.

While some rich nations are considered overpopulated, there are more developing and underdeveloped countries that are considered overpopulated precisely because they cannot afford a decent standard of living. Many suffered from the chronic inability to escape from the "Malthusian trap" via economic growth exceeding population growth. These countries simply lack the economic or infrastructural base to provide a rising standard of living for most of their people, especially in Africa, the Arab world, and parts of Latin America. Take Uganda for example. It had a population of approximately 7 million people at independence in 1962, and in 45 years the population of Uganda has grown to 30 million. By 2050, there will be a projected 130 million Ugandans, making Uganda the 12th most populated country in the world, with more people than Russia or Japan. The latter two countries are projected to have lower population by then. Uganda's population will have increased 18-fold in less than 90 years while its standard of living remains basically the same.

It should be noted that if developing countries were to consume resources and produce pollution at the current U.S. per-capita level, it would require several planet Earths just to sustain their economies.

The following article *A Crusade Against Overpopulation* is one view on the problem of overpopulation. It is reprinted with the tacit approval of the author.

The Earth's population is plagued by famines, energy shortages, epidemics, environmental pollution, degeneration, terrorism, dictatorship, anarchism, slavery, excessive increase of waste materials, racial hatred, food shortages, destruction of rain forests, the "greenhouse effect", pollution of lakes, streams and oceans, hatred towards asylum-seekers; radioactive emissions, chemical pollution of water, air, plants, food, human beings and animals. Crime, murder, mass murders, manslaughter; alcoholism, hatred of strangers, oppression, hatred of one's fellowman, extremism, sectarianism, drug addiction, overpopulation, annihilation of animal species, war, violence, torture and capital punishment, general mismanagement, water contamination, eradication of plant species; hatred, vice, jealousy, lovelessness, lack of logic, false humanitarianism, lack of housing, increased traffic, destruction of arable land, unemployment, the collapse of health care, the collapse of care for the elderly, destruction of nature, the collapse of solid waste removal, and the lack of living space, among others. In spite of the many efforts, mankind's problems are not decreasing but, instead, continue to rise steadily in direct proportion to population increases.

When an energy source becomes depleted, man on Earth simply plans and builds new, more powerful nuclear-, oil-, coal-, and hydro power plants. He does this regardless of the fact that through the utilization of these very same nuclear power plants, as well as the petroleum- and coal power plants, he immensely pollutes the environment even further. Additionally, nuclear radiation may leak from atomic power plants, thereby endangering all terrestrial life. Moreover, these new energy sources will have become partially outdated already, or inadequate, upon completion over a 3-7 year construction period. Furthermore, these plants tend not to meet the new energy demands because, very likely, birth rate increases have not remained stable during construction periods. Indeed, it is likely that overpopulation has busily escalated over this same period. Hundreds of millions of people are born worldwide during the construction phase of a power plant and, of course, these millions of newborn human beings once again will require additional energy. It is obvious also that the incessant increase in the Earth's population is sending the demand for energy into an upward spiral. Because of these tremendous energy demands, the earth must be exploited at an ever increasing speed. As a result, ever more nuclear power plants, along with other types of power plants, must be constructed and put into service, thereby increasingly endangering and destroying all life forms. Other sources of endangerment and destruction to the planet and all life yet exist, e.g., the unscrupulous use of chemicals, the American HAARP project in Alaska, nuclear testing and the commercial use of atomic bombs for the creation of lakes, waterways and subterranean expanses to be used as storage areas for rubble, sewage, solid waste and nuclear waste products. Mention must also be made of the clearing of rain forests and the burning of forests to criminally access parcels of land for construction sites, etc. Additionally, there are criminal sport activities which depend on combustion engines that burn gas, alcohol, gasoline or diesel oil, to name but a few.

It is an idiosyncrasy of the Earth human beings, due to their unreasonable and purely materialistic thinking processes, to think and act inappropriately in almost every matter. They act illogically in many ways as well, and as a result, they do so also with respect to the problem of hunger throughout the world. They create numerous humanitarian organizations in order to collect funds, food and other goods to help the starving and suffering population. Yet, all the while, they manage on one hand to legally siphon off 40% of the collected funds into their own pockets as expenses and, on the other hand, they abet, advance and tolerate the overpopulation explosion problem. Through these ostensibly humane acts, though truthfully inhumane acts of destruction, the suffering of humankind on Earth are not diminished and the problems of hunger are not being resolved. Instead, suffering and hunger continue to grow to even greater levels. Misunderstood charity and humanitarianism, as well as their subsequently misdirected assistance, are all primarily spawned by a totally false humanitarianism. As a rule, such false humanitarianism originates from the influence of religions, sectarianism and other false teachings, none of which are love, charity and humanitarianism. In fact, such false teachings spawn even greater and more difficult problems than those already in existence. Irresponsible and without a single thought to actual matters of truth, without true commitment or respect for life and the fulfillment of the natural-Creative laws and directives, many people carelessly give "relief", thereby furthering this "non-aid" and the destruction of life even more. Not only misunderstood sympathy and sectarian influences play a major role in this scenario, but also the fact that many people cling to such "relief campaigns" in order to calm their own guilty consciences for being more prosperous in some way. These people fail to realize that they and their countrymen have earned this higher standard of living in the civilized country where they live, mainly by keeping population growth figures low or at least on a more reasonable level than peoples of so-called underdeveloped countries. People in the underdeveloped nations carelessly and irresponsibly procreate like guinea pigs or rabbits, only to starve afterwards and shout for help. They lack real help in the format of a birthrate control.

Wherever possible, false humanitarians donate goods and funds to "Bread for Brothers", "Hunger Throughout the World" and similar programs. They have no idea that in so doing they are acting against reason and are interfering in nature's work which ultimately defends itself through famines. Likewise, they may not want to hear of such things. Starving people are procreated by the hundreds and millions through sympathy that is contrary to nature's ways, and a charity that results from false humanitarianism. Through a voluntary or forcibly decreed birthrate check these happenings could be avoided. Through the excess of the great human mass, mankind's problems are continuously increasing, and it must suffer privation and begins to slowly destroy faunal and floral life along with the planet itself.

Once the starving people have been saved from a death of starvation, they become well nourished, healthy and robust once again, and immediately begin through the lack of information regarding birth control to procreate in an uncontrolled manner by having children in large numbers that amount to many millions each year. Not only does this procreation immediately create further problems of hunger and energy demands, but it also leads to medical, spatial and financial problems, to name but a few. Likewise, the descendants of these people once again compound terrestrial mankind's excessive growth problem. Once these offspring become older and sexually mature, they also promptly begin procreating their own children and, once again, new descendants are conceived in even greater numbers, etc., etc. faster and ever faster. During an extremely brief time period the Earth will become even more overpopulated. In 1978, 4 billion people inhabited the Earth. In 2000, there will exist already 7 billion inhabitants. Because of this steady and incessant increase of overpopulation, each and every other problem becomes excessively, immeasurably and increasingly compounded. These problems will affect every facet of human life, indeed, the very life of the planet itself and its fauna and flora. In the coming decades as man's degeneration on Earth relentlessly increases, so will that of the planet and nature. Alone the looming ozone layer depletion caused by man's own actions will initiate unforeseen suffering upon the entire planet including all life forms, in much the same manner as a particular human immune deficiency, which today is already spreading epidemically. As a result of wars and revolutions, among other things, veritable migrations of entire nations will soon take place, as people begin to flee their homelands to seek asylum elsewhere. This migrant flow will lead to hatred of strangers, hatred of asylum-seekers and other races. It will result in severe unrest, murders by all types of extremists and others. The drug abuse epidemic and international political terrorism shall run rampant. Recession and inflation will reappear and millions of people will be without work and income. Criminality and organized crime will spread on a massive scale. The mass murder of individuals will become common place, including the mass murder of people for religious-sectarian and political-delusional reasons. The destruction of the environment will increasingly ensue, while the planet itself is exploited and tortured. However, nature and the planet will avenge themselves of this abuse through unusually severe storms, typhoons, cyclones, hurricanes, and huge infernos. Entire forests, fields and other territories will be incinerated. Many gigantic fires will be ablaze. Horrendously violent storms will sweep across the Earth with a severity not yet witnessed since time immemorial. Horrendous droughts, gigantic tsunamis, masses of snow, hail and much more, will plague the Earth and its inhabitants. Ancient, dormant volcanoes will reawaken and negatively influence the Earth's climate. Active volcanoes will rumble with increased activity, and savage earthquakes will shake the ground ever more frequently. The irresponsible commercial use and testing of atomic bombs and other explosives will contribute to this turmoil as they reverberate through the earth.

With a current population of about 6.5 billion terrestrial inhabitants (1998), the Earth is far beyond its capability to support and feed such a mass routinely, on a fundamental, natural and healthy basis. A basis, where neither human effort and intrusion into nature, the raping of nature nor the exploitation of its resources to produce more food need occur; and where no one need suffer from hunger. The truth is that Earth is a wondrous planet, but it has only the capacity to support and feed in every way and in abundance 529 million people. Mankind, on the other hand, has generated a gigantic, excessive population, and is now forced to spur all vegetable and fruit production to atypical, extreme achievements through the use of chemicals and hybrids. As though this were not enough, the exploitation of the planet has accelerated dramatically, including the expansion in recovery of raw materials from the earth, and the unrelentingly rising demand from the Earth for all types of other materials a direct result of the growing overpopulation. No one mentions the destruction of arable land due to this madness called overpopulation; no one speaks of the use of toxic chemicals nor of the expansion of housing areas and the like. Food for human consumption is laden with chemical additives and consists these days largely of artificially produced chemicals also a fact that is not mentioned.

Originally, the population of each region on Earth was only as large as that region could feed and support in accordance with nature's ways. Toxic chemicals, other types of poisons, new plant hybrids, as well as overly intensive exploitation of the ground, were completely unknown.

However, this condition changed dramatically during the Middle Ages, particularly at the time of the great French Revolution. For it was during this period that the crazy notion originated suggesting the need for a larger population who would rise up against the authorities. The masses wanted to overthrow the government. To have the capability of doing so, and to become powerful and mighty, the populace prodded themselves for larger numbers of progeny. Christianity and its sects, but Catholicism in particular, was party to this endeavor. Powerful as ever, Catholicism was preaching, as part of its false and insane teachings, that people should be "fruitful and multiply and replenish the Earth". This slogan, even today, is vigorously preached by the Catholic head honcho and his cassocked cohorts. The catchphrase remains in circulation throughout the world today for the sole purpose of acquiring little "sheep" and busy little tithing payers. The results have produced guinea-pig-like, human reproduction. Clearly, the ensuing overpopulation has meant large requirements for more food, energy, raw materials, as well as many other goods. In the way of food alone, mankind will ultimately arrive at a point where all natural produce becomes a rarity, since the insatiable demands for the provision of food for mankind's out-of-control masses, can only be satisfied by totally producing staples from chemicals. In part this already holds true today, for food requirements have soared relentlessly in the past few decades. Yet, food provision problems are not unique and have grown continuously, as have the problems of energy shortage.

Man on Earth is threatened by worldwide total contamination, destruction, and the manifold ills of extinction. Lists a yard long can be compiled that describe how every earthly life form is being endangered, destroyed, exterminated and annihilated. Yet, man continues to remain ignorant of the damage he has inflicted on nature, the planet and all types of life existing upon it. And now terrestrial man, the planet and life in general, have reached the point where everything stands on its last leg the direct result of people clinging to false charity and false humanitarianism. These individuals are behaving and acting in much the same criminal manner as those officials in responsible government positions, government agencies and relief organizations, which do their best to sound the death knell on the last remnants of life on planet Earth, now channeled into a path leading to its own final and irrevocable annihilation. The blame for this situation rests with those individuals also who, lacking responsibility and initiative, have relinquished their authority for making productive changes by uttering the primitive and absurd phrases: "What can I do by myself?" or "Of course, I'll help also if others go along with it," etc., etc. Anyone thinking in this manner is neither worthy nor fit to live, in the same way that people are unfit who relentlessly promote even further the madness of unremitting overpopulation through false humanitarianism, false charity and others. These individuals are contributing to the fact that terrestrial mankind's problems are reaching immeasurable levels, problems that surpass even those currently in existence and others yet to come. Anyone thinking like this or believing that the world is now in order is shunning progress and abetting the destruction and annihilation of the world and all life forms on it.

Mankind's horrendous ills originate from and exist through overpopulation with its unrelenting, irresponsibly continuing escalation. The situation dictates that any ill can only be fought and remedied by grasping it by its roots, ripping it out and destroying it: The numbers of terrestrial humankind must be drastically reduced. The only humane method by which this reduction goal can be achieved is through stringent birth control regulations that permit married couples, of a predetermined age, to have only a strictly specified number of children. This regulation must prevail over any excuse, argument, fear and/or stupid comment from those numbskulls who claim, for military, religious, social, egoistical, false humanitarian reasons, or those of false charity, that a large number of offspring is necessary, or that birth control is contrary to religious beliefs and is inhumane, etc. These inane claims are made singularly by rigid egotists, sectarians or people unfit to live those who have not the faintest idea of nature's laws, directives or truthful logic.

Terrestrial mankind's existing major problems can only be resolved through a purposeful birth control program, by which the population is reduced to an optimum level, and scaled according to the planet. All other problem-solving measures present trite, singularly miserable, pitiful and useless attempts that barely amount to the proverbial drop in the bucket. Such problem-solving attempts only serve instead to increase all ills and difficulties even further.

Is population control barbaric, inhumane and uncharitable? No! On the contrary, for it is only when a person begins to ponder these facts logically if he or she has not done so already and come to the same truthful conclusions that he or she finds the truth coinciding with the aforementioned argument. Only illogically thinking people, who cling to false charity and false humanitarianism, deny the truth. Such people are forced into this rut by sectarian machinations and false teachings, which cause them to grovel like dogs and rob them of all healthy, reasonable, normal and truthful thoughts, feelings and actions. In this manner they are dominated purely by pity, self-pity, feeblemindedness and illogic, in place of feelings of empathy for all life forms. Respect for and toward true life is ultimately destroyed by the illogical thinkers, who pave the way for false humanitarianism and false charity that turn into purulent boils capable of spreading as epidemics.

The truth, in regard to the clarification of mistakes and guilt, has always been damn hard to take, and seldom does an individual accept harsh truths without grumbling and complaining. Man on Earth has always felt attacked personally when someone speaks and offers the truth. He simply exalts himself above everything and believes to be free from error and guilt, which is the reason for his inability to bear the truth. He rebels against it if the truth does not correspond with his own, erroneous opinion. Truly, however, man's behavior is nothing more than sordid cowardice that infects everyone who is capable of comprehending issues in a halfway normal way.

Since times immemorial, the truth, along with true love, charity and humanitarianism, has invariably sounded harsh, because each one forces the human being to think and act in a logical manner. The same holds true also for the resolution of terrestrial humankind's problems. Only through population reduction, by way of the strictest birth control measures, can there be a remedy for all existing major ills. Inhumane aid must not be given to people.

The universal laws of nature apply to humans on Earth, too, and anyone with an open eye can easily recognize them: Wherever there is a region in which the population of a particular animal species suddenly increases, and the danger exists whereby the area involved cannot feed the increasing population, epidemics occur that decimate the increasing and excessive animal population. Furthermore, the same is evident also when excessively large populations simply starve to death or fall prey to their natural foes because they are weak from hunger. For it is through this method that nature keeps its natural populations in balance, allowing only as many faunal life forms to live in any one region as there is food for support. Only man, the thinking creature, acts contrary to this natural law and tramples upon it. Contrary to faunal life forms, man procreates his offspring to an excessive degree. For some time now, fertile regions capable of providing food have become so overpopulated that the land can no longer be cultivated nor can it provide sufficient food for everyone. The flip side of this coin is that people flock by the millions to cities built upon formerly fertile, arable ground. Man then imports food supplies from other regions where fields for gardening and agriculture have remained available; yet those demanding food have never even had to lift one finger towards the planting, maintenance or harvesting of it.

Man fancies himself as being the crown of Creation. Indeed, he believes that by having the capability to think he is allowed to regard himself as superior to everything else. Thus, he believes he is entitled to permit planet wide, human overpopulation, and that he can ignore the laws and directives of nature and trample them with his feet. In his megalomanic delusions of grandeur, man has already shown himself to be as inhumane, uncharitable and feebleminded as to allow everything around him to degenerate into limitless cowardice: His realistic and reasonable thinking, along with true love, charity, humanitarianism and love of truth, have all become completely desensitized. Hence, he is no longer able to recognize that terrestrial humankind's major problems are caused by the liability of overpopulation. This situation can only be relieved by the strictest birth control measures. Instead of acknowledging this truth, mankind criminally forms and supports relief organizations that create more harm than benefit. These organizations do not instruct and bring about birth control measures, to the effect that millions and millions are procreated all over the world and force all major problems beyond normal boundaries. Well-to-do individuals support the machinations of relief organizations with exorbitant sums merely to calm their guilty consciences, which is a direct result of their false humanitarianism and false charity. These so-called helpers cowardly cheat their own consciences because they are incapable of recognizing the truthful truth and acting accordingly. Hence, their aid is misdirected toward the wrong places and points of concern. Through their direct participation, therefore, they become guilty by being responsible for the unfolding of this increasing, unrelentingly multiplying, worldwide misery and plight, along with the many catastrophes and ills associated with it.

xxxxxx

It is because of mistaken, illogical people who have given relief aid, who scorn Creation, and who are pseudo-humanitarians and other types of overpopulation-mongers, that the earth is impregnated with the seeds of many different ills. From such seeds there sprout and mature the destruction that burdens the entire globe under an assortment of varying names. However, the most prominent ill of all, indeed the one that causes the greatest destruction worldwide, is overpopulation. It is from overpopulation that the delusion of hatred of strangers, racial hatred, hatred towards the asylum-seekers and one's fellowman originate, as well as sectarianism in the form of religious, profane, esoteric, ufological, philosophical, non-denominational or special interest groups, not to mention the sectarianism of major religions. This entire overpopulation phenomenon results in crime and wars, epidemics of drug addiction, prescription drugs abuse, alcoholism, tobacco addiction, solvent-sniffing, sadism, masochism and many other plights to which human beings fall prey. These epidemics are becoming more blatant and numerous through the unconstrained growth of the world's total population. This is a proven fact that cannot be ignored or kept secret any longer. It is those overpopulation-mongers only who close their eyes to this fact and truth and make themselves guilty of crimes against humanity. They wish neither to acknowledge this fact nor to admit to the truth of it. Why is this? Why do these overpopulation-mongers, who in this manner commit crimes against humanity, neither wish to see, hear, recognize, acknowledge nor accept the truth and the fact of global ills and destruction? The answer is not a simple one. It is a fact that the reasons vary greatly from falling prey to alcoholism, drug addiction, prescription drugs abuse, tobacco addiction, solvent-sniffing, sadism and masochism, to the sectarianism of a religious, non-denominational, special interest group, philosophical, esoteric, parapsychological, spiritualistic nature or sectarian ideologies of major religions. The reasons may vary also from war, murder and crime, hatred of strangers, racial hatred, hatred towards the asylum-seekers to hatred of one's fellowman. It is erroneous, therefore, to assume that only a single reason need apply to all the excesses mentioned. Truthfully, the reasons causing extremist, as well as sectarian ideologies and addictions of all types can have thousand variations.

These are many thousands of grounds, reasons, causes, bases and decisive factors leading to sectarianism and its various subtleties, as well as to drug addiction, tobacco abuse, alcoholism and solvent-sniffing. These reasons, etc., also apply, along with many other issues, to delusional hatred of strangers, racial hatred, hatred towards foreigners, the asylum-seekers and one's fellowman. Such ills are excessively represented in the Ku-Klux-Klan, anti-Semitism and neo-

Nazi movements to name but a few. These ills result in countless other ills and destruction, and frequently end in total despondency or suicide, murder, torture, capital punishment (a type of murder), crime, mass murder and genocide. The future will prove that these ills and destruction, along with many other grievances, are constantly increasing and becoming excessive. They include sectarianism of any type, along with vice and addictions such as drug abuse, prescription drug abuse, alcoholism and solvent-sniffing, and others. In the same manner will major criminal acts and all types of organized crime violence become excessive and cost many human lives, as will hatred of strangers, a hatred towards one's brother, the asylum-seekers, other races and one's fellowman. Tortures will take on malicious and far-reaching fatal forms, as will capital punishment, rape, simple murder, mass murder, religious, sectarian murder and genocide. Many different malicious ills of a religious-sectarian nature, along with those of a political and special-interest-group nature and implication, will increase horrendously. These ills will rule the world and its inhabitants, and will terrify everyone on Earth. Yet, the ills are mankind's own fault; that is to say, the fault of those individuals who must be branded as overpopulation-mongers, regardless of the manner in which they became guilty of it. For it is the overpopulation-mongers who must be blamed, those who deliberately endanger and threaten to destroy all life on the planet. Because of these irresponsible human beings on Earth, life-destructive ills are being consciously cultivated by a steady production of new human progeny and along with them a growing overpopulation. Man has to suffer these consequences because many people on Earth are in error and possess little sense of responsibility toward themselves, their progeny, their fellowman or the remainder of humankind. Moreover, they have no feelings of responsibility whatsoever for the planet Earth itself or its fauna and flora. All of this because irresponsible individuals, full of highhandedness and megalomania, depict themselves as being Creation itself, in the belief that their idiocy is equivalent to a true and reasonable thinking process. However, such individuals are incapable of willing or commanding even one hair to grow on their heads. These people truly cannot and must not be considered as being endowed with any powers of reasoning, otherwise they would not condone and instigate the many activities of a religious, sectarian and profane nature, or those with various delusional beliefs and the delusional extremism with all of their excesses. These individuals not only condone these issues, they actually foster and defend them. Life on Earth, indeed the entire planet, is being destroyed and annihilated. It is because of irresponsible people, such as the pseudo-humanitarians, sectarians, delusional followers, overpopulation- and havoc-mongers, along with the destroyers of life and the planet, who do everything in their power to drastically escalate every ill on Earth. They contribute to the planet's deterioration. Through their pseudo-humanitarian, sectarian beliefs, they threaten and destroy terrestrial life by supporting the rapidly increasing human population, which in itself is procreating ever faster more terribly and more unrestrainedly than guinea pigs and rabbits.

The real blame for the overpopulation ills and the steady but certain, persistent, increasingly destructive advance of life on Earth indeed the planet itself rests with mismanagement and corruption too, and with organizations and supporters of aid to Third World nations. However, the power elite does not wish to acknowledge this fact. In particular, as a result of the financial aid by industrial nations, the so-called civilized and economically sound world, devastation has befallen Third World nations ranging from the felling of rainforests trees to the total destruction and annihilation of formerly very fertile regions. In place of oxygen-rich rainforests that had regulated the climate, there remain only bleak, deserted, eroded, leached and barren soils today, devoid of the growth of even one blade of grass. In place of luxuriant fields and fertile ground (or at least arid soil that could provide sufficient life-sustaining grain and vegetable harvests through great struggles by the farmers) there now exist salt plains, deserted and dead landscapes or barren swamps, that are frequently the breeding ground for deadly pathogenic agents. These many situations have transpired due mainly to the relief aid from irresponsible people who have pumped industrial and other well-to-do nations' financial support into Third World countries, and who continue to do so even today. Members of relief programs are themselves carrying on with the mismanagement and corruption; or they permit such things to be perpetrated by others. People involved with these programs also want to build dams, model factories and companies to further Third World nations' development. They initiate the clearing of rainforests and the destruction of land and life, which ultimately cause ongoing, immense climatic changes that negatively influence the entire globe and all life upon it. These changes induce horrendous storms, hurricanes, typhoons, floods, landslides, earthquakes, droughts and many other catastrophes. With regard to mankind, a great many different catastrophes have been invoked and precipitated by these forms of developmental aid. For example, the "poor" farmers in Third World nations were being "developed" either by being chased from their land through social aid handouts, or by being prevented from cultivating their arid land to achieve meager harvests through which they had previously managed, more or less, to sustain themselves for centuries. By being chased away or prevented from accomplishing things that had to be done, these agricultural laborers, farmers and others, lost their basis for maintaining a livelihood. The same scenario applies also to situations where the "developed" farmers' meager, yet somehow still fertile, land was excessively built upon or destroyed and devastated by development aid.

xxxxxx

Within the same framework of the planet's destruction and every life form on it, blame for this overpopulation explosion rests also with the major religions and sects. Obstinately they advocate terrestrial mankind's breeding of a myriad of descendants, which generates overpopulation in the first place. Resembling degenerate beasts of prey, religions and sects lunge into Third World countries by sending missionaries to disseminate the madness of their religious and sectarian beliefs, along with their inhumane, degrading consequences and excesses. Such beliefs are based upon enslavement, mismanagement, corruption, exploitation, negative influence of the consciousness, deprivation of liberty of the consciousness, delusional beliefs, religious wars, murders and humankind's stultification. All of these are based on the sectarian madness' phrase "Be fruitful and multiply" the root-of-all-evil to overpopulation's stupidity.

This then is the truth: The Earth is incredibly overpopulated. It is propelling itself towards its own destruction and, as a result of overpopulation, is plummeting toward the destruction of all life on the planet. Humankind alone is guilty of this overpopulation for it knows no limit whatsoever in its own diverse excesses. In contrast to man, members of the animal world instinctively behave more reasonably and in accordance with nature's laws. By adjusting their urges and instincts, animals regulate their own population and adapt to prevailing food supplies and living conditions. When overpopulation arises for some reason, the death of many animals is effected, whereby a selection process comes into play that eliminates animal excess. Man, the creature of reason, ought to emulate this example. But in his megalomania he totally ignores it. He believes himself to be the crown of Creation, and feels entitled, therefore, to transgress against the natural laws. As a result, mankind unstoppably multiplies, and in doing so, they immeasurably and unrelentingly magnify all plights, misery, ills, crime, illnesses, epidemics, addictions, other wrongs and excesses once more, and create incredible chaos and total destruction to order and life itself.

The more development aid, famine relief and other forms of aid are provided throughout the globe and not birth control measures by the pseudo-humanitarians and other fools of compassion, the more horrendous become the plight, ills, misery of the people on Earth, along with all other catastrophic conditions and excesses that ruin and destroy life and the planet. Without relevant and really humane and pertinent help, neither underdeveloped countries nor their inhabitants can be turned into cultivated, civilized and economically balanced and progressive nations and peoples within a few short years or decades. Additionally, the population of these countries can be simply "revamped" and changed to adapt to the thinking and behavior of a world and its people who enjoy a healthy economy and politics without international direction. The privileged people enjoy extensive learning, comprehensive education, sound social systems, government leadership, legislation and guidelines for overall development each of which has had to evolve over centuries of painstaking effort.

xxxxxx

Hopefully, mankind on Earth will allow the pure, natural laws and directives to prevail in all matters, particularly as they apply to overpopulation, which can only be reduced by enforcing a drastic and rigorous, worldwide birthrate check program. It is in this manner that man can finally limit and eventually eradicate misery, privation and ills of every type on this beautiful, blue planet called Earth.

Overpopulation brings with it ethnic problems as well. Indeed, it actually induces them. It precipitates migration, war, bloodshed and murder. As a result of the world population's continuing growth, people are squeezed together ever closer, and the space for each person becomes ever smaller and more restricted. For this reason can situations not be avoided whereby inhabitants of various countries, tribes, religions, convictions, opinions, philosophies and outlooks increasingly crowd together only to infringe upon each other's personal space. Without fail, this type of close contact leads to friction, differences of opinion and arguments. These issues, in turn, automatically generate war, bloodshed, murder and migration. The migration issue alone leads to even more excessive, vicious, worldwide problems. For example, refugees do not simply leave their familiar homesteads merely to seek new ones within their own country. Instead, they flee to foreign lands and often to countries that are financially and economically more prosperous than their own homelands. So it transpires that thousands, tens of thousands, indeed hundreds of thousands, even millions of refugees abruptly flee their homelands and swarm into foreign, more prosperous nations. In turn, these nations become swamped with foreigners, causing almost insurmountable problems. Countries that accept these refugees are forced to expend billions of dollars that are paid for by the "host nation's" industrious inhabitants through hard-earned funds from horrendous taxes.

The refugees from nations where ethnic problems, wars, bloodshed, various types of persecution and murder prevail, swarm like locusts into the more prosperous countries and settle there, frequently through their lies and criminal activities. These people generate an escalating glut of foreigners within the world's prosperous nations, into which they often can enter only as illegal aliens. The surplus of foreigners, consisting of the refugees, brings renewed social, economic, political as well as religious or ethnic problems. Slowly but surely, the social structure within these nations begins to collapse. Living and housing expenses climb higher and higher, and the lack of housing increases. Equally slowly but surely, the refugees wipe out the lineage of the country's native people by intermingling with the local population. The refugees effect mixed marriages from which originate mixed progeny in numbers and masses that can no longer be condoned. It is normal and understandable that such mixed marriages do occur when individuals meet while travelling or working in various countries, and thereafter marrying as a result. This uncommon type of mixed marriage neither harms the lineage nor the native people themselves. But when the land becomes flooded with foreign refugees who embark upon mixed marriages with members of the local population and procreate mixed descendants, a new population of mixed races springs forth, and in no time at all this group displaces and eradicates the native population.

The type of refugee fleeing into foreign nations shows no homogeneity. Refugees come from all social levels, and their reasons for migrating are frequently very diverse. These reasons range from economic exodus and personal problems, broken hearts and drug problems, religious and military reasons, to fleeing for political and family reasons, a lust for adventure and leaving the homeland to avoid work. Thus, many diverse refugee groups flee their native lands to seek shelter in more prosperous countries. These nations ultimately suffer from the massive influx of foreigners and its vicious consequences, which endanger both government and the populace. The majority of refugees request political asylum, which costs the host nations and its hard-working tax payers billions of dollars. Of course, these unexpected costs are a burden to the various factions of local citizenry and cause hatred to flare up against the asylum-seekers, foreigners and other races. Such hatred becomes perpetuated and leads to fatal escalations, material damage and unimaginable disaster.

Another factor related to the refugee problem must be addressed as well, namely, that typically only somewhat affluent people flee from their homeland. Such refugees have limited personal financial security, e.g., a house or land which they have been able to sell in order to finance their escape. These people are not particularly humble. More often than not, they make brazen financial demands on the refugees' host nations, including for monetary donations, housing, vehicles, living expenses, clothing and social aid of various types. Yet, people who ought to flee their homeland for reasons of personal safety, rarely have the funds to pay for their escape, because their finances simply prevent them from doing so. They simply cannot afford to flee. For this reason they are arrested, tortured and murdered. Therefore, it is only people with financial means, as a rule, who then claim to be refugees. In general, they are the only ones who frequently flee to other economically and socially more prosperous nations, in order to achieve a more comfortable lifestyle than they previously enjoyed in their homelands. To obtain the same lifestyle while living in their native country would have required a great deal more effort and struggle. Even though they are obviously refugees for economic and related reasons and others, they make other people in the refugees' host nations believe, through their lying and cheating, that they have had to flee their homeland for reasons of religious, military and/or political persecution. In these cases are the claims, lies, fraud and deceit far from the truth. Furthermore, refugees frequently appear who are more than mere crooks. Indeed, they are major criminals who commit profitable and serious crimes within the host countries. Increasingly, refugees are appearing who gain unofficial access to the host nations, possibly even through official permission from the authorities, only to become involved in collecting horrendous sums of money with which they financially support wars, fratricide and revolutions in their homelands, or they purchase weapons and other war supplies.

Very few refugees indeed can truly be categorized as refugees. Among the many thousands there are but a few people who can genuinely be considered and classified as refugees. Only people who have had to flee for their lives when escaping from their homeland are actual refugees. This definition differs from that used by individuals controlling the host countries' refugee centers, where they provide legitimate refugee status to many thousands of bogus refugees. In doing so, these officials are really forcing the entire country to pay for the refugees' support. The individuals of authority are incapable of recognizing the fact that this type of refugee is simply a refugee for economic reasons or they simply decline to recognize this fact for pseudo-humanitarian reasons. These "economic" refugees are individuals who do not mind deserting their countries. They flee from their native lands especially in times of confusion and misery when their country really depends on the help and collaboration of each and every citizen, and at a time when their support is urgently needed to help the survival of land, country and life. These refugees cowardly flee their homeland, instead of helping to return the proper order needed to achieve and attain a prospering state and/or prospering nation. This goal can never be achieved by cowardly abandonment, regardless of what type of system is contemplated be that a somewhat normal country or a chaotic nation in the grip of a vicious dictatorship. Each and every country needs its citizens because it is only with their help, and the help of qualified leaders, that a civilized social structure can be secured and achieved, one that is worthwhile to live for because of a suitable economy, politics and a sound standard of living. However, when the cowardly citizens flee their homeland instead of standing up for it, helping it along, and in an emergency even fighting for it, chaos, misery, plight and every ill become subsequently even greater and more insurmountable.

Lastly, there are refugees who truly are unjustly persecuted victims of religious or political turmoil, wars and revolution. It goes without saying if for no other reason than for purely human empathy that such human beings must be granted support and asylum. However, this premise is justifiable only with the condition that the refugees return to their respective native lands after conditions in their own countries have normalized and improved. Such refugees would not be permitted to stay in the host country beyond the end of their term once a safe return to their homeland, without threats against life or limb, has been guaranteed, or once a state of somewhat normal economic and living standards has been re-established.

All evidence pertaining to the refugee problem clearly demonstrates that the flood of refugees and their illegal entry must be rigorously curtailed. If this does not occur, the problems of too many aliens, refugees and the asylum-seeking homeless, along with the generated hatred of strangers, hatred towards other races and the asylum-seekers, become uncontrollable and subsequently lead to unpreventable catastrophes.

Is it brutal and inhumane when the laws and directives of nature are followed? No. However, it is brutal, inhumane and uncharitable when mankind continues to cling to overpopulation, indeed even promotes it, regardless of the circumstances and consequences, in order that millions and millions of new children can be procreated. By failing to enact stringent birth control measures for sectarian reasons and feebleminded sentimentality, man precipitates all misery and problems that will eventually become even greater and more difficult to combat, and where finally no solution or salvation will be feasible.

xxxxxx

It is important to disseminate this text worldwide. Indeed, only through this action will it ever be possible to publicize the fatal overpopulation problem. This action will also allow deliberate, international measures to be taken against overpopulation and against torture and capital punishment. (The pamphlet Torture, Capital Punishment and Overpopulation can be obtained from FIGU. It may be copied, translated and distributed as well.) Please disseminate these writings to the best of your ability. Send copies of the texts to your relatives, acquaintances, friends, colleagues and associates; to physicians and scientists; to organizations of all types; to churches and sects that preach unrestrained human procreation; to environmental protection agencies and clubs of all types; to relief and peace organizations; to ministers, priests and clergymen; to radio and television stations, newspapers, journals, periodicals, tabloids and others; to the authorities, journalists, politicians, the military, legal authorities, schools and universities, attorneys, the government and all types of agencies; to private citizens, professors and officials; to businesses and corporations; to every Tom, Dick and Harry, and any other person of whom you may think. The overpopulation problem, along with the ensuing destruction of life on Earth and the planet itself, concerns all human beings, even those in the remotest and loneliest of hovels.

Please help us in our crusade against overpopulation and the destruction of all life on Earth. It is only through your help and that of every single person, that this suffocating monster and destroyer called overpopulation can be checked, reduced and normalized. This would permit life on Earth to once again become worthwhile for man and all other creatures, and the preservation of all life and the planet itself. The assistance of every single person is required for this task. If individuals participate and unite in this undertaking, the outcome will produce a gigantic mass and force capable of attacking and eradicating all ills on Earth. Nothing will ever be accomplished, however, unless each and every individual strives to fight against all current and future ills. In unity lies the strength to change and improve ills, i.e., when an individual ventures forth, undertakes a task and then meets like-minded persons; together they will slowly but surely form a great, vast force whose strength can then unfold. For this reason it is essential that every individual endeavors to act now and seeks like-minded individuals to powerfully attack all ills. Please help us, as an individual human being, by backing the fight against overpopulation through your own actions, and standing up against the subsequent, already partially evident destruction. Please support us in this task in every possible way.

Chapter 2

LIMITING FACTORS

Beside the natural death of every individual due to old age, diseases, accidents, crimes, wars, disasters, etc. are also taking their toll in reducing the population. Some of these factors have been overcome, which account for the spiraling of the human population, albeit at great cost to human lives, comforts and environmental degradation. There are also some benign factors that should influence some into limiting the size of their households. It is a reminder that not all is well for victims who are in dire strait to make ends meet. Unless people heed the growing signs of the coming catastrophe, they may just suffer the consequences of neglect and our *bahala* mentality.

Living Space

The total Earth's land surface is about 150 million km^2. Not all these lands are habitable or can be used beneficially. A significant portion of the Earth's exposed land is inhospitable and cannot be used for agricultural and habitation purposes such as the Arctic and Antarctic zones. Others are extremely arid and large portions are very mountainous, inhabited only land out of necessity due to the congested lowlands, high cost of ownership and attachment to their ancestral domain and their way of life.

Only about 90 million km^2 can be said to be habitable for the present population of 6.6 billion people. On the average, there is a density of 73.3 persons/km^2. A third or about 30 million km^2 are used for growing food and livestock and occupied by people for residential and other purposes. A small diminishing portion is devoted to the forest.

The Philippines is a small country of about 90 million people confined in a land area of about 300,000 km^2, giving us a density of 300 persons/km^2. We are also the 12th most populous country in the world with an annual growth rate of 2.04% since the year 2000, according to the August 2007 census. The growth rate translates to 3.5 children per family. This means that if the current trend continues, the population will double in about 70 years. Even if we decide to have a replacement level of two children per family in place immediately, the population will still increase for at least a generation before tapering off during the second generation as the people of the present generation start dying off.

Overpopulation and demand for shelter is the prime motive behind the spiraling cost of land and housing. It has become prohibitive for wage earners that many have resorted to squatting on government and private lands. Most of the government lands located along riverbanks, esteros, and beside railroad tracks have been invaded by hordes of squatters. In a move to improve the cities, many of these squatters are being forced out of these areas and relocated to remote areas, often without minimal sanitation and potable water supply. One example published in *Balatbat* is an article entitled *Rail Evictees: Dumped and Neglected* written by Dabet Castaneda. It has to do with a pet project of Vice President and Housing Secretary Noli de Castro in Southville, Cavite. This 55-hectare relocation center was created to shelter the squatters evicted from the North South Rail Linkage Project of the Philippines National Railways. Almost 7,000 families were evicted and their homes demolished along the railways in Makati, Manila and Cabuyao to make room for the project.

The project in Southville is located in the middle of an agricultural land and beside a former garbage dumpsite. Three other relocation centers are Towerville and Northville IV, which are located in the province of Bulacan. A fourth relocation center is in Imus, Cavite.

The Southville project was the scene of a dengue outbreak recently. It is one of the deadly diseases that annually kill thousands of children. According to one NGO, COHRE, the poor drainage system in the housing project and its proximity to the garbage dump pose health risks to the neighborhood. The Ecological Waste Coalition said residents of the Southville relocation site are exposed to "high levels of contaminants that are released through dump fires, landfill gas migration and surface and underground leachate migration." Because they have no sources of water, deep wells are dug to provide the needed water. Children have been developing skin diseases which their parents attribute to filthy water from the deep wells.

After the dengue outbreak, five health centers have been built but residents here said no doctors, nurses or even midwives were assigned. They only come when they conduct medical missions. Patients have to be transported to hospitals in other places with the facilities. Some of the parents of the patients were so poor they have to pawn the mobile phone of their neighbors just to be able to get the money to pay for the laboratory services.

Many of these relocation sites are located in the provinces and far from the places where most of the breadwinners worked. Most of them have to spend quite a sum of money to travel to work in Metro Manila. Some 70% have to rent a place in Metro Manila near their work places and return home during the weekends. One example of how difficult it is to stay away from the relocation site is the experience of Joel Alvarez, 35, who works as a driver in Makati City. He said he spends a minimum of P80 ($1.62) a day for transportation alone so he decided to leave his family in Southville and rented a space near his work. He goes home on weekends.

Due to the dengue outbreak, Alvarez decided to bring his family in Cavite, a neighboring province, until the outbreak subsides. His good intentions were misinterpreted by local officials of the National Housing Authority (NHA) who told him to vacate his house because he and his family were not occupying it. There were ten other cases similar to his.

In the three other relocation sites visited by *Bulatlat*, residents do not have access to electricity and potable water. A five gallon container of potable water costs P35 while residents pay another P35-P50 a day for use of the generator for 12 hours to supply electricity starting at 6 p.m. Others just depend on "jumpers" or illegal power connections.

There are many other inadequacies such as education and health services. In Southville, COHRE said 2,000 children attend school that is partially housed in tents. There is no water for the two small toilets and children must pay for drinking water. The teachers work in three four-hour shifts to cope with the sheer volume of pupils and lack of facilities.

During *Bulatlat's* visit to Northville IV in January, at least 16 families were still living in tents. Daisy Mariñas, community relations chief of NHA-Bulacan Task Force North Rail, admitted there is no budget yet for decent houses for these families categorized as "uncensused" - families who lived along the railways but were not at their homes when NHA conducted its survey in July 2004. She said there are 110 "uncensused" families in Balagtas alone. Of these, 65 families still live along the railways because there are no more lots allotted for them.

Because of the depressing conditions experienced by thousands of relocatees, the government has received flak from local and international groups supporting the cause of the urban poor. COHRE said the right to adequate housing is, in fact, enshrined in an extensive body of international law, including the Universal Declaration on

Human Rights and the International Covenant on Economic, Social and Cultural Rights (ICESCR).

The Government of the Philippines has ratified the ICESCR, COHRE said, and the right to adequate housing as provided by the Constitution and the Urban Development and Housing Act of 1992. The plight of the displaced urban poor in the country is seen by President Arroyo's critics as one more glaring example of how she has bartered away the life and well-being of a sector most in need in exchange for the questionable benefits of modernization.

I personally do not think it is easy to solve the housing problem of the urban poor because there are just too many of them and there is not enough funding to help all of them. As soon as one family is relocated, other urban poor sprout out to replace them. This vicious cycle will not be solved until the population of the urban poor stabilized.

Food Supplies

The FAO of the United Nations states in its report *The State of Food Insecurity in the World 2006*, that while the number of undernourished people in the developing countries has declined by about three million, a smaller percentage of the populations of developing countries is undernourished today compared with 1990–1992: 17% against 20%. Furthermore, FAO's projections suggest that the proportion of hungry people in developing countries in 2015 could be about half of what it was in 1990–1992: a drop from 20% to 10%. The FAO also states "We have emphasized first and foremost that reducing hunger is no longer a question of means in the hands of the global community. The world is richer today than it was ten years ago. There is more food available and still more could be produced without excessive upward pressure on prices. The knowledge and resources to reduce hunger are there. What is lacking is sufficient political will to mobilize those resources to the benefit of the hungry." Despite the optimism, the food and oil crisis of 2007-2008 just renege the FAO prediction with a vengeance. Even if there is enough food supply, the problem is that there are not enough funds for the poor to buy the needed food.

According to the U.S. Department of Agriculture, the number of people in the world's 70 poorest countries lived with persistent hunger increase by more than 130 million between 2006 and 2007 - from 849 million to 982 million. They consumed less than 2,100 calories daily, the minimum requirement for a healthy life as defined by FAO. This is in contrast to the 2006 Food Security Assessment of the USDA that the number of hungry and malnourished people worldwide would fall to 800 million by 2017. In a complete turnabout, it now estimates that the number of food-insecure people in developing countries will expand to 1.2 billion within a decade.

In Asia, we are still one of the most successful producers of babies but still least successful when it comes to producing the staple food. As basically an agricultural economy, we still have to annually import rice and corn to feed the people does not speak well of our government as an institution. Even the National Food Authority (NFA), sets up to subsidize farmers have failed to encourage farmers to produce enough. The rising incident of hunger is mainly due to the rise in the cost of foods. The price of rice soared by 43% because of the growing demand for the staple and the high cost of the input partly due to the oil price increases. Families in Metro Manila posted the largest number of hungry people comprising 22% or 530,000 families or 2.65 million people. (*Philippine Daily Inquirer*, July 22, 2008)

A survey made by the Social Weather Station shows that the period between April and June 2008, the involuntary hunger (due to lack of food) rose to a record of more than one in every five households or a total of 16.3% of the families nationwide, or around 14.5 million people. This survey is based on the experienced of a person who had at least suffered hunger once in the previous quarter. This is up from the 15.7% reported a month earlier.

Hunger and malnutrition kill nearly 6 million children a year, and more people are malnourished in sub-Saharan Africa this decade than in the 1990s, according to a report released by the FAO. In sub-Saharan Africa, the number of malnourished people grew to 203.5 million people in 2000-02 from 170.4 million 10 years earlier says *The State of Food Insecurity in the World* report.

The latest survey by the Gallup International-Voice of the People 2008 ranked the Philippines as the 5th on the list of the top 10 hungriest countries in the world with 40% of the people feeling hunger at least once during the last twelve month period prior to the survey. It is surpassed only by Cameroon with 55%, Pakistan (53%), Nigeria (48%), and Peru (42%). (*Philippine Star*, November 5, 2008)

Part of the reasons for hunger is the inability of the government to properly channel the subsidized rice to deserving recipients. According to a World Bank study made last November 2008, only a third of the subsidized rice sold by the NFA went to the poorest 20% of Filipino households. In 2006, as much as 41% ended up in non-poor households while an estimated 16% went to the two highest income groups. Leakage in the Food for Poor program was placed by the World Bank at 40%. (*PS*, December 24, 2008)

It does not take much to change a country from stable to chaos, from the status of a producer to importer of grain. Political upheaval and civil unrest can change all that overnight. One example is the Zimbabwe affair. According to the BBC, the famine in Zimbabwe was caused by government seizure of farmland, compounded by the drought. Prior to both events, Zimbabwe had been exporting so much food that it was called "the breadbasket of southern Africa." With the food production failure, even the neighboring countries depending on it were affected.

Prior to President Robert Mugabe's seizure of the farmland in Zimbabwe, the farmers had been using irrigation to deal with drought, but during the seizures of the farmland, much of the irrigation equipment was either vandalized or looted. A 2006 BBC article reported that Mugabe's seizure of farmland have devastated the economy and led to massive hunger. Much of the formerly white-owned land is no longer being productively used - either because the beneficiaries have no experience of farming or they lack finance and tools. Many farms were wrecked when they were invaded by government supporters.

In contrast, Mauritius, a densely populated country in Africa has no problem with food supplies. It is a rich country with a first world standard of living. The reason that Mauritius is doing so well is because it has strong protection of property rights, and its utilization of science and technology, and industrialization to achieve the goal.

Today, over half of the arable land in the world is in fact not under cultivation. This is because immense tracts of forests or jungles have been otherwise cleared to bring the rest of the arable land on that continent to productive use.[6] This is compounded by the growing population in many parts of the continent. However, bringing the unused land into service in many cases would require huge investments of money and effort, and would do considerable damage to the environment. For example, only about 28% of the arable land on the African continent is used for growing crops.

The steadily increasing human population is putting great pressure on our ability to feed the people of the world. Even though there are enough grains to feed everyone, the uneven income of consumers and the uneven distribution system coupled with economic,

---

[6] http://pages.prodigy.net/jhonig/bignum/qland2.html

political and military policies of some of the poorest countries have caused unprecedented starvation around the world. With steeply rising energy and fertilizer prices, some analysts doubt that future production can keep pace with the growing population. Each year, new cities, roads, airports, golf courses, suburbs and other human needs swallow up vast tracts of prime agricultural land. Soil degradation such as erosion takes away important soil nutrients forcing the farmers to import fertilizers and pesticides to increase production. The expanding deserts are abetting the shortfall in agricultural land. The per capita water has been shrinking as more people are consuming the vital fluid. In many places, competition among rural and urban dwellers for water is becoming acute especially during dry seasons. Likewise, the affluent citizens have been consuming their disproportionate available food and water making obesity a new problem. As a result, total grain reserve stocks have fallen by 53 million tons in 2007 alone. This scant reserve could easily be wiped out when famine struck at several regions simultaneously or crop failures in some of the grain producing countries. The energy crisis that sporadically occurs has forced many countries to shift some of their agricultural land into food production for biofuels.[7] One solution is to change the consumption patterns of those who consumed more than their shares for the benefit of others.

High consumption patterns of those with higher income can only worsen the food crisis because not only because of their bigger appetite but also they have a preference for high value food such as meat and dairy, which make heavy demands on feed grains and land for grazing. An average American consumes about 275 pounds of meat each year, while people in Denmark consumed 321 pounds. In contrast, the average Nigerians consumes 19 pounds and an Indian consumes only 11 pounds (2002 data). Not only that, the rich also demand other rich and varied food such as fresh fruits, exotic coffees, nuts, and wines, and other high value items. They eat more frequently in restaurants, where large and wasteful portions are routinely served. The practice has found favors with many millions of middle class from the developing countries.

China, with one-fifth of the world's population may be way behind in living standard than most developing countries in Asia, but their eating habits have improved a lot. Their meat consumption has

---

[7]

http://www.globalpolicy.org/socecon/hunger/general/2008/07paulwahlberg.pdf

increased more than 150% since 1985 while their importation of animal feed grain has steadily increased. In 2007, China imported 35 million tons of soybean oilseeds, mostly as animal feed. It is one of the driving forces for worldwide grain consumption and with it the spiraling price.

The new middle classes also eat more processed foods, which require energy inputs and create more food waste. Supermarkets and fast-food restaurants are also part of the new lifestyle, which is not necessarily healthier. A global obesity pandemic attests to the new dietary problems. Some 1.6 billion adults around the world are now overweight (400 million of them obese), says WHO. Yet some 800 million worldwide are chronically undernourished.[8]

It is not enough to be fully fed, but the food must be nutritious enough to improve the health leading to brighter children. Children need protein to build up their brain cells that is badly needed if they are to compete in this crowded world.

The uneven distribution of wealth is one cause of the food crisis. There are many people who cannot afford to buy the needed food because they usually came from poor families with too many mouths to feed. Even in rich countries there are tens of millions of people who are considered "food insecure." Poor families have the added burden of balancing their budget, and better food consumption is often sacrificed for other necessities of life. There are many difficult choices to make with their meager budgets. Many have cut back on their diets, even reducing the number of daily meals. Misery and severe malnourishment, if not outright starvation, are the inevitable result. Those that survived face serious long-term health consequences, like stunting and mental retardation.

Grain prices rose about 50% between 2005 and 2007, and USDA long-term projections indicate about 90% of the price increase will persist over the next 10 years, thanks in part to the biofuel boom and to increased consumption of grain-fed meat by the rapidly expanding Asian middle class. This is expected to increase further with the rise of oil prices in 2008. Fortunately, on the latter part of the year, the price of oil felled to around $40-$50 which allows the ordinary workers to save some money for food and other needs. However, in many Third World countries the cost of food accounts for more than half of the total household expenses, especially those

---

[8]

http://www.globalpolicy.org/socecon/hunger/general/2008/0718crowded.htm

countries that has to import the much needed oil and food like the Philippines.

The sea was once touted as the source of unlimited food for the runaway population. However, overfishing has drained the sea of many food sources, especially the valuable ones. It will take years to replenish the stocks. Many less valuable commercial species are now targeted for depletion. To safeguard against overfishing, marine patrols are used in many developed countries to check on violation of overfishing. Protection of some species has been imposed, their minimum sizes for harvesting as well as the fishing gears used to catch them.

The rising fuel cost for fishing vessels have added to the difficulties for fishermen to go further to catch profitably the needed fish for the people. The more economical solution is to plant more crops. Planting crops have their own unique problems. Pesticides and fertilizers are needed to improve crop production. Most of our pesticides are imported, some of them banned for use from the countries of origin. Banned pesticides that can cause cancer, birth defects and brain damage are often exported to poor countries with less stringent environmental laws. Farmers are often ignorant of the health risks of pesticides until it is too late.

Worldwide, approximately three million cases of pesticides poisoning occur annually with over two hundred thousand deaths. While 80% of pesticides and other agricultural chemicals are used in developed countries, more than 99% of all deaths from pesticide poisoning occur in developing nations. Most of the pesticides used in developing countries are imported from the U.S. In a three months time in 1990, over 120 million pounds were exported from the U.S. with 12 million pounds classified as extremely toxic including banned cancer-chemicals such as chlordane, mirex, and heptachlor. Half of them can cause either cancer or birth defects. Chlordane has been banned in the U.S. since the 1980s, but we are still using them in treatment against termite at home and during construction where it is spray on the soil to kill the termites. The pesticide can only move downward and contaminate the groundwater. Another pesticide used at home is methyl bromide. This colorless gas or liquid is used against termite and can be found in carpets, drapes and leather. It is suspected of causing cancer, and is toxic to lungs, skin and brain. (Steinman and Wisner, 155, 187, 192)

The harmful effect of pesticides was first documented by Rachel Carson with her book *Silent Spring*. But the war against insects invading our food supply has to be fought with new and deadlier form of pesticides. Many of today's pesticides are systemic in the sense that they do not just kill the insects outside the fruit trees and crops but can penetrate to become part of the fruit or crop that cannot be washed or peeled off. They are not biodegradable and can remain on the environment for a long time. This means they can be active for years after it is applied and eventually washed down by rainfall or wind to contaminate rivers and streams leading to lakes, seas and oceans. Others may just percolate to contaminate ground water. (Weintraub, 294)

Since pests have the remarkable ability to adapt to toxic chemicals, more and powerful pesticides have to be used to produce the same degree of crop protection. In order to produce more food, the use of pesticides has increased some 3,300% since 1945, but crop loss due to insects has still increased some 20% over the same period. Clearly, there must be a better way of producing food for consumption and it is organic farming. More on this in the section on Food Supplies.

One example of how pesticides are recklessly handled is the recent sea tragedy of July 21, 2008 near the Sibuyan Island. It is the sinking of the *M. V. Princess of the Stars* with their illegally stowed 10 tonnes of toxic endosulfan. The toxic chemical endosulfan was imported by Del Monte from a firm in Israel.

The use of pesticides and other chemicals is needed to save mankind from hunger, especially those from the Third World because of their overpopulated problem. But many of these chemicals are toxic and have to be handled with care. Endosulfan is a neurotoxic organochlorine insecticide of the cyclodiene family of pesticides. It is a highly acutely toxic to insects and mammals as well as humans. Symptoms of acute poisoning include hyperactivity, tremors, convulsions, lack of coordination, staggering, difficulty breathing, nausea and vomiting, diarrhea, and in severe cases, unconsciousness. Doses as low as 35 mg/kg have been documented to cause death in humans, and many cases of sub-lethal poisoning have resulted in permanent brain damage. Farm workers with chronic endosulfan exposure are at risk of rashes and skin irritation.

It is banned in the European Union, Cambodia, and several other countries, while its use is restricted in other countries, including the Philippines (where it will be banned after September 2008 accident). It is still used extensively in many countries including India, New Zealand and the United States. It is made by Bayer CropScience, Makhteshim-Agan, and Hindustan Insecticides Limited among others, and sold under the trade names Thionex, Thiodan, Phaser, and

Benzoepin. Because of its high toxicity and high potential for bioaccumulation and environmental contamination, a global ban on the use and manufacture of endosulfan is being considered under the Stockholm Convention.

Endosulfan has been used in agriculture around the world to control insect pests including whiteflys, aphids, leafhoppers, Colorado potato beetles, cabbage worms, and other pests. It has also seen use in wood preservation, home gardening, and tse-tse fly control, though it is not currently used in any vector control campaigns.

In the United States, endosulfan is only registered for agricultural use. It is used extensively on cotton, potatoes, tomatoes, and apples according to the Environmental Protection Agency (EPA). The EPA estimates that 1.38 million pounds of endosulfan were used annually from 1987 to 1997. In California, annual use of endosulfan dropped from 104 tons in 1995 to just 38 tons in 2005.[9]

It is an endocrine disruptor. Theo Colborn, an expert on endocrine disruption, lists endosulfan as a known endocrine disruptor, and both the EPA and the Agency for Toxic Substances and Disease Registry consider endosulfan to be a potential endocrine disruptor. Numerous *in vitro* studies have documented its potential to disrupt hormones and animal studies have demonstrated its reproductive and developmental toxicity, especially among males. A number of studies have documented that it acts as an anti-androgen in animals. It is not known whether endosulfan is a human teratogen (an agent that causes birth defects), though it has significant teratogenic effects in laboratory rats.

Several studies have documented that endosulfan can also affect human development. Researchers studying children from an isolated village in Kerala, India have linked endosulfan exposure to delays in sexual maturity among boys. Endosulfan was the only pesticide applied to cashew plantations in the hills above the village for 20 years and had contaminated the village environment. The researchers compared the villagers to a control group of boys from a demographically similar village that lacked a history of endosulfan pollution. Relative to the control group, the exposed boys had high levels of endosulfan in their bodies, lower levels of testosterone, and delays in reaching sexual maturity. Birth defects of the male reproductive system including cryptorchidism were also more prevalent in the study group. The researchers concluded that suggest that endosulfan exposure in male children may delay sexual maturity

---

[9] http://en.wikipedia.org/wiki/Endosulfan

and interfere with sex hormone synthesis. Increased incidences of cryptorchidism have been observed in other studies of endosulfan exposed populations.

In 2001, in Kerala, India, endosulfan spraying became suspect when linked to a series of abnormalities noted in local children. Initially endosulfan was banned, yet under pressure from the pesticide industry this ban was largely revoked. The tragedy was regarded as next in magnitude only to the Bhopal gas tragedy. In 2006, in Kerala, compensation of Rs 50,000 was paid to the next kin of each of 135 people who were identified as having died as a result of endosulfan use. The government also assured the other victims affected that they will be taken care of and rehabilitated.

A 2007 study by the California Department of Public Health found that women who lived near farm fields sprayed with endosulfan and the related organochloride pesticide dicofol during the first eight weeks of pregnancy are several times more likely to give birth to children with autism. This is the first study to look for an association between endosulfan and autism, and additional study is needed to confirm the connection.

On the same day of the tragedy, another vessel, the *MV Ocean Papa*, carrying 16 metric tons of the toxic substance toluene di-isocyanate (TDI) sunk near Mararison Island on its route to Iloilo from Manila. It has many useful purposes but is primarily concentrated in the manufacture of polyurethane, flexible foams used in upholstery, mattresses and automotive seats. Lesser uses include polyurethane elastomers and coating functions. The chemical can cause inflammation of the skin and burning of the eyes, cause asthma when inhaled, and damage the gastrointestinal and central nervous systems when ingested. It has been found to be carcinogenic in experimental rats when ingested.

The use of biotechnology or genetic engineering to increase food production is being harnessed to solve the growing hunger problem. It is achieved by manipulation of plant and animal reproduction processes to increase output or strengthen the plants and animal against pests and diseases. Until now, it is being opposed by many including the Catholic Church because of the potential harmful effects of genetically modified (GMO) food products and the idea of tampering with God's plan for nature. There are several controversies regarding the health problem of GMO. Unless we can find some way to increase food production without tinkering with nature, we have little choice but to accept GMO food products until a final verdict has been arrived.

Other methods and schemes to produce more food are taking place. High crop yield vegetables like potatoes and lettuce do not waste space with inedible plant parts, like stalks, husks, vines, and inedible leaves. New varieties of selectively bred and hybrid plants have larger edible parts (fruit, vegetable, grain) and smaller inedible parts; however, many of the gains of agricultural technology are now historic, with new advances being more difficult to achieve. With new technologies, it is possible to grow crops on some marginal land under certain conditions. Aquaculture could theoretically increase available area. Hydroponics and food from bacteria and fungi, like Quorn, may allow the growing of food without having to consider land quality, climate, or even available sunlight, although such a process may be very energy-intensive.

Land are needed not only for residential purposes but more so for food production. World Resources Institute claimed that agricultural conversion to croplands and managed pastures has affected some 3.3 billion hectares - roughly 26% of the world's land area. All totaled, agriculture has displaced one-third of temperate and tropical forests and one-quarter of natural grasslands. Global warming may cause flooding of many of the most productive agricultural areas. Thus, available useful land for food production may become a limiting factor. Sea water flooding may intrude into the agricultural land making the land infertile for farming.

Fortunately, most of the net food producers and exporters are not affected. These countries such as the U.S. with vast tracts of idle land have programs to hold farmland fallow in reserve. The current crisis has prompted proposals to bring some of the reserve farmlands back into use. The American Bakers Association has proposed reducing the amount of farmland held in the US Conservation Reserve Program. Currently the US has 140,000 km² in the program. In Europe about 8% of the farmland is reserved. Farmers have proposed freeing up all of this for farming. Two-thirds of the farmers who were on these programs in the UK are not renewing when their term expires. These idle lands can be used to produce more food to lower the prices and stockpile grain for emergency uses.

Some claim that not all arable land will remain productive if used for agriculture, as they argue that some marginal land can only be made to produce food by unsustainable practices like slash-and-burn agriculture. Even with the modern techniques of agriculture, the sustainability of production is in question. Some scientists have said that in the future, densely populated cities will use vertical farming to grow food inside skyscrapers. Some countries, such as Dubai have constructed large artificial islands, or have created large dam and dike systems, like the Netherlands, which reclaim land from the water to increase their total land area. All these are not going to make a large dent on the need for more arable land if the population does not stop growing.

Because of the high cost of food and the use of pesticides, many urban homes have resorted to planting organic food from their spare space at home. Even in skyscrapers, many have opted to use vertical farming to grow food on their floor. Personally, I doubt this would make a big dent on food production although it could be a great help for the urban poor by allowing them to use many of the idle land. Otherwise, the high cost of floor space also negates the use of space for food production. There would not be enough room to plant the needed food even to ease the food shortage for a large population. It can only mitigate shortages should the need arises.

Organic food business has been growing worldwide due to health conscious consumers' demand for pesticide-free food. However, this has not caught on in the Philippines because of limited demand and expensive. The demand for the growing population has forced farmers to produce more food with the use of synthetic fertilizers and pesticides. In contrast, organic farming uses crop rotation, beneficial insects to control predators, and plant biodiversity to increase organic food production free of pesticides that could harmful to human health. It could also help the environment without harming this fragile ecosystem that is constantly being assaulted by humans. (Weintraub, 290-292)

Most farmers have relied on synthetic fertilizers to increase food production. However, there is little benefit to the soil except residues and contamination of the soil and eventually the over-fertilization of the oceans leading to red tide. While increasing food production temporarily, these fertilizers also repel and kill beneficial soil microorganism and earthworms that could enrich the soil.

Pesticides can also destroy the beneficial as well as harmful microorganisms of the soil. Each year, U.S. farmers use more than 200 million pounds of insecticides, 450 million pounds of herbicides, and 40 million tons of chemical fertilizers on cropland. Manufacturers produce new and stronger pesticides every year, which find their way into our food chain. They are often persistent in the environment and there is no adequate toxicity evaluation on these substances before they are spread on the crops.

Many of the pesticides, whether evaluated for toxicity or not, have been detected in fruits and vegetables in the U.S. More than 80% of apples, peaches, and celery samples contain unsafe levels of pesticide residues even after washing and peeling. Over 70% of non-organic foods have unsafe residues. Many people with food sensitivities find that they are actually sensitive to the toxic pesticides or herbicides and not to the food itself.

About 95% of the toxic chemicals found in U.S. food came from meat, fish, dairy products and eggs. Most of these chemicals were once applied to plants and fed to the animals. They are then accumulated in the tissues of the animals. Beef contains the highest concentration of herbicides than any other food and ranks third in insecticides contamination. Farm animals receive an average of 30 times more antibiotics that are meant to fatten them than people do. Up to 80 drugs have been used on dairy cows in the U.S. but only a few have been tested by the government. European countries have banned most of the beef, poultry, and dairy products from the U.S. precisely because some of these drugs have been detected.

The present food crisis has three interrelated components at work. They involved the use of agricultural lands in some countries. Many peasant farmers have lost their land to land speculators. A new market for agriculture-based energy supplies have some land used once used for food crops converted into crops for energy conversion. The high price of commodity or more commonly known as cash crops has also turned some farmers into producing commodity for the more lucrative export markets. The result is that the poor countries have to import food crops from food producing countries with their high subsidy from government. Land speculators continue to set their eyes on agricultural land in the hope of converting them into more lucrative undertakings. Lastly, governments and corporation abroad have been buying or leasing up agricultural plantations in the poorer countries for food crops and commodity for their own consumption back home. It not only displaced the farmers and those depending on them, but also the production of food crops for the rest of the population.

There is a lot of speculation going on in the commodity market with big money involved. Food crops that are essential for the ordinary people have become a speculated commodity. According to a leading commodities broker, the amount of speculative money in commodities futures has risen from US$5 billion in 2000 to US$175 billion in 2007. Half the wheat now traded on the Chicago commodities exchange is controlled by investment funds. At the Agricultural Futures Exchange of Thailand, speculation on rice has, within one year, tripled the average number of contracts traded daily on the exchange, with hedge funds and other speculators now representing up to half of the daily contracts being traded. All of this speculative activity can only send the prices up and few governments and international agencies are doing anything about it.

The situation is becoming even more critical as land grabbing is going global and becoming official. Many poor farmers and landowners willingly sell their patrimony for top dollars. According to some sources, Japan has acquired 12 million hectares of land in Southeast Asia, China and Latin America to produce food for export to Japan. In effect, Japan has now three times more croplands than its mainland counterpart. The Libyan government has leased 200,000 hectares of cropland in Ukraine to meet its own food import needs, and the United Arab Emirates is buying large landholdings in Pakistan with Islamabad's support. China, with its huge population and diminishing agricultural land is also looking elsewhere for agricultural land. Chinese corporations have also been acquiring rights to productive farmland across Africa and in other parts of the world. In 2007 the Philippine government signed a series of deals with Beijing to allow Chinese corporations to lease land for rice and maize production for export to China, triggering a huge national outcry. The Beijing government is about to make the buying of land overseas to produce food for export to China a central and official government policy.[10] Undeterred, President Arroyo visit to Qatar in December 2008 opened talks over the lease of at least 100,000 hectares of agricultural land to the emirate. (PDI, January 5, 2009)

One of South Korea's biggest conglomerates, Daewoo Logistics wants to invest about $6 billion to develop 1.3 million hectares of land in Madagascar to produce 4 million tons of corn and 500,000 tons of palm oil a year out for export out of Madagascar. This despite the country being highly impoverished and needing the food relief from the World Food Program (WFP). In Cambodia, where the WFP is still supplying aid, oil-rich Kuwait was granted a $546 million loan in return for crop production. Other countries where Cambodia was interested in pushing land concessions to attract foreign investments include talks with South Korea, Indonesia and the Philippines. In Laos, some 2 to 3 million hectares have been parceled out by the impoverished and corrupt dictatorship before it was suspended. The FAO has sounded alarm over the loss of land in countries full of poor rural people who have little access to land for foraging that could lead to tree cutting and replaced with industrial crops. (Ibid)

---

[10] http://www.globalpolicy.org/socecon/hunger/general/2008/07grain.htm

The input of modern machineries could only displace many farmers. Their displacement could only mean more migration of rural people to urban areas, thereby aggravation the problems of urbanization in the cities. The only solution is land reforms. But giving land to the farmers may not be enough without government input such as capital, fertilizer, subsidies and price support for their products. It is also a short term solution as the increasing population of the farmers will only dilute each individual share holdings in the future. It has always been a paradox why those who are producing the staple for people are the ones who are the poorest in our country.

As in any crisis, there are always people who would try to take advantage of a bad situation. Some of these are the big suppliers of agricultural inputs and the speculators trying to make a windfall profit. The sad part of the speculation is that few farmers ever benefit from the crisis, partly because of government regulation and subsidy to the consumers while the middlemen made most of the profit. One example is that of the Thai farmers who are getting less for their rice while consumers pay three times more. The farmers in Honduras, once the bread basket of Central America, cannot afford to buy seed or fertilizer any more, as prices for these inputs have soared. Corporations, on the other hand, are making record profits at every link in the food chain – from fertilizers and seeds to transport and trading. In the first quarter of 2008, while many hungry people were further cutting back on the amount of food they eat, the major food and fertilizer companies were reporting even increasing their already spectacular profit.

In our bid to feed everyone on earth, modern agriculture uses large amounts of fertilizer and pesticides. Since much of this fertilizer is made from petroleum, the problem of oil running out is of great concern. The old ways of using manure as fertilizer should be adopted. But they are good only for small scale farming making it less adaptable for large-scale plantation. Crops rotations have been useful in many instances, but in today's monoculture of production, it is seldom used. Integrated Pest Management (IPM), which uses a wide range of ecological insights have proven successful in eliminating the use of pesticides in Indonesia's rice crop production. (North, 52) Some plants such as legume can fix nitrogen from the air to the soil. New ways must be found. According to a 2003 article in *Discover* magazine, it is possible to use the process of thermal depolymerization to manufacture fertilizer out of garbage, sewage, and agricultural waste.

Beef

More people mean more protein necessary for our healthy life. Protein is an important ingredient in our food consumption. It is necessary for our body to be healthy and for our brain to grow intelligently. Most of the land-based protein came from the animal kingdom, usually chicken, swine, and cattle. Except for a few incidents of double dead, pigs being sold in the open market, there are few complaints about the cleanliness of our foodstuffs. One source is the beef from the cattle industry. But unknown to many, the cattle industry employs a lot of chemicals to fatten and to keep the animals from getting sick.

Toxic chemicals such as pesticides are often applied to the animals directly or indirectly through the feeds grown on land. In the U.S., about 80% of the pesticides used in the US are applied to four major feed crops - corn, soybean, cotton, and wheat. Many of these pesticides can accumulate in our bodies after eating contaminated beef.

Modern factory farming of cattle is treated with chemicals with little regard to the animals and therefore the human consuming the beef. The animals are often castrated to promote growth and packed like sardines inside feedlots. They are fed with chemically-treated grains that promote the growth of fats and hasten their growth and weight before they are slaughtered. The muscles of these animals produce stearic acid fat, which promotes elevated cholesterol and especially LDL in those who eat it.

Most of these pesticides and hormones end up in their fat. In 1991, a 36-country study reported a strong and direct correlation between consumption of dietary and animal fat and the incidence of prostate, colorectal, lung and breast cancers. The more animal products we consume, including all dairy items, the greater is our toxic burden. Eating organic meat and dairy products reduces this toxic load.

Even dioxin, a by-product of the modern industrial age has actually travelled great distances to contaminate the food we ate, most notably red meat, fish and dairy products. Dioxins have been implicated in heart disease, endometriosis, immune dysfunction, diabetes, thyroid disorders, reproductive and birth defects.[11]

Animals are also routinely treated with antibiotics to control sickness and disease, and to make them grow faster. Penicillin, tetracycline, drug-resistant bacteria and countless other substances are routinely found in America's meat supply. Livestock consumes 50%

---

[11] http://findarticles.com/p/articles/mi_m0ISW/is_2001_Oct/ai_78900860

of all the antibiotics used in the U.S., leading to new virulent strains of bacteria that are resistant to all modern antibiotics.

Most hormones are endocrine disrupters and can upset the delicate balance of our hormonal functions. Some of the hormones allowed by the Food and Drug Administration (FDA) to be implanted in beef cattle include the female hormones estradiol, estrogen and progesterone; norgestomet, a synthetic progestin; the male hormone testosterone; and the synthetic anabolic steroids, zeranol and trenbolone.

Estradiol, the hormone most commonly used to "fatten" cattle, is a potent cancer-causing estrogen. The FDA insists that any residues in meat fall within the "normal" range. However, confidential industry reports reveal high hormone residues in meat products. A USDA survey of 32 large feedlots revealed nearly half the cattle had visible illegal "misplaced implants" in muscle tissue rather than in the ear. This could result in very high hormone levels in steak and hamburger. Federal regulators are now looking more closely at the estrogenic effects of pesticides on fruits and vegetables while completely ignoring the contamination of meat products with the far more potent estradiol hormone.

Estrogen is a chemical messenger hormone in the body. It is important for normal sexual development and is essential for the normal functioning of the female organs needed for childbearing such as the ovaries and uterus. Estrogen helps control a woman's menstrual cycle. It is important for the normal development of the breast. It also helps maintain healthy bones and the heart. From puberty to menopause, the ovaries are producing the female hormone estrogen. After menopause, when the ovaries no longer make estrogen, the body fat is the primary source for estrogen made by the body.[12]

The effect of ovarian hormones, such as estrogen, on breast cancer risk was first shown over 100 years ago when researchers found that removing the ovaries of women with breast cancer improved their chances of survival. Recent studies have shown that women who had their ovaries removed early in life have a very low incidence of breast cancer.

One recent study showed that women who developed breast cancer tended to have higher levels of estrogen circulating in their bodies than women without breast cancer. Another recent study showed that women treated for breast cancer, and who had higher levels of estrogen in their bodies, had a return of the disease sooner

---

[12] http://envirocancer.cornell.edu/FactSheet/General/fs9.estrogen.cfm.

than women treated for breast cancer and who had lower levels of estrogen.

This evidence suggests that life-long exposure to estrogen, and perhaps other ovarian hormones, plays an important role in determining breast cancer risk. Studies identifying risk factors for breast cancer have found that women who experience menarche at an early age, or menopause at a later age have a higher risk of breast cancer. This also supports the theory that the number of menstrual cycles a woman has, and hence the length of exposure to estrogen during her lifetime, affects her risk for breast cancer.

Since the 1950s reproductive cancers have escalated dramatically: breast cancer - 55%; testicular cancer - 120%; prostate cancer - 190%. Many of the risk factors for breast cancer outlined by The American Cancer Society and the National Cancer Institute revolve around estrogen dominance - early menarche/late menopause; previous history of breast cancer; advanced years/lifetime accumulation of estrogen, all of which are secondary risk factors. Completely ignored are the primary sources of these hormones coming from the food supply and other environmental exposures.

Recombinant Bovine Growth Hormone is a genetically engineered copy of a naturally occurring hormone produced by cows. It is manufactured by Monsanto Company under the name POSILAC. Other names are BGH, rBGH, BST and rBST. This hormone is intended to increase milk production by as much as 10-15%. It was approved by the FDA in 1993 and immediately put into use by 1994. With a glut of milk already on the market it is inconceivable why this drug was allowed in the first place. Unfortunately for the cows, the extra milk production creates enormous stress on their bodies, interferes with reproduction, promotes mastitis requiring increased use of antibiotics, and causes premature death of the animals. To counteract the increased physical demand on the animals from excessive milk production the agricultural industry took another bold step against the laws of nature and decided to feed the dairy cows a high protein diet of ground up dead cows including sick and diseased animals.

Monsanto and the FDA insist that rBGH milk is indistinguishable from natural milk and safe to cows and consumers. Yet, Monsanto was forced to admit to about 20 veterinary health risks on its Posilac label including mastitis and udder inflammation. The milk is contaminated by pus from mastitis induced by rBGH, and antibiotics used to treat the mastitis. The rBGH milk is contaminated by the GE hormone which can be absorbed through the gut and induce immunological effects. Some rBGH milk is chemically and nutritionally very different from natural milk and is supercharged with high levels of a natural growth factor (IGF-1), excess levels of which have been incriminated as major causes of breast, colon, and prostate cancers.[13]

The genetically engineered version of a natural hormone, rBGH was renamed somatotropin (BST), dropping the word hormone, lest the public should become alarmed over this latest tampering with the food supply. The European Union has refused to use this drug on their dairy herds on the basis of no long-term human studies and because of its adverse effect on the animals. There is no reason why it should be used in the first place considering that there are so many problems encountered since its introduction.

Howard Lyman, a former cattle rancher turned vegetarian and animal rights advocate made a study on Mad Cow Disease. He indicated that this disease which is similar to Cruetzfeldt-Jakob disease (CJD), made its appearance in cows following the cannibalistic procedure of adding animal protein to their diets. The first few cases of Mad Cow Disease, bovine spongiform encephalopathy (BSE), first appeared in Great Britain in 1989. It was suspected that feeding scrapie-infected sheep remains to the cows might have been a cause. Scrapie can be passed onto offspring (vertical transmission). In 1991 the first indications of BSE in vertical transmission was noted, a significant occurrence suggesting the infectious prion was blood borne, and could be passed from mother to calf.

In 1992 BSE was successfully transmitted by injection to animals from seven mammalian species, including pigs and monkeys, which share a high percentage of biological traits with humans. Although the British government denied the obvious, the risk of CJD was a serious possibility to the public. In 1993 two British dairy farmers whose herds were infected with BSE died of CJD. The natural incidence of CJD is one in a million, and generally over age 63. In 1993 a fifteen year old was diagnosed with the disease, followed by two more teenagers in 1995. On March 20, 1996 ten people under age 42 reportedly died from a new, particularly virulent strain of CJD. In 1989 the US rendering industry voluntarily decided to stop using sheep heads in an effort to avoid scrapie-infected feed. An FDA review three years later found 15 of 19 plants inspected were not following this ban. No action was taken.

---

[13] http://www.shirleys-wellness-cafe.com/bgh.htm

In 1997 the FDA banned feeding of ruminant protein to ruminants. But cattle are still fed animal parts from other species, including horses and pigs. Spongiform disease suggests that all mammalian species may be susceptible to them and these diseases transmit easily across species barriers. There is no ban against feeding scrapie infected sheep to pigs, which then can be fed to beef cattle. Worse yet, claims Lyman, bovine bloodmeal has been excluded from the ban. Spray-dried blood products are increasingly used in the feed industry. "Until we stop the transformation of cattle into carnivores, until we can be 100% sure that they are no longer consuming the blood and fecal material of their own species and the meat and bonemeal of any other animal, the risks of Mad Cow Disease and a consequent epidemic of CJD will be with us," claims Mad Cowboy Lyman.

Mad Cow Disease may also be connected to the use of pesticides. Mark Purdy, a Somerset farmer, has been arguing since 1988 that scientists have overlooked the root cause of BSE. He asserts that BSE arose in British herds in the 1980s when the Ministry of Agriculture required all cattle to be treated with the pesticide, phosmet at greater doses than previously used. The pesticide was poured along the spinal cord. Phosmet captures copper. At the same time cattle feed was being supplemented with chicken manure from birds dosed with manganese to increase egg yield. The prion proteins in the cow's brains were deprived of copper while being dosed with extra manganese.

Evidence supporting Purdey's hypothesis comes from Cambridge University where a team of biochemists found that when manganese substituted for copper in prion proteins, the prions took on the distinguishing features that identify the infective agent in BSE. More information on the phosmet/BSE connection can be obtained from http://ny.nofa.org.

Scientists studying the problem of global warming in Australia claimed to have a solution by replacing meat from cattle to eating the meat from kangaroos and wild camels. Raising these animals can reduce damage to the environment because kangaroos emit negligible amount of methane gas compared to cattle. This has been a practice since ancient history. In the case of camel, this imported animal is now a million strong and running wild in the outback of the country. This new eating habit will reduce the population of cattle by 7 million and sheep by 36 million and thus allow the population of kangaroos to increase to 240 million from the present 34 million. The kangaroo's meat is much healthier because it is low in fat and got in protein levels. (*PDI*, January 5, 2009)

Famine and Starvation

A famine is a widespread shortage of food that deprived the people of food necessary for survival. It is usually accompanied by malnutrition, starvation, diseases, epidemic, and increased mortality. It can also be man-made due to bad economic policies or military policy that has deprived certain populations of sufficient food to ensure survival. It can also happen during periods of drought, crops failure, pestilence, war and flood. The 20th century alone took the lives of an estimated 70 million people with 30 million of them coming from the famine of 1958-61 in China.[14]

Famine is another great equalizer to the growing population. As more people are inhabiting this finite earth, the probably of more mass starvations can be expected, especially in countries ruled by dictatorship or under a state of war as is happening in many places in Africa. Dictatorship of the Manchu dynasty was responsible for the greatest famine ever recorded, the 1876-1879 famine of Northern China where 9 to 13 million died. The main cause of the famine was a drought the seared the land for two years from 1876 to 1878 over a vast area in northern China even while flooding was occurring in southern China. In response to the starvation, children have been sold in exchange for food. Cannibalism was practice on a large scale while suicide became a way of death for many. The Manchu dynasty attempted to cover up the famine help fueled the starvation until she was exposed before foreign aids started to pour in. (Spignesi, 14-15) Aside from drought, flooding is also a cause of famine as crops are destroyed before harvesting and topsoil washed away.

Most of the famines today occur in countries that have poor governance. In countries under dictatorship the people are the first to suffer during period of famine. War has also devastating effect on farming and food production and food ration are often diverted to soldiers to appease the military under dictatorship such as in North Korea. At times, emergency food aids are delayed due to inadequate logistics and violence that disrupt the food distribution processes.

Famine has a very destabilizing and devastating effect. The prospect of starvation led people to take desperate measures. When scarcity of food became apparent to peasants, they would sacrifice

---

[14] http://en.wikipedia.org/wiki/Famine

long-term prosperity for short-term survival. They would kill their draught animals, leading to lower production in subsequent years. They would eat their seed corn, to satisfy their immediate need and hope that aids will be forthcoming for the next planting season. Once those means had been exhausted, they would take to the road in search of food. Cities tend to have administered relief programs and grain for immediate emergency reliefs to keep the populations in civil order. With the confusion and desperation of the migrants, crime would often follow them. Many peasants resorted to banditry in order to acquire enough to eat.

Greed often plays a part in famine and starvation. Foods have been diverted to areas where people can afford and willing to pay a higher price. The Great Famine in Ireland, which began in 1845 and occurred as food was being shipped from Ireland to England because only the English could afford to pay higher prices. In a similar manner, the 1973 famine in Ethiopia was concentrated in the Wollo region, although food was being shipped out of Wollo to the capital city of Addis Ababa where it could command higher prices.

Famine can be caused by the plague of locusts that swarm the agricultural fields leaving nothing behind. Famine is sometimes used as a tool of repressive governments as a means to eliminate opponents, as in the Ukrainian famine of the 1930s. In other cases, such as Somalia, famine is a consequence of civil disorder as food distribution systems break down.

Soil degradation has put approximately 40% of the world's agricultural land is jeopardy. In Africa, if current trends of soil degradation continues, the continent might be able to feed just 25% of its population by 2025, according to UNU's Ghana-based Institute for Natural Resources in Africa. As of late 2007, increased farming for use in biofuels, along with world oil prices at nearly $100 a barrel, has pushed up the price of grain used to feed poultry and dairy cows and other cattle, causing higher prices of wheat (up 58%), soybean (up 32%), and maize (up 11%) over the year. Food riots have recently taken place in many countries across the world. An epidemic of stem rust on wheat caused by Ug99 is currently spreading across Africa and into Asia and is causing major concern.

Hunger can be caused by people not having enough money to buy the foodstuff. While it may not cause massive starvation, still it is a cause for alarm. The cost of food has risen 57% in 2007, aggravated by the soaring freight rates. Some donors are also having a hard time to deliver the goods to their intended beneficiaries. The cost of food has jumped by 74% in poor countries that rely on imported foods, according to FAO. Roughly 100 million people are tipping over the survival line. Some food grain importers are Eritrea (88%), Sierra Leone (85%), Niger (81%), Liberia (75%), Botswana (72%), Haiti (67%), and Bangladesh (65%). This Malthusian crunch has been building for a long time. Instead of slowing the population growth, the world is adding 73 million more mouths ever year to the 6.5 billion today and they are expected to reach 9.5 billion or more in 2050. Asia's bourgeoisie is switching to an animal-based diet to survive.[15]

The rich and favored members of the world can help in alleviating starvation in many cases. A lot of grain has been diverted to produce animal proteins. It takes about 7 kilos of grain to produce a kilo of beef, 3 kilos to produce a kilo of pork and 2 kilos to produce a kilo of chicken meat. By reducing the intake of meat, especially beef, there will be more grain for the starving poor. It would even be a healthy lifestyle for the rich considering that meat has been tainted with so much unhealthy chemicals. Prices of grain would not be going up and may even go down.

War against famine has been going on for decades. Beginning in the 20th century, fertilizers, new pesticides, desert farming, and other agricultural technologies began to be used as weapons against famine. The start of the Green Revolution in 1950 saw the increase in grain production until it reaches 250% more in 1984. These agricultural technologies temporarily increased crop yields, but there are signs as early as 1995 that not only are these technologies reaching their peak, but they may now be contributing to the decline of arable land such as the persistence of pesticides leading to soil contamination and decline of area available for farming. Developed nations have shared these technologies with developing nations to solve the food shortage problem.

Some believe that the Green Revolution was an answer to famine in the 1970s and 1980s. The Green Revolution began with the introduction hybrid strains of high-yielding crops. Some criticize the process because they require more chemical fertilizers and pesticides that are harmful to the environment. These high-yielding crops make it technically possible to feed much of the world population. They can be developed to provide enhanced nutrition, and a well-nourished, well-developed population would emerge. However, there are indications

---

[15] http://www.globalpolicy.org/socecon/hunger/general/2008/0414rage.htm

that some regional food production has peaked due to certain strategies associated with intensive agriculture such as groundwater overdrafting, overuse of pesticides and other agricultural chemicals.

Droughts and water deficits are some prime reasons for the shortages of grain harvest. The global warming, coupled with the El Niño and La Niña effects are wrecking the weather pattern around the world. Their repercussions are widespread droughts and flooding in unexpected places. They are already spurring heavy grain imports in numerous smaller countries, may soon do the same in larger countries, such as China or India.

The water tables are falling in scores of countries (including Northern China, the US, and India) due to widespread overpumping where powerful diesel and electric pumps were used. Other countries affected include Pakistan, Iran, and Mexico. This will eventually lead to water scarcity and cutbacks in grain harvest. Even with the overpumping of its aquifers, China has developed a grain deficit, contributing to the upward pressure on grain prices. Just China, India and Pakistan alone probably pump out around 400 cubic kilometers of underground water a year from the new tubewells. They account for more than half of the world's total use of underground water for agriculture. Vietnamese farmers have quadrupled the number of tubewells to more than a million. Iran, Sri Lanka, Indonesia and Bangladesh are doing the same just so to have enough water for drinking and irrigation. It is only a question of time before these groundwater runs out as recharging is not enough to replenish the rate of extraction. Perhaps, 100 million Chinese eat food grown using underground water while 200 million Indians are doing the same. (Pearce, 79-80)

Most of the three billion people projected to be added worldwide by mid-century will be born in countries already experiencing water shortages. After China and India, there is a second tier of smaller countries with large water deficits - Algeria, Egypt, Iran, Mexico, and Pakistan. Four of them already import a large share of their grain. Only Pakistan remains marginally self-sufficient. But with a population expanding by 4 million a year, it will also soon turn to the world market for grain.

Overpumping of deep wells and groundwater are expected to cause the intrusion of salt water that could destroy the arable land once the salt saturated them. Global warming and the rise of sea water are expected to make it easier to contaminate the wells and groundwater with salt water. Even without the rise of sea water level or the sinking of the land, the septic tanks of households are often located near the wells can easily contaminate the wells with fecal matters. Industrial wells channel through the canal and esteros can also percolate and contaminate the wells in the future as they slowly seep down. Using disease contaminated water for food production may just add to the unhealthy production of food crops.

Famine strikes Sub-Saharan African countries the hardest. With the exhaustion of food resources, overdrafting of groundwater, wars, internal struggles, and economic failure, famine continues to be a regional problem with millions at risk of starvation. These famines cause widespread malnutrition and impoverishment in the past. Modern African famines are characterized by widespread destitution and malnutrition, with heightened mortality confined to children, the weak and the elderly. Relief technologies including immunization, improved public health infrastructure, general food rations and supplementary feeding for vulnerable children, has blunted the mortality impacts of famines. Humanitarian crises also arise from civil wars, refugee flows and episodes of extreme violence and state collapse, creating famine conditions among the affected populations.

Despite repeated stated intentions by the world's leaders to end hunger and famine, famine remains a chronic threat in much of Africa and Asia. In July 2005, the Famine Early Warning Systems Network labeled Niger as well as Chad, Ethiopia, South Sudan, Somalia and Zimbabwe on an emergency status. In January 2006, FAO warned that 11 million people in Somalia, Kenya, Djibouti and Ethiopia were in danger of starvation due to the combination of severe drought and military conflicts. In 2006, the most serious humanitarian crisis in Africa is in Sudan's region Darfur. The combination of decades of drought, desertification, and fast population growth are among the causes of the Darfur conflict as the Arab Baggara nomads searching for water have to take their livestock further south to compete for land mainly occupied by non-Arab farming communities. As a result of these conflicts, a civil war is going on with genocide being committed against the civilians. The Sudan's government and its proxy militias in Darfur had done almost nothing to stop the carnage in Darfur. More than 5,000 displaced persons die each month out of the 2.7 million driven from their homes. So far, the U.N. estimated that up to 300,000 people have been killed. (*PS*, December 12, 2008)

Famine has been abetted by the introduction of cash crops to supply the needs of the developed countries. Landlords are the only beneficiaries while leaving the farmers to fend for themselves. Most of these cash crops have no edible value as food. They include tobacco, cotton, coffee, cocoa, sugar cane, tea, jute, oil-yielding crops such as palm oil and other oil-yielding trees. There are also the illicit cash crops such as marijuana and opium poppy. The introduction of these legitimate cash crops has impoverished the peasantry in many areas, such as northern Nigeria, contributing to greater vulnerability to famine when severe drought struck. Because these cash crops are traded as commodity in the world's market, they are subject to fluctuation in the prices. An oversupply of these products can severely lower the prices leading to bankruptcy and poverty for the landlord/farmer.

Many African countries are not self-sufficient in food production, relying on income from cash crops to import food. Agriculture in Africa is susceptible to climatic fluctuations, especially droughts which can reduce the amount of food produced locally. Other agricultural problems include soil infertility, land degradation and erosion, swarming locusts which can destroy whole crops, and livestock diseases. The most serious famines have been caused by a combination of drought, misguided economic policies, and conflict. The 1983–85 famine in Ethiopia, for example, was the outcome of all these three factors, made worse by the Communist government's censorship of the emerging crisis. At the same time in Sudan, drought and economic crisis combined with denials of any food shortage by the government of President Gaafar Nimeiry created a crisis that killed perhaps 250,000 people - and helped bring about a popular uprising that overthrew Nimeiry.

The relationship between overpopulation and famine may be recounted in the history of Chinese and Indian famines. Most of these great famines happened in these countries by virtue of their huge population. Chinese scholars had kept count of 1,828 famines since 108 B.C. to 1911, or an average of close to one famine per year. From 1333 to 1347 a series of terrible calamities striking different parts of the country ranging from famine, flooding and an earthquake opening up the earth killed 6 to 9 million Chinese. The four famines of 1810, 1811, 1846, and 1849 are said to have killed no fewer than 45 million people. During the 1850 to 1873 Taiping Rebellion, coupled with drought, and famine, the population of China drop by over 60 million people. A few years later, famine in northern China claimed 13 million lives. China's Qing Dynasty bureaucracy, which devoted extensive attention to minimizing famines, is credited with averting a series of famines following El Niño-Southern Oscillation-linked droughts and floods. These events are comparable, though somewhat smaller in scale, to the ecological trigger events of China's vast 19th century famines. (Pierre-Etienne Will, *Bureaucracy and Famine*) Qing China carried out its relief efforts, which included vast shipments of food, a requirement that the rich open their storehouses to the poor, and price regulation, as part of a state guarantee of subsistence to the peasantry.

When a stressed monarchy shifted from state management and direct shipments of grain to monetary charity in the mid-nineteenth century, the system broke down. Thus the 1867–68 famine under the Tongzhi Restoration was successfully relieved but the Great North China Famine of 1877–78, caused by drought across northern China, was a vast catastrophe. The province of Shanxi was substantially depopulated as grains ran out, and desperately starving people stripped forests, fields, and sold their very houses for food. Estimated mortality was 9.5 to 13 million people. (Mike Davis, *Late Victorian Holocausts*) In 1936, a famine resulted in the death of 5 million Chinese.

The largest famine of the 20th century was the 1958–61 Great Leap Forward famine in China, causing an estimated 30 million deaths. It was only when the famine had wrought its worst that Mao reversed the agricultural collectivization policies, which were effectively dismantled in 1978. The official statistics is 20 million deaths, as given by the late President Hu Yaobang. China has not experienced a major famine since 1961 (Woo-Cummings, 2002).

The immediate causes of this famine lay in Chairman Mao Zedong's ill-fated attempt to modify agricultural production with the attempt to industrialize. Farmers were forced to abandon their farms by Communist Party cadres across China. Farms were turned into collective farms while the farmers were ordered to produce steel in small foundries, often melting down their farm instruments in the process. Collectivization undermined incentives for the investment of labor and resources in agriculture. Coupled with unfavorable weather conditions and overconsumption in communal hall, led to starvation of unprecedented scale. (see Chang, G, and Wen, G (1997), "Communal dining and the Chinese Famine 1958-1961"). Such was the centralized control of information and the intense pressure on party cadres to report only good news - such as production quotas met or exceeded - that information about the escalating disaster was effectively suppressed. When the leadership did become aware of the scale of the famine, it did little to respond, and continued to ban any discussion of the cataclysm. This blanket suppression of news was so effective that very few Chinese citizens were aware of the scale of the famine, and the greatest peacetime demographic disaster of the 20th century only became widely known twenty years later, when the veil of censorship began to lift.

Like China, India, with the second largest population had been visited by famines killing million in its wake. Owing almost entirely upon the monsoon rains, India is more liable than any other country in the world to crop failures. There were 14 famines in India between 11th and 17th century. During the 1022–1033 great famines in India entire provinces were depopulated. Famine in Deccan killed at least 2 million people in 1702-1704. The first Bengal famine of 1770 is estimated to have taken around 10 million lives - one-third of Bengal's population at the time. During the British rule, there were approximately 25 major famines spread through states such as Tamil Nadu in the south, and Bihar and Bengal in the east during the latter half of the 19th century.[16]

The famines were a product of both uneven rainfall and British economic and administrative policies, which since 1857 had led to the seizure and conversion of local farmland to foreign-owned plantations, restrictions on internal trade, heavy taxation of Indian citizens to support unsuccessful British expeditions in Afghanistan during the Second Anglo-Afghan War, inflationary measures that increased the price of food, and substantial exports of staple crops from India to Britain. Some British citizens, such as William Digby, agitated for policy reforms and famine relief, but Lord Lytton, the governing British viceroy in India, opposed such changes in the belief that they would stimulate shirking by Indian workers.

The 1896 drought leading to famine and the proliferation of sick people intertwining with healthy people claimed that lives of 8,250,000 in a span of five years. The initial drought covering 300,000 $mile^2$ of land affected 61 million people resulting in the death of 6 million people. After a short respite, it was followed by another two years of drought that claimed another 2,250,000 Indians. (Spignesi, 20)

The few poorhouse set up by the government soon overflow with destitute and helpless people. It soon turns into dens of criminal activities as well as brothels and hospices for the terminally ill. Many suffering from leprosy and other diseases were mixing with all kinds of people and infecting them. Cannibalism was resorted to by some to survive as corpses were literally littering the streets. Those who were able to find work were paid too little to buy the necessary food for sustenance of the family. (Ibid)

The famines continued until independence was granted by the Great Britain in 1947. The Bengal Famine of 1943-1944 - even though there were no crop failures, killed 1.5 million to 3 million Bengalis

---

[16] http://en.wikipedia.org/wiki/Famine_in_India

during World War II.[17] The man-made famine in British-ruled Bengal ultimately took the lives of more than 4 million people, about 90% of the total British Empire casualties during World War II and was accompanied by a multitude tales of horrors, not the least being massive civilian and military sexual abuse of starving women and young girls that compares unfavorable with the comfort women abuses of the Japanese Army.[18]

Ultimately, millions of Bengalis died because their British rulers did not give a damn to their welfare and had other more important strategic imperatives. The Bengal Famine and its aftermath for the debilitated Bengal population consumed its victims over several years in the case of complete British inaction through most of 1943 or insufficient subsequent action. Churchill had a confessed hatred for Indians and during the famine he opposed the humanitarian attempts of people such as the Prime Minister of Canada, Louis Mountbatten, Viceroy General Wavell, and even of Japanese collaborationist leader Subhash Chandra Bose. The hypothesis can be legitimately advanced that the extent of the Bengal Famine derived in part from sustained, deliberate policy. Another theory advanced by Nobel Laureate Amartya Sen was that there was no shortage, but the peasants and laborers were just too poor to buy them.

In 1966, there was a close call in Bihar, when the United States allocated 900,000 tons of grain to fight the famine. Three years of drought in India resulted in an estimated 1.5 million deaths from starvation and disease.

Famine struck North Korea in the mid-1990s, set off by unprecedented floods. This autarkic urban, industrial society had achieved food self-sufficiency in prior decades through a massive industrialization of agriculture. However, the economic system relied on massive concessionary inputs of fossil fuels, primarily from the Soviet Union and the People's Republic of China. When the Soviet collapse and China's marketing switched to trading in hard currency, full price basis, North Korea's economy collapsed. The vulnerable agricultural sector experienced a massive failure in 1995–96, expanding to full-fledged famine from 1996 to 1999. An estimated 600,000 died of starvation (other estimates range from 200,000 to 3.5 million). North Korea has not yet resumed its food self-sufficiency and relies on external food aid from China, Japan, South Korea and the United

---

[17] Ibid

[18] http://www.abc.net.au/rn/science/ockham/stories/s19040.htm

States. Recently, North Korea requested that food supplies no longer be delivered. (Woo-Cummings, 2002)

Various famines had occurred in Vietnam. Japanese occupation during World War II caused the Vietnamese Famine of 1945, which caused 2 million deaths. Following the unification of the country after the Vietnam War, Vietnam briefly experienced a food shortage in the 1980s, which prompted many people to flee the country.

Droughts and famines in Imperial Russia are known to have happened every 10 to 13 years, with average droughts happening every 5 to 7 years. Famines continued in the Soviet era, the most notorious being the *Holodomor* in various parts of the country, especially the Volga, and the Ukrainian and northern Kazakh during the winter of 1932–1933. The last major famine in the USSR happened in 1947 due to the severe drought.

Although large-scale famines in peaceful countries is a thing of the past, countries where people do not have enough fund to buy the needed food continue to suffer silent hunger. Starvations have been occurring more frequently now than in the past as more people are populating the Earth. All the famines before the 17th century does not add up to what had happened later. The trend is expected to continue until the end of the world. Some of the lists of recorded famines in the past are given below.[19]

17th century

- 1599-1600 famine in Spain
- 1601-1603 one of the worst famines in all of Russian history; famine killed as many as 100,000 in Moscow and up to one-third of Tsar Godunov's subjects. Same famine killed about half Estonian population.
- 1611 famine in Anatolia
- 1618-1648 famines in Europe caused by the Thirty Years' War
- 1619 famine in Japan. During the Tokugawa period, there were 154 famines, of which 21 were widespread and serious.
- 1623-1624 famine in England

---

[19] http://en.wikipedia.org/wiki/List_of_famines

- 1630-1631 Deccan famine in India kills 2,000,000 (Note: There was a corresponding famine in northwestern China, eventually causing the Ming dynasty to collapse in 1644.)
- 1636 famine in Spain
- 1648-1660 Poland lost an estimated 1/3 of its population due to the wars, famine, and plague
- 1649 famine in northern England
- 1650-1652 famine in the east of France
- 1651-1653 famine throughout much of Ireland during the Cromwellian conquest of Ireland
- 1661 famine in India, when not a drop of rain fell for two years
- 1661-1662 famine in Morocco
- 1661-1662 famine in France
- 1669 famine in Bengal
- 1680 famine in Sardinia
- 1680 famine in Japan
- 1680s famine in Sahel
- 1690s famine in Scotland which may have killed 15% of the population
- 1693-1694 famine in France which killed 2 million people
- 1695-1697 Great Famine of Estonia killed about a fifth of Estonian population (70 000 – 75 000 people). Famine also hit Sweden (80 000 – 100 000 dead)
- 1696-1697 famine in Finland wiped out almost a third of the population

18th century

- 1706-1707 famine in France
- 1708-1711 famine in East Prussia killed 250,000 people or 41% of its population
- 1709-1710 famine in France
- 1740-1741 famine in Ireland
- 1722 famine in Arabia
- 1727-1728 famine in England
- 1732 famine in Japan
- 1738-1739 famine in France
- 1738-1756 famine in West Africa, half the population of Timbuktu died of starvation
- 1741 famine in Norway
- 1750 famine in Spain
- 1764 famine in Naples

- 1769-1773 Bengal famine of 1770
- 1770-1771 famine in Czech lands killed hundreds of thousands people
- 1771-1772 famine in Saxony and southern Germany
- 1773 famine in Sweden
- 1779 famine in Rabat, Morocco
- 1780s Great *Tenmei* Famine in Japan
- 1783 famine in Iceland caused by the eruption of Laki killed one-fifth of Iceland's population
- 1783-84 *Chalisa* famine in South Asia
- 1784 widespread famine throughout Egypt
- 1784-1785 famine in Tunisia killed up to 20% of its population
- 1788 famine in France. The two years previous to the French Revolution saw bad harvests and harsh winters, possibly because of a strong El Niño cycle or caused by the 1783 Laki eruption at Iceland.
- 1789 Famine in Ethiopia afflicted all the provinces
- 1789-92 *Doji bara* famine or Skull famine in India

19th century

- 1800-1801 famine in Ireland
- Four famines - in 1810, 1811, 1846, and 1849 - in China claimed nearly 45 million lives.
- 1811-1812 famine devastated Madrid, taking nearly 20,000 lives
- 1815 eruption Tambora, Indonesia. Tens of thousands died of subsequent famine
- 1816-1817 famine in Europe (Year Without a Summer)
- 1830 famine killed almost half the population of Cape Verde
- 1830s Tenpo famine (Japan)
- 1835 famine in Egypt killed 200,000
- 1845-1849 Great Irish Famine killed more than 1 million people
- 1846 famine led to the peasant revolt known as "Maria da Fonte" in the north of Portugal
- 1846-1857 Highland Potato Famine in Scotland
- 1866 Orissa famine of 1866 in India; one million perished
- 1866-1868 Famine in Finland. About 15% of the entire population died

- 1869 Rajputana famine of 1869 in India; one million and a half perished
- 1870-1871 famine in Persia is believed to have caused the death of 2 million persons
- 1873-1874 famine in Anatolia
- 1879 Famine in Ireland
- All mortality avoided in Bihar famine of 1873–74 in India.
- 1876-1879 Famine in India, China, Brazil, Northern Africa (and other countries).
- 1888 famine in Sudan
- 1888-1892 Ethiopian Great famine. About one-third of the population died. Conditions worsen with cholera outbreaks (1889-92), a typhus epidemic, and a major smallpox epidemic (1889-90).
- 1891-1892 famine in Russia caused 375,000 to 500,000 deaths
- 1896-1897 famine in northern China
- 1896-1902 famine in India

20th century

- 1907 famine in east-central China
- 1914-1918 Mount Lebanon famine during World War I which killed about a third of the population
- 1914-1918 famine in Belgium
- 1916-1917 famine caused by the British blockade of Germany in WWI; up to 750,000 Germans starved to death
- 1916-1917 winter famine in Russia
- 1917-1919 famine in Persia. As much as 1/4 of the population living in the north of Iran died in the famine
- 1917-1921 a series of famines in Turkestan at the time of the Bolshevik revolution killed about a sixth of the population
- 1921-1922 Famine in Tatarstan
- 1921-1922 famine in Volga German colonies in Russia. One-third of the entire population perished
- 1928-1929 famine in northern China. The drought resulted in 3 million deaths.
- 1921-1923. A Soviet famine in 1921 began with a drought that caused massive crop failures. But there were then enough food that the Soviet leadership back in Moscow forcibly took the food from the peasants to sell them elsewhere, leaving them with little subsistence food. The initial death toll was greatly magnified when Lenin refused to acknowledge the famine and sent no aid. The starving people resorted to cannibalism to

survive. Disease became a secondary killer. Typhus and cholera resulted in hundreds of thousands of death. Medicine was not available for many of them. The Soviets later estimated that 5.1 million died.

- 1928-1929 famine in Ruanda-Burundi, causing large migrations to the Congo
- 1932-1933 Soviet famine in Ukraine (Holodomor), some parts of Russia and North Caucasus area. As many as 10 million people may have died. It was caused by Stalin's collectivization that forced the peasants to give up 70% of everything they harvested. Although there was ample food, most of them were shipped to feed the Soviet people. Those who protested were shot dead and their villages were burned to prevent them from fleeing to another country.
- 1932-1933 famine in Kazakhstan killed 1.2-1.5 million
- 1940-1943 famine in Warsaw Ghetto
- 1941-44 Leningrad famine caused by a 900-day blockade by Nazi and Finnish troops. About one million Leningrad residents starved, froze, or were bombed to death in the winter of 1941-42, when supply routes to the city were cut off and temperatures dropped to -40 degrees.
- 1941-1942 famine in Greece caused by Nazi occupation. An estimated 300,000 people perished
- 1942-1943 famine killed one million in China
- 1943 famine in Ruanda-Urundi, causing migrations to the Congo
- 1944 famine in the Netherlands during World War II, more than 20,000 deaths
- 1946-1947 famine in Soviet Union
- 1958 Famine in Tigray, Ethiopia, claimed 100,000 lives
- 1965-1967 three years of drought in India responsible for 1.5 million deaths
- 1966 famine in Bihar, India
- 1967-1970 Biafran famine caused by Nigerian blockade
- 1968-1972 Sahel drought created a famine that killed a million people
- 1973 famine in Ethiopia; failure of the government to handle this crisis led to downfall of Emperor Haile Selassie and to Derg rule
- 1974 famine in Bangladesh
- 1980 famine in Karamoja, Uganda
- 1984-1985. Famine killed at least one million in Ethiopia as severe drought led to desperate food shortages.

- 1991-1993 Somalian famine
- 1992-1996 North Korean famine, mostly due to flood caused the death of 2-3 million
- 1998 famine in Sudan caused by war and drought
- 1998-2000 famine in Ethiopia. The situation worsened by the Eritrean-Ethiopian War
- 1998-2004 Second Congo War. 3.8 million people died, mostly from starvation and diseases
- 2000-2008 Zimbabwe's food crisis caused by Mugabe's land reform policies

The 21st century had a few small-scale famines as the world has been prepared for any eventuality. Most of the food crises have been caused by the high energy and rising food prices. A few of them such as the famine in Sudan/Darfur has been caused by the conflict going on. A major food crisis was caused by the military junta of Myanmar following a devastating cyclone Nargis that destroyed her rice-producing region.

Starvation is a severe reduction of food with their accompanying vitamins, nutrients that energized the body. It is the most extreme form of malnutrition that often last for months leading to permanent organ damage and eventually death. According to FAO, more than 25,000 people died of starvation every day in 2003 with another 800 million chronically undernourished. The WHO also claimed that malnourishment is the biggest contributor to child mortality and is present in half of all cases.[20]

Scientists say millions of people face starvation following an outbreak of a deadly new strain of blight, known as Ug99, which is spreading across the wheat fields of Africa and Asia.

Individuals experiencing starvation lose substantial fat (adipose) and muscle mass (atrophy) as the body breaks down these tissues for energy. *Catabolysis* is a medical condition where the body is breaking down muscles and other tissues in order to keep vital systems - such as the nervous system and heart muscle (myocardium) in working condition. Catabolysis will not begin until there are no usable sources of energy coming into the body. Vitamin deficiency is also a common result of starvation, often resulting in anemia, beriberi, pellagra, and scurvy. These diseases collectively may cause diarrhea, skin rashes,

---

[20] http://en.wikipedia.org/wiki/Starvation

edema, and heart failure. Individuals are often irritable and lethargic as a result.

Atrophy (wasting away) of the stomach weakens the perception of hunger, since the perception is controlled by the percentage of the stomach that is empty. Victims of starvation are often too weak to sense thirst, and therefore become dehydrated.

All movements become painful due to atrophy of the muscles, and due to dry, cracked skin caused by severe dehydration. With a weakened body, diseases are commonplace. Fungi, for example, often grow under the esophagus, making swallowing unbearably painful.

The energy deficiency inherent in starvation causes fatigue and renders the victim more apathetic over time. Interaction with one's surroundings diminishes as the starving person becomes too weak to move or even eat.

Low-volume, high-density food is provided slowly to sufferers of severe malnutrition, concurrently with water and control of diseases. The atrophic stomach is unable to accept large quantities of food. Organs and tissues weakened by starvation may, in a manner similar to that of a heart attack, rupture if food is provided too quickly. This can potentially cause death.

The glycogen storage is used up and the level of insulin in the circulation is low and the level of glucagon is very high. The main means of energy production is lipolysis. The TCA cycle helps the gluconeogenesis convert glycerol and fatty acids the acetyl CoA produces the energy used. Two systems of energy enter the gluconeogenesis, proteolysis provides alanine and Lactate produced from pyruvate. Too much Acetyl CoA produces ketone bodies, which can be detected in urine exam. The brain starts to use ketone bodies as a source of energy leading to ketoacidiosis and coma.

Starvation has been used as a weapon against those who opposed the rule of the dictators. This is the case of the Ukraine Famine of 1932-1933 during the reign of Joseph Stalin. Stalin, leader of the Soviet Union, set in motion events designed to cause a famine in the Ukraine to destroy the people there seeking independence from his rule. As a result, an estimated 7,000,000 persons perished in this farming area, once the breadbasket of Europe, with the people deprived of the food they had grown with their own hands.

The Ukrainian independence movement actually predated the Stalin era. Ukraine, which measures about the size of France, had been under the domination of the Imperial Czars of Russia for 200 years. With the collapse of the Czarist rule in March 1917, it seemed the long-awaited opportunity for independence had finally arrived.

Optimistic Ukrainians declared their country to be an independent People's Republic and re-established the ancient capital city of Kiev as the seat of government.

However, their newfound freedom was short-lived. By the end of 1917, Vladimir Lenin, the first leader of the Soviet Union, sought to reclaim all of the areas formerly controlled by the Czars, especially the fertile Ukraine. As a result, four years of chaos and conflict followed in which Ukrainian national troops fought against Lenin's Red Army, and also against Russia's White Army (troops still loyal to the Czar) as well as other invading forces including the Germans and Poles.

By 1921, the battles ended with a Soviet victory while the western part of the Ukraine was divided-up among Poland, Romania, and Czechoslovakia. The Soviets immediately began shipping out huge amounts of grain to feed the hungry people of Moscow and other big Russian cities. Coincidentally, a drought occurred in the Ukraine, resulting in widespread starvation and a surge of popular resentment against Lenin and the Soviets.

To lessen the deepening resentment, Lenin relaxed his grip on the country, stopped taking out so much grain, and even encouraged a free-market exchange of goods. This breath of fresh air renewed the people's interest in independence and resulted in a national revival movement celebrating their unique folk customs, language, poetry, music, arts, and Ukrainian orthodox religion.

But when Lenin died in 1924, Joseph Stalin, one of the most ruthless humans ever to hold power, succeeded him. To Stalin, the burgeoning national revival movement and continuing loss of Soviet influence in the Ukraine was completely unacceptable. To crush the people's free spirit, he began to employ the same methods he had successfully used within the Soviet Union. Thus, beginning in 1929, over 5,000 Ukrainian scholars, scientists, cultural and religious leaders were arrested after being falsely accused of plotting an armed revolt. Those arrested were either shot without a trial or deported to prison camps in remote areas of Russia.

Stalin also imposed the Soviet system of land management known as collectivization. This resulted in the seizure of all privately owned farmlands and livestock, in a country where 80% of the people were traditional village farmers. Among those farmers, was a class of people called Kulaks by the Communists. They were formerly wealthy farmers that had owned 24 or more acres, or had employed farm workers. Stalin believed any future insurrection would be led by the Kulaks, thus he proclaimed a policy aimed at liquidating the Kulaks.

Declared "enemies of the people," all their possessions were confiscated by the State. It was also forbidden by law for anyone to aid dispossessed Kulak families. Some researchers estimate that ten million persons were thrown out of their homes, put on railroad box cars and deported to "special settlements" in the wilderness of Siberia during this era, with up to a third of them perishing amid the frigid living conditions. Men and older boys, along with childless women and unmarried girls, also became slave-workers in Soviet-run mines and big industrial projects.

Back in the Ukraine, once-proud village farmers were by now reduced to the level of rural factory workers on large collective farms. Anyone refusing to participate in the compulsory collectivization system was simply denounced as a Kulak and deported. Continuing resistance by the Ukrarians finally put them in direct conflict with the power and authority of Joseph Stalin.

Soviet troops and secret police were rushed in to put down the rebellion. They confronted rowdy farmers by firing warning shots above their heads. In some cases, however, they fired directly at the people. Stalin's secret police (GPU, predecessor of the KGB) also went to work waging a campaign of terror designed to break the people's will. GPU squads systematically attacked and killed uncooperative farmers.

But the resistance continued. In Moscow, Stalin responded to their unyielding defiance by dictating a policy that would deliberately cause mass starvation and result in the deaths of millions. By mid 1932, nearly 75% of the farms in the Ukraine had been forcibly collectivized. On Stalin's orders, mandatory quotas of foodstuffs to be shipped out to the Soviet Union were drastically increased in August, October and again in January 1933, until there was simply no food remaining to feed the people of the Ukraine.

Much of the hugely abundant wheat crop harvested by the Ukrainians that year was dumped on the foreign market to generate cash to aid Stalin's Five Year Plan for the modernization of the Soviet Union and also to help finance his massive military buildup. If the wheat had remained in the Ukraine, it was estimated to have been enough to feed all of the people there for up to two years.

Ukrainian Communists urgently appealed to Moscow for a reduction in the grain quotas and also asked for emergency food aid. Stalin responded by denouncing them and rushed in over 100,000 fiercely loyal Russian soldiers to purge the Ukrainian Communist Party. The Soviets then sealed off the borders of the Ukraine, preventing any food from entering, in effect turning the country into a gigantic concentration camp. Soviet police troops inside the Ukraine also went house to house seizing any stored up food, leaving farm families without a morsel. All food was considered to be the 'sacred' property of the State. Anyone caught stealing State property, even an ear of corn or stubble of wheat, could be shot or imprisoned for not less than ten years.

Starvation quickly ensued throughout the Ukraine, with the most vulnerable, children and the elderly, first feeling the effects of malnutrition. The once-smiling young faces of children vanished forever amid the constant pain of hunger. It gnawed away at their bellies, which became grossly swollen, while their arms and legs became like sticks as they slowly starved to death.

Mothers in the countryside sometimes tossed their emaciated children onto passing railroad cars traveling toward cities such as Kiev in the hope someone there would take pity. But in the cities, children and adults who had already flocked there from the countryside were dropping dead in the streets, with their bodies carted away in horse-drawn wagons to be dumped in mass graves. Occasionally, people lying on the sidewalk thought to be dead were actually alive, were also carted away and buried.

While police and Communist Party officials remained quite well fed, desperate Ukrainians ate leaves off bushes and trees, killed dogs, cats, frogs, mice and birds then cooked them. Others, gone mad with hunger, resorted to cannibalism, with parents sometimes even eating their own children.

Meanwhile, nearby Soviet-controlled granaries were said to be bursting at the seams from huge stocks of 'reserve' grain, which had not yet been shipped out of the Ukraine. In some locations, grain and potatoes were piled in the open, protected by barbed wire and armed GPU guards who shot down anyone attempting to take the food. Farm animals, considered necessary for production, were allowed to be fed, while the people living among them had absolutely nothing to eat.

By the spring of 1933, at the height of the famine, an estimated 25,000 persons died every day in the Ukraine. Entire villages were perishing. In Europe, America and Canada, persons of Ukrainian descent and others responded to news reports of the famine by sending in food supplies. But Soviet authorities halted all food shipments at the border. It was the official policy of the Soviet Union to deny the existence of a famine and thus to refuse any outside assistance. Anyone claiming that there was in fact a famine was accused of spreading anti-Soviet propaganda. Inside the Soviet Union, a person could be arrested for even using the word 'famine' or 'hunger' or 'starvation' in a sentence. Such was the customary practice of countries under totalitarian regimes as is happening in many countries today.

The Soviets bolstered their famine denial by duping members of the foreign press and international celebrities through carefully staged photo opportunities in the Soviet Union and the Ukraine. The writer George Bernard Shaw, along with a group of British socialites, visited the Soviet Union and came away with a favorable impression, which he disseminated, to the world. Former French Premier Edouard Herriot was given a five-day stage-managed tour of the Ukraine, viewing spruced-up streets in Kiev and inspecting a 'model' collective farm. He also came away with a favorable impression and even declared there was indeed no famine.

Back in Moscow, six British engineers working in the Soviet Union were arrested and charged with sabotage, espionage and bribery, and threatened with the death penalty. The sensational show trial that followed was actually a cynical ruse to deflect the attention of foreign journalists from the famine. Journalists were warned they would be shut out of the trial completely if they wrote news stories about the famine. Most of the foreign press corps yielded to the Soviet demand and either did not cover the famine or wrote stories sympathetic to the official Soviet propaganda line that it did not exist. Among those was Pulitzer Prize winning reporter Walter Duranty of the New York Times who sent one dispatch stating "...all talk of famine now is ridiculous."

Outside the Soviet Union, governments of the West adopted a passive attitude toward the famine, although most of them had become aware of the true suffering in the Ukraine through confidential diplomatic channels. In November 1933, the United States, under its new president, Franklin D. Roosevelt, even chose to formally recognized Stalin's Communist government and also negotiated a sweeping new trade agreement. The following year, the pattern of denial in the West culminated with the admission of the Soviet Union into the League of Nations.

Stalin's Five Year Plan for the modernization of the Soviet Union depended largely on the purchase of massive amounts of manufactured goods and technology from Western nations. Those nations were unwilling to disrupt lucrative trade agreements with the Soviet Union in order to pursue the matter of the famine.

By the end of 1933, nearly 25% of the population of the Ukraine, including three million children, had perished. The Kulaks as a class were destroyed and an entire nation of village farmers had been laid low. With his immediate objectives now achieved, Stalin allowed food distribution to resume inside the Ukraine and the famine subsided. However, political persecutions and further round-ups of 'enemies' continued unchecked in the years following the famine, interrupted only in June 1941 when Nazi troops stormed into the country. Hitler's troops, like all previous invaders, arrived in the Ukraine to rob the breadbasket of Europe and simply replaced one reign of terror with another.

Many measures have been used to increase food production. Supporting farmers in areas of food insecurity through measures such as free or subsidized fertilizers and seeds to increase food harvest could reduce food prices to help fellow consumers. One example is Malawi. After almost five million of its 13 million people needed emergency food aid in the past, the government tried fertilizer subsidies and lesser ones for seed, abetted by good rains, helped farmers produce record-breaking corn harvests in 2006 and 2007, according to government crop estimates. Corn production leapt to 2.7 million metric tons in 2006 and 3.4 million in 2007 from 1.2 million in 2005, the government reported. The harvest also helped the poor by lowering food prices and increasing wages for farm workers. Malawi became a major food exporter, selling more corn to the World Food Program and the United Nations than any other country in Southern Africa. Over the previous 20 years to this change in policy, the World Bank and some rich nations Malawi depended on for aid have periodically pressed to cut back or eliminate fertilizer subsidies, in the name of free market policies even as the United States and Europe extensively subsidized their own farmers. However, many, if not most, of its farmers are too poor to afford fertilizer at market prices. Proponents for helping the farmers include the economist Jeffrey Sachs, who has championed the idea that wealthy countries should invest in fertilizer and seed for Africa's farmers. He also conceived the Millennium Villages Project (MVP), where good seeds and fertilizers are applied, and farmers trained to use them. In a Kenyan village, where this was experimented, the project resulted in a tripling of its corn harvest, even though the village had previously had a cycle of hunger.

To save lives due to famine and other disasters, it is necessary to have the reserve grain on hand and the logistics to deliver them in short notice. But most countries are too poor to store enough of these life-saving grains and in sites where they are needed. It is often too late once the emergency starts, especially if the foods haves to be imported. By the time they arrive, many would have perished. This was shown during the 1985 Ethiopia's famine when massive shipment of food has little effect on the starving people because many have died before they arrived and distributed.

Studies of every recent famine have shown that food was available in country - though not always in the immediate food deficit area. Usually, merchants begin hoarding food as a crisis develops not only to keep it from being stolen but also to command higher prices. Sometimes, it would usually be cheaper for a donor to buy the hoarded food at the inflated price than to import it from abroad.

One way to increase the availability of grains is to reduce meat intake by being a vegetarian. A vegetarian diet can provide food for larger populations, with the same resources, compared to omnivorous diets. Except for chicken and other fowls which have a better feed conversion, most animals takes in more grain to produce an equivalent in meat. But the problem is that the more affluent people are not about to change their eating style. The rise of the middle class in many developing countries is expected to increase the consumption of meat thereby aggravating the poor man's need for cheaper foodstuff.

Safe Water Supplies

The Earth may be covered mostly with water, but only a small portion of about 2% are freshwater found in lakes, rivers and in the polar regions. This amount is fairly constant throughout the ecological history of the planet. They are constantly replenished from the evaporation-transpiration of the weather pattern.

According to the World Bank, as many as two billion people lack adequate sanitation facilities to protect them from water-borne disease, while a billion lack access to clean water altogether. Eighty percent of all diseases in developing countries are related to unsafe drinking water and poor sanitation. This is compounded by another report of the United Nations that 95% of the world's cities still dump raw sewage into their water systems leading to some 80% of all the health maladies in developing countries.[21] Prevention of diseases is always cheaper and better than treatment. In the U.S. the waterborne infectious diseases such as giardiasis cost the nation nearly $20 billion annually.[22] More people could only mean more sewage and other pollutants. Whether they are dumped on land or on the ocean, they are contaminating the environment. Untreated sewage dumped into the ocean can be absorbed by marine creatures that are later consumed by

---

21

http://environment.about.com/od/biodiversityconservation/a/watersupply.htm
[22] http://dieoff.org/page5.htm

people. This would account for so many contaminants absorbed by humans consuming seafood.

Some pollutants came mostly from major companies that that discharge deadly chemicals directly to the sewage systems that drain into the oceans. Household sewage does not only include human excrement, they often contain industrial chemicals and household products such as detergents, oil-based solvents, cleansers, etc. that are flushed into the septic tank and sewage system. These contaminants accumulate in the fatty tissues of organisms and work their way up the food chain leading to extremely high concentrations when consumed by people. Many of these contaminants are heavy metals and pesticides that cause cancer and birth defects.

Researchers have also found that as the living standard of the developed world improved, the demand for water will increase six folds over the next 30 years. In the U.S., researchers found a six-fold increase in water use with only a two-fold increase in population size in the United States since 1900. Sometime in the future, as many developing countries developed into First World economy, the demand of water is expected to show up with more water scarcity problems, even among neighboring countries being supplied with water from the rivers flowing through each country. This is becoming a source of conflict among neighboring countries and countries downstream sharing the same source.

Clean freshwater is just as important as clean air and food for human needs. Water deficits, which are already spurring heavy grain imports in numerous smaller countries, may soon do the same in larger countries, such as China and India. The diminishing freshwater is aquifers and the falling water tables in scores of countries including China, the US, and India is mainly due to widespread overpumping utilizing powerful diesel and electric pumps. Other countries in similar situation include Pakistan, Iran, and Mexico. This will eventually lead to water scarcity and cutbacks in grain harvest. Even with the overpumping of its aquifers, China is developing a grain deficit. This will certainly drive grain prices upward. Most of the 3 billion people projected to be added worldwide by mid-century will be born in countries already experiencing water shortages.

To get an idea on how water is indispensable for food production, here are some statistics. It takes between 2,000 and 5,000 liters of water to grow one kilo of rice, 1,000 liters to grow a kilo of wheat, 3,000 liters for sugar, 20,000 liters for coffee and 500 liters to grow a kilo of potatoes. It takes 24,000 liters to grow the feed consume by cow to make a kilo of beef, and between 2,000 and 4,000 liters for the cow to fill its udders with a liter of milk. As for cheese, it will take another 5,000 liters just to make a kilo of it. To top it all, we still water to turn these into consumer goods for consumption. (Pearce, 1-2) Fortunately, most of water came from the rainfall. But because of the uneven rainfall, farmers have to rely on irrigation to keep the land productive all year round.

Unless population growth can be slowed quickly by investing heavily in female literacy and family planning services, there may not be a humane solution to the emerging world water shortage. Desalinization is an effective solution to the problem of water shortages, but it is costly and most developing countries cannot ill afford it.

The Philippines is an island surrounded by seas. With two types of seasons, rainy season with high average rainfall and dry season with periods almost evenly shared. With a large watershed areas scattered throughout the country, it is theoretically assured of enough freshwater throughout the year. Most of the water is used in the agricultural sector, consuming about 86%, 8% for the commerce and industry, while 6% is for domestic use. The problems lie not in the quantity but in the quality and distribution among those who needed the most. There have been numerous outbreaks of water-borne diseases such as cholera and typhoid fever in the past. As a result, diarrhea is the number one cause of illness among the people, and a source of high mortality among the children of the poor families. Outside of the metropolitan areas, the source of drinking water came mostly from deep wells. Contamination of drinking water is caused mostly by improper disposal of human waste. Unsanitary handling of food because of lack of safe water is behind most transmission of infectious diseases, especially in slum areas.

Drinking water from deep wells is often regarded as universally safe because it has never come into contact with human pollutants. Even then, it is possible for nature to pollute the water with its inherent makeup of the rock formation. Some rocks naturally contain fluoride and arsenic that unless properly tested may be just as poisonous to humans. In India, thousands are suffering from knock-knee disease or fluorosis caused by fluoride poisoning. Some sixty millions could be suffering to some degree. In China, there are probably a million victims. (Pearce, 73-74)

A more serious problem is arsenic poisoning. It is found mostly in Bangladesh and western India. The arsenic began in the rocks of the Himalayan mountains and washed downstream over thousands or millions of years to the plains and deltas of Bangladesh. Due to the heavy toll from sewage bacteria poisoning, the government decided to tap water from the deep wells. Tubewells sunk to depths of between 20 and 100 meters contain the most arsenic, which happen to be the case. Deeper tubewells could have been spared from the poison. Very few tubewells have been tested while tens of thousands of Bangladeshis have developed skin lesions, cancers and other symptoms. Many have died, and many are expected in the future. Despite the damage, in 2003 efforts to find and replace the estimated five million poisoned tubewells were making little headway. The government has so far spent less than $7 million of the $32 million given by the World Bank in 1998 for immediate clean-up. (Ibid, 74-75)

Almost all the waterways running through the cities are biologically dead due to pollution. Nearly half of the rivers around the country are classified as below normal quality and are expected to compromise the water resources needed for agriculture, industrial and domestic uses.

Metro Manila can be said to be the representative of the country to the megacities of the world. It is only in the cities where fresh water needs of the people are safeguarded for human consumption. However, there have never been enough supplies to give everyone a decent share of this precious fluid. In many areas of the metropolis, there are still no water services to supply the needs of the residents. Some have been forced to buy bottled water for drinking while tankers are trucked in many outlying subdivisions to supply the needed water for use in their daily consumption. As for other chores, water from the deep wells is pumped from the aquifers. The unregulated and excessive extraction of groundwater lead to the decline in the water table caused many places to sink and possibly increase the earth fissures and aggravate the earthquake fault in some places. Since Metro Manila lies near the sea which are connected to the rivers, salt water intrusion is a great possibility. Even though there are two concessionaires supply water to the needs for the people, it is still inadequate. Massive extraction of groundwater is still going in many places.

There has also been a dispute over the alleged sinking of the Camanava (Caloocan-Malabon-Navotas-Valenzuela) area allegedly reported by the scientific findings of the University of the Philippines Marine Science Institute. Some 70-80% of Malabon and Navotas are reclaimed from the Manila Bay and most parts are perennially flooded during high tide and rainy days. Federico Pascual is one of his columns in *Postcript* claimed that at present, Metro Manila and as far as Cavite have been sinking ten times faster than during the 1960s.[23]

Most of the suburban areas which were not supplied by the concessionaires of MWSS have long been extracting water from the aquifers. Inadequate supply of water has also forced some 3,000 companies to operate deep wells. More than half of them are not licensed by the government. Some of them have been identified by the DENR/NWRB in government reports are Manila Electric Co. (Meralco), St. Luke's Medical Center, Corinthian Gardens, Manila Peninsula Hotel, Citibank Makati and Quezon City, The Landmark, Araneta Center in Cubao, and the Greenhills Shopping Center. Some of them have been ordered shut down, but what actions have been undertaken are not known.[24]

It does not take much engineering calculations to arrive at a logical conclusion to the sinking problem. In coastal areas surrounding Metro Manila, the foundation is mostly sandy making the land prone to subsidence whenever water is extracted unless the water is replenish with saltwater from the sea. This is the reason why there are few deep wells being introduced along the coastal areas. On the other hand, inland aquifers are not prone to seawater intrusion, making subsidence, sinkhole and creating fissures a grave reality. If the waters are in confining layers composed of compressible silt or clay, the loss of water reduces the water pressure in the confining layer, causing it to compress from the weight of overlying geological materials. In severe cases, this compression can be observed on the ground surface as subsidence. This subsidence is more or less permanent unless replenish with water from overhead immediately. The subsidence could lead to buildings tilting and eventually collapsing from their own weight. In the Datun coal mining district in East China, the level of subsidence since 1976 to 2006 has reach a maximum of 863 mm with an accumulated subsidence of more than 200 mm reaching an area of 33.1 km^2 by the end of 2006. Over ten cases of building crack due to ground subsidence have been observed.[25] A U.S. Geological Survey reported that more than 80% of the identified subsidence in the U.S. is a consequence of human impact on subsurface water extraction. The increasing development of the land and the water resources threatens to exacerbate existing land-subsistence problems and initiate new ones. More than 17,000 mi^2 in 45 States have been directly affected by subsidence. The three principal causes are aquifer-system compaction, drainage and subsequent oxidation of organic

---

[23] http://www.manilamail.com/archive/mar2006/06mar16.htm
[24] Ibid
[25] http://sciencedirect.com........

soils, and dissolution and collapse of susceptible rocks. The compaction of unconsolidated aquifer systems due to excessive groundwater pumping is by far the single largest cause of subsidence, according to the Geological Survey.[26]

Hope of fully recharging the aquifers with clean rain water is no longer feasible in highly urbanized metropolis. Most of the lands have been built on and paved over and the rainwater is often drained to the storm drainage system and into the estero and on to the river and sea. Beside, most of the asphalt roads contain toxic chemicals that may carry its runoff to the aquifers or drained to the river that has been responsible for the death of many waterways. Once an aquifer is contaminated, even boiling the water may not remove all the toxic chemicals.

Asphalt is made up of asphaltenes, resins, and other hydrocarbons that are suspected of causing cancers in large quantity. Contact with asphalt can cause irritation to the eyes and skin. Toxic asphalt fumes are more dangerous because it can cause headaches, dizziness, anesthesia, drowsiness, and when acting of the central nervous system can cause death in some.[27] Fumes can be inhaled during very hot weather when the sunlight hit the asphalt road.

Speaking of asphalts which are made from petroleum products, the tires used in motor vehicles also came from petroleum. One passenger tire uses about seven gallons of oil to produce. Some 6.7 million tires being spent annually on the roads, and many are disposed by burning at the end of its lifetime. Not only is the oil wasted, about two gallons can leach into the ground contaminating the groundwater.[28]

Despite advances in agriculture, the fresh water supplies that people depend on are running low worldwide because of overpopulation. The freshwater available around the world is constant and every time someone is born, the per capita available is lowered proportionally. There is also the problem connected with abnormal weather pattern and uneven rainfall that is responsible for floods and droughts around the world. There are times when water is so abundant during rainy seasons while negligible during dry season. The water crisis could have disastrous consequences for agriculture.

---

[26] http://water.usgs.gov.ogw/pubs/fs00165/
[27] www.petron.com/HSEpdf/Petron_AS_115.pdf -
[28] http://www.sunstar.com.ph/static/pam/2005/10/28/oped/rox.pena.html

Desalinization of sea water is one solution. Desalinization refers to any of several processes that remove excess salt and other minerals from water. Water is desalinated in order to be converted to fresh water suitable for human consumption or irrigation. It is often used on many ships and submarines on a small scale. For the more populous areas and drier regions of the world, desalinization is focused on developing cost-effective ways of providing fresh water for human use.

Large-scale desalinization typically uses large amounts of energy as well as specialized, expensive infrastructure, making it very costly compared to the use of fresh water from rivers or groundwater. Therefore this process is not for every country. Only the rich and the energy-rich can afford them. The large energy reserves of many Middle Eastern countries, along with their relative water scarcity, have led to extensive construction of desalinization in this region. Saudi Arabia's desalinization plants account for about 24% of total world capacity.

The world's largest desalinization plant is the Jebel Ali Desalinization Plant (Phase 2) in the United Arab Emirates. It is a dual-purpose facility that uses multi-stage flash distillation and is capable of producing 300 million cubic meters of water per year. The largest desalinization plant in the United States is the one at Tampa Bay, Florida, which began desalinizing 25 million gallons (95000 m^3) of water per day in December 2007. A January 17, 2008, article in the Wall Street Journal states, "World-wide, 13,080 desalinization plants produce more than 12 billion gallons of water a day, according to the International Desalinization Association."

The high costs of desalinization technologies, especially for poor third world countries made it impractical. There is also the high cost of transporting or piping massive amounts of desalinated seawater throughout the interiors of large countries. It is only suitable for coastal cities or near the sea to reduce cost of delivery. After desalinization, dumping back the saline brine into the ocean can be a major cause of marine pollution.

Most of the efforts to make desalinization practically are focused on reducing cost. In Perth, Australia, a wind powered desalinization plant was opened in 2007. The water is sucked in from the ocean at only 0.1 meter per second, which is slow enough to let fish escape before they are sucked into the plant. The plant provides nearly 140,000 m^3 of clean water per day. The development of cheaper desalinization plant using solar energy is in the work. One example of newer theoretical approaches for desalinization is the Passarell Process. This tedious process involves vaporizing water at lower temperature by reducing pressure in an evaporation chamber set up for the purpose. Through an intricate process of compression and vaporization, fresh water can be vaporized from the salt water and collected to other fresh water chambers.[29]

According to a June 5, 2008 article in *Globe and Mail*, a Jordanian-born chemical engineer at the University of Ottawa has invented a new desalinization technology that is alleged to be 6-7 times more efficient than current technology. According to the article, General Electric is looking into similar technology, and the U.S. National Science Foundation announced a grant to the University of Michigan to study it as well. On June 23, 2008 it was reported that Siemens Water Technologies had developed a new technology that desalinizes one cubic meter of water while using only 1.5 kwh of energy, which, according to the report, is one half the energy that other processes use.

Another solution is the use of reverse osmosis technology that does not produce "hot water" as a byproduct. Additionally, depending on the prevailing currents of receiving waters, the seawater concentrate byproduct can be diluted and dispersed to background levels within relatively short distances of the ocean outlet. The city of Perth has been successfully operating a reverse osmosis seawater desalinization plant since 2006. The Perth desalinization plant is powered partially by renewable energy from the Emu Downs Wind Farm. Other desalinization plants are to be built is in Australia's largest city, Sydney and in Wonthaggi, Victoria in the near future. The Sydney plant will be powered entirely from renewable sources, thereby eliminating harmful greenhouse gas emissions to the environment, a common argument used against seawater desalinization due to the energy requirements of the technology. The Queensland state government recently announced that the Gold Coast desalinization plant will be powered entirely from renewable sources.

Israel is now desalinating water for a cost of $0.53/m³. Singapore is desalinating water at a cost of $0.49/m³. According to a May 9, 2008 article in *Forbes*, a San Leandro, California company called Energy Recovery has been desalinizing water for US$0.46/m³.

It would be a matter of time before the cost of natural flow of water goes up forcing countries to look to the sea for more supply. In the meantime, there are many ways that can be employed to reduce the wastage of water for agriculture and other activities. Agricultural

---

[29] http://www.waterdesalinization.com/theory.htm

technologies have made it possible to grow food with little water such as hydroponics and the use of green houses.

While comparing ocean water desalinization to wastewater reclamation for drinking water shows desalinization as the first option, using reclamation for irrigation and industrial use provides multiple benefits. Urban runoff and storm water capture also provide multiple benefits in treating, restoring and recharging groundwater. Increased water conservation and water use efficiency remain the most cost effective priority for stretching the water supply.

Water leakage is probably the single source of water wastage in the supply of water for the households. From its source to the users, leakage may account for up to 40% of waste due to old pipes and pilferage. For a few pesos, employees of water concessioners or their contractors are willing to illegal bypass the water meter by "jumping" the supply lines. Most consumers are thus made to shoulder for these losses through higher rates. It is only recently that something is being done in Metro Manila by one of the concessioners to plug these leaks and pilferages. The use of plastic instead of metal pipes has also prevented leakages from rusting pipes.

At home, one way to check leak is to read the water meter before and several hours later. There should be no discrepancy. If there is any discrepancy there must be some leakages, probably in the bathroom areas. To check the toilet for leakage, put a little coloring in the toilet tank. The coloring should not appear on the bowl if there is no leak. If none can be found, the leakage could be through the house piping system that cannot be seen. Most modern model of water closets uses a smaller toilet tank for flushing. For existing water closet, place a plastic bottle with something heavy to displace some of the water in the tank. A flushing needs only about three gallons of water to flush properly instead of five to seven gallons of the old model.

Avoid using the toilet for other wastes. If you do, at the very least, no do flush the wastes unless it stings. Using separate urinals for men would be cheaper and less wasteful. Some modern urinals do not even need flushing.

Insulate the hot water pipes to minimize heat loss. Have the heater install near the shower room to minimize wastage as cold water is being drained or use the instant water heater that is connected to the shower head. The instant heater also saves energy. Most of the water we used at home came from showering. It is advisable to take only one shower a day. After wetting the body, close the shower as you soaped up before water rinsing. An aerator fitted on the shower head and faucet can help save water. Try to cut down the time for shower. Even brushing the teeth can be wasteful if we allow the water to drain while brushing the teeth. Keep the tap off before rinsing. Better yet, use a glass of water for rinsing instead of free-flowing water from the tap.

Minimize the use of water for gardening. Use low-water or drought resistant plants to avoid using too much water. Avoid using sprinklers. If there is a way to collect rainwater, use it for watering the garden. It is cost effective. Water the garden during the early hours and evening to minimize evaporation. Avoid also watering during windy hours to minimize evaporation.

Avoid hosing the cars during washing. A wet sponge and a bucket of water can be just as effective. Use a low flow nozzle to save on water. The same goes for washing other equipments.

Be water conscious and conservation can come naturally. There are many ways an individual can save on water simply by being aware of the importance of water and how not to be wasteful. It does not take much effort to save water. Close the water if it is not needed as one would turn off the light if not needed.

Rainwater has become an important resource for water starved regions. It is the only source for recharging the underground aquifers. In urban areas not service by the water concessioners, the construction of houses and road has left little exposed earth for water to soak in. In the rural areas, floodwater quickly flows to the rivers, which then dry up soon after the rains stop. If this water can be held back by levees, it can seep into the ground and recharge the aquifers.[30]

Another way of harvesting the water is collecting rainwater from the roofs of building and funneling it to the groundwater tanks or buckets for later outdoor use. In many water-poor countries where rainfall does not come often, the people have to devise ingenious ways to collect water. At the ages of the Sahara region, the farmers laid low stone walls on the hillsides to capture water long enough to soak in and nourish crops. This has made it possible for thousands of hectares across the arid Sahel to grow crops and trees where nothing grows before. Digging ponds and terracing are other effective means of water harvesting.

In India, town planners and civic authority in many cities are introducing bylaws making rainwater harvesting compulsory in all new structures. No water or sewage connection would be given if a new building did not have provisions for rainwater harvesting.

---

[30] http://www.edugreen.teri.res.in/explore/water/conser.htm

Agriculture uses a comparative large amount of water and conservation measures can minimize wastage. Water is essential growing plants and crops. A lowering water table and a rise in salinity due to overuse of chemical fertilizers and pesticides has worsen the matter. Various methods of water conservation have been devised throughout the world to meet regional needs.

In India's arid and semi-arid areas, the "tank" system is traditionally the backbone of agricultural production. Tanks are constructed either by bunding or by excavating the ground to collect rainwater. Large bunds (embankment) to create reservoirs known as khadin, dams called johads, tanks, and other methods were applied to check water flow and accumulate run-off. At the end of the monsoon season, water from these structures was used to cultivate crops.

Simple techniques can be used to reduce the demand for water. The underlying principle is that only part of the rainfall or irrigation water is taken up by plants, the rest percolates into the deep groundwater, or is lost by evaporation from the surface. Mulching or the application of organic or inorganic material such as plant debris, compost, etc., slows down the surface run-off, improves the soil moisture, reduces evaporation losses and improves soil fertility. Soil covered by crops, slows down run-off and minimizes evaporation losses. Hence, fields should not be left bare for long periods of time.

Ploughing helps to loosen and move the soil around. As a consequence it retains more water thereby reducing evaporation. Shelter belts of trees and bushes along the edge of agricultural fields slow down the wind speed and reduce evaporation and erosion. Planting of trees, grass, and bushes breaks the force of rain and helps rainwater penetrate the soil instead of carrying the rainwater away with the precious soil.

Fog and dew contain substantial amounts of water that can be used directly by adapted plant species. Artificial surfaces such as netting-surfaced traps or polyethylene sheets can be exposed to fog and dew. The resulting water can be used for crops. Contour farming is adopted in hilly areas and in lowland areas for paddy fields. Farmers recognize the efficiency of contour-based systems for conserving soil and water.

Salt-resistant varieties of crops have also been developed recently. Because these grow in saline areas, overall agricultural productivity is increased without making additional demands on freshwater sources.

Water Conflicts

The demand for fresh water is expected to grow and the potential for conflicts remain a great possibility among bordered nations sharing freshwater supplies through the great rivers of the world and the aquifers beneath their ground. More than 50 countries on five continents around the world might soon be caught up in water disputes unless they can establish binding agreements on how the available water can be shared equitably. Even with the agreements, there is always the possibility of unilateral abrogation of the treaty caused by other issues. Issues such as sharing reservoirs, rivers, and underground water aquifers and the damming of riverways need to be addressed. Within these countries, the points of conflicts are numerous that could easily spark into armed conflict especially among belligerent countries. Most of these countries are located in Africa and the Middle East.

In Asia, the conflict that could spark the use of atomic weapons is between Pakistan and India as mostly people feared. This has to do with the Indus River where Pakistan's 150 million people depend for irrigating most their crops and generating the needed electricity. The gateway to this river is Kashmir. The first conflict arose when India intervened in Kashmir to cut the flow of tributaries of the Indus to Pakistan. It was finally settled by the World Bank as it brokered the 1960 Indus Waters Treaty between the two countries. It was the World Bank's refusal to grant any loan to the countries for new dams unless the treaty was signed that finally succeeded. Water from one of the three tributaries, the River Chenab was given to Pakistan for irrigating the Punjab, the breadbasket for Pakistan. But geographically, India has the potential to stop water from flowing to Pakistan, especially now that India is building a 160-meter dam on the Chenab just across the border. Pakistan sees it as a breach of the treaty. India countered that the dam is only to be used for generating electricity and has no intention of using the water. Pakistan wanted to issue to be resolved but India refused and continues the building program. Likewise, Bangladesh receives more than 90% of its water from India which has also built a dam on the Ganges right on the border. (Pearce, 201-202)

Ethiopia and Kenya are two countries at the forefront of the world's coming water crisis. Here, women often walk for miles each day to collect drinking water while the farmers are pushed into deadly conflict by the dwindling river flows, and city water supplies are drained by overzealous irrigation trying to produce enough food for survival. The problem is abetted by the conflict between Ethiopia and Somalia that sometimes flare up into armed conflicts. Many Somalis fleeing the inter-clan war caused by the conflict in water and pastureland have setup camps inside the fertile highland of Ethiopia, thereby causing frictions between the two countries. Their long stay has not been welcome despite the hardship. To get water to drink and wash they have to dig into the sandy bottom of the dry riverbed to reach the muddy water that flows beneath. This is not an isolated event but is happening across Ethiopia and northern Kenya.[31]

Even within countries, water deficit is causing conflicts between different groups. In Africa, most of the conflicts are between the pastoralists and the farmers and sometimes politically motivated. This is true in the Oromia and the Ogaden region of Ethiopia, both long-neglected lowland areas with large pastoralist populations. Even the genocides in Darfur and Rwanda were born from the cultural collisions between pastoralists and farmers. In highland urban capitals like Addis Ababa and Nairobi, where temperatures are cool and rains are plentiful, access to clean drinking water and sanitation facilities tops the list of problems cited by slum dwellers who make up half the population of some cities. Deaths from waterborne disease usually receive less attention, although they typically exceed deaths from AIDS.

In Uganda, the drying of the second largest lake in the world, the Lake Victoria has destroyed the breeding grounds for fish, and endangering the 30 million East Africans who live around

---

[31] http://www.globalpolicy.org/security/natres/water/2008/0619ethiopconflict.htm

the lake. Kenyans chasing fish into deeper Ugandan waters have been arrested and allegedly tortured by Ugandan military. In addition to rising temperatures, decreased rainfall, and watershed deforestation, scientists and fishermen alike blame new hydroelectric projects at the source of the River Nile in Uganda from draining too much water out of the shrinking lake.

Conflicts over the water resources of the Lake Victoria/Nile River system seem almost inevitable. The nine countries that share the system (Egypt, Ethiopia, Sudan, Tanzania, Kenya, Uganda, Burundi, Rwanda, and the Democratic Republic of Congo) all needed water for farming, irrigation, reclamation of the deserts, feeding their dams, and have nowhere to get the badly needed water. They are some of the world's poorest nations and their populations are exploding, increasing stress on endangered water resources.

Under the present setup, the current international treaty on the Nile River is a relic of British rule on the river giving the lion's share of the flow to Egypt, a modicum to Sudan and nothing else for the others, even Ethiopia where three-quarters of the river's flow begins. (Ibid, 204)

The Middle East where Israel is considered an outsider is fraught with conflict not only over land but also over fresh water. Some of the driest and hottest places can be found here. Israel, in order to survive needed all the water it can lay its hand on has been in conflict with her neighbors for water rights. With its growing population, the Jordan-Yarmouk watershed is an important source of water for the four neighboring countries. Several wars have been fought until the Israelites took control of the area. Several regional water-sharing proposals failed in part because Israel linked them to recognizing the Jewish state. It also rejected solutions not in its strategic interest and acted unilaterally instead. Israel began constructing its largest water project in the 1960s to transfer water from the Sea of Galilee northern water to highly populated areas in the center and south and to facilitate efficient water use. It was considered a hostile act by the Arab neighbors and they responded with their own diversion plans. Israel viewed them as a national security threat. Fighting broke out as the Arab tried to destroy the Israel's project called the National Water Carrier. Israel retaliated against Syrian construction sites. Skirmishes broke out, and the 1967 war resulted. Officially it began on June 5, 1967. Others, including Ariel Sharon, said it started two and a half years earlier when Israel acted against diverting the Jordan River. Earlier, Ben-Gurion warned that Jews and Arabs would battle over strategic water resources and determine Palestine's fate. Aside from other strategic aims for land and regional control, Israel secured water rich lands in southern Lebanon, Jordan, the Golan, and West Bank. It fully exploited them and is a key reason why the Golan was never returned. West Bank water is another issue. It has three principle aquifers supplying about one-quarter of Israel's needs, including for its settlements and nearly all of what West Bank Palestinians get.[32]

The conflict is expected to continue as the Palestinians have been shortchanged with the use of the vital fluid. The Israelites are getting five and half times more water than their Palestinians counterpart. By integrating Occupied Territory water resources into its legal and bureaucratic system and denying Palestinians the right to develop them for their own use, Israel violates international law under Articles 43 and 55 of the 1907 Hague Regulations. Palestinian rights are severely compromised but the survival of the Israelites in a hostile environment made the move necessary.

One source of water for the Palestinians in Gaza lay beneath the sand. Its million-plus inhabitants have one of the lowest per-capita natural fresh water in the world. They are pumping at least 125 million m^3 of water a year but the recharge rate is only 90 million m^3. With the lowering water table, sewage from the towns and refugee camps and the salty sea water from the coast are invading the aquifer. Bacteria count and salinity level have risen considerably, making the water nasty to drink and increasingly poisonous for crops. (Pearce, 84)

The Israelis have enough water for their needs and some more for their luxurious lifestyle. In contrast, Palestinians have precious little. During summer it problem gets worse. This is expected to maintain the animosity among them.

Israel need for more people to populate the country for its own survival has made it crucial to have all the water needed for Jews to immigrate to the country. Its aggressive need for water is said to be partly responsible for the 1982 Lebanon invasion - to control the Litani River in the southern part of the country. It remains out of reach today, but a richer resource would be to secure access to major rivers like the Nile, Euphrates or Seyhan and Ceyhan in Turkey. In October 1994, it concluded a peace treaty with Jordan that included five annexes; two

---

[32] http://www.globalpolicy.org/security/natres/water/2008/0718westbank.htm

of them include water and environmental concerns. The water rich Golan has been a stumbling block toward a similar deal with Syria as is the bilateral talk with the Palestinians.

The Jordan River since Biblical time has served the people well until today. Sadly, today the lower Jordan River is almost dry. There is not enough water left in the river to turn a hamster wheel let alone an electric turbine. Of the 1.3 billion cubic meters of water that historically would flow down the river to replenish the Dead Sea each year, as little as 70,000 to 100,000 cubic meters is all that remains. The river has seen over 90% of its water sources diverted by Israel and Jordan. Since the 1950s the water of the Jordan River has been diverted largely to support large-scale irrigated agriculture. Competition for scarce water resources in the midst of conflict allowed little room to think about the needs of the river. The cultural belief in "making the desert bloom," supported by the economic necessity of conquering nature, was the prevalent ideology on both banks of the Jordan.[33]

The Euphrates and Tigris Rivers may fare a little better. The source of the water comes from Turkey, gives it an important role in any future negotiation. The interaction between the three co-riparians on the Euphrates and Tigris Rivers reflects the fundamental upstream-downstream characteristic of their relationship. This geographic asymmetry is reinforced by the economic and military advantages that favor the upstream riparian, Turkey. A combination of upstream projects in Turkey (GAP Project) and Syria impact the lowest downstream riparian (Iraq). Officially, the GAP Project is scheduled for finalization in 2014, while unofficial sources anticipate that the project would be completed in 2050 if it were to be fully implemented. The consequences for downstream Syria are also highly problematic in light of the centrality of the Euphrates Basin for the country's overall water supply (65% of total water volume). Considering the actual level of completion of the GAP (45%), the current issue is less quantitative than qualitative, as waters reaching Syria and Iraq are increasingly

---

[33]

http://www.globalpolicy.org/security/natres/water/2008/062008waterconflict.pdf

being polluted with pesticides and herbicides. Meetings have been going on between the three countries on cooperative use of the water allocation for each country.

Poor Health and Diseases

Disease is another great equalizer to the runaway population, claiming more lives than any other natural and man-made disasters. Poor health not only shortened the lives of many, it made the victims easily succumbed to infectious diseases. Plague is one of the deadliest diseases when it first strike in 541 and wiped out 50 to 60% of the world's population. During the Middle Ages, starting in 1348, the Black Death caused by bubonic plague was known to decimate 25 million Europeans and 50 million non-Europeans, 13 million of them in China before it subsided. (Levy, 60) The 75 million deaths is one-third of the existing population then. So far, this is still the number one disaster known to mankind. The agent of the disease was the bacterium *Yersinia pestis* carried by a small flea that is transported from region to region through the ubiquitous rat.

There are two forms of plague: bubonic and pneumonic. Both are caused by the bacterium mentioned above. In bubonic plague, fleas become infectious when they bite an infected animal and transmit the disease by biting people. The bacteria make their way from the skin to the lymph nodes where they multiply rapidly, swelling the lymph nodes. From the lymph nodes, they start moving into the bloodstream to destroy small blood vessels, cutting off the blood supply to extremities like the fingers, toes, and the nose, which develop gangrene and turn black. It is this reason that it is often referred to as the Black Plague. (Levy, 60)

Pneumonic plague is rarer but far more fatal is not treated immediately. The chance of fatality is 57% even when treated with antibiotics compared to 14% for bubonic plague. It can be spread by inhaling droplets from a coughing infected person. (Ibid, 61)

The second deadliest toll is the Great Influenza Epidemic or the Spanish flu epidemic of 1918-1919. It was caused by a virus. It probably started in Haskell County, Kansas and spread to Europe during the First World War brought in by U.S. soldiers to help the Allied forces. It later spread worldwide and cost the lives of at least 20 million people. Some estimates put the death toll at 50 million and an estimated 20 to 40% of the world's population became sick.

In India alone, about 12 million died of flu. In some U.S, cities, people died so quickly that morticians could not cope with the bodies. The corpses were piling up in a warehouse until they could get coffins for them. The disease started with a cough, then headache. Temperature, breathing and heart rate increased rapidly. In the worst cases, pneumonia came next, the lungs filling with liquid, drowning the patients and turning them blue from lack of air. Patients bled from every orifice: mouth, noses, ears, and eyes. Those who survived often suffered temporary or permanent brain damage. Several million developed encephalitis lethargic, in which victims were trapped in a permanent sleeplike and rigid state, as portrayed in the 1990 movie *Awakening*.[34] The 1957-1958 pandemic Asian flu caused by H2N2 virus killed as many as 4 million people.[35] Experts believed that a major pandemic flu outbreak could kill as many as a billion people, because of the ease of travel and the huge population of people in the world.

Then there is the new scourge of mankind known throughout the world as AIDS. This is the first pandemic disease to inflict every country on earth. It has killed more than 25 million so far with even more infected. Most of the deaths are coming from Africa where the Catholic Church is active in recruiting new members and refused to condone the use of condoms that would greatly reduce the numbers of infections. The disease is incurable and any hope of controlling the disease is remote, especially with the Church's teaching on contraceptives. The death toll caused by this disease is expected to outnumber the record held by the bubonic plague of 1348-1351.

One of the most frightening diseases ever to inflict a person is smallpox. The first episode of epidemic of the disease was the 1520 Mexican smallpox that killed 4 million people and brought the downfall of the Aztec civilization. The disease was unwittingly brought to Mexico by the Spanish conquistador, Hernando Cortes, who brought an infected black slave from Puerto Rico as he tried to conquer the country. Many Aztecs contracted the disease that killed so many of them that they were helpless to defend their city. (Spignesi, 29)

Medical advances have kept many diseases in check and increase the life span of people such that there are more people being born than dying. But the poor health of people from the developing countries made them vulnerable to many infectious diseases even though many

---

[34] http://ideaesplore.net/news/041116.html#Pop

[35] http://www.america.gov/st/washfile-english/2005/April/20050415154315 cmretrop0.3807642.html

of them are preventable and curable. Access to the proper medicine and health care are sorely lacking in many of these deaths.

Poor malnourished people are among those who easily succumbed to diseases. They are the least in society to have the best health care when worse come to worse. Children born to them are the first victims of diseases. It is for this reason that many poor parents continue to have children in the hope that some of them may survive to old age.

Despite the new medical advances and sanitary conditions around the world, new diseases are waiting to unleash. The severe acute respiratory syndrome (SARS) of 2003 caused so much fear and social disruption than any other disease of modern time. Although only a few succumbed to the disease, it nevertheless buckled economies, crippled international trade and travel, and emptied the streets of some of the world's most prosperous cities.

The following article by Ronalyn V. Olea has been reprinted here with the permission of the editors of *Bulatlat* from their August 2, 2008 issue.

People's Health, Least in GMA's Priorities

While Mrs. Gloria Macapagal-Arroyo has repeatedly claimed that health and other social services are her priorities, records show otherwise. The budget for health has been consistently meager, causing dire effects on the people's conditions.

In 2007, the United Nations ranked the Philippines 90th out of 177 countries for the Human Development Index (HDI). The HDI is a survey on the quality of life of citizens in UN member countries. It measures life expectancy, educational attainment, and GDP per capita. It was developed by the United Nations Development Program (UNDP) as a standard means of measuring human development, a concept, which according to the UNDP, refers to the process of widening the options of persons, giving them greater opportunities for education, health care, income, employment, etc.

Data from United Nations International Children Fund (UNICEF) reveals that in 2006, infant mortality rate in the Philippines is 24 per 1,000 live births. At least 20% of infants born between 1999 and 2006 are with low birth weight. From 2000 to 2006, 28% of children under five are underweight.

According to the Health Alliance for Democracy (HEAD), ten mothers die daily of pregnancy- and child-related causes. The group also said that seven out of ten Filipinos die without medical attention.

Malnutrition and hunger remain perennial in the Philippines. UNICEF Representative in the Philippines Nicholas K. Alipui said in a statement in May 2006, "The malnutrition situation in the Philippines is devastating."

The Philippines is among the ten countries severely affected by malnutrition, which is considered a disease caused by inadequate intake of food. More than three million Filipino children are suffering from undernourishment, the worst form of malnutrition. A recent survey by the Social Weather Station (SWS) showed that 14.5 million Filipinos experienced involuntary hunger or hunger due to lack of food between April and June this year.

The number accounts for 16.3% of families nationwide or approximately 2.9 million households. It must be noted that it is higher than the 10-year average hunger rate of 12.1%. Severe hunger also increased from 3.2% to 4.2% (760,000 families or 3.8 million people) Metro Manila has the highest hunger incidence, hitting a record high of 22%. This is equivalent to 530,000 families or 2.65 million people.

A survey by IBON Foundation in April this year showed that 75.3% of families could not buy enough food. Undeniably, poverty has affected the health conditions of the Filipino people. Based on the 2004 data of the Department of Health (DOH), most of the ten highest causes of morbidity remain to be communicable but preventable diseases such as dengue, diarrhea, bronchitis and tuberculosis.

Pittance

Amid these conditions, the Arroyo government has neglected the people's health as data from the Department of Budget and Management (DBM) showed. From 2001 to 2007, the annual average allocation for health is only P13 billion. ($293,918,155 at an exchange rate of $1=P44.23) The budget for 2007 was the lowest in seven years at P11.66 billion ($263,621,976). While the budget for 2008 has increased to P19.77 billion ($446,981,686), this is still a meager P219.66 ($4.966) per person health budget for the year considering that the country's population is estimated at over 90 million. In addition, this meager budget is fast becoming nil because of runaway inflation. The Bangko Sentral ng Pilipinas said the inflation rose to 11.4% this June and could even reach 12%.

For this year, the allocation for disease prevention and control is only P4.91 billion ($111,010,626) while P120.13 million ($2,716,029) is allotted for monitoring and surveillance of diseases and outbreaks.

For the same year, the 12 specialty government hospitals have a combined budget of P2.79 billion ($63,079,357). These include the Jose Reyes Memorial Medical Center, Rizal Medical Center, East Avenue Medical Center, Quirino Memorial Medical Center, Tondo Medical Center, Jose Fabella Memorial Hospital, National Children's Hospital, National Center for Mental Health, Philippine Orthopedic Center, San Lazaro Hospital, Research Institute for Tropical Medicine, and Amang Rodriguez Medical Center.

Five of these hospitals have not received funds for capital outlay. Tondo Medical Center has the lowest budget of P102.44 million ($2,316,075) and the National Center for Mental Health is allotted P461.65 million ($10,437,485).

The budget for the Philippine General Hospital (PGH) for this year is P1.07 billion ($24,191,725), of which P810 million ($18,313,361) is allotted for personnel services and only P3 million ($67,827) for capital outlay.

In 2007, the PGH budget included a measly P15.5 million ($350,440) for medical and dental assistance, including hospitalization, for indigent patients. For this year, no such item is reflected in the PGH's budget. Meanwhile, the Veterans Memorial Medical Center would receive P 629.33 million ($14,228,577) and the AFP Medical Center, P713.34 million ($16,127,967).

Subsidies for indigent patients for confinement in specialty hospitals and for the use of specialized equipment is only P6 million ($135,654). The overall subsidy for indigent patients is only P139 million ($3,142,663).

This is a pittance compared to allocations for defense and debt interest payments. From 2001 to 2008, the average allocation for debt interest payments is P257.10 billion ($5,812,796,744) and for defense, P43.58 billion ($985,304,092).

IBON Foundation revealed that debt service increased by 100% from 2001 to 2005. The independent think-tank estimated that during the same period, $48 billion had been paid for debt, equivalent to 11.8% of the country's gross domestic product (GDP) each year.

Payments for the principal amortization of foreign and local debts in 2007 amounted to P303.83 billion ($6,869,319,466) and for this year, principal amortization is pegged at P328.34 billion ($7,423,468,234).

Year	Health	Debt Interest Payments	Defense
2001	13.64 B	181.60 B	32.78 B
2002	14.49 B	185.86 B	38.91 B
2003	12.40 B	226.41 B	44.42 B
2004	12.88 B	271.53 B	43.85 B
2005	12.93 B	301.69 B	44.19 B
2007	11.66 B	318.18 B	49.34 B
2008	19.77 B	269.85 B	50.93 B
Ave. allocation per year	13.84 B	257.10 B	43.58 B

Source of basic data: Department of Budget and Management The Congress re-enacted the 2005 budget for 2006.

Due to the meager budget for health, government hospitals have imposed charges such as operating room deposits, emergency room fees and laboratory fees. Based on a primer released by the Council for Health and Development (CHD), a national organization of community-based health programs (CBHPs), the PGH charges P1,500 ($33.91) for the use of its operating room and Jose Reyes Memorial Hospital charges P3,500 ($79.13) for the same item.

The CHD further revealed that patients at the National Kidney and Transplant Institute (NKTI) are suffering because of the hospital's "no pay, no hook policy" referring to the hospital's policy of not giving dialysis treatment to patients who cannot pay the treatment. One dialysis session at the NKTI costs P2,700 ($61.04). A patient with a serious kidney problem usually has to undergo dialysis treatment twice a week.

The health group also said that patients in public hospitals have to pay even for the cotton balls, syringe and gauze they consume. Indeed, health services in government hospitals have become prohibitive for many of the country's poor.

A survey conducted by the Kilos Bayan para sa Kalusugan (KBK or People's Health Movement) in August 2007 revealed that 70% of patients paid P1,000 to P50,000 ($22.60 to $1,130) for hospital expenses and 5% spent P50,000 to one million pesos ($1,130 to

$22,609). Only 15% were charged one peso to one thousand pesos ($0.02 to $22.60).

Sixty-one percent of the respondents of the survey are unemployed, 27% are low-income earners while the remaining 13% are low-income professionals. The survey results showed that 76% of the respondents have to borrow money from friends and relatives, sell their property or beg for mercy from charitable institutions to be able to pay the expenses they incurred while in the hospital.

The April 2008 survey by IBON Foundation also showed that 73.38% of families are having difficulty paying for medicines and treatment. Even the Philippine Health Insurance Corporation (PhilHealth) cards prove to be insignificant, the CHD primer stated. The PhilHealth claimed to cover 80% of the population.

According to Dr. Gene Nisperos, HEAD vice chairperson, the National Institute of Health maintained that the PhilHealth's claim of coverage is overestimated by at least 20%. Nisperos noted that the PhilHealth coverage has been bloated to 80% during the election period in 2006. In the past years, the coverage is only 61%. He added that the PhilHealth does not include outpatient services.

Independent surveys conducted by the KBK also showed that in Metro Manila's seven government hospitals, seven in every ten poor families are not members of PhilHealth.

Another study commissioned by the European Commission regarding PhilHealth coverage in Mindanao showed that only 10% of the poor in Tawi-Tawi, 12% in Davao Oriental and 15% in Zamboanga del Norte and Maguindanao are covered by PhilHealth.

In a press conference, July 25, Dr. Eleanor Jara, CHD executive director, criticized the Botika ng Barangay program of the Arroyo government. She said, "There is no truth in government's claim that the poor benefits from this program." Jara cited as an example the Botika ng Barangay in Payatas. She said that residents complained that the pharmacy is empty.

She also slammed the profiteering of the government from the said program. She revealed that while mefenamic acid costs P11 ($0.248) in some branches of the Botika ng Barangay, the actual cost of the said medicine, which is imported from India or Pakistan is only two pesos ($0.045).

The Arroyo government has continued the implementation of the Health Sector Reform Agenda (HSRA) through the Fourmula One Program. The HSRA was formulated in 1999 and ended in 2005. The

CHD maintained that the HSRA "laid down the conditions where the people have to foot for all their health needs and expenditures."

The HSRA paved the way for the privatization of specialty hospitals. The CHD said, "In the guise of corporatization, the Philippine Heart Center, Lung Center of the Philippines, National Kidney and Transplant Institute at Philippine Children's Medical Center, East Avenue Medical Center and the Quirino Memorial Medical Center were corporatized and provided autonomy in management and financial aspects."

Mechanisms were implemented to collect and earn more revenues, including increasing the number of pay wards while reducing the number of beds for charity and allowing the DoH by virtue of Executive Order 197 to increase fees in public hospitals up to 20%.

The CHD further stressed, "The aspects of health reforms are characterized by increasing the people's out-of-pocket spending for health and decreasing funds and responsibility of the government for people's health." (End of article)

Natural Disasters

There are many types of natural disasters that have been responsible for millions of deaths. The death tolls are increasing along with the increasing number of people on earth. Those in the poor world are expected to suffer more because of the lack of logistics and disaster control. They are often at the mercy of nature. The following is a list of some of the worst natural calamities to strike the world since 1900. The list is by definition arguable.

Earthquakes and tsunamis

Earthquakes have been occurring more frequently than ever before. The death tolls are also increasing because of overpopulation. Statistics can easily bear out that more deaths occurred when the areas are densely populated. No one is really safe when a devastating earthquake struck. They not only took away precious lives but destroy properties that took years of saving. The poor are particularly vulnerable to devastating earthquakes with their low quality of houses. Earthquakes almost always occurred in places where and when the people least expect them, often overwhelming rescue efforts. Some of these devastating earthquakes are listed below:

- May 12, 2008. A 7.9 earthquake on the Richter scale in Sichuan claimed the lives of at least 69,197 confirmed dead and 374,176 injured, with 18,222 listed as missing. The earthquake left about 4.8 million people homeless, though the number could be as high as 11 million. It is the deadliest and strongest earthquake to hit China since the 1976 Tangshan earthquake.
- Oct. 8, 2005. At least 80,000 people were killed and three million left homeless after a quake struck the mountainous Kashmir district in Pakistan.
- Dec. 26, 2004. A magnitude 9.0 quake struck off the coast of Sumatra, triggering tsunamis that swept through the coastal regions of a dozen countries bordering the Indian Ocean. The death toll has been estimated at between 225,000 and 275,000.
- Dec. 26, 2003. An earthquake devastated the ancient city of Bam, in central Iran, leaving between 31,000 and 43,000 people dead.
- July 28, 1976. The 20th century's most devastating quake with a magnitude 7.8 hit the sleeping city of Tangshan in northeast China. The official death toll was 242,000. Unofficial estimates put the number as high as 655,000.
- May 22, 1960. The biggest earthquake with a magnitude of 9.5 occurred in Chile.
- Oct. 5, 1948 - More than 110,000 were killed when a 7.3 quake rolled through the area around Ashgebat in Turkmenistan.
- May 22, 1927. A magnitude 7.9 quake near Xining, China, killed 200,000
- Sept. 1, 1923. A third of Tokyo and most of Yokohama were leveled when a magnitude 8.3 earthquake shook Japan. About 143,000 were killed as fires ravaged much of Tokyo.
- Dec. 16, 1920. China was also the site for the world's third deadliest quake of the 20th century. An estimated 200,000 died when a magnitude 8.6 temblor hit Gansu, triggering massive landslides.
- Dec. 28, 1908. Southern Italy was ravaged by a 7.2 magnitude quake that triggered a tsunami that hit the Messina-Reggio-Calabria area, killing 123,000.
- 1556. The world's deadliest recorded earthquake was in central China that killed an estimated 830,000 people.

Volcanic eruptions

- July 15, 1991. Mt. Pinatubo on Luzon Island in the Philippines erupted, blanketing 750 km^2 with volcanic ash. More than 800 died. The effects of the eruption were felt worldwide. It ejected roughly 10 billion metric tons of magma, and 20 million tons of SO_2, bringing vast quantities of minerals and metals to the surface environment. It injected large amounts of aerosols into the stratosphere - more than any eruption since that of Krakatoa in 1883. Over the following months, the aerosols formed a global layer of sulfuric acid haze. Global temperatures dropped by about 0.5° C, and ozone layer temporarily increased substantially.

- Nov. 13-14, 1985. At least 25,000 are killed near the town of Armero, Colombia, when the Nevado del Ruiz volcano erupted, triggering mudslides.

- May 8, 1902. Mt. Pelee erupted on the Caribbean island of Martinique, destroying the capital city of St. Pierre. Up to 40,000 were killed, most of them instantaneously. The day before, a volcano erupted had killed 1,600 people on the nearby island of St. Vincent.

- October 1902. Mt. Santa Maria erupted in Guatemala, killing 6,000 people. A subsequent outbreak of malaria killed many more. The eruption was one of the largest of the 20th century and comparable in magnitude to that of Mount Pinatubo in 1991. Both volcanoes were dormant for at least 500 years.

- August 26-27, 1883. The eruption of the volcano in the island of Krakatoa destroyed two-thirds of the island. The eruption ejected more than 25 km^3 of rock, ash, and pumice and generated the loudest sound in history that could be heard as far the island of Rodriguez near Mauritius, approx. 5,000 km away. Near the eruption area, according to official records, 165 villages and towns were destroyed and 132 seriously damaged. At least 36,417 people died, according to official Dutch authorities, although some put the figures at 120,000 death and many thousands were injured, mostly from the tsunamis that followed the explosion.

- 1783. The lava from the eruption of Laki Volcano in south-central Iceland caused little direct damage, but the ash and sulfur dioxide spewed out over most of the country caused three-quarters of the island's livestock to perish. In the following famine, around ten thousand people died, one-fifth of the population of Iceland. The 122 megatons of sulfuric acid cooled the planet by 1°C that lasted for 2-3 years.

- 79 CE. Mt. Vesuvius, located near Naples in southern Italy is the only active volcano in the mainland European continent. Its most notable eruption destroyed the ancient Roman cities of Pompeii, Oplontis and Herculaneum. Pompeii was buried under 10 feet of ash while Herculaneum was buried under 75 feet of ash. No official figures of death were reported since the number of inhabitants of the three towns was unknown at that time. The toll was estimated at 20,000. This active volcano erupted again in 1631 and killed about 4,000 people. The next eruption could easily kill tens of thousands as the population near the Mt now stood at over three million people, a sign that the population has grown so large.

Hurricanes, typhoons, cyclones and floods

To get an idea of what these terms are referring, it is best to define them. Hurricanes, typhoons, and cyclones are actually all the same phenomena except their places of origin. Hurricanes are tropical cyclones formed in the Atlantic or Caribbean areas while typhoons have their origin in the Pacific Ocean. Those originating from the Indian Ocean are simply called cyclones. In order to be classified as a hurricane, the wind speed of the storm must be at least 74 mph (119 kph).

As the world's temperature continues to rise, the number of hurricanes is expected to increase and with more ferocity. This seems to be confirmed with the presence of Hurricane Catarina that struck the coast of Brazil. There has never been any hurricane forming in this area in the past. It is the warming of the atmosphere that made it possible for Catarina to form in such unusual area, according to two Australian-based meteorologists. Another study by Kerry Emanuel of the Massachusetts Institute of Technology, concluded that storms were in fact more intense and lasting for longer, due in large part to rising sea temperatures driven by global warming. The storm intensity index in the last 30 years has also doubled. Still another team from the Georgia Institute of Technology in Atlanta, analyzing data for the past 30 years found that despite an overall decrease in the number of cyclones, there is a large increase in the number of Categories 4 and 5 hurricanes (supertyphoons). They also found that there were near doubling of the strongest storms between 1970 and 2004. (Lynas, 43-46) To understand why, it is necessary to know how hurricanes are formed.

The two essential ingredients in every typhoon are warm water and moist warm air (water vapor). During the summer months, the water is naturally warmer especially in the tropics which accounts for why typhoons start in the tropical seas. As the sun heats the water to at least 82°F, it will evaporate to form water vapor and rise up. The water vapor is what fuel the typhoon as it absorbed heat from the evaporated sea water. Usually, the heat released in this way in tropical thunderstorms is carried away by wind shear, which blows the top off the thunderstorms. But when there is little wind shear, this heat can build up, causing low pressure to form. The low pressure causes wind to begin to spiral inward toward the center of the low pressure area called the eye. These winds help to evaporate even more water vapor from the ocean, spiraling inward toward the center, feeding more showers and thunderstorms, and warming the upper atmosphere still more. The cycle continues until it forms into a tropical depression leading to typhoons in some cases. It is no wonder why global warming is abetting the rise of supertyphoons. It is well known that typhoons draw strength from heat in ocean surface waters and the higher the heat, the greater is the strength of the typhoon. One example is the case of the Hurricane Katrina that rampaged through New Orleans. At the time of Katrina, as it was gathering force on its way, the surface waters in the Gulf of Mexico were about 20°F warmer than the historical average for that time of the year. Many climatologists believed that the warming ferocity was attributed to global warming. (Friedman, 112)

Unless accompanied by huge rainfall leading to flooding, typhoons cause mostly damage to properties. But flooding and storm surge are different. Even below this wind speed, thunderstorms can be very destructive because of the deluge of rainwater has been responsible for more deaths.

In the 20th century more than a million died directly from earthquakes. In the same period, death from disasters caused by hurricanes, typhoons, cyclones, tornadoes, and especially flood took the lives of more than nine million people directly worldwide. These disasters probably killed many more millions from diseases and famine as a result of these catastrophes. Destructive cyclones followed by flooding not only destroy lives but also farmlands that often lead to famine and starvation. Topsoil is washed away and will take centuries to replenish. The most destructive flood around the Yangtze River affected 180 million Chinese. A tropical cyclone in Bangladesh in 1970, followed by a tidal wave left about half a million people dead. An estimated 138,000 people died as a result of a cyclonic tidal wave in 1991. Last November 23, 2007, another cyclone followed by a 20-foot tidal wave may have killed up to 10,000 people in Bangladesh.[36] (Robinson, 8) The following are some of the casualties in the past.

- Typhoon Fengshen (locally named Frank) that hit the Philippines in June 2008 killed over a thousand people as one ship, the *MV Princess of the Stars* sunk off the coast of Romblon carrying over eight hundred passengers. Damaged to agriculture and infrastructure cost more than $100 million.
- May 3, 2008. Cyclone Nargis, swept along by winds that exceeded 190 kph and waves six meters high struck the Burmese peninsula and may have left as many as 100,000 dead, according to U.S. estimates. Many more could have died from starvation as the military junta was slow to allow foreign aids to come in. A delegation from the Philippines was allowed into the country and was the only country where the Philippine flag was also allowed to be hoisted in the camp.
- Oct. 26-Nov. 4, 1998. Hurricane Mitch was the deadliest hurricane to hit the Americas. It killed 11,000 in Honduras and Nicaragua, with around 8,000 still unaccounted and left 2.5 million homeless. Damage to properties is estimated at $5 billion.
- Aug. 5, 1975. At least 85,000 were killed along the Yangtze River in China when more than 60 dams failed following a series of storms, causing widespread flooding and famine. This disaster was kept secret by the Chinese government for 20 years.
- Nov. 13, 1970. The Bhola cyclone in the Ganges delta killed an estimated 500,000 in Bangladesh (East Pakistan then). Some put the complete death toll as high as one million. Another million dead cows floated in the Ganges River and Delta turning the water into red. It was followed by a tsunami that did away more properties, animals and lives. The neglect of the government at Karachi to help the stricken East Pakistan results in a revolution and the birth of Bangladesh.
- 1954. The overflowing Yangtze River killed 40,000 people, but not before the government ordered 600,000 workers to use their bodies to form a levee to hold back the water. It did not

---

[36] http://www.isiswomen.org/index.php?option=com_content&task=view&id=834&Itemid=204

work. Interestingly, before the Communist took over, the U.S. was planning to build the largest dam in the world then. (Spignesi, 36)

- August 1945. An estimated 600,000 died as a result of the famine following the severe flooding in what was then North Vietnam caused by the breaching of 79 dikes that flooded 312,000 hectares of land cross 17 provinces.

- 1939. Massive flooding from the Yellow River caused an estimated 500,000 death in northern China. The famine that followed killed even more millions. All the rice crops and houses hit by the flood were wiped out and left 25 million homeless.

- June 1938. During the Second Sino-Japanese War, Nationalist Chinese soldiers, under the direction of Chiang Kai-Shek, blew up dikes around the Yellow River to stop Japanese troops from advancing. The flooded area covered 54,000 km^2 and killed about 890,000 people including a number of Japanese troops. Famine and disease followed probably killed even more.

- May-August 1931. The Yellow River is sometimes called "Chinese Sorrow" for good reason. After a two year drought, massive flooding of China's Yellow and Yangtze Rivers led to almost four million deaths from drowning, disease and starvation. Charles Lindbergh flew food and medicine into the devastated area.

- 1911. The flooding of the Yangtze River after it overflowed inundated four provinces as well as the city of Shanghai killed an estimated 200,000 and starved another 100,000 in the weeks that followed.

- 1887. The flooding of North China Plain by the Yellow River and followed by starvation killed nearly 2 million.

The Philippines is visited by about 20 typhoons annually. Each strong typhoon that hit directly the country often incurs death and destruction mostly to the poor inhabitants. Those living in the upland and lowland surrounding the mountainous areas are likely to suffer from muddy landslides. Destruction to farm crops often runs into the millions. Floodwater often causes death by drowning, followed by famine and diseases. Some of the dreaded typhoons are listed below.

- Super Typhoon Joan (locally called Sening) was the first of two super typhoons to strike the country within a week in October 1970. It is the strongest typhoon to ever hit the country with maximum wind speed of 275 kph. The second to hit the country a week later is the Super Typhoon Kate. The death toll from Typhoon Sening was 768 people and damage to property is estimated at $373 million (2005 rate). More than 90% of the agricultural crops were destroyed along its path.

- Super Typhoon Angela (locally called Rosing) battled the island of Luzon for five continuous days of sustained wind of 260 kph. By the time it left the country, 936 people died with damage to properties estimated at more than P10 billion. It was the most expensive typhoon to hit the country so far.

- Super Typhoon Durian (locally called Reming) was an intense storm that caused massive loss of life when mudslides from the Mayon Volcano buried many villages. After causing massive damage in the Philippines and killing 734 people (unofficial figure put it at more than 1,200) and P5 billion in damage, it exited into the South China Sea and weakened slightly, before managing to reorganize and re-strengthen into a typhoon shortly before its second landfall in Vietnam causing further damage of more than US$400 million. In all, the typhoon killed at least 1,497 people, and left hundreds more missing. Preliminary damage estimates total about US$508 million.[37]

- The provinces hardest hit by Super Typhoon Ike (locally called Nitang) are Surigao del Norte and the Negros Island, from August 31 to September 4, 1984. It killed 1,363 people (unofficial figure at 1,492-3,000) and damaged properties worth P4.1 billion. Its mighty wind first ravaged Surigao City leaving hundreds of death behind before crossing Cebu, on its way to the Negros Island. In Negros Occidental, the Ilog River burst its bank and sent a deluge of water and mud, debris and thousands of unharvested logs to the municipalities of Kabankalan and Ilog killing hundreds of people. Some survivors clambered to rooftops and attics of two storey houses while others clung on tall trees for almost two days without food and water before being rescued.

- Super Typhoon Mike (locally called Ruping) was probably the most devastating since 1947 in terms of damage to properties that was estimated at P10.846 billion. It occurred on November 10-14, 1990 with wind speed of 240 kph. It also

---

[37] http://en.wikipedia.org/wiki/Typhoon_Durian

claimed 748 lives. Everywhere the typhoon passes, the howler rampaged to destroy everything on its path. Its devastation was so widespread that it affected more than one million families.

- Sometimes, it does not have to be a strong typhoon to bring devastated to the country. A tropical storm could do just as much damage to lives and properties. This is the case of tropical storm Uring. Uring was a weak tropical storm but because of heavy precipitation, it flooded many places along its path. On the morning of November 5, 1991, it descended on Ormoc City in Leyte. The river bisecting the city burst its banks and overflowed, drowning the whole city in more than 10 feet of water laden with mud and debris. Thousands were caught flatfooted and perished. The storm then moved through Cebu, northern Negros, Iloilo, northern Palawan and on to the South China Sea, but not before flooding these provinces. Ormoc City was the hardest hit with a quarter of its population drowned and their bloated bodies were littered everywhere. Those washed out to the sea where feasted by sharks. The final official death toll was 5,100, but may rise to 8,000 plus because entire family members may have perished.[38] These are just some of the devastating typhoon with their death tolls and devastating damages to properties. The death tolls in the future are expected to rise as more people inhabit the country.

Flooding in a way is caused by overpopulation. As urbanization continue to proliferate, underdeveloped areas such as forest lands and wetlands are often converted to other uses to accommodate more people. These areas that used to serve as sponges for excess rainwater have been eradicated permanently by houses and paved roads. The result is that the only channel for excess water is through the storm drainage. One study estimated that flooding over open space was to occur once in a 100 years is down to five years should the impervious cover reaches 25% and could be an annual event when the impervious cover reaches 65%.[39] This is an indication of how urban cities like Metro Manila are getting flooded all the time.

Metro Manila is a good example of how urbanization has caused annual flooding even in the absence of typhoon. The poor urban stormwater management lacks the needed drainage system to siphon

---

[38] http://www.typhoon2000.ph/stats/11WorstPhilippineTyphoons.htm
[39] http://www.nrdc.org/water/pollution/storm/chap3.asp

water to the sea when the rain stops. The small pipes gathering the stormwater only channel the water from one area to flood another area until it is finally channel to the sea. There are no water retention facilities to mitigate the floodwater. Except for some well developed subdivisions were water can quickly flow through paved channels, large stormwater pipes and other techniques, the local and national governments are probably too poor to undertake massive floodwater control projects despite the years of trying to solve the problem with a special levy for flood control. What are needed are massive steel pipes and automated pumping stations strategically located to harness all the flood prone areas to solve the flooding problem once and for all. In the U.S. the steel pipes are often large enough for vehicles to pass through and runs throughout the city.

Accidents

Thomas Malthus probably never anticipated that accidents could be such a big factor in limiting population growth. The world at the time he wrote his *Principle* was not such an overcrowded world with new forms of transportation, machineries and equipment that would have caused such great number of accidents that took millions of lives annually. The most common type of accidents today involved the motor vehicles. In the U.S. where statistics were easily obtained, there were more than 6.3 million vehicle accidents annually with roughly more than 41,000 deaths and 2.9 million injuries. In 2005, the financial cost of these crashes is more than $230 billion.[40] According to WHO, there are about 1.2 million people killed in traffic accidents every year with 50 million of them injured and the medical cost is estimated to be $520 billion.[41] Some 480,000 of these deaths and 20 million of the injured are caused by drunk driving, according to Ray Butch Gamboa, again citing WHO, in his article on *Motoring Today*. (*PS*, December 24, 2008)

Accidents took the lives of about 830,000 children annually and injured millions more that require long-term hospitalization and rehabilitation. Ninety-five percent of these accidents occur in developing countries because there are few laws preventing them from harm. A majority of the unintentional victims of road accidents are children. According to WHO and UNICEF, road accidents kill some 260,000 children and injured around 10 million others every year. It

---

[40] http://www.car-accidents.com/pages/stats.html
[41] http://www.car-accidents.com/accident_photo_country.html

was followed by drowning with 175,000 children and fire-related burns claiming 96,000 children. The death rate is 11 times higher in low- and middle-income nations than in high-income nations. (*PS*, December 26, 2008)

China is the world's most populous country with over 1.3 billion people, leads the world with the most number of fatal car accidents. According to Chinese official studies there are about 450,000 car accidents on Chinese roads each year resulting in 470,000 injuries and 100,000 deaths. Most of the accidents were due to poor driving skills. The latest figure released by the traffic administration bureau under the Ministry of Public Security claimed that the accidental deaths have declined by 19% in 2008, resulting in the death of 73,484 people and injured 304,919. The lion share of fatalities involved pedestrians, followed by bicyclists and motorcyclists. The traffic administration bureau attributed the decreases to stepped-up road safety campaigns and better management of commercial vehicles. (*South China Morning Post*, January 7, 2009) These figures are disputed by a WHO study. The WHO study reported that the actual number of fatalities on China's roads is more than twice the official figure or about 250,000 killed each year. Road traffic crashes are believed to be the leading cause of death for people 15 to 45 years old. The direct and indirect costs of these accidents are estimated at between $12 to $21 billion or about 1.5% of China's GNP. This accident rate means that roughly 20% of the world's fatal car accidents take place in China. The Chinese Government has formed a new ministry committee and introduced a major new Road Traffic Safety Law throughout the country in an effort to reduce the accident rate.[42]

India, with the world's second largest population of about 1.2 billion people has its large share of motor vehicle accidents. The India Department of Road Transport and Highway, reports that there are about 406,730 accidents each year with 86,000 people killed. Philippine National Police reported about 15,000 traffic accidents in 2006 resulting in 674 fatalities, 3,767 injuries and 10,623 instances of property damage. Road accidents are expected to continue to rise as more vehicles are being introduced into the world everyday.

Aside from the road accidents caused by motor vehicles, there are the railroad accidents that often kill dozens in a single incident especially in the highly congested countries such as India. It is the main mode of

---

[42] http://www.car-accidents.com/country-car-accidents/china-car-accidents-crash.html

transport in the country. The railways criss-cross the Indian subcontinent stretch for more than 62,000 route kilometers and carryover 11 million passengers and another million tonnes of freight each day. The trains are often overcrowded and overused. Passengers are often packed to twice its capacity. In the United States, statistics show that approximately every two hours a railroad accident occurs in which a pedestrian or vehicle is struck by a train. In 2007, there were 13,067 railroad related accidents, according to the Federal Railroad Administration's Office of Safety Analysis. These railroad accidents resulted in 851 deaths and 8,801 non-fatal injuries. Of the deaths, 338 occurred at highway railroad crossings and 473 were a result of trespassing on railroad rights-of-way and property. The statistics show that of the railroad accident injuries in 2007, 1,031 happened at highway railroad crossings and 398 of the injuries occurred due to trespassing.[43]

Trains are one of the cheapest forms of transport on land. It has also its fair share of accidents that often kill dozens of people. The reasons for these accidents vary. In many instances, derailment is the prime suspect. At times it is collision with other motor vehicles along its track. Human errors cannot also be ruled out in some cases. The trains have also been targets for terrorists. Thousands have been killed annually, especially in India.

Ships and small boats have their fair share of accidents. The Philippines has the distinction of having the worst sea mishap in the world. *MV Doña Paz* is considered the worst maritime disaster ever in terms of lives lost. The 23-year old ferry had already had one serious accident, but after a reconstruction it was declared fully safe.

On 20 December 1987, she was on her way to Manila, when she collided with *Vector*, a motor tanker, carrying 8,800 barrels of petroleum products. The collision ignited a fire, from which it was virtually impossible to escape. Only 21 persons from *Doña Paz* survived by diving under the sea of flames surrounding the two ships. The extent of the accident was increased by the sloppiness of the crew. Although *Doña Paz* was licensed to carry only 1,518 passengers, subsequent interviews have revealed that the total number of casualties was 4,375. Many of the victims were families on their way home for Christmas holiday. Officials from the maritime authorities said that the number of passengers was impossible to control. Survivors' testimonies have revealed that the crew of the ship were drinking beers and watching videotapes prior to the accident. The fire was so intense,

---

[43] http://www.totalinjury.com/trains.asp

that it annihilated the two ships. Only 270 bodies washed ashore. After the accident, an investigation was commenced, which very quickly faded away. Very few survivors and relatives went to court, because they had little faith in the legal system.[44]

I cannot understand why maritime authorities cannot easily spot an overloaded ship. It is a common practice to have the sides of the ship delineated with different colors of lines to establish their capacity and the weight of their cargoes. The maximum load can be determined just by looking at the lines for maximum load. If the ship is not overloaded, other causes are probably the culprit. One possibility is that the cargoes are not secured enough to prevent them from tossing during rough seas. Another possibility is that the ship is not seaworthy despite the thorough investigation. Taking chances by the ship captain or corrupting the inspectors is not farfetched.

War, WMD, and Genocide

War and genocide have been two of the greatest destructive forces in reducing the population of the world. Since time immemorial, the planet has only experienced less than 300 years of utopia where war has never occurred anywhere in the world. The greatest and deadliest war was the Second World War that killed more than 70 million people, most of them civilians. This global military conflict involved a majority of the world's nations and the most widespread that lasted for six years from 1939 to 1945. The total financial cost of the war is estimated at about US$1 trillion, making it the most expensive war then.[45] Some historians claimed that the war started much earlier, during the Japanese invasion of Manchuria. It soon spread to other cities culminating with the Nanking Massacre. More than 20 million Chinese civilians were killed without remorse. Few Japanese war criminals were ever punished as a result of the Red Menace, the rise of communism.

The other Great War was the First World War that left more than 20 million military and civilian deaths in the aftermath. It lasted from 1914 to 1918. It was supposed to be the war to end all wars. That never happened and the destructions continued. Other great wars mostly occurred during the Middle Ages in the so-called religious wars.

---

[44] http://www.hazardcards.com/card.php?id=14
[45] http://en.wikipedia.org/wiki/World_War_II

Religious war is mostly triggered by differences in religious beliefs. It can involve one state with an established religion against another state with a different religion or a different sect within the same religion, or a religiously motivated group attempting to spread its faith by violence, or to suppress another group because of its religious beliefs or practices. Examples of these are the Muslim conquests of Europe followed by the expulsion of the Muslin from Europe during the Reconquista, the Crusades against the Muslim control of the Holy Land, the French Wars of Religions, the Protestant revolt called Reformation and its Catholic counterpart called Counter-Reformation.

The Muslim concept of Jihad, or Holy War was set down in the 7th Century and is sometime used by Arabs in its war against Israel. On the other hand, two of the Catholic greatest Church Fathers are St. Augustine and St. Thomas Aquinas. Saint Augustine is credited as being the first to adopt a "Just War" theory within Christianity to justify the killing among Christian sects on religious grounds. This was followed by Saint Thomas Aquinas elaboration on these criteria and his writings were used by the Roman Catholic Church to regulate the actions of European countries.[46]

The Vietnam War claimed that lives of more than three million Vietnamese including 86,580 American GIs. One of the notable event was the March 16, 2970 My Lai Massacre were around 450 to 500 children, women and elderly were massacred. Only two little girls were spared after they showed up after the massacre. The massacre was led by Lt. William L. Calley, Jr. who was later court-martialed.

Weapons of Mass Destruction

Before the atomic bombs were dropped on Hiroshima and Nagasaki in Japan during the Second World War, there are two other weapons considered as weapons of mass destruction. They are the chemical weapons such as the use of poison gases to maim and kill enemies. The other weapons which were in use much earlier are the biological weapons found in nature. Some of these biological weapons are viruses and bacteria that have killed countless people in the past and curable have been enhanced against any antidote.

Many countries have entered the nuclear weapon clubs while others are trying to develop for themselves such as Iran and North

---

[46] http://en.wikipedia.org/wiki/Reconquista

Korea. There are also those who may be developing crude nuclear weapons called dirty bombs that could be developed by rogue states.

The use of unconventional weapons of mass destruction has come a long way since the use of poison gas during the First World War. At the Battle of Ypres in Belgium, the German unleashed mustard gas on April 15, 1915 against the British soldiers. It wounded 10,000 and killed some 5,000. Not to be outdone, the British counter with its own poison gas. When the war ended, more than 100,000 were dead. The gasses caused the victims to suffer vomiting and choking followed by blistering of the skin and singeing of the lungs. The deaths were slow and ghastly. (Power, 205-206)

Modern bioterrorism was first used by the Japanese in its war with China during the 1930s. However, its earliest interest in biological warfare began at the end of World War I with the rise of the now notorious Shiro Ishii. Despite being signatory to the 1925 Geneva Disarmament Convention outlawing both chemical and biological warfare, the Japanese went on to use these banned weapons. This just goes to show that rogue nations will use whatever weapons at their disposal to win the war. The same goes on in Communist Russia during the Cold War. Through lies and deceits, the Soviets was able to build up an arsenal of biological weapons that could destroy mankind several times over despite signing a treaty banning biological weapons with the U.S. and UK. The fuller account of biological warfare can be found in the book *Plague Wars* by Tom Mangold and Jeff Goldberg.

Despite the adoption of the Biological Weapons Convention by many rogue states, this toothless treaty has been violated by many members to this treaty. Many of these biological agents include anthrax, Q fever, botulinum toxin, Plague, Ebola and Marburg virus, the dreaded smallpox that was supposed to be eliminated to extinction a few decades, etc. Some of these viruses have even been developed to be vaccine resistance, making them incurable. The Soviet was said to have produced sufficient Marburg virus to wipe out the world. North Korea was suspected to have reduced anthrax to the micron range making them ideal for human inhalation, thus making them more lethal in aerosol form than the spores. They were also able to coat the anthrax with special organic compounds to shield the spores from harmful UV rays. In the development of these lethal viruses, in some cases, human guinea pigs were used. (Mangold, 191, 330) The Japanese were notorious for using humans as guinea pigs during the Second World War. A more detailed account can be found in the book *The Brutal Holocaust*, about Japanese atrocities during the Second World War.

Genocide

Genocide is the deliberate and systematic destruction, in whole or in part, of an ethnic, racial, religious, or national group. It has often been resorted to by the overpowering of the dominant states against the ethnic few. The most famous genocide is the destruction of the Jews throughout Europe during the Middle Ages culminating with the Holocaust during the Second World War. Were it not for the genocides committed against the Jews, the population of the Jews around the world would have been more than 200 million instead of the roughly 20 million plus scattered around the world. They would have been roughly equal to the total population of the Arab states since both started at the same number of people during Biblical times.

One of the most gruesome massacres happened during the Second World War under the reign of Ante Pavelic, a Catholic dictator in Croatia. A puppet of Hitler, he massacred around 800,000 Jews, Orthodox Christians and gypsies and even boasted to Hitler that he was able to solve the Jewish problem faster than the Nazis. He was greatly abetted by the prelates of the Catholic Church, mostly Franciscans who took up armed to massacre the unarmed civilians. Even the Nazis in the occupied country could not stomach the atrocities committed by the priests. Some prelates even tried to contest who among them could kill the most number of non-Catholics. After the war, none of the leaders of these massacres were ever brought to justice. A fuller account can be found in my book, *The Dark Side of Catholicism*. Most of the documents on the account of this massacre can be found in the Internet under the Pavelic Papers.

Other victims of genocides are the Armenian genocide where some 1.5 million Armenians were killed by the Turks, the Rwandan genocide where more than 800,000 Tutsis killed in a matter of 100 days beginning on April 6, 1993. In the latter case, some of the deaths were abetted by members of the Catholic Church who pinpointed where the Tutsis are hidden, even within the sanctuary of the Church. In fact, two Hutu nuns, Sister Getrude and Sister Maria, were later convicted and sentenced them to life Imprisonment by a Belgian court that uses its universal jurisdiction over genocide. They offered their church as sanctuary for hundreds of Tutsi refugees and then bought petro to incinerate them. (Robertson QC, xxvii) The conflict has not ended even after the Tutsis were able to control the country because many of those who committed the genocide fled to the border countries and has initiated two Congo wars that are still going on today.[47]

The Armenian Genocide (1915-1918), was the first genocide of the 20th century. It was directed against the Christian minority of Armenians when two million Armenians living in Turkey were eliminated from their historic homeland through forced deportations with the massacre of about 1.5 million of them. In the 1890s, young Armenians began to press for political reforms and calling for constitutional reforms. The despotic Sultan Abdul Hamid II (1876-1909) responded to their pleas with brutal persecutions. Between 1894 and 1896, 100,000 to 300,000 inhabitants in Armenian villages were massacred during widespread pogroms conducted by the Sultan's special regiments.[48] The Humidian Massacre as it is known today made the sultan infamous by being branded as the "Red Sultan" or "Bloody Sultan."

But the Sultan's days were numbered. In July 1908, reform-minded Turkish nationalists known as "Young Turks" forced the Sultan to allow a constitutional government and guarantee basic rights. The Young Turks were ambitious junior officers in the Turkish Army who hoped to halt their country's steady decline.

Armenians in Turkey were delighted with this sudden turn of events and its prospects for a brighter future. Both Turks and Armenians held jubilant public rallies attended with banners held high calling for freedom, equality and justice.

However, their hopes were dashed when three of the Young Turks seized full control of the government via a coup in 1913. This triumvirate of Young Turks, consisting of Mehmed Talaat, Ismail Enver and Ahmed Djemal, came to wield dictatorial powers and concocted their own ambitious plans for the future of Turkey. They wanted to unite all of the Turkic peoples in the entire region while expanding the borders of Turkey eastward across the Caucasus all the way into Central Asia. This would create a new Turkish empire, a "great and eternal land" called Turan with one language and one religion.

But there was a big problem. The traditional historic homeland of Armenia lay right in the path of their plans to expand eastward. And on that land was a large population of Christian Armenians totaling some two million persons, making up about 10% of Turkey's overall population.

Along with the Young Turk's newfound "Turanism" there was a dramatic rise in Islamic fundamentalist agitation throughout Turkey.

---

[47] http://en.wikipedia.org/wiki/Rwandan_Genocide

[48] http://www.unitedhumanrights.org/Genocide/armenian_genocide.htm

Christian Armenians were once again branded as infidels (non-believers in Islam). Young Islamic extremists, sometimes leading to violence, staged anti-Armenian demonstrations. During one such outbreak in 1909, two hundred villages were plundered and over 30,000 persons massacred in the Cilicia district on the Mediterranean coast. Throughout Turkey, sporadic local attacks against Armenians continued unchecked over the next several years. The real aim of these massacres was to loot, destroy and seize Armenia properties and businesses and to eliminate a culturally superior civilization.

There were also big cultural differences between Armenians and Turks. The Armenians had always been one of the best-educated communities within the old Turkish Empire. Armenians were the professionals in society, the businessmen, lawyers, doctors and skilled craftsmen. And they were more open to new scientific, political and social ideas from the West. Children of wealthy Armenians went to Paris, Geneva and America to complete their education.

By contrast, the majority of Turks were illiterate peasant farmers and small shopkeepers. Leaders of the Ottoman Empire had traditionally placed little value on education and not a single institute of higher learning could be found within their old empire. The various autocratic and despotic rulers throughout the empire's history had valued loyalty and blind obedience above all. Their uneducated subjects had never heard of democracy or liberalism and thus had no inclination toward political reform. But this was not the case with the better-educated Armenians who sought political and social reforms that would improve life for themselves and Turkey's other minorities.

When World War I broke out in 1914, leaders of the Young Turk regime sided with the Central Powers (Germany and Austria-Hungary). The outbreak of war provided the perfect opportunity to solve the "Armenian question" once and for all. With war at hand, unusual measures involving the civilian population would not seem too out of the ordinary.

As a prelude to the coming action, Turks disarmed the entire Armenian population under the pretext that the people were naturally sympathetic toward Christian Russia. Every last rifle and pistol was forcibly seized, with severe penalties for anyone who failed to turn in a weapon. Quite a few Armenian men actually purchased weapons from local Turks or Kurds at very high prices so they would have something to turn in.

At this time, about forty thousand Armenian men were serving in the Turkish Army. In the fall and winter of 1914, all of their weapons were confiscated and they were put into slave labor battalions building roads or were used as human pack animals. Under the brutal work conditions they suffered a very high death rate. Those who survived would soon be shot outright. For the time had come to move against the Armenians.

The decision to annihilate the entire population came directly from the ruling triumvirate of ultra-nationalist Young Turks. The actual extermination orders were transmitted in coded telegrams to all provincial governors throughout Turkey. Armed roundups began on the evening of April 24, 1915, as 300 Armenian political leaders, educators, writers, clergy and dignitaries in Constantinople (present day Istanbul) were taken from their homes, briefly jailed and tortured, then hanged or shot.

Next, there were mass arrests of Armenian men throughout the country by Turkish soldiers, police agents and bands of Turkish volunteers. The men were tied together with ropes in small groups then taken to the outskirts of their town and shot dead or bayoneted by death squads. Local Turks and Kurds armed with knives and sticks often joined in on the killing.

Then it was the turn of Armenian women, children, and the elderly. On very short notice, they were ordered to pack a few belongings and be ready to leave home, under the pretext that they were being relocated to a non-military zone for their own safety. They were actually being taken on death marches heading south toward the Syrian Desert.

Some young Armenian children were spared from deportation but were coerced into denouncing Christianity and becoming Muslims, and were given new Turkish names. For Armenian boys the forced conversion meant they each had to endure painful circumcision as required by Islamic custom.

Turkish gendarmes escorted individual caravans consisting of thousands of deported Armenians. These guards allowed roving government units of hardened criminals known as the "Special Organization" to attack the defenseless people, killing anyone they pleased. They also encouraged Kurdish bandits to raid the caravans and steal anything they wanted. In addition, an extraordinary amount of sexual abuse and rape of girls and young women occurred at the hands of the Special Organization and Kurdish bandits.

Most of the attractive young females were kidnapped for a life of involuntary servitude such as sex slaves. The death marches during the Armenian Genocide, involving over a million Armenians, covered hundreds of miles and lasted months. Indirect routes through mountains and wilderness areas were deliberately chosen in order to prolong the ordeal and to keep the caravans away from being seen by Turkish villagers.

Food supplies being carried by the people quickly ran out and they were usually denied further food or water. Anyone stopping to rest or lagging behind the caravan was mercilessly beaten until they rejoined the march. If they couldn't continue they were shot. A common practice was to force all of the people in the caravan to remove every stitch of clothing and have them resume the march in the nude under the scorching sun until they dropped dead by the roadside from exhaustion and dehydration.

An estimated 75% of the Armenians on these marches perished, especially children and the elderly. Those who survived the ordeal were herded into the desert without a drop of water. Others were thrown off cliffs and burned alive. Some were promised newfound land to be shipped away. Enroute to the promise land, they were drowned by sinking their ships.

During the Armenian Genocide, the Turkish countryside became littered with decomposing corpses. At one point, Mehmed Talaat responded to the problem by sending a coded message to all provincial leaders: "I have been advised that in certain areas unburied corpses are still to be seen. I ask you to issue the strictest instructions so that the corpses and their debris in your villages are buried."

But his instructions were generally ignored. Those involved in the mass murder showed little interest in stopping to dig graves. The roadside corpses and emaciated deportees were a shocking sight to foreigners working in Turkey. Eyewitnesses included German government liaisons, American missionaries, and U.S. diplomats stationed in the country.

Warnings of future punishments for those responsible were ignored. Temporary relief for some Armenians came as Russian troops attacked along the Eastern Front and made their way into central Turkey. But the troops withdrew in 1917 upon the Russian Revolution. Armenian survivors withdrew along with them and settled in among fellow Armenians already living in the provinces of the former Russian Empire. There were about 500,000 Armenians gathered in this region.

But peace did not come to them for long. In May 1918, Turkish armies attacked the area to achieve the goal of expanding Turkey eastward into the Caucasus and also to resume the annihilation of the Armenians. As many as 100,000 Armenians may have fallen victim to the advancing Turkish troops. However, the Armenians managed to acquire weapons and they fought back, finally repelling the Turkish invasion at the battle of Sardarabad, thus saving the remaining population from total extermination with no help from the outside world. Following that victory, Armenian leaders declared the establishment of the independent Republic of Armenia.

World War I ended in November 1918 with a defeat of the Central Powers including Turkey. Shortly before the war had ended, the Young Turk triumvirate; Talaat, Enver and Djemal, abruptly resigned their government posts and fled to Germany where they had been offered asylum.

In the months that followed, repeated requests by Turkey's new moderate government and the Allies were made asking Germany to send the Young Turks back home to stand trial. However all such requests were turned down. As a result, Armenian activists took matters into their own hands, located the Young Turks and assassinated them along with two other instigators of the mass murder. Talaat was killed in Berlin by an Armenian in revenge for killing his family on March 21, 1921.

Meanwhile, representatives from the fledgling Republic of Armenia attended the Paris Peace Conference in the hope that the victorious Allies would give them back their historic lands seized by Turkey. The European Allies responded to their request by asking the United States to assume guardianship of the new Republic. However, President Woodrow Wilson's attempt to make Armenia an official U.S. protectorate was rejected by the U.S. Congress in May 1920.

But Wilson did not give up on Armenia. As a result of his efforts, the Treaty of Sevres was signed on August 10, 1920 by the Allied Powers, the Republic of Armenia, and the new moderate leaders of Turkey. The treaty recognized an independent Armenian state in an area comprising much of the former historic homeland.

Turkish nationalism once again reared its ugly head. The moderate Turkish leaders who signed the treaty were ousted in favor of a new nationalist leader, Mustafa Kemal, who simply refused to accept the treaty and even re-occupied the very lands in question, then expelled any surviving Armenians, including thousands of orphans.

No Allied power came to the aid of the Armenian Republic and it collapsed. Only a tiny portion of the easternmost area of historic Armenia survived by becoming part of the Soviet Union.

After the successful obliteration of the people of historic Armenia during the Genocide, the Turks demolished any remnants of Armenian cultural heritage including priceless masterpieces of ancient architecture, old libraries and archives. The Turks even leveled entire cities such as the once thriving Kharpert, Van and the ancient capital at Ani, to remove all traces of the three thousand year old civilization.

Referring to the Armenian Genocide, the young German politician Adolf Hitler duly noted the half-hearted reaction of the world's great powers to the plight of the Armenians. After achieving total power in Germany, Hitler decided to conquer Poland in 1939 and told his generals: "Thus for the time being I have sent to the East only my 'Death's Head Units' with the orders to kill without pity or mercy all men, women, and children of Polish race or language. Only in such a way will we win the vital space that we need. Who still talks nowadays about the Armenians?" Today, some 25 countries recognize the Armenia Genocide as a historic fact, but Turkey still refuses to acknowledge it happened. Even the U.S. was forced by political reasons not to pass a bill recognizing the genocide ever occurred.

Cambodia

One of the greatest genocides to occur in Asia is the massacre of a quarter of the population of Cambodia during the reign of Pol Pot from 1975 to 1979. The resulting deaths number more than 2 million people. It was his attempt to form a Communist peasant farming society that resulted in their death as the people were forced into starvation, overwork and executions.[49]

Pol Pot was born in 1925 (as Saloth Sar) into a farming family in central Cambodia, which was then part of French Indochina. In 1949, at age 20, he traveled to Paris on a scholarship to study radio electronics but became absorbed in Marxism and neglected his studies. He lost his scholarship and returned to Cambodia in 1953 and joined the underground Communist movement. The following year, Cambodia achieved full independence from France and was then ruled by a royal monarchy.

By 1962, Pol Pot had become leader of the Cambodian Communist Party, becoming its secretary-general, and was forced to flee into the jungle to escape the wrath of Prince Norodom Sihanouk, leader of Cambodia. In the jungle, Pol Pot formed an armed resistance movement that became known as the Khmer Rouge (KR, Red Cambodians) and waged a guerrilla war against the government of Prince Sihanouk.

---

[49] http://www.unitedhumanrights.org/Genocide/pol_pot.htm

In 1970, Prince Sihanouk was ousted, not by Pol Pot, but due to a U.S.-backed right-wing military coup led by Lon Nol. An embittered Sihanouk retaliated by joining with Pol Pot, his former enemy, in opposing Cambodia's new U.S.-backed military government. Sihanouk, the father of Cambodia's independence, was even made the figurehead leader of an unlikely coalition. That same year, the U.S. invaded Cambodia to expel the North Vietnamese from their border encampments, but instead drove them deeper into Cambodia where they allied themselves with the KR.

From 1969 until 1973, the U.S. intermittently bombed North Vietnamese sanctuaries in eastern Cambodia, killing up to 150,000 Cambodian peasants with 540,000 tons of bombs dropped on the countryside. (Ibid, 94) As a result, peasants fled the countryside by the hundreds of thousands and settled in Cambodia's capital city, Phnom Penh. All of these events resulted in economic and military destabilization in Cambodia and a surge of popular support for upcoming despotic Pol Pot.

By 1975, the U.S. had withdrawn its troops from Vietnam. Cambodia's government, plagued by corruption and incompetence, also lost its American military support. Lon Nol's government, in trying to engineer a peaceful transition welcomes the Communist rebels for a peace talk. Taking advantage of the opportunity, Pol Pot's Khmer Rouge army, consisting of teenage peasant guerrillas, marched into Phnom Penh had other plans and on April 17 effectively seized control of Cambodia.

Upon arrival, the KR cadres carried out swiftly the order from higher-ups demanding that all citizens in the city to leave the capital immediately on the pretext that American B-52 bombers were about to "raze the city." The KR insisted that only a citywide exodus would guarantee citizens safety. Over the next few days, 2 million people were herded on the road on foot to the countryside. Tires of motor vehicles were slashed to prevent anyone from using them. Even patients from the hospital, under gunpoint, were not spared. The patients, dressed in wispy hospital gowns, wheeling their own IVs, carrying fellow patients in their arms, or being pushed in their hospital beds by their trembling loved ones. The infirm collapsed for lack of water, babies were born at the side of the road, heat-struck children squealed for material succor, and fathers and husbands cowed before the guns in command. The entire city was emptied in a few days. Other major towns throughout Cambodia met similar fate. (Power, 88)

A week earlier, Lon Nol fled the city with a tidy sum of U.S. money in his pocket "retired" to Honolulu, buying a home in an upper-middle-class suburb east of Honolulu. Some of the refugees, including senior Cambodian government officials, took refuge at the French embassy did not fare any better. They were forced out of the embassy after threat from the KR that they will be starved to death unless the refugees were booted out. The officials who trusted the American assurances were taken to the back of a sanitation truck and executed. (Ibid, 89-90)

Once in power, Pol Pot began a radical experiment to create an agrarian utopia inspired in part by Mao Zedong's Cultural Revolution, which he had witnessed first-hand during a visit to Communist China.

Mao's "Great Leap Forward" economic program included forced evacuations from Chinese cities and the purging of "class enemies." Pol Pot would now attempt his own "Super Great Leap Forward" in Cambodia, which he renamed the Democratic Republic of Kampuchea. He began by declaring, "This is Year Zero," and that society was about to be "purified." Capitalism, Western culture, city life, religion, and all foreign influences were to be extinguished in favor of an extreme form of peasant Communism. Whole villages were burned so that the people have nothing to return back for. Children were separated from their parents, monks defrocked, and those who disobeyed were killed. New irrevocable living arrangement was created. (Power, 96)

All foreigners were thus expelled, embassies closed, and any foreign economic or medical assistance was refused. The use of foreign languages was banned. Newspapers and television stations were shut down, radios and bicycles confiscated, and mail and telephone usage curtailed. Money was forbidden. All businesses were shuttered, religious practices were banned, education halted, health care eliminated, and parental authority revoked. Thus Cambodia was sealed off from the outside world for 3-1/2 years while killings were going on.

All the people within the cities were forcibly evacuated. At Phnom Penh, two million inhabitants were evacuated on foot to the countryside at gunpoint. As many as 20,000 died along the way. Millions of Cambodians accustomed to city life were now forced into slave labor in Pol Pot's "killing fields" where they soon began dying from overwork, malnutrition and disease, on a diet of one tin of rice (180 grams) per person every two days.

Workdays in the fields began around 4 a.m. and lasted until 10 p.m., with only two rest periods allowed during the 18-hour work, all under the armed supervision of young Khmer Rouge soldiers eager to kill anyone for the slightest infraction. Starving people were forbidden to eat the fruits and rice they were harvesting. After the rice crop was harvested, Khmer Rouge trucks would arrive and confiscate the entire crop.

Throughout Cambodia, deadly purges were conducted to eliminate remnants of the "old society" - the educated, the wealthy, Buddhist monks, police, doctors, lawyers, teachers, and former government officials. Ex-soldiers were killed along with their wives and children. Anyone suspected of disloyalty to Pol Pot, including eventually many Khmer Rouge leaders, was shot or bludgeoned with an ax. "What is rotten must be removed," a Khmer Rouge slogan proclaimed.

In the villages, unsupervised gatherings of more than two persons were forbidden. Young people were taken from their parents and placed in communals. They were later married in collective ceremonies involving hundreds of often-unwilling couples.

Up to 20,000 persons were tortured, often electrocuted as they hung by their feet, their heads submerged in jars of water. They were forced into giving false confessions at Tuol Sleng Examination Center, one time a girls' high school in Phnom Penh, which had been converted into a jail, became notorious emblem of terror. Some were forced to self-confessed as CIA or Vietnamese agents. Of the 16,000 Cambodians brought there, only five survived. Most of the deaths were killed with farm implements. When the Vietnamese journalists visited the place in 1979, they found these tools beside bloodied victims whose cadavers lay shackled to the bed posts. The prisoners' throats had been slit, and their blood still dripped slowly from the beds onto the mustard-and-white-tiled floors. Elsewhere, suspects were often shot on the spot before any questioning. Intellectuals or those who had completed seventh grade were killed. Even their supporters who are suspected of even momentary disloyal were shot. There seems to be enemies everywhere for the paranoid KR. They have a reversed adage that goes "It is better to arrest ten people by mistake than to let one guilty person go free." (Power, 120, 143)

Ethnic groups were attacked including the three largest minorities; the Vietnamese, Chinese, and Cham Muslims, along with twenty other smaller groups. Fifty percent of the estimated 425,000 Chinese living in Cambodia in 1975 perished. Khmer Rouge also forced Muslims to eat pork and shot those who refused. The single-mindedness with which the regime turned against the ethnics was unexpected. Even the Buddhist monks, where Buddhism is the state religion were not spared. They were branded as reactionary. Those who refused to disrobe were executed. All religious practice, were prohibited, monks; libraries burned, temples destroyed or turned into prison or killing sites. Pagodas were used as silos for grain. (Ibid, 119)

On December 25, 1978, Vietnam launched a full-scale invasion of Cambodia seeking to end Khmer Rouge border attacks. On January 7, 1979, Phnom Penh fell and Pol Pot was deposed and fled to Thailand with his remnant army. The Vietnamese then installed a puppet government consisting of Khmer Rouge defectors.

After 17 years trying to regain Cambodia, he finally lost control of the Khmer Rouge. In April 1998, 73-year-old Pol Pot died of an apparent heart attack following his arrest, before he could be brought to trial by an international tribunal for the genocide he and his henchmen committed from 1975 to 1979.

Kurds

The Kurds are a stateless people scattered throughout Turkey, Iran, Syria, and Iraq. Some 25 million of them are residents in an estimated area of 200,000 mi^2 in these places. At the time of the Armenian genocide in Turkey, the Kurds have been fighting for an autonomous homeland for themselves. In 1922, Turkey refused to ratify the Treaty of Sèvres granting them a homeland, forcing the Kurds numbering about 4 million, to stage frequent rebellions throughout the century in Iraq. Their crime for wanting a homeland for made them traitors in the eyes of Saddam Hussein. (Power, 174)

There is little doubt that the Kurds are a difficult people to manage, even fighting among themselves often since there were two groups under two different leaders. In 1970 Iraq offered them self-rule in a Kurdistan Autonomous Region that covered half of the territory Kurds considered theirs excluding the Kurdish populated oil-rich provinces. It was rejected by the Kurds. However Saddam Hussein imposed the plan unilaterally in 1974. The Kurds not only refused but revolted, thinking they could receive support from Iran, Israel and the U.S. The support never came after Iraq and Iran came to a border agreement. Soon, Hussein ordered 4,000 mi^2 of the Kurdish territory in northern Iraq taken over by Arabs and the Kurds forced out. The Kurds were deported to the south. (Power, 175)

The overthrow of the Shah of Iran and the breakdown of the border agreement lead to the Iraq-Iran war in 1980. Just as in many wars in many countries, Hussein found an opportunity to destroy the Kurds, especially when the U.S. was turning a blind eye to the atrocities against the Kurds when it decided to support Iraq against Iran that the U.S. considered an enemy and a threat to the region.

When the Kurds sided with Iran during the war, Hussein was furious. After one faction of Kurds under Mullah Mustafa Barzani helped Iranian fighters capture an Iraqi border town, Iraqi forces swiftly responded by rounding some 8,000 Kurdish men, including 315 children and they were never seen again.

During the war, Iraq was able to use chemical weapons against Iran without getting condemnation from the U.S. In May 1987 Iraq became the first country ever to attack its own citizens with chemical weapons. The task was given to Ali Hassan Al-Majid (aka Chemical Ali), whom Hussein appointed as secretary-general of the Northern Bureau with order "to solve the Kurdish problem and slaughter the saboteurs." The Kurds would dubbed him "Anfal (spoils) Ali." Ali Hassan was hung sometime in 2008, a few years after the Hussein regime was toppled by the U.S.

The Kurds were deported from their ancestral homes to collective centers so that they can easily be monitored. Some 500 villages were bulldozed, dynamited and/or bombed with poison gas. Those who refused were considered traitors and marked for death. Thousands of Kurdish villages and hamlets were destroyed and close to 100,000 Iraqi Kurds, all were unarmed and many of them women and children were killed. The U.S., by backing Iraq against Iran refrained from protesting and even denying there is conclusion proof that chemical weapons were used. It was even considered as an "internal affair." (Ibid, 172-173)

The most notorious and deadliest single gas attack against the Kurds was in Halabja. It was only one of the more than forty chemical assaults ordered by al-Majid. The chemicals include mustard gas, which burns, mutates DNA, and causes cancers and malformations; the nerve gas sarin and tabun, which can kill, paralyze, or cause immediate and lasting neuropsychiatic damage. Doctors suspected that the dreaded VS gas and the biological agent aflatoxin were also used. Some 5,000 Kurds civilians were killed immediately while thousands were injured. The attack was justified on the grounds that it aimed to destroy the saboteurs aligned with the Iranians. Those who aligned with the Iranians were given gas masks. This is often the case. Instead of pursuing the militants into the mountains, civilians are easier to deal with because they are usually unarmed.

Crimes and Terrorism

Every year, hundreds of thousands of people are killed by criminals and terrorists. This is one way of limiting the population, albeit in a violent way. Too many people have a tendency to produce some degenerates who willingly took the lives of many innocent victims. It takes only a few to take the lives of millions. The likes of dictators such as Hitler, Stalin, Mao, Idi Amin, Tamerlane, Ante Pavelic, Popes Innocent III, IV, VIII and Urban II can with one stroke of the pen caused the death of millions or start a chain of events they cannot stop. Pope Innocent III ordered the destruction of the Cathars for refusing to vow down to Catholicism while Pope Urban II unleashed the Crusaders to take back Jerusalem that started off several other crusades and killed numberless Jews, Muslims, and other Christians. Pope Innocent IV sanctioned the use of torture to get confession that lead to more innocent deaths. Pope Innocent VIII started the witch hunt with one stroke of his pen when he issued a bull condemning witchcraft and set of a reign of terror. Even good intentions have a way of going awry.

Many religious fanatics or fundamentalists have been killing others in the name of God or some other sacred entity. There is little room for compromise when it comes converting people to what they think is the "true" religion or faith. For centuries, Catholics have been harassing and killing Jews as a race of deicide (killers of Christ) and for refusing the Christian faith or be converted into Catholicism. The same treatment has been accorded by the Muslim to the Jews since Muhammad founded Islam in the Middle East. The Quran offers texts to justify a range of attitudes toward Jews. In some passages, Muhammad sharply criticizes the Jews because they refused his call to Islam. They are accused of subverting and falsifying their own scripture and rejecting their own prophets, as well as Jesus and, of course, Muhammad himself. Violent clashes that led to the destruction of the Jewish community of Media at the hands of Muhammad and his followers. (Benjamin, 66-67)

There have been several religious wars in Europe where Catholics tried to impose its form of Catholic worship on the Protestants culminating with the Thirty Years' War. The war was fought in Germany from 1618 to 1648. Almost two-thirds of the population of Germany was wiped out without a decisive victory except to agree that the faith of each inhabitant should follow the faith of the leaders.

The world is full of people with anti-social tendencies that led them to kill others. Crimes are often committed by people who know each other while terrorists have no qualms about who gets killed. They are often motivated by greed, envy, jealousy, crime of passion, ideology, etc. It is not a normal way of depopulating people but society cannot help it because there are just too many people around.

Crimes around the world have been on the increase with the increasing population. The United States Crime Index Rates per 100,000 inhabitants went from 1,887.2 in 1960 to 5,897.8 in 1991. This is a rise of more than 300% the 1960 crime rate. In 1996 the risk of being a victim of a crime in the United States was 5.079%, and of a violent crime 0.634%. It used to be 1.89% in 1960 for being a victim of a crime and 0.161% of becoming a victim of a violent crime. Crime in the United States accounts for more death, injuries and loss of property then all natural disasters combined. Approximately thirteen million people (approximately 5% of the U.S. population) are victims of crime every year. Approximately one and a half million are victims of violent crime. In 2005, the number of homicides in the U.S. was 16,740 and 17,034 in 2006. There was a slowdown of violence compared to the 1990s where in 1991, the homicide cases peaked at 24,700 cases.[50] The crime of homicides in the Philippines is even worse and it will be discuss under the topic on *Poverty and Crime.*

The world is inhabited with many ethnic groups, minorities, and of different ideology who wanted a homeland for themselves or a change of government. In many instances, these terrorist groups are allegedly involved in drug trafficking to raise funds for their activities. The NPA, the MNLF, MILF and the Abu Sayyaf Group have been tagged as drug traffickers for cultivating marijuana in the hinterland and have branched out into crystal methamphetamine or better known as shabu. (David Robbins, 319) Since they cannot get it through peaceful means, some have resorted to violence to overthrow the government. Hardly a day passed by without reading news of acts of terrorism somewhere in the world that killed scores of individuals, many of them innocent civilians. Grenade throwing has become common occurrences in parts of Mindanao.

The Philippines is now in the midst of a civil war in some provinces in Mindanao. The MILF and the government forces are battling each other after a misguided peace negotiation went awry. The supposedly negotiated peace could not be implemented because an amendment to the constitution is needed to consummate the agreement. The Muslim, especially the MILF felt betrayed and is now using force and fighting the government for control of territories promised them by the accord. Thousands of people are being displaced from their homes every time

---

[50] http://www.disastercenter.com/crime/

a gun battle erupts. The latest report has it that half a million people are displaced and the government does not have facilities to take care of them. Their homes are pillaged and sometimes burned by the rebels. Sanitation such as clean water and medicine are often in short supply. Most of the killings involved civilians who were defenseless. Like most wars, the refugees are always at the mercy of the humanitarian efforts. Many of these efforts always come short.

So far, our refugee problem is manageable compared to the refugee problems happening in other parts of the world. In Vietnam, at one time, the problem has to do with the unwanted ethnic group cast out to the sea to find a new homeland elsewhere. Thousands of these boat people who were lucky to be temporarily absorbed were able to be relocated to other countries. Many died in the high seas when their boat capsized.

The Philippines also has her fair share of bombings, usually by people who used timed bombs to explode after they are long gone. One of the most serious bombings was the December 30, 2000 bombings within several hours in five places including the Light Railway Transit station in Blumentritt, Manila that killed 12 people and injured more than 100 others. In all, more than 20 people were killed. Based on the globalsecurity.org website, the bombings were carried out by the Special Operations Group of the Philippines-based Moro Islamic Liberation Front on behalf of Indonesia-based Jemaah Islamiyah. (January 23, 2009) Sporadic bombings have been going on in Mindanao. Others simply used grenades by throwing them indiscriminately into crowds of people. Three of the suspects were later convicted of the main attack on an LRT station only by the Manila Regional Trial Court and sentenced to life imprisonment. Seven other suspects remain at large.

In parts of Africa, the civil war and fighting for supremacy has been responsible for millions of refugees crossing borders to find refuge. They are often unwanted by their neighboring countries and have to be taken care of by humanitarian efforts of the West. Many died of starvation and diseases before help arrived. Food and clean water is constantly in short supply. Food aids are sometimes diverted or forcibly taken to the fighting soldiers.

One of the latest forms of terrorism is the proliferation of bombing to kill not only the enemies but also civilians to force the government to act for their interest. Traditional terrorism has its aim at ideological or separatist movements for the purpose of effecting political or social aims such as establishment of a separate state or starting a new social order or intimidating the government to make changes for the benefit of a minority group. Terror is a weapon of intimidation and fear to force government to change its policies. Terrorists tried to bring fear to the ordinary civilians to force the government to change. This is what is happening to most of the terrorism going today.

Terrorism is not confined to the Middle East, but have been going on in the India/Pakistan conflict, religious conflict between Catholics and Protestants in the past, the two major sects of Islam, Israel and the Palestinians, separatists in Sri Lanka, some of the Russian states such as Chechnya wanting a statehood for themselves.

In some cases where car bombs can be ineffective, humans as suicide bombers can be more effective as they can move around and target as much people as possible. The suicide bombers in Israel often attack buses where people are enclosed together giving greater impact to the bombs in an enclosed place. Israel has been victims of this kind of terrorism. It was alleged that Iraq under Saddam Hussein financed some of these suicide bombers. The bombers pack themselves with explosives, and visit areas crowded with people such as mall, bus station, or marketplace and explode themselves to kill as many civilians as possible. Between 2000 and 2004, about 1,000 Israelis have been killed this way. This is also the form of terrorism in India with their highly congested train.

Most of these suicide bombers are Muslims who willingly sacrificed their lives to kill their enemies. They are supposed to be greatly rewarded in the next life with virgins in paradise. These enemies are usually Israelites and Americans who some Muslims considered as their number one enemies. It could also be religious rivalries especially between the two sects of Islam in Iraq. Suicide killings have been going since the toppling of Saddam Hussein. One of the latest happened on January 4, 2009 in the latest suicide bombing in Iraq where 40 people were killed. The bombing occurred in Baghdad at the doorstep of one of Iraq's hottest Shiite shrines. The targets were allegedly Iranian pilgrims visiting the shrine of Imams Musa al-Kadhim and Mohammed al-Jawd in Baghdad.

The attack was perpetuated by a man in a long, black winter coat when he stepped into a crowd of Iranian pilgrims about to enter the golden-domed shrine. He was stuffed with explosives on his body. An earlier attack on December 22, 2009 on the same site employed a car bomb attack that killed 24 people. (*PS*, January 6, 2009)

On the morning of March 20, 1975, five skilled scientists and disciples of Shoko Asahara, a messianic pretender and leader of a quasi-Buddhist apocalyptic cult called Aum Shinrikyo, boarded separate Tokyo subway trains heading to the center of the city. They were carrying plastic containers with 30% solution of sarin, a nerve gas that kills by blocking the chemical reactions that enable muscle tissues to relax after flexing. It can kill within minutes. If disseminated effectively by aerosol spray, a few quarts would kill thousands of unprotected people. In this case, each carried a sharpened umbrella tips to pierce the plastic containers. As the trains converged on Kasumigaseki station underneath the heart of the Japanese government, they were released. Twelve people were killed and 5,500 were injured, many seriously. (Benjamin, 433) the group has actually at least nine attacks using biological weapons. These attacks failed because of insufficient the bacteria in not sufficiently virulence and they attackers were persistently amateurish. (Mangold, 336)

Suicide is considered a crime in the laws of many countries. Every year, hundreds of thousands of people commit this ultimate crime on themselves mostly out of desperation due to poverty or failure in business or even schooling. In China alone, 250,000 to 300,000 suicides occurred every year, accounting for about a quarter of the world's total, according to one medical report. It is the only country where more women than men take their own lives, with women representing 58% of the total. This is due to the stress imposed on women. Additionally, most suicides happened in the rural areas. (*The Foreign Post*, December 11-17, 2008)

According to the United Nations 1996 *Demographic Yearbook*, Lithuania has the highest suicide rate at 45.6 per 100,000 population, followed by Russia at 41.2, Latvia, 40.7, Estonia, 401, Hungary, 32.9. The U.S. has 11.9 while the Philippines 1.3, China, 17.6, Hong Kong has 11.8, Japan 16.7, and Switzerland, 21.4.[51]

Japanese suicides account for about 30,000 annually. These are not isolated events. There are many cults that believe in the end of the world or whatever that is bothering them to commit mass suicides such as the People's Temple of Jim Jones were more than 900 people were killed in a case of mass poisoning. There is also the Heaven's Gate were 38 members and followers of the founder, Marshall H. Applewhite believed they were angels in container bodies and committed suicide in the belief that their souls would be beamed to a spacecraft passing near the earth in the wake of the comet Hale–Bopp. The Branch Davidians of David Koresh killed more than 100 men, women and children after the government lay siege on their farms for 51 days in Waco, Texas. Earlier in 1994, about fifty members of this sect committed mass suicide.

---

[51] www.haciendapub.com/stolinsky.html

The worst attack happened on September, 2001 with the collapse of the Twin Tower buildings at the World Trade Center in New York City. More than two thousand casualties were reported. It started with the hijacking of four commercial airplanes fully loaded with jet fuel and used like a missile to target four buildings in the U.S. Two of them succeeded in destroying the twin towers in Manhattan, New York. The attack was carried out by the notorious terrorist group called al-Qaeda, whose leader is the billionaire Saudi heir, Osama bin Laden.

The leader of the hijackers was an Egyptian, Muhammad Atta with fifteen Saudi Arabians, two Emirates, and one Lebanese. They were separated into four groups with specific targets. One plane, a Boeing 757 with sixty-five people abroad, owned by American Airlines, hit the west side of Pentagon killing 189 people. A fourth plane, crashed in Pennsylvania was not able to reach its target as passengers struggle with the hijackers after learning about the attacks at the World Trade Center through their cell-phone conversations, helped by the forty-minute delay in the takeoff. (Benjamin, 34-35)

Terrorism is nothing new. It has been going on for centuries. Unfortunately, most of the victims of terrorisms are civilians. Other notable acts of terrorism are enumerated below:

- February 22, 1970. A Swissair plane flying to Tel Aviv was blown out of the sky with the loss of forty-seven passengers and crew including fifteen Israelis. The attack was planned by George Habash, the Marxist leader of the Popular Front for the Liberation of Palestine (PLFP).

- May 30, 1972. Three Japanese belong to the Japanese Red Army disembarked from an Air France flight at the Lod Airport in Tel Aviv and started firing indiscriminately after gathering their luggage where weapons were hidden. Twenty-four people were killed, most of them Puerto Rican pilgrims and seventy-eight were wounded. In the mayhem, Yasuiki Yashuda was accidentally shot by his comrade while Takeshi detonated a grenade next to his head. Kozo Okamoto, after firing all his bullets into the crowd ran outside to the airport tarmac trying to blow up a parked jet with a grenade was tackled around the neck by an El Al official and arrested. He was later convicted and sentenced to life imprisonment.

- September 5, 1972. A band of Palestinian terrorists calling themselves Black September, an extremist faction within the Palestinian Liberation Organization (PLO) took eleven Israeli athletes and coaches as hostage during the Summer Olympic in Munich. All eleven were killed including five of the terrorists. The Black September name was taken from the massacre of four thousand Palestinian *fedayeen* in Jordan who tried to take over the country from King Hussein of Jordan.
- July 1976. A plane carrying more than 100 Jews was hijacked and flown to Entebbe, Uganda, then under the reign of Idi Amin. They were later rescued by Israelite commando in a daring flight from Israel. A Hercules plane was allowed to refuel by the Kenyan government on the return trip without which the plan would not have been possible. The Israeli commandos suffered one fatality, Jonathan Netanyahu, brother of Benjamin Netanyahu.
- December 21, 1988, Pan Am Flight 103 exploded in mid-air over the Scottish town of Lockerbie killing 243 passengers, 16 crew members, and 11 people on land. It was caused by a bomb planted on the plane allegedly by two Libyan terrorists, Abdel Baset Megrahi and Al Amin Khalifa Fhimah. Megrahi, a Libyan intelligence officer was convicted and sentenced to life imprisonment. Fhimah was acquitted. The Libyan government was fined $2.3 billion in compensation. Megrahi is now appealing his case on the ground of miscarriage of justice.[52]
- February 1992. A bombing attack, carried out by the Hezbollah of Lebanon against the Israelite embassy in Buenos Aires, Brazil, resulted in the killing of twenty-nine person.
- April 19, 1995. Timothy McVeigh, with his favorite guide novel, *The Turner Diaries*, detailing a guerilla war waged in the U.S. by white supremacists decided to put it in actual action. He conspired with Terry Nichols to bomb the Alfred P. Murrah Federal building in Oklahoma City. They bought 108 pieces of 50-pound bags of explosive-grade ammonium nitrate fertilizer, 3 drums of

---

[52] http://en.wikipedia.org/wiki/Pam_Am_flight_103

55-gallon liquid nitromethane, Tovex, ANFO, and diesel oil. With the proper mixture, they loaded them into the rented Ryder truck and McVeigh parked it at the front of the north side of the building. The blast was so powerful it destroyed one-thirds of the building, damage to 324 buildings in a sixteen block radius, burned 86 cars, and shattered glass in 258 building. The final death toll was 168 lives including 19 children and 800 injuries. McVeigh was sentenced to death by lethal injection on June 11, 2001 while Terry Nichols was given life imprisonment. A third conspirator, Michael Fortier who was not active in the plot received 12 years for failing to report the plot. He was convicted on May 27, 1998, served and released on January 20, 2006 for good behavior. He is currently under the Witness Protection Program because he once acted as state witness.

- June 25, 1996. The bomb attack employing a fuel truck packed with explosives by militants on the U.S. military complex at Khobar Tower in Dharan, Saudi Arabia killed nineteen servicemen. The servicemen were from the 4404th Fighter Wing enforcing the no-fly zone in southern Iraq. It was the largest truck bomb the FBI had ever seen.

- July 30, 1997. Two suicide bombers detonated explosives in the busy Mahane Yehuda market in Jerusalem killing sixteen shoppers and wounding 178 others. The massacre was allegedly carried out by the militant Palestinian organization Hamas that has been responsible for the ongoing missiles attacks into Israel in 1996 leading to the invasion of Lebanon and the 2009 invasion of the Gaza by the Israelite forces. Two-thirds of the victims of these invasions are children.

- March 11, 2004. A series of 10 explosions in four commuter train system of Madrid, Spain killed 191 people and injured more than 1,700 others.

- July 11, 2006. A series of seven bombs exploded along the Suburban Railing in Mumbai (Bombay) that took the lives of 209 people and injured 700 others. The bombs were made up of 2.5 kg mixture of RDX and ammonium nitrate and placed inside a pressure cooker to maximize the explosion. It was allegedly carried out by Lashkar-e-Toiba and the militant Students Islamic Movement of India.

Hardly a week passed by without news of incidents of terrorism occurring somewhere in the world. Those who are interested to read more may find a list of the terrorist incidents in the website: en.wikipedia.org/wiki/List_of_terrorist_incidents and other websites.

Chapter 3

SIGNS OF OVERPOPULATION

Despite the many efforts being done by governments and non-governmental organizations (NGOs) to mitigate the problems of overpopulation, few overpopulated developing countries have succeeded in solving them. The fertility rates have been dropping in many developing countries, but it is not enough for many countries in Asia such as the Philippines because we have long reached our carrying capacity. We need not only to slow down and stabilize our population but eventually we have to reduce our population to a manageable level and give everyone in this country a worthy life where everyone can enjoy the amenities the earth has to offer.

Some countries such as Japan may be highly industrialized and enjoy a high living standard, but life in their competitive and overcrowded atmosphere is not what they are seeking. It is why less Japanese are getting married and bring up new families. Many have opted to remain single leading to the graying of the population and the falling birth rate. The population of Japan and many countries in Europe are expected to decline in the coming decades. Their fertility rates are way below the replacement rate of 2.1 children per family. They have experienced the folly of having a huge population with their accompanying problems and doing something about it. God created us and the earth for us to enjoy the fruit of our labor. Unless we do so, we will experience the folly of our runaway population and continuing to wallop in poverty and make believe that the future will turn for the better or work out by itself. The many crises we faced are expected to continue well beyond the 21st century unless we take the initiative to reduce our population to a more manageable level. The country cannot hope for some miracles to happen in the near future to solve the predicament we are facing today. Otherwise, only disasters await the people like the visit of the four horsemen of the apocalypse.

Poverty and the Food Crisis

Poverty can be defined as a serious need for money to buy the basic necessities of life such as food, shelter, clothing, education, and healthcare. Others would include income security, economic stability with continuing means to meet basic needs and some amenities to go along with it. Under this definition, the basic need of $2 per day per individual does not come close to alleviating the poverty threshold of many in the Philippines. There is just not enough good and services created to give everyone more money than the country can afford. Otherwise, inflation will just negate the oversupply of the paper currency. There are either too many people for the limited resources or too many greedy people refusing to share their wealth. In either case, there are just too many mouths to feed.

Overpopulation often breeds more poor members of society because most of the newborn babies came from their ranks. This is the findings of the Harvard School of Public Health when they made a study of a typical India village of farmers in Manupur. In the thirty years of keeping track of the families, they found that the poor head of families tend to have bigger families to take care of them in old and as helping hand for them in their farming. This is also true in the Philippines. On the other hand, the rich farmers have farming machineries and farmers to work for them typically have smaller families. In short, the study concluded that poverty causes population growth causes poverty.[53]

Even with their dire economic situation, the poor continue to have more children because they do not have the amenities of life to enjoy and keep themselves occupied except to copulate. There is also the lack of opportunities and activities to uplift their standard of living. This is mostly due to the lack of education that would have allowed the bread-earners decent and high-paying jobs. They are often bogged down on minimum wage jobs that have little chance of improving their livelihood. The minimum wage law is only enough to allow them a decent day to day subsistence with little room for improvements. This is reflected in the unofficial new poverty threshold set at P10,000 per month for those living in the National Capital Region set by the National Statistics Coordination Board. This translates to about P400/day for 25 days work per month. The present daily minimum wage is pegged at P382 which is close enough. This amount only covers the basic needs for a family of five and includes only food, clothing, shelter and transportation. It does not include spending money for recreation and emergencies. The last official threshold limit sets in 2006 was P8,569. The next official figures would be determined in 2009 since it is supposed to be done every three years.

---

[53] http://www.sustainer.org/dhm_archive/index.php?display_article= vn126manupured

With the new threshold limit, after so many inflationary situations and high prices of food and energy, it is feared that more families would fall below the poverty line, especially when rice, one of the criteria in determining the threshold limit has risen more than 50%. Already, a survey made in March 2008, shows that 50% of the population rated themselves as poor, a 4% increase from the 46% of December 2007.

Those who refused to acknowledge that overpopulation is behind the poverty problem often blamed bad governance, corruption, poor economic policies, and injustice to the lower income group. This may be partly true, but the fact that too many people competing for the limited resources are not going to reduce the number of people stricken with poverty. If all the gross national products generated every year were divided among the people, the per capita income would make all the people in this country poor. The only way to increase the per capita income is to reduce the number of people sharing the limited income. This is simple logic. A family of two children would have twice the food available for the children compared to a family of four children. The same is true with per capita income.

A World Bank research into the world's civil wars since 1960 found that poverty and economic stagnation were two of the main risk factors. When the income of the people doubles, the risk of civil war halves. Likewise, when the economic growth increases by one point, so does the conflict falls by one point. (Guest, 56)

Rice, together with wheat and corn are the three staples needed to alleviate hunger in the world. It is also the mainstay of food for Asians and the Filipino people. Yet, as a basically agrarian country, we have yet to achieve self-sufficiency in rice production. Between 1950 and 1984, as the world was undergoing Green Revolution to produce more food for the tables, we were able to increase rice production enough for two years during the 1970s. But it took a lot of energy that is provided by fossils fuels in the form fertilizers, pesticides and energy for irrigation.

Today, we have become the number one rice importer in the world, even begging the United Nations to force our Asean neighbors to export to us because of the food and oil crisis. What has led to this crisis? With one-third (36% according to the *New York Times 2008 Almanac*) working in the agriculture sector, we could not even produce enough to feed the population. One obvious reason is that there are just too many mouths to feed and there are not enough capital and land devoted to food production. Some arable lands are devoted to raising tobacco and cash crops to earn foreign exchange. Another reason is that the need of the residential, commercial and industrial sectors for prime land. This has cause widespread land conversion that forced President Arroyo to take drastic steps to put an end to it for a while.

The Philippines had experienced an unprecedented rice crisis during the first half of 2008, forcing the prices of international rice to go up as high as $1,400 per ton from the current price of about $400. It goes to show the vulnerability of the country to potential food crisis. Even though there is no large scale hunger going on, the country has long been suffering from a silent famine. Most of the people in the country are either malnourished or faced hunger most of the time. This is aggravated by the financial crisis and the rising food prices. The years 2007 and 2008 saw dramatic world food price rises, bringing a state of global crisis and causing political and economical instability and social unrest in both poor and developed nations. The latest survey by Pulse Asia had 66% of the Filipino families cutting back on food consumption because of the high prices brought about by oil price hikes and inflation. (*PS*, August 7, 2008) Initial causes of the late 2006 price spikes included unseasonable droughts in grain producing nations and rising oil prices. Oil prices further heightened the costs of fertilizers, food transport, pesticides, and industrial agriculture.

Other causes include the increasing use of biofuels in developed countries and an increasing demand for a more varied diet (especially meat) due to the expanding middle-class populations of Asia. These factors, coupled with falling world food stockpiles have all contributed to the dramatic world-wide rise in food prices. Long-term causes remain a topic of debate. These may include structural changes in trade and agricultural production, agricultural price supports and subsidies in developed nations, diversions of food commodities to high input foods and fuel, commodity market speculation, and climate change.

The Philippines, a densely populated and land-poor country cannot afford to give land and shelter to everyone without infringing on other important land uses such as food production, parks and wilderness, and wildlife sanctuaries. Because of the food crisis, President Arroyo ordered a stop to the conversion of agricultural land into housing projects, industrial parks, shopping malls, and other projects for the benefit of the middle and upper classmen. Most of the rural areas were once forested land and forested land are being converted to other uses. Land conversion has been going on for decades because of the uncontrolled population growth. As a result, we have a difficult time being rice independence despite the great subsidies being allocated to the farmers or the farmers being cheated out of their share of the subsidies from unscrupulous government officials in connivance with businessmen such as the fertilizer scam where money are skimmed off and fertilizer sold at inflated prices.

The tug-of-war between land conversion and the need for more arable land to sustain the growing population can only be resolved by controlling the population growth. This is especially acute for a highly densely populated country like ours. Under the Comprehensive Agrarian Reform Law of 1988 (RA 6657), the recipient landowner is entitled to a maximum of 5 hectares and each of his children is entitled to a limit of three hectares provided he is at least 15 years old and is actually tilling or directly managing the farm. The rest is then divided among his tenant holders and farmers, which could just a few hectares each. Problems arise when they are old with other children. His progenies are expected to inherit the same plot of land which will have to be subdivided further into smaller units. This will not be able sustain more mouths and to survive, other children will have to migrate to the urban areas for employment. This is the main cause of urbanization. Another problem is that there is not enough available land for the agrarian reform program to give every farmer a sustainable share.

There is just not enough land for food production to meet our goal of sufficiency in food production. If we aim to live like the ecological standard of the American, each person will need 4.5 hectares.[54] For 90 million Filipinos, we need 405 million hectares which is way above the 300,000 km^2 or 30 million hectares we have. There is no hope for everyone to have an average lifestyle diet of the Americans. For this criterion alone, we have long exceeded our carrying capacity. The other criteria that we have long exceeded its carrying capacity include housing, education, employment, energy supplies, etc. The problem is compounded by the lack of internally generated capital to tackle each problem. Most of these problems could be resolved easily if we have a smaller population to deal with in the first place.

One good solution to the food crisis is to be a vegetarian. It is much healthier and takes less land to grow vegetable than it does to raise cattle or other animals. It is even less costly than raising animals. There is also less land degradation.

The rice crisis is not a new phenomenon. This has been going on sporadically in the past. The following article was written in 2005 and

---

[54] http://dieoff.org/page5.htm

reprinted with the permission of the management of the *Balatbat* magazine.

Palit-Bigas' Prostitution

Or how rural women are trading sex for rice due to hunger

The Philippines observed World Food Day this year amid an atmosphere of increasing hunger. Amid worsening hunger, a number of women in the rural areas – where food crops are grown – have been turning to what is called *palit-bigas* prostitution.

BY ALEXANDER MARTIN REMOLLINO
Bulatlat

More and more Filipino rural women are driven to prostitution due to hunger. This stark reality has come about as the Philippines joined other nations on Oct. 16 to observe the 25th World Food Day and as thousands of farmers from provinces south and north of Manila marched several kilometers last week to Metro Manila for a big protest rally near the gates of the presidential palace. A national federation of peasant women, Amihan, estimates the number of prostituted women in the country at 800,000. This is 200,000 more than the 600,000 estimate given by Gabriela, the national women's alliance, last year. Both groups state that many prostituted women come from the provinces.

The Gabriela Women's Party (GWP), represented in Congress by Liza Largoza-Maza, had warned even last year of the rise of *palit-bigas* prostitution. The phenomenon of *palit-bigas* (or selling bodies for rice) was first documented by Gabriela following the 1992 eruption of Mt. Pinatubo in Central Luzon, said Maza. She also said that in some cases these sexual "favors" were done in exchange for a cup of coffee. How have Filipino women been coping so far with increasing hunger? Are the cases of women like Julie Ann and Gina indicators?

Julie Ann (not her real name), 18, works as a "guest relations officer" (euphemism for bargirl) in Nasugbu, Batangas, some three hours south of Manila. She hails from a family of corn farmers in Quezon province. Her family, Julie Ann told *Bulatlat*, earns some P200 ($3.61) for every sack of corn sold. While she could not recall how much they would earn after every corn harvest season, she did say that it was never enough to feed all of them, and she recalls several instances when they would have only one meal for a whole day. From her job as a bargirl, Julie Ann says, she could earn as much as P1,500 ($27.05) just by letting customers take her out for a night. "That's certainly more than half of what our family earns by selling sacks of corn," she said.

Residents of nearby Calatagan town, also in Batangas, interviewed by *Bulatlat* told of women in a number of villages there resorting to *palit-bigas* prostitution. In some cases, they said, the kilogram of rice which they get for trading sex would come with a few cans of sardines.

Julie Ann's case is similar to that of Gina, 26, who comes from a family of rice farmers in Montalban, Rizal (about an hour north of Manila). She appeared in a recent press conference sponsored by Amihan.

Gina recently went back to the job she left seven years ago, that of a dancer at a nightclub in Caloocan City, so she could buy medicines for a daughter sick of urinary tract infection. From that job she earned some P700 ($12.62), a far cry from the five kilograms of rice for each week that she earns in Montalban's upland rice farms, and the additional two kilograms she gets from hiring herself out as a laundrywoman. She also chops wood for charcoal and gets some P15 ($0.27) for every 100 pieces of chopped wood. Most of the time her family has only one meal a day, she said.

An October 2004 study by Jose Ramon Albert and Paula Monina Collado of the government Statistical Research and Training Center (SRTC) noted that seven out of every 10 poor Filipinos live in the countryside. Data from the socio-economic think tank IBON Foundation for the same year place the number of poor Filipinos at 88% of the then 81-million population, which is reported to have grown to 84 million.

Based on 2004 data from Amihan, 68% of people in rural areas are poor. The high and increasing incidence of poverty in the countryside is blamed by peasant groups on landlessness and globalization. Amihan reveals that eight out of ten farmers in the Philippines are landless. More than 13 million hectares of agricultural land in the Philippines, Amihan further discloses, is controlled by big landlords and comprador businessmen, while multinational corporations also control vast tracts of land.

It is disturbing that women in the rural areas, where food crops are planted and grown, are increasingly turning to prostitution to cope with hunger. Based on the October 2004 SRTC study, seven out of ten poor Filipinos come from the rural areas. The same study shows that half of all rural dwellers are poor.

"The overwhelming numerical importance of the rural poor means that poverty programs must be concentrated in improving...(people's) living standards in rural areas and that we ought to promote policies on rural development, which include support for rural entrepreneurial activities and rural competitiveness, as well as enabling the improvement of farmers' access to markets through infrastructure development and the creation of farmers' markets in the cities (to ensure that less middle men reap the fruits of farmers' labors)," Albert and Collado said in their study.

The Philippines observed World Food Day this year (2005) amid an atmosphere of increasing hunger. Last month, the results of the Social Weather Stations' Social Survey for the third quarter of 2005 showed 15.5% of household heads reporting that their families experienced hunger, without having anything to eat at least once during the said period. This is equivalent to some 2.6 million families or nearly 16 million individuals experiencing hunger in this year's third quarter. The hunger percentage for this year's third quarter is higher than that registered for the same period last year, which stood at 15.1%. The SWS reports that this is also the highest national hunger percentage since March 2001.

The results of the SWS surveys on hunger from 1998 to the third quarter of 2005 also show that hunger incidences for the third quarter of every year since then have always been the lowest compared to other parts of the year – until 2004, when it recorded a 15.1% hunger incidence for the year's third quarter, as compared to 7.4% for the first quarter, 13% for the second quarter, and 11.5% for the last quarter.

It was in the third quarter of 2004 that President Gloria Macapagal-Arroyo admitted that the country was mired in a fiscal crisis. For this year, the SWS reported a hunger incidence of 13% for the first quarter and 12% for the second quarter.

© 2005 Bulatlat ■ Alipato Publications

The latest SWS report on hunger for the 4th quarter of 2008 shows that 18.5% of Filipino families experienced at least once or a few times (moderate hunger) in the previous three months while 5.2% suffered involuntarily often or always (severe hunger) during the same period. (*PDI*, December 27, 2008) Another survey by the same outfit concerning poverty shows about 9.4 million or 52% of Filipino families considered themselves poor while 24% rate themselves on the "borderline" and another 24% considered themselves not poor. The 52% who considered themselves poor are the same as the surveyed made in September 2008. For the whole year of 2008, the average poverty level stood at 53%. (PS, January 13, 2009)

One major indicator of overpopulation is the inability to feed the local population despite being an agrarian nation. The article written by Ronalyn V. Olea from the July 27-August 2, 2008 issue of the newsmagazine *Bulatbat* is reprinted here.

Scientists Call for Thoroughgoing Reforms to Resolve Rice Crisis

To address the rice crisis, a group of Filipino scientists joined farmers in calling for a genuine agrarian reform program, mechanization and development of agriculture and support for farmers, among others.

Scientists belonging to AGHAM or Samahan ng Nagtataguyod ng Agham at Teknolohiya para sa Sambayanan (Association for the Promotion of Science and Technology for the People) said that the measures being implemented by the Arroyo government would not resolve the rice crisis. They proposed several alternatives, including subsidy for farmers, mechanization of agriculture and a genuine agrarian reform program.

In a forum, July 24, Reynan Calderon, an agricultural economist teaching at the Bataan Peninsula State University (BPSU) said that the continuing rice deficiency is the pre-condition for the rice crisis. He said that from 1991-2006, there was a 42% increase in the consumption of rice. Calderon said that in the 70s and 80s, imported rice accounted for 5% of the total consumption. He said that this increased to 14% by 2007.

Calderon explained that the crisis is actually an "effect of a more deepening poverty problem." He said that most of the poor have nothing else or very little to eat except rice. *"Walang maiulam, damihan ang kanin."* (No viand to eat, eat more rice.) He cited Bataan as an example. Bataan has a 4% net surplus of rice. The Central Luzon region is a net exporter of rice, providing 18% of the country's total supply. Calderon disclosed that even so, the poor in Bataan would line up to buy rice from the NFA and still many go hungry. Calderon said, "Bataan and Central Luzon are a microcosm of Philippine society. Not everyone can afford to buy rice... As long as there is a deepening poverty problem, even if there is enough food supply, the poor cannot avail of rice."

In the same forum, Fines Cosico, NFA grains operations officer and AGHAM project officer, agreed that there was no rural development and the poverty level is high in farming communities. Citing data from the Kilusang Magbubukid ng Pilipinas (KMP-Philippine Peasant Movement), she said that farm workers in Negros receive only P20-P90 ($0.45 to $2.03 at an exchange rate of $1=P44.23) per day; in Cagayan Valley, P69 ($1.56) per day; and, in Samar, P50 ($1.13). Cosico attributed this to the problem of landlessness, with 1/3 of landlords owning 80% of agricultural land. She said 51% of farmlands are under tenancy. She said that multinational corporations also control the land, with 220,000 hectares in Mindanao occupied by Dole and Del Monte.

Cosico said that local production is backward and stunted. Philippine agriculture has a low mechanization level with only 2% of farms mechanized. She said that there are only 102 tractors, six harvesters/threshers per 1,000 hectares of agricultural land.

Irrigation is very low, too. BPSU's Calderon cited that while 19% of the total irrigated area in the Philippines is in Central Luzon, still, 85% of agricultural lands in the region are not irrigated.

Cosico further said that 56.53% of farms are operated through manual labor; and 78% of the 4.61 million hectares of agricultural land in 1991 are divided into farmlands constituting less than 3 hectares each.

Cosico said that there was a 3% decrease in the number of farm areas in the past decade due to land use conversion. In Southern Tagalog, for example, more than 1.30 million hectares of agricultural land are under conversion while 172,967.30 hectares have already been converted to real estate. Cosico said that while the government uses modernization as byword in its policies on agriculture, the government is not actually modernizing agriculture.

She cited the Agricultural and Fisheries Modernization Act (AFMA) and the Medium Term Development Plan, supposedly the government's program for modernization. Under these programs, the catchwords are "food security, agricultural mechanization, rural development and global competitiveness."

Under the AFMA, Cosico explained, food security is to be achieved through importation instead of increasing local rice production. With regards agricultural mechanization, she said that she has not seen anything concrete yet that has improved technical efficiency in farms.

She criticized the inclusion of global competitiveness in the definition of modernization under AFMA. "It will only strengthen the import-dependent and export-oriented character of the Philippine economy." She asserted that the Philippine government should prioritize food production for local consumption.

Cosico blamed the globalization policies for the devastation of agriculture. She cited the structural adjustment programs (SAPs) in 1981 to 1985, which removed price control on rice and farm inputs; the General Agreement on Tariff and Trade (GATT) in 1995 and the Agreement on Agriculture under the World Trade Organization, which removed quantitative restrictions on agricultural imports and the charging of tariffs on rice.

The Arroyo government's measures in addressing the crisis would not work, scientists said. Calderon criticized the government's proposal to replace the staple food. Government officials said that cassava, banana, sweet potato may be staple substitutes. "This is politically, economically and culturally wrong." Calderon said.

He said that likewise population control management would not resolve the problem. Even if the population growth would register zero, the deficit in supply would remain at 10 to15%. The real issue, Calderon said, is food security. He said that the converted agricultural lands in Calabarzon region alone could produce enough rice for the country. "Government must intervene not only in rice trading and in providing subsidies, but also in providing the facilities needed." He added that the P50 billion budget of the NFA to import rice could be diverted to help increase local production.

In a statement, Dr. Chito Medina, national coordinator of Magsasaka at Siyentipiko para sa Pag-unlad ng Agrikultura (MASIPAG or Farmers and Scientists for the Development of Agriculture) criticized the International Rice Research Institute (IRRI) for calling for another Green Revolution. He said that the Green Revolution, implemented in the 70s, and its introduction of high-yielding varieties nearly wiped out the country's traditional varieties.

For Anakpawis Representative and KMP Chairperson Rafael Mariano, IRRI is doing nothing good for Filipino farmers and the Philippine agriculture. "It continues to be the number one perpetrator of anti-farmer rice research in Asia."

For Cosico, lasting solutions include the outright rejection of globalization policies, providing economic and political reforms to local agriculture through the genuine agrarian reform program, and re-energizing agricultural science and technology for national industrialization.

Cosico maintained that agriculture is the base for industrialization. It will provide the means of subsistence for the people and raw materials for industries. With the development of agriculture the rural population would become a vast market for industrial products and the main reservoir of the labor force for industry and other sectors of the economy.

In a statement, AGHAM and RESIST (Resistance and Solidarity Against Agrochemical Transnational Corporations) expressed support for House Bill No. 3059 or the Genuine Agrarian Reform Bill (GARB) and for the House Bill No. 3958 or the Rice Industry Development Act (RIDA). Both bills are being sponsored by progressive partylist representatives from Anakpawis (Toiling Masses), Bayan Muna (People First) and Gabriela Women's Party.

Antonio Flores, spokesperson and lead convenor of Bantay Bigas, said, "The RIDA will pave the way for the development and protection of our rice industry into a self-reliant and sustainable economic element of our national development." Dr. Giovanni Tapang, AGHAM president, maintained that GARB is the solution to the age-old problem of landlessness and feudal exploitation in the country.

Speaking at the forum, Mariano said that the Arroyo government must not take pride in the so-called accomplishments of the Comprehensive Agrarian Reform Program (CARP). He said that of the 3.8 million hectares covered by CARP, only 2.1 million hectares are private agricultural lands. This, he said, is equivalent to only 20% of the privately owned lands and 80% still remain outside the CARP.

Mariano said that certificate of land ownership awards (CLOA), emancipation patents (EP) and certificate of land titles (CLT) are being confiscated from farmers. *"Walang security of tenure ang magsasaka, babalik at babalik sa panginoong maylupa."* (Farmers have no security of tenure, the land will go back into the hands of the landlords.)

Mariano said that it is essential to break up land monopoly control of foreign and local agricultural corporations. He said that while the GARB aims to do this, the peasant mass movement is implementing various levels of land reform. Mariano said, *"Ang masang magsasaka ay nagpapatupad ng bersyon ng tunay at puspusang reporma sa lupa. Kung sapat ang angking lakas, naipagtatagumpay ang kanilang pakikibaka."* (The masses of peasants implement their own version of genuine and thoroughgoing land reform. If they have enough strength, they succeed in their struggles.) He said that the farmers' campaign for the defense of land continues and develops amid violence from the state and landlords. He cited the experience of Hacienda Luisita farmers and farm workers who have asserted their right to till thousands of hectares of land. More than 2,000 hectares are now planted to rice, vegetables and other crops.

In Hacienda Looc, Mariano said that farmers refused to leave even as their EPs and CLOAs were taken. The same is true with farmers at the Central Mindanao University (CMU) in Bukidnon and in Ha. San Antonio Sta. Isabel in Isabela. "*Nakakapanatili sila dahil organisado.*" (They are able to stay because they are organized.) Mariano maintained that farmers should not be made to pay for the land they till. After all, their ancestors were the ones who developed the land, he said.

The peasant leader also cited successful campaigns for the decrease in land rent, decrease in interest of debt, for the increase in the farm gate prices of agricultural products, and increase in the wages of farm workers. Mariano said that peasants also have asserted their right to organization despite threats and harassments from state security forces. He said that the GARB is a response to the peasant mass movement's campaign for land reform. The central objective of GARB is the free distribution of agricultural land. Mariano said that free distribution will correct the historical social injustice against farmers who till and develop the land as the landlords wait for their share by virtue of pieces of paper. (End of article)

Another special report on agrarian reform by Zelda R.T. Soriano is reproduced below:

16 Years of Agrarian Reform Lands are Back in the Hands of the Lords

The government claims that the Comprehensive Agrarian Reform Program (CARP) is a success, even if it was supposed to end in 1998 but got extended until 2008 due to delays in the distribution of land and lack of funds. Farmers, on the other hand, claim to still experience feudal bondage and brand CARP as a bogus reform program. What is the truth behind the CARP's accomplishment? How are the tenant-beneficiaries doing at present? This special report seeks to shed light on what has happened to the program, and, more importantly, the farmers, 16 years after CARP's supposed implementation. (Author's note: Congress has passed a resolution extending the CARP program for another six months and is awaiting the approval of the President.)

Sixteen years ago - or just two years after the fall of the Marcos dictatorship - an agrarian reform law was passed. The Comprehensive Agrarian Reform Act (CARP) was the fifth land reform law in 50 years after those proclaimed under Presidents Manuel Quezon, Ramon Magsaysay, Diosdado Macapagal and Ferdinand Marcos. CARP was declared the centerpiece program of then President Corazon C. Aquino but organized peasants and other sectors did not expect much from it, however. As a farmer leader then quipped, how can a genuine agrarian reform program be legislated by a landlord-dominated Congress and signed by a landlord President?

Fast forward to 2004. If official pronouncements were to be believed, genuine agrarian reform is a pipe dream no more. A full-page government advertisement in a leading newspaper last June 10 described CARP as "a tribute to the sturdy and resilient Filipino farmers." "After 16 years of meeting the challenges of providing productive lives to millions of farmers all over the country, the farmers are finally realizing their dreams," the ad, published by the Department of Agrarian Reform (DAR), said further.

Remembering the past

CARP was mandated by Republic Act No. 6657 signed by President Aquino on June 10, 1988. Upon its passage, the government promised to distribute lands in 10 years, i.e., until 1998, to about 8.5 million landless peasants, share tenants and agricultural workers "to liberate them from the clutches of landlordism and poverty."

CARP covered "all public and private lands regardless of tenurial arrangement and commodity produced." It included "the totality of factors and support services" such as credit extension, irrigation, roads, bridges and marketing facilities, among others. Overall, it envisioned "a nation where there is equitable land ownership with empowered agrarian reform beneficiaries who are effectively managing their economic and social development for a better quality of life."

The next three presidents after Aquino echoed the promise of distributing lands and a better life to Filipino farmers. However, something else happened under Aquino herself and the presidencies of Fidel V. Ramos, Joseph Estrada and now, Gloria Macapagal-Arroyo. First, the original land distribution target of 24 million hectares was reduced by phases until it became just 4.7 million hectares. Then the 1998 deadline for the "full implementation" of CARP was extended by Congress for another 10 years. The main reason cited is the lack of budget allocations.

DAR figures: "distorted, bloated and unreliable"

According to DAR, around 3.4 million hectares of lands have been distributed to some 1.9 million beneficiaries as of May this year. DAR Policy Research Officer Narcisa S. Martinez said that these statistics are best proof that the agency is doing well on its task to implement the land reform act.

On closer look, however, the DAR reports tend to hide the fact that only half of the reported figures (or the final target after a process of reductions) have actually been distributed. Tenant-beneficiaries, on the other hand, are losing their lands back to the landlords, industrialists and real estate developers. A DAR insider dismissed the department's accomplishment reports as "distorted, bloated and unreliable." Its latest accomplishment report, according to the agrarian reform officer in Central Luzon who spoke to this author on condition of anonymity, is unreliable. Having been assigned in various local and regional DAR offices in the past 21 years, he admitted witnessing "so many ways of fooling around with the law."

In Zambales province, for example, some 12,755 hectares of land reportedly distributed by the agrarian department have been under investigation since 1999. The lands are supposed to be inalienable, being seashores, rivers, roads, titled properties and protected areas. In other words, they cannot be used for agricultural production. Initial investigation confirmed the bogus land distribution in this case. Surprisingly, those responsible were not sanctioned.

The provincial DAR office was believed to carelessly rely on *barangay* (village) census as basis of land distribution targets. The local agrarian officials overlooked the fact that many supposed beneficiaries were no longer residing in the targeted CARP communities.

The DAR source cited many other land distribution cases including CLOA cancellations that remained unsolved due to lack of evidence and witnesses. Eventually, many lands were excluded from CARP coverage after secret deals between land reform officials, local government executives and landowners, he said. The whistleblower ends up in hot water as "corruption is systematic from the field surveyor/technician up to the high levels. *Ang matapat ang siya pang maiiba at mapapahamak."* (The true public servant is the one who finds himself intimidated).

Laments the DAR official: "It is a lonely, frustrating battle...When I was assigned in the province some years back, the regional director called me a few times. He said I should play it cool and that I should refrain from touching some landowners. *Huwag ko daw isama sa CARP coverage."* (Their properties should be exempted).

There are other ways by which DAR accomplishment reports are distorted. David Erro, executive director of the Sentro para sa Tunay na Repormang Agraryo (Sentra – Center for Genuine Agrarian Reform) - a Quezon City-based foundation offering legal services and assistance to poor farmers said, for instance, that to beat targets and deadlines, the DAR in the past released many certificates of land ownership award (CLOAs) although the beneficiaries have neither paid the required amount nor met other requisites.

To differentiate these CLOAs from those held by complying beneficiaries, DAR officials stamped the label "encumbered" or other annotations of encumbrances on the back of the certificates. The latter are as good as the original, many holders of encumbered CLOAs were told. The number of holders of the defective CLOAs is then padded to the accomplishment report.

Erro, who is a lawyer, clarified however that holders of this kind of CLOAs "cannot exercise acts of ownership unlike those holding regular certificates." In fact DAR officials withhold the generated titles until the farmers themselves fulfill the requirements such as documents and payments.

Another serious concern in CARP is the pattern of farmer-beneficiaries losing lands for different reasons. One of such reasons is government cancellation of the farmers' land titles.

In a March 2004 report titled, "Cancellation of Land Titles: Pulling the Rug from Under Agrarian Reform," peasant group Kaisahan tungo sa Kaunlaran ng Kanayunan at Repormang Pansakahan (Kaisahan or coalition for rural progress and land reform) described the alarming trend of title cancellation among holders of CLOA and of emancipation patent (EP) as *"bigay tapos bawi"* (give, and then take back) scheme.

EPs have been issued since 1972 under Presidential Decree No. 27, the land reform program of the late President Ferdinand Marcos. The issuance of EPs lasted until 1989 when the Supreme Court (SC) ruled to stop their release.

As of May this year, DAR's Management Information System (MIS) revealed that titles for about 380,000 hectares of farmlands have been cancelled. The incidence of title cancellation was highest in Southern Tagalog, followed by CARAGA region which comprises the provinces of Surigao del Norte and Sur and Agusan del Norte and Sur.

While DAR has yet to show disaggregated data on the current numbers and the reasons for cancellation, the usual reasons for the department's action to cancel included erroneous coverage of land, erroneous entry of data and transfer action (or change of documents from EP to CLOA). Decisions of the DAR Adjudication Board (Darab) on cases involving retention, exemption, re-issuance of owner's title, and correction of farmer-beneficiaries were also cited.

Yet another reason was the reclassification of land under which lands distributed, for unknown reasons, have suddenly been reclassified for residential, commercial and industrial uses by a local zoning ordinance or land use plan.

In the past 16 years, around 800,000 hectares of agricultural lands have been converted to other uses, based on government records. Land conversion, according to a source from DAR, is the "easiest way of circumventing the law."

Based on DAR records, foreclosed properties due to non-payment of amortization totaled around 100,000 hectares. This implies that the economic conditions of farmer-beneficiaries did not improve significantly to enable them to sustain payment.

Recent surveys by the Center for Peasant Education and Services (CPES) in Southern Tagalog and Central Luzon regions showed that three out of five holders of CLOA or EP have sold their rights or mortgaged then abandoned their properties without payment.

Asked to explain why they sold their land, farmers surveyed by CPES said they lack capital to sustain or improve farm production. Some farms were also converted to residential or commercial uses. This was resorted to often because farming prospects were compromised by water drain, pollution and other problems brought about, so the farmers said, by non-agricultural activities around the farms.

The same surveys revealed that those who bought the CARP-awarded lands were the landlords themselves as well as businessmen and real estate developers. Corroborating the CPES surveys, the DAR source said that when a beneficiary sells his farm to his former landlord, the latter pays the remaining obligations of the farmer. When fully paid, the landlord, through the farmer, applies for change of owner's name after claiming wrong identification of the beneficiary.

Project Development Institute (PDI), a non-government organization, shared the same observation. In an interview with this author, Julio Rodrigo de Guia of PDI said that in one of the institute's areas of operation in Tarlac, about 30 out of 100 CARP beneficiaries gave up their lands in the past five years after realizing that farming was no longer a viable source of income. But in other areas where PDI facilitated socio-economic projects to improve production and to introduce other sources of income, the farmer-beneficiaries stayed.

For PDI, DAR's mishandling the delivery of support services could partly explain CARP's failure. The law allots only 25% of the total CARP funds to be used exclusively for support services like farm-to-market roads, bridges, irrigation facilities, etc. The remaining 75% will be sourced out from the donor communities or international funding agencies.

Poverty, according to Research Officer Raul Espere of CPES, remains the major reason why tenant-beneficiaries are forced to surrender their rights and lands to buyers and mortgagees. "It is quite ironic that this is the reason why CARP was implemented - to solve rural poverty. If this is the same reason why lands are being given up, then, it only shows that CARP dismally failed in meeting its objectives," Espere said.

Danilo Ramos, secretary general of the militant Kilusang Magbubukid ng Pilipinas (KMP – Peasant Movement in the Philippines), offered his own assessment of CARP. He said: "*Pagkatapos ng CARP sa 2008* (when the extension period ends), *naibenta na ulit ng mga benepisyaryo ang lupa sa mayayaman dahil wala namang pag-asang umunlad ang kabuhayan ng magsasaka sa taas naman ng gastos sa produksyon. Wala namang suportang pautang at iba pang serbisyo ang gobyerno kaya magigipit uli ang benepisyaryo, mababaon sa utang, mapipilitang ibenta ang lupa.*" (When the CARP ends in 2008, the beneficiaries would have re-sold the land to the rich because their livelihood cannot be expected to improve with the high cost of production.

There is no credit support and other services from the government so the beneficiaries end up in a tight fix, go indebted and are forced to sell the land.)

Ramos argues that the root of this flawed land reform program is in the very concept of compensating the landlords and making the farmers pay for the lands. *"Nasaan naman doon ang katarungan? Ang naging papel lang ng gobyerno sa programang ito ay ang pagiging middleman sa bentahan ng lupa sa pagitan ng may-ari at ng magsasaka. Reporma ba 'yun?"* (Where is justice in this case? The only role of the government in this program is to serve as a middleman in the sale of land between the owner and the farmer. Is this reform?), he says.

Given a distorted DAR accomplishment report, Ramos said the sum of failures would offset the claimed number of distributed lands or outbalance whatever "little gains" CARP has accomplished.

By 2008, the KMP leader says, another land reform program would be needed as the CARP lands – or those that government claims were transferred to tenants - are back in the hands of the landlords. *"Wala nang katapusan ang pagrereporma sa lupa dahil ayaw naman talaga ng gobyerno na tapusin."* (Land reform is never-ending. The government does not want to end it anyway). (End of the Article)

Looking back at the problem on hand, I can only conclude that one factor behind the impoverishing of the poor is the greed and selfishness of the few rich people who would do anything to take advantage of the poor. They tried to frustrate the land reform programs because there would not be any farmers left to till the soil for them.

Blood is thicker than water and the thickest of them is money. Even the Christian virtue of sharing cannot be found in most of the hearts of people here and around the world. Public contributions to legitimate victims are sometimes siphoned off and sold to the public by local officials. This is often abetted by corruption of funds intended for the poor such as the rice scam that recently hit the newspaper a few days ago (September 2008), the fertilizer scam that started a few years back, and the market road scams supposedly intended for the improvement the road network from the producer to the market place. So much money meant to help the poor have been siphoned off by greedy politicians and abetted by some private individuals. It often takes years to end an investigation and punish the culprit/s before another one hit the limelight.

There is now under investigation by the Citizen's Debt Audit Commission (CDAC) a possible fertilizer scam involving the $121-million Small Coconut Farms Development Project, a World Bank-funded project intended to help the coconut farmers. According to the group, the money was supposed to help the farmers through the distribution of free farm inputs like fertilizers sometime in 1990. But the farmers claimed during the public hearing that the project was riddled with irregularities and widespread corruption involving government officials and private contractors. The alleged irregularities ranged from complete non-delivery, sale of fertilizers to private companies engaged in trading or manufacturing fertilizers, and an estimated 40% of the funds had been malversed. A fund of P275,730 was allegedly used to finance the campaign for Charter change during the Ramos administrator. (*PS*, December 9, 2008) This is not surprising because many politicians are power-hungry.

Energy Crisis

Signs of poverty and overpopulation of the masses are the number of poor consumers unable to pay for their electricity need. Many of them are so poor that they consume only enough for lighting, a TV set or an electric fan in their small living quarter. This has forced the government to come to their aid with an unprecedented additional subsidy for the payment of power bills. The electricity power subsidies have been on the energy bills for Meralco-franchised consumers for many decades. Those who consumed less than 200 kwH per month have been paying lower rates than others. Now, the government is planning to aid some 1.9 million lifeline users with P2 billion cash transfer. Each recipient will receive P1,000 a year to help defray some of the electricity expenses for those consuming less than 100 kilowatts per month.

Even with the low power rates, some more desperate consumers still resort to stealing electricity by using "jumper" to bypass the electric meter. This just goes to show that there are so many poor people in this country who could not afford to live a decent life.

Fossil fuels may not run out soon in the near future, but it is becoming more expensive and hard to find and explore. Many new oil fields are found in very volatile and disputed areas and therefore unreliable. As a result, there have been moves to find a renewable replacement for fossil fuels. Even the drop in oil prices due to economic meltdown is no comfort for consumers in the long run. These renewable energy resources include solar, wind, biomass, tidal energy, etc. Most of them are not cheap to build on a large scale without government or foreign financial helps. It will also take decades before we can be called self-sufficient in energy. Most of the alternative energy are not easily stored or transported such as gasoline for the transportation industry.

After pending in Congress for 23 years, it was finally signed into law by President Arroyo on December 16, 2008. It is hoped that Republic Act No. 9513 or the Renewable Energy Act of 2008 will improve the self sufficiency of the country's energy to 60% by the year 2010. The current supply of renewable energy is pegged at 57%. The law provides incentives for investors in renewable energy such as geothermal, hydropower, solar, biomass, wind and tidal energies. These incentives include a seven-year tax holiday, no tax on carbon credits generated from renewable energy sources, and a 10% corporate income tax. There will also be a cap of 1.5% real estate tax on the cost of equipment and facilities used to produce these energies and duty-free importation of machinery, equipment and materials. The energies produced from these firms will be given priority in the purchase, grid connection and transmission of electricity to consumers. The purchase of local supplies and sales from the renewal energy are also exempted from value-added tax. With the incentives, the country hopes to add more than 4,000 MW of renewable energy in the next few years of which 1,200 is expected to come from geothermal sources. The Philippines is currently the world's second largest geothermal producer for power generation with a capacity of 1,958 MW. On July 10, 2008, three geothermal contracts were signed and awarded for exploration in three areas with the expected generation of 100 MW of electricity. This will save the country about $1.8 billion in import bills. The country imported about $7.5 billion worth of oil last year (2007). (*PDI*, December 17 and 18, 2008)

The country with plenty of mountainous terrain can be ideal for wind farms. It has been features in many countries in Europe, the U.S. China, and recently in the Philippines. In 2002 alone, investors spent $7 billion to install equipment with 7,000 MW of wind power capacity to supply electricity for nearly 4 million homes in Europe. At the core of the wind power is the simple wind turbine. A tower-mounted wind turbine, attached to a two to three large blades spinning on an axis drive an internal generator and produce electric current. The harder the wind blows, the more electricity is generated. The efficiency of each turbine has also increased from 100 kW in the 1980s to 1.2 MW or more today. With the growing efficiency of the wind turbine, it is possible to harness the wind energy for home use simply by erected one on the backyard or the rooftop. (Roberts, 196-197)

The Philippines is at present the top wind power producer in Southeast Asia with a total of 33 MW generating capacity. One of the wind turbine plants with a capacity of 25 MW is located in Bangui, Ilocos Norte. Except for the initial investment for the tower and equipment, there is no other fuel input necessary except the natural blowing wind. Another shortfall is the land required for setting up these towers. However, wind power pollution free and maintenance is also very minimal.

Except for nuclear energy, all other energy sources have their origin from the sun, through photosynthesis, heating of the ocean, changing weather pattern, etc. Direct harnessing of the sun energy is one common form of energy that is being touted as the best sources of alternative renewal energy that could last for as long as the sun shines. On the average, the sun produces one kW of solar energy per m^2 as it reaches the earth. It will take only 0.3% of the sunlight falling on the Sahara and Middle East deserts to provide all of Europe's energy needs.

Solar energy requires large initial investment and is not dependable during cloudy days and at night. Cagayan de Oro City is host to a 1-MW solar photovoltaic power plant that is connected to the grid. Another plant, the Sunpower Solar Wafer Fabrication Plant in Sta. Rosa, Laguna, boast of producing 214 MW in 2007 from 108 MW in 2006. Individual solar photovoltaic to date numbered about 42,531 units nationwide. (*PDI*, December 18, 2008)

All these is going to change as scientists tried to harness the solar energy off Sahara Desert where some patches of the desert reach 113°F on many afternoons. A few years ago scientists were astounded that a 35,000 mi^2 chunk of the Sahara could yield the same amount of electricity as all the world's power plants combined. Just 6,000 mi^2 could provide all the energy need for Europe's 500 million people. Instead of using solar panels which convert sunlight directly into electricity, concentrating solar power (CSP) will be used. CSP utilizes mirrors to focus light on water pipes or boilers, generating superheated steam to operate the turbines of generators. Small CSP plants have produced power in California's Mojave Desert since 1980s. The Sahara Forest Project proposes building CSP plants below sea level so that seawater can flow into them and be condensed into distilled water for powering turbines and washing dust off the mirrors. Wastewater would be used to irrigate areas around the stations, creating lush oases.

The estimated cost is $59 billion to bring the power Europe by 2020. (TIME, January 26, 2009)

Aside from the cost, there are other problems such as the distance the power have to travel to reach Europe. Just to supply Europe with 20% of its electricity needs, more than 12,000 miles of high-voltage direct-current cables would be laid under the Mediterranean. Europe will also need to build completely new electrical grids because the aging alternating-current lines built largely for the coal-fired plants that supply 80% of Europe's power are inadequate for a larger load. One estimates put the additional cost of about $465 billion over the next 40 years. Government subsidies may be needed. Delays are inevitable with the pending high investment needed especially with government support. (Ibid)

The mainstay of our renewal energy needs come from the hydroelectric power plants. Currently there is an installed capacity of 3,289 MW with more mini-hydro in the pipeline. The Department of Energy (DOE) has approved five mini-hydro plants with a capacity of 13.5 MW and 29 reconnaissance permits. It is also monitoring 35 existing mini-hydro projects as well as the on-going construction of four others.

The first gas-to-power project harnessing the methane gas from landfill located in the Payatas dumpsite was commissioned in May 2007. A one-megawatt La Suerte Rice Hull Cogeneration Plant in San Manuel, Isabela was commission in April 2008. The success of these ventures will probably lead to more plants.

Even before the passage of the law, TeaM Energy in partnership with Tokyo Power Company and Marubeni Corporation has installed more than 2,000 MW of electricity servicing 300,000 households and benefiting over one million Filipinos. Through their Project BEACON, they have energized 1,500 barangays in several regions around the country. Since 2002, BEACON has stringed 18,000 km of wire, erected, 60,000 poles, and installed more than 10,000 solar home systems. (*PDI*, December 18, 2008)

The oil crisis is not a new phenomenon. It happened during the Yom Kippur War when the price of oil quadrupled. Then there is the Iranian Revolution that toppled the Shah and caused another price increase. Since then, the price of oil has been fluctuating upward. Every time there is a crisis somewhere in the oil-producing countries, such as the bombing of oil pipelines in Nigeria, the tendency is for the oil price to increase. We are at the mercy of the oil producing countries as long as we have to rely on them for most of our energy needs.

In the U.S. the expected energy shortages, especially of oil have prompted many to call for the opening of the American wilderness in Alaska for oil exploration. Other places included are the offshore or continental shelves in the Mexican Gulf area where oil may be plentiful. Even our own Spratly Islands are being disputed by several countries for possible hidden oil that could even lead to war if the claimants cannot agree on how the dispute is to be resolved.

Unlike in the Middle East, most of the oil and energy supplies are found in the forested areas of the world like in Africa and South America. It is here where the exploitation of oil come into conflict with the environment and laws protecting them. Changes to the laws have to be put into effect before oil exploration can be undertaken. In the Philippines, it is geothermal power that is at stake. There is a battle now raging in Negros Occidental, between the "Save Mt. Kanlaon Coalition," an environmental group, against the proponents of geothermal power development, aided by the DOE and Department of Environment and Natural Resources (DENR). At stake are some four thousand plus trees in a 12.5 hectares buffer zone that have to be cut down to make room for the geothermal plant. The debate is now centered on the interpretation of the public law that established the national park as protected areas while one provision of the law allows for the exploration of geothermal energy in the buffer zone area. (*PDI*, August 16, 2008) Conflicts in laws are common in judicial system and the SC has been time and time again called to interpret the law.

Another aspect of oil exploration is the delivery of the crude oil for refinement to the intended buyers. Many of these crude oils have to be delivery thousands of miles through the sea lanes. Whether they are traveling in the ocean or inland, there is the possibility of oil spill. There are more than 10,000 oil spills in the sea going on around the world every year.

The two greatest oil spills were the 1991 Gulf War oil spill that was deliberately set by the Iraqi to prevent the Americans from landing from the Persian Gulf. It caused considerable damage to wildlife in the areas surrounding Kuwait and Iraq. Estimates on the volume spilled range from 42 to 462 million gallons; the slick reached a maximum size of 101 by 42 miles and was 5 inches thick. It was five to 27 times the size of the Exxon Valdez oil spill and more than twice the size of the 1979 Ixtoc I blow-out in the Gulf of Mexico.[55]

---

[55] http://en.wikipedia.org/wiki/Gulf_War_oil_spill

Birds and mammals are often the first victims of oil spill. The oil penetrates and opens up the structure of the plumage of birds, reducing its insulating ability, thus so making the birds more vulnerable to temperature fluctuations and reduces their buoyancy in the water. It also impairs birds' flight abilities, making it difficult or impossible to forage and escape from predators. As they attempt to preen, birds typically ingest oil that coats their feathers, causing kidney damage, altered liver function, and digestive tract irritation. This and the limited foraging ability quickly cause dehydration and metabolic imbalances. Most birds affected by an oil spill die unless there is human intervention.

Marine mammals exposed to oil spills are affected in similar ways as seabirds. Oil coats the fur of sea otters and seals, reducing its insulation abilities and leading to body temperature fluctuations and hypothermia. Ingestion of the poisonous oil causes dehydration and impaired digestion.[56]

Cleanup along the coastal areas usually takes years and can be very expensive. Unless they affect coastal areas, the spill is often left alone to break down by natural means. A combination of wind, sun, current, and wave action will rapidly disperse and evaporate most oils. Another way is to skim up the oil slick with skimmer equipment such as various types of brooms. Skimmers float are used on top of the slick and suck or scoop the oil into storage tanks on nearby vessels or on the shore. Dispersants are used to break up the oil and speed its natural biodegradation. They are most effective when used within an hour or two of the initial spill. Dispersants act by reducing the surface tension that stops oil and water from mixing. Small droplets of oil are then formed, which helps promote rapid dilution of the oil by water movements. The formation of droplets also increases the oil surface area, thus increasing the exposure to natural evaporation and bacterial action. The introduction of biological agents to hasten biodegradation takes a longer period to accomplish. The oil is broken down by bacteria and other microorganisms into harmless substances such as fatty acids and carbon dioxide. This action is called biodegradation. The natural process can be speeded up by the addition of fertilizing nutrients like nitrogen and phosphorous, which stimulate growth of the microorganisms concerned.[57] Whatever methods to be adopted usually

---

[56] http://en.wikipedia.org/wiki/Oil_spill
[57] http://www.ocean.udel.edu/oilspill/cleanup.html

depend on the weather conditions and the capability and logistics of those involved.

Oil import bill is the single largest foreign exchange outflow of the country. Most of these imported oils are used by householders using the automobiles. They consumed more than 60% of all oil imports. For more than a century now, the internal combustion engines have been the mainstay of our mobility. Every time there is a crisis, talks of alternative forms of transport system have been advocated. The auto industry is at the forefront to find an alternative form of energy for the automobiles. One of the earliest proposed alternatives is the gas-electric hybrid. The power of the vehicle is taken over by the electric car for about fifty miles before it is fully drained and the gasoline takes over. It can then be recharged by plugging into the electric current outlet.

Because of the high cost of these Plug-in Hybrid Electric Vehicles (PHEV), demand has not caught on. Work to reduce the cost and increase the power mileage is on-going and may become a reality soon. Toyota, the leader in the hybrid technology plans to introduce a hybrid vehicle in 2010 using the lithium-ion batteries which is much more efficient than any hydride batteries in the market. The former battery is used in almost all cell phones and laptops today. The problem is that these hydride batteries need electricity for recharging and most of the energy came from fossil fuels.

The use of hydrogen power in the form of the fuel cell has been touted as one solution to the energy problem. Hydrogen is the building block of the universe and can be found in many compounds such as water, organic compounds such as carbohydrates and is the root of all fossil fuels or hydrocarbons such as oil, gas and coal. The downside of hydrogen energy is that it does not exist alone in nature and splitting the hydrogen from the compounds such as water requires a great deal of energy. This 150-year-old energy technology is clean, quiet, and nearly three times as energy efficient as even the best internal-combustion engine (ICE). The fuel cells can be built to any scale making them easy to transport and utilized in all almost any energy consuming items. (Roberts, 68-69)

Work on automobiles using hydrogen power has been going on for years. The power plants of such vehicles convert the chemical energy of hydrogen to mechanical energy (torque) in one of two methods: it can be used like the combustion engine where the hydrogen is burned in engines like the traditional gasoline cars or as in a fuel-cell conversion where the hydrogen is reacted with oxygen to produce water and electricity, the latter of which is used to power an electric traction motor.

There had been some demonstration models of hydrogen powered motors used in buses, trains, bicycles, golf carts, motorcycles, wheelchairs, ships, airplanes, submarines, and rockets. They are very expensive such as the one used in the Space Shuttles by NASA into launching them. There is even a working toy model car that runs on solar power, using a reversible fuel cell to store energy in the form of hydrogen and oxygen gas. It can then convert the fuel back into water to release the solar energy.

The current land speed record for a hydrogen powered vehicle is 333.38 km/h (207.2 mph) set by a prototype Ford Fusion Hydrogen 999 Fuel Cell Race Car at Bonneville Salt Flats in Wendover, Utah in August 2007.

There are several problems that need to be resolved before commercialization can be realized. One of them is size, weight and the high cost of producing fuel cells. Some prototypes are in operation. The Japanese auto makers, Toyota and Honda have started leasing them to the public in Japan and California, each costing upwards of $1 million to produce. Toyota hopes to reduce its costs per fuel-cell vehicle to around $50,000 by 2015, which would make them more economically viable. General Motors plans to sell hydrogen-powered vehicles in the United States by 2010.[58] So far, the cost is prohibitive for most buyers.

The lack of hydrogen refueling stations is another hurdle. The extra cost of setting them up could also be prohibitive if there is not much demand. The oil companies with their highly lucrative gasoline stations are not about to let the hydrogen eat into their profits. Nevertheless, some 38 independent hydrogen fuel stations have been set up in California as part of a network created by the nonprofit California Fuel Cell Partnership, a consortium of automakers, state and federal agencies, and other parties interested in furthering hydrogen fuel-cell technologies.

At present 95% of the hydrogen available in the United States is either extracted from fossil fuels or produced by the electrolytic processes powered by fossil fuels, thus negating any real emissions savings or reduction in fossil-fuel usage. Only if renewable energy sources - solar, tidal, wind, geothermal, hydroelectric, and others - can

---

[58] http://environment.about.com/od/fossilfuels/a/fcv.htm?nl=1

be harnessed to provide the energy to process hydrogen fuel can the dream of a truly clean hydrogen fuel be realized.

Another drawback is that the capacity of the fuel cells could be limited in range before recharging. It takes several hours, even overnight to completely recharge the fuel cells. This tedious process would have to be done daily and using electricity only shifted the pollution emitted from the automobile to the power plants.

Most of today's hydrogen is produced using fossil energy resources. While some advocate hydrogen produced from non-fossil resources, there could be public resistance or technological barriers to the implementation of such methods. Hydrogen produced in this fashion would still incur the costs associated with transportation and compression or liquefaction assuming direct (molecular) hydrogen is the on-board fuel. Recently, alternative methods of creating hydrogen directly from sunlight and water through a metallic catalyst have been announced. This may eventually provide an economical, direct conversion of solar energy into hydrogen a very clean solution for hydrogen production.

ICE-based hybrid cars use both gasoline and electricity to power the vehicle. Electricity can be plugged into the electric grid (Plug-in hybrid electric vehicles, or PHEVs) and achieve much higher overall gas mileage and lower emissions than other hybrids. A 2006 article in *Scientific American* argues that PHEVs, rather than hydrogen vehicles, will soon become standard in the automobile industry. One reason is the lower cost of the hybrid vehicles.

Electric vehicles have been promoted in the past as one solution. So far, they are very expensive and will not put a dent on the oil and pollution problems in the near future. Several prototypes have been invented such as the General Motors EV1 which is more efficient than fuel cell-powered vehicles on a well-to-wheel basis. As *Technology Review* noted in June 2008, they have an enormous advantage over hydrogen fuel-cell vehicles in utilizing low-carbon electricity. That is because of the inherent inefficiency of the entire hydrogen fueling process, from generating the hydrogen with that electricity to transporting this diffuse gas long distances, getting the hydrogen in the car, and then running it through a fuel cell—all for the purpose of converting the hydrogen back into electricity to drive the same exact electric motor you will find in an electric car. For this reason, battery powered vehicles are gaining popularity, particularly with the introduction of new models like the Tesla Roadster.

One innovation is the use of propane or liquefied petroleum gas (LPG). Another is the compressed natural gas (CNG). Propane is a byproduct of natural gas processing and crude oil refining. It is also a byproduct of oil exploration. Already widely used as a fuel for cooking and heating, propane is also a popular alternative fuel for vehicles. Propane produces fewer emissions than gasoline, and there is also a highly developed infrastructure for propane transport, storage and distribution. The government is also encouraging the conversion of diesel-run public utilities with a P1 billion loan fund for drivers and operators of public utility vehicles. In her meeting with the jeepney operators groups, President Gloria Macapagal-Arroyo says that since LPG and CNG are cheaper than diesel or gasoline, this project will help the transport sector cope with the surging prices of oil products.

The cost of converted a carburetor type motor vehicle is about P23,000 while that of the fuel injection type is about P55,000. There are now 13,886 vehicles running of LPG with 165 Auto-LPG dispensing stations operating nationwide. On the other hand, CNG-fed buses in operation numbered 19 and they are plying the Batangas/Laguna/Manila route. There are so far only two stations servicing them: one in Laguna and the other in Batangas. The government hopes to increase the units to 5,000 buses by 2025.

In fact, LPG has other uses beside cooking and running the vehicles. It is also being promoted for home appliances as way of cutting the energy bills while reducing the carbon footprint of greenhouse gases. It is being used as laundering, heating homes, running boiler, and generating hot water and steam, in other countries.

There are many things an individual can do to mitigate the energy crisis. The best solution to the energy crisis while reducing air pollution is to reduce the use of motor vehicles. High tax on gasoline is one way by incorporating the cost of cleaning up air pollutants. Car pooling, biking, using motorcycle, commuting with the mass transport or by the railways, teleconference instead of physical presence, scheduling the trip, home delivery instead of eating out, etc. are just some simple acts. Other alternatives of saving gasoline include proper tune-up, proper tire pressure, defensive driving, drive at 80 kph in the highway for maximum efficiency, avoiding traffic congested areas, higher taxes for gushy vehicles like SUV, etc. A vehicle traveling at 120 kph uses 20% more gasoline than one traveling at 80 kph, besides more accidents prone. It is well known that higher traveling at high speed are more likely to meet accidents and often fatally. The government can also help fix the traffic congestion by proper maintenance of road and traffic lights. Lack of discipline is one reason for congestion. MMDA and city traffic enforcers should be directing traffic instead of busy apprehending motorists for "swerving." It is a scheme for corruption and the violation does not add much to traffic congestion. If there is one good reason for disciplining motorists, it is to stop them from clogging the intersections. This is one issue the traffic czar fears to face because their personnel will be end up exhausted and exasperated.

Our streets are also laden with potholes and uneven patch works. Instead of grouting the potholes to smooth out the cracks, which is less expensive, an oversize asphalt patch tends to cause more bumps and slow down the traffic once they deteriorate after a few downpours. With many potholes and uneven roads, drivers are forced to slow down causing unnecessary fuel consumption. Every time the brake is applied, there is a loss of momentum that can only be picked up again by applying the gas accelerator.

There is a need to carefully analyze the time and motion of each traffic lights. Some traffic lights are much longer than necessary while others are too short, especially along streets with synchronized lighting. The use of U-turn slots in many roads are not actually helping the free flow of traffic, especially when the intersections they are supposed to take over are heavy with traffic. The vehicles are forced to jam-pack around the U-turn slots, reducing the traffic lanes and slowing down the traffic flow not only to the entrance of the U-turn slot but also the exiting slot. The MMDA claimed to save the motorists P40 to P50 million in gasoline cost annually with the 23 U-turn slots that have been setup so far and another P2 billion in terms of opportunity and productivity. It is highly paradoxically to be able to save gasoline while traveling more distances. At each U-turn slot, every time a vehicle has to slow down, gas is wasted to accelerate to the normal speed again. It is like slowing down because of potholes which waste a lot of energy.

In the case of gasoline savings, I have my doubts because many of these U-turn slots take more than half a kilometer to traverse the same distance to the point of origin and the time and gasoline wasted, and the depreciation of the engine, is more than compensated by waiting at the traffic light intersections. Idling is less expensive than having the car travel around the U-turn slots. One U-turn slot going to Tramo in Pasay City from the domestic airport takes 2.2 kilometers to traverse and more than ten minutes when it will only take at most five minutes waiting at the traffic intersection. That is pure wastage of about three liters of gasoline. Traffic lights should not take more than 1-1/2 minutes to change as practice in many foreign countries with smooth traffic flow. Complaints about this long span of U-turn have not heeded. As for the time saved, I have the same doubts. To top it all, the traffic lights have been kept on for more than a month, leading to energy wastage. This was the same scenario when the U-turn slots were first constructed along Quezon Avenue. The traffic lights have been on for more than a year before the authority decided to shut them down. The barricade in front of the intersection is enough to show the driver there is no thru street. A road sign posted on the barricade would have done the same trick. In fact, each approach to the U-turn slots should have an elevated sign post indicating their presence before drivers are apprehended by enterprising MMDA enforcers looking out for "swerving" motorists. It is obvious the MMDA is not energy conscious when it comes to solving the traffic situation.

The compact fluorescence lamps (CFLs) have been around for quite some time but it is only very recent that householders have switched to this new product. They may be more expensive initially, but have proven to be economical in the long run. The CFLs produced more lighting that the comparable incandescent bulbs with the same wattage and uses two-thirds less energy. They also came in all sizes and shapes and have a much longer life, up to eight to ten times than the standard incandescent bulb. One statistics claimed that if every U.S. family replaced one regular light bulb with a CFL, it would eliminate 90 billion pounds of greenhouse gases, the same as taking one million cars off the road for one year or lighting 2.5 million homes for one year. (Bongiorno, 147)

Disposing of spent CFLs can posed environmental problems. It is partly produced with neurotoxic mercury vapor and if broken indoors they contaminate the air while adding to the mercury pollution when disposed improperly to the dumpsite. They require special clean up procedure.

By far the best effort in reducing carbon dioxide is by planting trees. Only the trees can soak up carbon dioxide effortlessly from the atmosphere through photosynthesis. Trees can absorb 15 times more carbon dioxide in the urban areas and the rural areas because it is here where most carbon dioxide gases are emitted and concentrated. (Zimmerman, 81) The chopsticks that Japanese restaurants wantonly disposed after each use should be replaced with reusable plastic or metal chopsticks like in South Korea. There energy spent in producing recycled paper is cheaper and does not entail cutting down trees. The trees are also great absorber of carbon dioxide since half the trees are made up of carbon. Were it not for the trees, we would be living in a dead planet.

There are other ways, directly or indirectly an individual can do to save the environment from further harm. The battle cry of the environmentalists: the 3Rs can be put into effect. These are reduce, reuse and recycle. We can reduce the use of disposables, buy products with minimum packaging or buy in bulk, reuse the things as often as possible such as bottles and cans for other purposes, using the papers fully before they are discarded for recycling, etc. At lot of household waste can be recycled if we just take a few minutes to think about them instead of throwing to the garbage bins. A lot of energy can be saved from recycling papers, aluminum and plastic cans while saving the natural resources. Even the mining of the natural resources requires energy. Even conserving water is conserving energy as energy is needed to deliver the water to our faucet.

Turn off the lights or TV, or computer when not in use. Adding insulation to the house and particularly the rooms where air-conditioning units are used saves energy. Lowering the thermostat helps too.

The high prices of gasoline a few months back have forced many to use public transport, saving us about 10% in additional gasoline consumption while emitting less pollution to the atmosphere and less traffic on the road. Walking, biking, and the use of motorcycle have reduced the need for fossil fuels. Planning the trip can also help.

Each gallon of gasoline weights 6.3 pounds can actually produce 20 pounds of carbon dioxide when burned. This is because the carbon in the gasoline combines with oxygen in the air to produce carbon dioxide. It takes a carbon atom with an atomic weight of 12 and two atoms of oxygen each with an atomic weight of 16 to form carbon dioxide with an atomic weight of 44. To calculate the amount of CO_2 produced from a gallon of gasoline, the weight of the carbon in the gasoline is multiplied by 44/12 or 3.7. Since gasoline is about 87% carbon and 13% hydrogen by weight, the carbon in a gallon of gasoline weighs 5.5 pounds (6.3 lbs. x .87). We can then multiply the weight of the carbon (5.5 pounds) by 3.7, which equal 20 pounds of CO_2.[59] Each gallon is equivalent to 3.78 liters and each kilo is 2.2 pounds, therefore, each liter of gasoline should produce 20/3.78 or 5.29 pounds or 5.29/2.2 or 2.4 kilos of carbon dioxide.

---

[59] http://www.fueleconomy.gov/Feg/co2.shtml

Food and Energy Controversy

Demand for fuel around the world is now competing against demand for food mostly in poor countries. Cars, not people, used most of the increase in world grain production in 2006. The grain required to fill a 25-gallon SUV gas tank with ethanol will feed one person for a year. This is expected to increase the number of poor consumers as food price increases. The World Bank estimated that in 2001 there were 2.7 billion people who lived in poverty on less than $2 per day. This was nearly half the 2001 world population of 6.2 billion. The poor people spend a higher portion of their income on food, so higher food prices hurt them more. If a poor person spends 60% of their money on food and then the food prices double, they will be in trouble. Aid organizations that buy food and send it to poor countries are only able to send half as much food on the same budget if prices doubled. High prices mean more people in need of aid.

The impact is not all negative. Farmers in poor countries that do substantial farming have increased profits due to biofuels. If vegetable oil prices double, the profit margin could more than double. In the past rich countries have been dumping subsidized grains at below cost prices into poor countries and hurting the local farming industries. With biofuels made from grains, the rich countries might run out of stockpile grain surpluses for use in case of emergencies. Farming in poor countries is seeing healthier profit margins and expanding, but this does not seem to be the case with our farmers.

The United States and Brazil lead the industrial world in global ethanol production, with Brazil as the world's largest exporter and biofuel industry leader. In 2006 the U.S. produced 18.4 billion liters, closely followed by Brazil with 16.3 billion liters, producing together 70% of the world's ethanol market and nearly 90% of ethanol used as fuel. These countries are followed by China with 7.5%, and India with 3.7% of the global market share.

This alliance between the U.S. and Brazil generated some negative reactions. While Bush was in São Paulo as part of the 2007 Latin American tour, Venezuela's President Hugo Chavez, from Buenos Aires, dismissed the ethanol plan as "a crazy thing" and accused the U.S. of trying "to substitute the production of foodstuffs for animals and human beings with the production of foodstuffs for vehicles, to sustain the American way of life." Chavez' complaints were quickly followed by then Cuban President Fidel Castro, who wrote that "you will see how many people among the hungry masses of our planet will no longer consume corn." "Or even worse," he continued, "by offering financing to poor countries to produce ethanol from corn or any other kind of food, no tree will be left to defend humanity from climate change." Daniel Ortega, president of Nicaragua and one of the preferential recipients of Brazil technical aid, said that "we reject the gibberish of those who applaud Bush's totally absurd proposal, which attacks the food security rights of Latin Americans and Africans, who are major corn consumers." However, he voiced support for sugar cane based ethanol during Lula's visit to Nicaragua.

As a result of the international community's concerns regarding the steep increase in food prices, on April 14, 2008, Jean Ziegler, the United Nations Special Rapporteur on the Right to Food, at the Thirtieth Regional Conference of FAO in Brasília, called biofuels a "crime against humanity," a claim he had previously made in October 2007, when he called for a 5-year ban for the conversion of land for the production of biofuels. The previous day, at their Annual IMF and World Bank Group meeting at Washington, D.C., the World Bank's President, Robert Zoellick, stated that "While many worry about filling their gas tanks, many others around the world are struggling to fill their stomachs. And it's getting more and more difficult every day."

German Chancellor Angela Merkel said the rise in food prices is due to poor agricultural policies and changing eating habits in developing nations, not biofuels as some critics claim. On the other hand, British Prime Minister Gordon Brown called for international action and said Britain had to be "selective" in supporting biofuels, and depending on the U.K.'s assessment of biofuels' impact on world food prices, "we will also push for change in EU biofuels targets." Stavros Dimas, European Commissioner for the Environment said through a spokeswoman that "there is no question for now of suspending the target fixed for biofuels," though he acknowledged that the EU had underestimated problems caused by biofuels.

On April 29, 2008, U.S. President George W. Bush declared during a press conference that "85% of the world's food prices are caused by weather, increased demand and energy prices," and recognized that "15% has been caused by ethanol." He added that "the high price of gasoline is going to spur more investment in ethanol as an alternative to gasoline. And the truth of the matter is it's in our national interests that our farmers grow energy, as opposed to us purchasing energy from parts of the world that are unstable or may not like us." Regarding the effect of agricultural subsidies on rising food prices, Bush said that "Congress is considering a massive, bloated farm bill that would do little to solve the problem. The bill Congress is now considering would fail to eliminate subsidy payments to multimillionaire farmers," he continued, "this is the right time to reform our nation's farm policies by reducing unnecessary subsidies."

Just a week before this new wave of international controversy began, U.N. Secretary General Ban Ki-moon had commented that several U.N. agencies were conducting a comprehensive review of the policy on biofuels, as the world food price crisis might trigger global instability. He said, "We need to be concerned about the possibility of taking land or replacing arable land because of these biofuels," then he added "While I am very much conscious and aware of these problems, at the same time you need to constantly look at having creative sources of energy, including biofuels. Therefore, at this time, just criticizing biofuel may not be a good solution. I would urge we need to address these issues in a comprehensive manner." Regarding Jean Ziegler's proposal for a five-year ban, the U.N. Secretary rejected that proposal.

A report released by Oxfam in June 2008 criticized biofuel policies of rich countries as neither a solution to the climate crisis nor the oil crisis, while contributing to the food price crisis. The report concluded that from all biofuels available in the market, Brazilian sugarcane ethanol is far from perfect but it is the most favorable biofuel in the world in term of cost and greenhouse gas emission. The report discusses some existing problems and potential risks, and asks the Brazilian government for caution to avoid jeopardizing its environmental and social sustainability. The report also says that: "Rich countries spent up to $15 billion in 2007 supporting biofuels while blocking cheaper Brazilian ethanol, which is far less damaging for global food security."

A World Bank research report published on July 2008 found that from June 2002 to June 2008 "biofuels and the related consequences of low grain stocks, large land use shifts, speculative activity and export bans" pushed prices up by 70 to 75%. The study found that higher oil prices and a weak dollar explain the 25-30% total price rise. The study said that "...large increases in biofuels production in the United States and Europe are the main reason behind the steep rise in global food prices" and also stated that "Brazil's sugar-based ethanol did not push food prices appreciably higher." The Renewable Fuel Association (RFA) published a rebuttal based on the version leaked before its formal release. The RFA critique considers that the analysis is highly subjective and that the author "estimates the impact of global food prices from the weak dollar and the direct and indirect effect of high petroleum prices and attributes everything else to biofuels."

An economic assessment by the OECD also published on July 2008 agrees with the World Bank report regarding the negative effects of subsidies and trade restrictions, but found that the impact of biofuels on food prices are much smaller. The OECD study is also critical of the limited reduction of greenhouse house gas emissions achieved from biofuels produced in Europe and North America, concluding that the current biofuel support policies would reduce greenhouse gas emissions from transport fuel by no more than 0.8% by 2015, while Brazilian ethanol from sugar cane reduces greenhouse gas emissions by at least 80% compared to fossil fuels. The assessment calls on governments for more open markets in biofuels and feedstocks in order to improve efficiency and lower costs. The OECD study concluded that "...current biofuel support measures alone are estimated to increase average wheat prices by about 5%, maize by around 7% and vegetable oil by about 19% over the next 10 years."

The gradual and sometimes abrupt increase in fossil fuels since 2003 due to the disturbances in their supply has prompted many governments to accelerate the use of biofuel in conjunction with fossil fuels in the transport industry. It has also a direct link to the price increase of food and other products. Coupled with the increasing demand for oil and the expected depletion in the future, the price of oil is expected to go up along with the vegetable oil, including those crops that have no relation to biofuels such as rice and fish. Transforming vegetable oil into biodiesel is not difficult or costly such that many farmers have switch to growing vegetable oil crops if those are more profitable than food crops. A World Bank study concluded that oil prices and a weak dollar explain only 25-30% of total price rise between January 2002 and June 2008. The global economic meltdown is only a temporary setback for oil producers. It is no comfort since the price is still considered relatively stiff due to the recession.

In some countries with surplus of grain such as Germany and Canada, it is much cheaper to heat a house by burning grain than by using fuel derived from crude oil. At $120/barrel a savings of a factor of 3 on heating costs is possible. However, this is not a compassionate way discarding excess grain considering that there are many poor and hungry people needing the foodstuff in the developing world.

The U.S. is the largest consumer of oil and also the number one grain producer in the world. Therefore it is necessary for her to act prudently in helping solve the energy crisis. It used 75% of its crude oil that is converted to fuel for motor vehicles. Its large stock of food grains have been converted to biofuel. There are many pros and cons when it comes to resolving the problem between food and energy.

The advantage of biofuel is that it is mostly derived from organic matter and therefore renewable. Another advantage of is that most of them are biodegradability and therefore relatively harmless to the environment. Agricultural products used to produce biofuels include corn, soybeans, cassava, sugarcane, coconut, sweet sorghum, beet sugar, wheat, jatropha, *malunggay*, and possibly others not discovered yet. The important thing to remember is that they should be newly cultivated idle land devoted to biofuel instead of converting land already devoted to other food crops.

Sugar and starch are the main ingredients in making ethanol as biofuel. Any crops or plants that contain a large amount of sugar, starch and even cellulose are great candidates. Sugar beets and sugar cane contain natural sugar and therefore less expensive to turn into ethanol. Crops such as corn, wheat and barley contain starch that can also be converted to sugar. Most trees and grasses are made of cellulose, which can also be converted into sugar, although not as easily as starch. Producing ethanol requires the ethanol feedstock to be ground into for easier processing. Then the sugar is dissolved from the ground material, or the starch or cellulose is converted into sugar. Microbes are introduced to feed on the sugar, producing ethanol with carbon dioxide as byproducts. The ethanol is purified to achieve the correct concentration.

It is also possible to produce ethanol through a wet-milling process, which is used by many large ethanol producers. This process also yields byproducts such as high-fructose corn syrup, which is used as a sweetener in many prepared foods.

According to Goldman Sachs, the cost of producing ethanol from corn is about $81 a barrel of oil equivalent, with wheat at $145, soybeans at $232 and the cheapest is sugar at $35. New technology is needed to open the way for the use of non-edible grain stalks to make ethanol, but for now the only biofuel crop that genuinely pays its way is sugar cane, which at one time is abundantly available in the Philippines. Sugar is carbohydrate and is ideal for fuel. Grains containing proteins made of nitrogen are useless for fuel, but vital for people.[60] A lot of R&D efforts are currently being put into the production of second generation biofuels from non-food crops, crop residues and waste.

---

[60] http://www.globalpolicy.org/socecon/hunger/general/2008/0414rage.htm

Using ethanol has many benefits for the environment. Ethanol-fueled vehicles produce lower carbon monoxide and carbon dioxide emissions, and the same or lower levels of hydrocarbon and oxides of nitrogen emissions. There is no net production of carbon dioxide emitted to the atmosphere because the carbon dioxide was taken from the atmosphere during the production of ethanol. Adding ethanol to gasoline in lower percentages, such as 10% ethanol and 90% gasoline (E10) reduces carbon monoxide emissions from the gasoline and improves fuel octane. As the gasoline crisis continue, ethanol will become widely use and available in the future to motorists and prolonged the availability of gasoline in the market.

As the country move toward using locally produced ethanol, it should bring more support to the impoverished farmers and creates domestic jobs while cutting our dependence on foreign oil. This renewable alternative energy not only reduces our dependence on foreign oil, it could also save us from spending too much foreign currency in buying foreign oil.

Methyl Tertiary Butyl Ether (MTBE)

One of the beneficial uses of ethanol is as an additive to gasoline in place of methyl tertiary butyl ether (MTBE.) According to a document published by the U.S. Department of Energy, MTBE ground water contamination was a significant motivator encouraging U.S. gasoline suppliers to switch to ethanol as a fuel oxidant. By year 2000, MTBE use, as a gasoline additive, had contaminated many of the water wells throughout the U.S. As a result, bans on using MTBE within a number of local jurisdictions followed. There was also concern that widespread and costly litigation might be taken against the U.S. gasoline suppliers. Thus the suppliers agreed to eliminate the use of MTBE by year 2006 by switching to ethanol. The corn growers recognized the potential of this new market and delivered accordingly. This was a significant event contributing to the wide spread use of corn as a fuel additive to gasoline within the U.S. California was one of the first State to ban the gasoline oxygenate additive MTBE after it was detected in ground water. Ethanol, a non-petroleum product usually made from corn, is being used in place of MTBE. Gasoline with ethanol requires changes in the way gasoline is produced and distributed.[61]

---

[61] http://www.eia.doe.gov/bookshelf/brochures/gasolinepricesprimer/

MTBE, is a volatile, flammable and colorless chemical compound. It is immiscible, yet reasonably soluble in water. MTBE has a minty odor vaguely reminiscent of diethyl ether, leading to unpleasant taste and odor in water. MTBE is an important gasoline additive used as oxygenate to raise the octane number, although its use has declined in the United States in response to environmental and health concerns. It has been found to easily pollute large quantities of groundwater when gasoline with MTBE is spilled or leaked at gas stations. MTBE is also used in organic chemistry as a relatively inexpensive solvent with properties comparable to diethyl ether but with a higher boiling point and lower solubility in water. It is also used medically to dissolve gallstones.[62]

MTBE is derived from fossil fuel because it came from the chemical reaction of methanol and isobutylene. Both are derived from natural gas or crude oil. Due to widespread releases of MTBE-containing gasoline from underground storage tanks all over the US, various jurisdictions banned the use of MTBE and production was greatly reduced. MTBE contamination in drinking water aquifers is a serious concern in many states (the most famous cases are Lake Tahoe and Santa Monica). By late 2006, most American gasoline retailers had ceased using MTBE as an oxygenate. MTBE production has also declined in Western Europe. It was not due to environmental concerns but because the alternative ethanol-derived ether ETBE has been given more favorable tax treatment. Nevertheless, in other parts of the world, which account for about a half of 2004 production, the use of MTBE will continue and even grow.

A World Bank policy research working paper released in July 2008 concluded that large increases in biofuels production in the United States and Europe are the main reason behind the steep rise in global food prices. Some commodities like maize, sugar cane or vegetable oil can be used either as food, feed or to make biofuels. Rice prices have gone up by a factor of 3 even though rice is not directly used in biofuels. The prices of rice and corn always go in tandem. Since 2006, land that was also formerly used to grow other crops in the United States is now used to grow maize for biofuels, and a larger share of maize is destined to ethanol production, reaching 25% in 2007. The UN says it takes 232 kg of corn to fill a 50-litre car tank with ethanol. That is enough to feed a child for a year. Something has to be done before more starvation sets in.

---

[62] http://en.wikipedia.org/wiki/MTBE

Corn is abundantly grown in the U.S. and is used to produce ethanol to the tune of nearly two billion gallons a year. Some of this ethanol is blend with gasoline to make gasohol; some is further refined to make gasoline octane boosters, and some is burned, either in pure form or mixed with a small percentage of gasoline in fleets of research and demonstration vehicles.[63]

When corn was used to make ethanol, prices went up by a factor of three in less than 3 years. Reports in 2007 linked stories as diverse as food riots in Mexico due to rising prices of corn for tortillas, and reduced profits at Heineken the large international brewer, to the increasing use of corn (maize) grown in the US Midwest for ethanol production. (In the case of beer, the barley area was cut in order to increase corn production. Barley is not currently used to produce ethanol. Wheat is up by almost a factor of three in 3 years, while soybeans are up by a factor of two in 2 years.

Corn is also commonly used as feed for livestock causing the rise in prices of animal food sources. Vegetable oil is used to make biodiesel and has about doubled in price in the last couple years. The price is roughly tracking crude oil prices. The 2007- 2008 world food price crisis is blamed partly on the increased demand for biofuels.

Another major hurdle is to find the necessary arable land to plant these biofuel crops without offsetting the crops for human consumption. Some skeptics fear that more forests would have to be cut down to make room for these plantations. Some farmers may even shift the selling of their food crops for biofuel purposes should they make more money out of it, thereby worsening our food crisis. One study is the U.S. claimed that replacing 5% to the nation's diesel with biodiesel would require diverting approximately 60% of today's soy crops to biodiesel production. Soy crops have been a good source of plant protein, especially for developing countries.

Another problem that has to be licked is whether producing the biofuel would be more expensive in terms of energy input that can be generated from biofuel. According to Cornell University researcher David Pimentel in his 2005 study, he found that producing ethanol from corn required 29% more energy than the end product itself is capable of generating. He found similarly troubling numbers in making biodiesel from soybeans. "There is just no energy benefit to using plant biomass for liquid fuel," Pimentel says. Others analyzing the problem seem to agree with this assessment.

---

[63] http://bioenergy.ornl.gov/papers/misc/switgrs.html

R.A. 9367, otherwise known as the Biofuels Act of 2006 was signed on January 12, 2007. It was authored by Rep Miguel Zubiri and Sen. Miriam Santiago. It was one of the components of the government's policy of reducing the country's dependence of imported fuel by 60% by 2010. This optimism is not well-founded because only 10% ethanol is mandated by law. The law requires oil companies to use biofuels in all "liquid fuels for motors and engines sold in the Philippines." All gasoline sold in the country must contain at least 5% ethanol by February 2009, and by 2011, the mandated blend can go up to 10%. In fact, this has been reached before the mandated as many gasoline stations are already selling the 10% ethanol blend. The new law is expected to bring a number of benefits to the country. Commercial production of ethanol from sugarcane, cassava or sorghum will help the island nation diversify its fuel portfolio and help to ensure its energy security. It could also generate employment, particularly in rural regions, as investors put up biofuel crop plantations and processing plants. Also, the shift to these plant-based fuels for transportation will help reduce pollution.[64]

Four feedstocks - sugarcane, corn, cassava and sweet sorghum - were initially identified for ethanol production, but sugarcane is expected to be the predominant source of ethanol. The Philippines is a sugar-producing country, and sugarcane is grown mainly in the islands of Negros, Luzon, Panay and Mindanao. Despite growing demand for sugar, there are still an estimated 90,750 hectares of sugarcane available that can be used for ethanol production, and high-yielding varieties of sugarcane are available. Sugar has been branded as one of the worst additives in the world. It has been implicated as the source of many diseases and health problems such as diabetes, tooth decay, etc.

At least 400,000 hectares have been identified by the Department of Agriculture around the country as suitable for investment by the private sectors in the planting of these agricultural products for biofuels. Investors can choose several forms of investment such as straight purchase, lease, contract growing and joint venture. Agriculture Secretary Arthur Yap expects that the growing of biofuel crops will not only be used to energize vehicles but also benefits the small farmers, who accounts for 35% of the labor force and the agricultural industry accounts for 25% of the gross national product.[65]

---

[64] http://en.wikipedia.org/wiki/Ethanol_fuel_in_the_Philippines
[65] http://frankahilario.com/?p=209

With the passage of the law, local manufacturer, Leyte Agri Corp. is producing 800,000 liters annually. Another project under constructed and will be operational by the first quarter of 2009 has a capacity of 30 million liters. There are also 10 projects in the pipeline with a production capacity of 535 million liters. (*PDI*, December 18, 2008) While the law mandated only 5% blend, in July 2008, 10% ethanol blend gasoline was made available in the market. Pilipinas Shell has the Super Unleaded E10 while Petron Corporation introduced 95 Octane E10 Gasoline alongside their Unleaded (93 Octane) and Premium Unleaded (95 Octane) variants. There are currently 273 gasoline stations nationwide selling the ethanol blended gasoline. Pilipinas Shell has also made available biodiesel with 1% coconut methyl ester (CME) on the market since 2006. The country is presently producing biodiesel from eleven accredited manufacturers. In 2007, biodiesel displaced a total of 43 million liters of diesel equivalent to $23.65 million. (Ibid)

US scientists have developed a technology that would turn glycerin, a biodiesel production by-product, into another biofuel which is ethanol. Rice University Assistant Professor Ramon Gonzalez and colleagues identified the metabolic processes and conditions that allow a strain of E. coli to convert glycerin into ethanol. He estimated the operational costs to be 40% cheaper than those of producing ethanol from corn. Gonzalez noted US biodiesel production is at an all-time high. At the same time, the industry faces a significant problem on how to utilize the glycerin as a by-product. One pound of glycerin is produced for every 10 pounds of biodiesel.[66]

Other alternative fuels include biodiesel and P-Series. Biodiesel is an alternative fuel based on vegetable oils or animal fats, even those recycled after restaurants have used them for cooking. Vehicle engines can be converted to burn biodiesel in its pure form, and biodiesel can also be blended with petroleum diesel and used in unmodified engines. Biodiesel is safe, biodegradable, reduces air pollutants associated with vehicle emissions, such as particulate matter, carbon monoxide and hydrocarbons.

P-Series fuels are a blend of ethanol, natural gas liquids and methyltetrahydrofuran (MeTHF), a co-solvent derived from biomass. P-Series fuels are clear, high-octane alternative fuels that can be used

---

[66] http://www.ucap.org.ph/062807.htm

in flexible fuel vehicles. P-Series fuels can be used alone or mixed with gasoline in any ratio by simply adding it to the tank.

The second generation biofuels are now being produced from the cellulose of desiccated energy crops (such as perennial grasses), forestry materials, the co-products from food production, and domestic vegetable waste. Advances in the conversion processes will almost certainly improve the sustainability of biofuels, through better efficiencies and reduced environmental impact of producing biofuels, from both existing food crops and from cellulosic sources. Lord Ron Oxburgh suggests that responsible production of biofuels has several advantages.

Far from creating food shortages, responsible production and distribution of biofuels represents the best opportunity for sustainable economic prospects in Africa, Latin America and impoverished Asia. Biofuels offer the prospect of real market competition and oil price moderation. According to the Wall Street Journal, crude oil would be trading 15 per cent higher and gasoline would be as much as 25 per cent more expensive, were it not for biofuels. A healthy supply of alternative energy sources will help to combat gasoline price spikes.

A few countries with food surpluses and hedge against future food failure can afford to divert some of the crop foods for making ethanol. But the rest of the world may not survive long without self sufficiency in food should disaster struck. The only alternative is to use different feedstock such as non-food crops to produce biofuel. This avoids direct competition for commodities like corn, sorghum, wheat and edible vegetable oil people needed. However, as long as farmers can make more money by switching to biofuels they will do so at the expense of the poor especially those in the developing countries. The law of supply and demand dictates that farmers will try to make more money either from crops for biofuel or for food whichever commands a better price. In the meantime, the poor will be suffering from high prices of both food and energy.

Non-food crops like Camelina and Jatropha, used for biodiesel, can thrive on marginal agricultural land where many trees and crops find it hard to grow. Camelina is virtually 100% efficient in this type of land. It can be harvested and crushed for oil and the remaining parts can be used to produce high quality omega-3 rich animal feed, fiberboard, and glycerin. Camelina does not take away from land currently being utilized for food production. Most camelina farms can be set up in areas previously not utilized for farming. Areas that receive limited rainfall that cannot sustain corn or soybeans without irrigation can grow camelina and add to their profitability. Jatropha, which is indigenous to the Philippines will benefit local communities.

Jatropha is a genus of approximately 175 succulent plants, shrubs and trees (some are deciduous, like Jatropha curcas L.) The hardy *Jatropha* is resistant to drought and pests, and produces seeds containing up to 40% oil. When the seeds are crushed and processed, the resulting oil can be used in a standard diesel engine, while the residue can also be processed into biomass to power electricity plants. Goldman Sachs recently cited *Jatropha curcas* as one of the best candidates for future biodiesel production. However, despite its abundance and use as an oil and reclamation plant, none of the *Jatropha* species have been properly domesticated and, as a result, its productivity is variable, and the long-term impact of its large-scale use on soil quality and the environment is unknown.[67]

The Biofuel Act of 2006 mandated the use of plants in making biodiesel. The *Jatropha curcas* seed is one good candidate. It is also being promoted as an easily grown biofuel crop in hundreds of projects throughout India and other developing countries. The railway line between Mumbai and Delhi is planted with *Jatropha* and the train itself runs on 15-20% biodiesel. In Africa, cultivation of *Jatropha* is being promoted and it is grown successfully in countries such as Mali.

Estimates of *Jatropha* seed yield vary widely due to the genetic diversity of the crops and their yield can range from 1,500 to 2,000 kilograms per hectare, corresponding to extractable oil yields of 540 to 680 liters per hectare. They can also be intercropped with other cash crops such as coffee, sugar, fruits and vegetables, therefore without taking over new land.

Air New Zealand test flight a passenger jet from Auckland International Airport using a 50-50 blend of this fuel with the standard A1 jet fuel in one of the four engines. The two-hour flight on December 31, 2008 was a success. It is an experimental flight in the hope of finding a cheap and environmentally friendly blend to be added to the fossil fuel. Earlier in February, Boeing and Virgin Atlantic carried out similar test flights using a biofuel mixture of palm and coconut oil. Biofuels were once regarded as impractical for aviation because most freeze at low temperatures encountered at cruising altitudes. (*PDI*, December 31, 2008) Continental Airlines also made a successful 1 hour, 45 minutes on a Boeing 737-800 on January 7, 2009 with biofuel derived from algae and jatropha plants in one of

---

[67] http://en.wikipedia.org/wiki/Jatropha

the two engines of the plane and the other half using traditional jet fuel. The biofuel exceeded specifications for regular jet fuel and no modifications to the plane or its engines were needed. (*MB*, January 9, 2009)

It has an even lower freezing point than jet fuel. Biofuel made from jatropha oil and algae are second generation fuel, is also significantly cheaper than crude oil. Other sources of include switch grass and salt-tolerant plants called halophytes. It could also mean less carbon released to the atmosphere, even against ethanol. The Air New Zealand's proposed blend could mean a one-quarter reduction in carbon compared to the standard jet fuel. The cost is an estimated $43 a barrel is way below the current prices of over $100 per barrel of crude oil before the economic meltdown.

Since 2006, the Philippine National Oil Co. (PNOC) has been planning to build a refinery to process jatropha into biodiesel. It is hoping to develop 118,000 hectares of land for planting jatropha to process into about 250,000 tons of biodiesel annually. The refinery would have to come much later after the trees have grown up. A thorough feasibility study is needed to determine if it is competitive and profitable.

An initially experimental in Cabangcalan, Negros Occidential has been planted to three varieties of jatropha to find out which one would give the maximum oil yield. President Arroyo has ordered the allocation of P1 billion from the PNOC and the National Development Corp. (NDC) for the development of jatropha into biodiesel.[68] In many parts of rural India and Africa, about 200,000 people now find employment through jatropha planting. Moreover, villagers often find that they can grow other crops in the shade of the trees. Their communities will avoid importing expensive diesel and there will be some for export too.

Cellulosic ethanol is a type of biofuel produced from lignocellulose, a material that comprises much of the mass of plants. Corn stover, switchgrass, miscanthus and woodchip are some of the more popular non-edible cellulosic materials for ethanol production. Commercial investment in such second-generation biofuels began in 2006/2007, and much of this investment going beyond pilot-scale plants. Cellulosic ethanol commercialization is moving forward rapidly. The world's first commercial wood-to-ethanol plant began operation in

---

[68] http://philippineenergynews.blogspot.com/2006/06/pnoc-mulls-construction-of-jathropa.html

Japan in 2007, with a capacity of 1.4 million liters/year. The first wood-to-ethanol plant in the United States is planned for 2008 with an initial output of 75 million liters/year.

Other second generation biofuels may be commercialized in the future and compete less with food. Synthetic fuel can be made from coal or biomass and may be commercialized soon. Switchgrass, a tall, native grass of the American prairie once fed millions of bison is making a comeback. It is a big and tough and can grow up to ten feet high with stems as strong as hardwood with plenty of cellulose that can be liquefied, gasified or burned directly. It is also reaches deep into the soil for water and used it very efficiently. Switchgrass is undergoing experiments at the Auburn University and 18 other research sites in Eastern and Central United States to improve its yields. So far there is an average of five-year yields of 11.5 tons, enough to make 1,150 gallons of ethanol per acre per year.[69]

Switchgrass is already being grown by farmers as forage for livestock and as control for erosion. Cultivating switchgrass as an energy crop would require only minor changes. Advances in technology of gastification could allow switchgrass to yield a variety of useful fuels such as synthetic gasoline and diesel fuel, methanol, methane gas, and even hydrogen as well as chemical by-products useful for making fertilizers, solvents, and plastics. It has also the added feature of removing more carbon dioxide as it grows and harvested because some of carbon are retained in the roots and soil, and recycling the carbon dioxide when it is used as alternative fuel. It also takes about 10 years for replanting. Besides, making ethanol from switchgrass can produce about five times more energy than putting it in unlike corn which requires almost as much energy to produce as it yields. With other factors considered such as energy required to make tractors, transport farm equipment, plant and harvest, etc., the net energy output of switchgrass is about 20 times better than corn.

Biofuels can also be produced from the waste byproducts of food-based agriculture (such as citrus peels or used vegetable oil) to manufacture an environmentally sustainable fuel supply, and reduce waste disposal cost. Collocation of a waste generator with a waste-to-ethanol plant can reduce the waste producer's operating cost, while creating a more-profitable ethanol production business. This innovative collocation concept is sometimes called holistic systems engineering. Collocation disposal elimination may be one of the few cost-effective, environmentally-sound, biofuel strategies, but its

---

[69] http://bioenergy.ornl.gov/papers/misc/switgrs.html

scalability is limited by availability of appropriate waste generation sources. For example, millions of tons of wet Florida-and-California citrus peels cannot supply billions of gallons of biofuels. Due to the higher cost of transporting ethanol, it is a local partial solution, at best.

Third generation biofuels coming from algae could use much less land and freshwater and does not compete for farmland with food production. One of the pioneers in this field is Algenol. Algae are microscopic plant-like organisms that feed off sunlight and carbon dioxide. The experiment had the algae growing in tubs fitted with plastic windows to let sunlight in. on a bigger scale, algae can be grown anywhere warm and sunny and can even thrive in saline water rather than precious fresh water. Most algae firms harvest the organisms and squeeze them to extract oil that is processed into fuel. At Algenol, the oil is sweat out into a gaseous form that can be condensed into a liquid. Their system can yield 6,000 gallons (22,700 liters) of ethanol per acre annually compared to 370 gallons per acre for corn ethanol. (TIME, January 26, 2009)

Oil, gas, and other mineral resources are running scarce and more expensive. It is fuelling a new cold war as the economic superpowers are moving aggressively to secure their sources and creating new economic alliances over the dwindling natural resources found around the world.

Oil, by far the most important natural resources needed by the world is the engine that drives the modern civilization and is constantly under threat. In Nigeria, the sub-Saharan country is the largest oil producer there and its pipelines are being targeted by rebels. Every time a pipeline is disrupted, the price of oil and gas go up which partly trigger the oil price crisis. The rebels have been fighting government troops for years for a bigger share in the petrodollars generated from the oil fields. They even went further by demanding secession for a homeland, demanding billions of dollars from multinationals such as Shell and Agip, the Italian oil company operating in the country.[70]

Natural resources such as natural gas have the potential of becoming a weapon for heating during the winter months. This is what happened to Europe caused by the row over the pipelines running through Ukraine. The experiences of Georgia in 2006 and Ukraine in 2003 and 2009 over prices and alleged pilferages can damage a

---

[70] http://www.spiegel.de/international/0,1518,394403,00.html

country. When two pipelines supplying oil to Georgia and Germany were shut down allegedly by Muslim rebels, according to Russian President Vladimir Putin, the country suffer cold for a week forcing many households to burn their own furniture to stay warm. Georgia, on the other hand, charged Russia for instigating the bombing to teach the West just how dependent they are on Russia for their energy needs.

When Russia shut off the flow of natural gas to one of its satellite, the Ukraine over pricing, it sent a shock wave throughout Western Europe, especially Germany that imported 40% of its natural gas from Russia. She also imports 10 times more oil from Russia than from Saudi Arabia and 60% of her coal. Although the deal was resolved to the satisfaction of both countries, Russia made it known that she is willing to use her dominance in petroleum products as a weapon.

All major states have long realized the importance of oil and natural gas to their country especially after the 1973 Yom Kippur War when the Arab countries embargoed oil to the United States and shoot up oil prices by fivefold. It was followed up by the Iranian revolution of 1979 when Ayatollah Khomeini's took over Iran followed a year later with the Iran-Iraq war from 1980 to 1988. The world knows that petroleum and natural gas products are the driving force behind the coming conflicts. This is why the world's powerful nations are staking their claims wherever vital reserves of resources can be found through aggressive diplomacy.[71] However, the use of arms can never be discounted, especially by the superpowers.

New stages of possible conflicts are coming into play with many new discoveries of petroleum products around the world. Discoveries in West Africa, Sudan, Venezuela or the region surrounding the Caspian Sea are some examples. Not all of the rulers of these places are run by well meaning leaders or dictators. In Azerbaijan, the corrupt 44-year-old ruler Ilam Aliyev demonstrated his brutality by putting down demonstrations against the construction of a $3.6 billion pipelines from Azerbaijan through Georgia to the Turkish port of Ceyhan. It was inaugurated with plenty of pomp and circumstance and in the presence of the US Secretary of Energy in May 2005. For political reasons, the great pipeline is one of Washington's pet projects to reduce the West dependence of natural gas from Iran and Russia.

In Turkmenistan, another country rich in resources is ruled by a bizarre 65-uear old dictator, Saparmurad Niyazov, is being wooed by Americans, Europeans, Chinese and Russians. He is cultivating a

---

[71] http://www.spiegel.de/international/spiegel/0,1518,429968-2,00.html

bizarre cult of personality that could even make North Korea's notoriously self-obsessed Kim Jong Il envious. He has ordered the erection of golden monuments bearing his likeness all over the country. His writings are taught in school and his people are even quizzed on those writing when they take a driving test.

Where there is money, there is sure to be some adventurers willing to risk their lives to enrich themselves. In the West African state of Equatorial Guinea, a country rich in natural resources, a strange group of mercenaries from the former South African elite soldiers consisting of Armenian warriors and even a few Britons, one of which the son of former British prime minister, Mark Thatcher was involved in the plot to overthrow the government in March 2004. The coup failed and the corrupt President Theodoro Obiang continues to hold office and steal the coffer of the national government to the tune of an estimated $500 million, according to the *Los Angeles Times*. Dictators stealing from the coffers of the nation are such common phenomena that often lead to the impoverishment of the people. This would accounts for why many nations once under dictatorship cannot rise from the yoke of poverty and backwardness.

The U.S. is the largest consumer of oil in the world, accounting for about 26% or 19.5 million barrels of oil a day. On the other hand, it possesses only 2% of the world's oil reserves and has to imports 9.8 million barrels of oil a day to fill the gap. The importation is expected to increase in the coming years to 17 million barrels a day or 2/3 of daily oil consumption by 2020. This could be one of the reasons why the U.S. invaded Iraq, not just to topple the dictator Saddam Hussein, but to secure the oil supply of the second largest oil reserves in the world. The U.S. refused to acknowledge the reason but British Foreign Secretary Jack Straw acknowledged in a recent speech to British ambassadors that oil is the main motivation for Blair's support for Bush's war, much more so than any threat of weapons of mass destruction.[72]

Housing Shortages

Shelter is an important element in sustaining life. The only reason some people survive in overcrowded urban centers is their willingness to live in dilapidated houses or squatting in squalor houses on government and private lands and even sidewalks. Others are forced to

---

[72] http://www.progress.org/2003/greenp19.htm

live alongside dangerous places such as riverbanks, railways and esteros. Still others have no shelter and sleep anywhere even in and around dumpsites.

According to government statistics for Metro Manila, there are approximately 14,132 families living alongside canals; 11,340 along road rights of way or sidewalks, 67,949 along waterways; 14,072 along transmission lines, 2,821 near airports; and about 16,506 spread in areas of priority development, dumpsites, sewerage systems and market places. (*PS*, December 28, 2008) Collectively, they account for about half a million squatters, which is a very conservative estimates because there are many more squatting on private and public lands that are not of immediate concern to the authority.

One sign of overpopulation is the dwindling supply of large tract of residential lots in the metropolitan areas. Many have been subdivided or used for mass housing projects. Even the sizes of new homes are getting smaller because of the high cost. To accommodate the rising population, high rise buildings are being built to house the higher echelon of society while low cost houses are being built for the poorer sector of society. This only hides the fact that the cities are suffering from overpopulation. Most economical houses are small and highly congested and unsuited for a decent life even for the poor.

The cost of owning a decent home has become exorbitant because of the overpopulated population. With more than three million squatters in Metro Manila, there would not be enough land to give them a decent plot. Even plans to give them low cost housing will never be enough to settle the issue as long as the population kept on increasing. If we were able to give a family of four a home of 30 m^2 each, we still need an equivalent of half a million homes annually (90 million x 2.36%/4) just to house the new generation annually. This is on top of the millions of housing backlog. Even the government plan for economic housing with an area of 18 m^2 and long term payment and tax-free property taxes is not adequate for a family of four. They would only be living in overcrowded unit that is not conducive to improving their livelihood. More need to be done for them, but land is in short supply.

While the middle classes used to be able to own a small plot of land to build a home, today, they can only manage to buy a condo or townhouse under long term repayment schemes where they are being ripped off by most of the developers. Whereas before, it is cheaper to buy a lot and build on their own, today, the cost of owning a lot is so exorbitant, buyers have to buy overpriced homes from developers who more often sell these units several times the prevailing cost, partly due to large taxes imposed by government. A normal house and lot of 100 m² would cost less than half a million, but when developed into condo or townhouses, it would cost several times more because of excessive profits and taxes. In fact, buying from a developer would cost an additional 12% VAT, 20% more net profit (net because all the expenses are passed on to the buyers) for the developer, transfer tax, stamp tax, and documentary tax. The three latter taxes and the VAT would amount to an additional 20% for the buyers compared to one build by the homeowners themselves. In most instances the buyers are also cheated on the materials and labors by some unscrupulous contractors/developers which could easily adds up the cost of the house by half. It would not be surprising to find developers conniving with contractors to cheat on the buyers with cheap materials. They often advertised their finishes with imported fixtures which often turn out to be cheaper than the local ones.

There is at present a housing backlog of more than four million houses and the needed financing to construct all these units. At 150,000 per unit for low cost housing, we need P600 billion to build the needed homes just to accommodate the old backlog. With the population growing at nearly two million annually, there will be another shortfall of roughly 500,000 units for a family of four, also annually. That is an additional of at least P75 billion annually. The actual outlay could be several times more expensive since not everyone will be willing to live in low cost housing that is not conducive to health. There is no way we can solve the housing shortage as long as the runaway population is not kept in check as long as the runaway population is not kept in check.

Like all the other shortages, there is a need to act drastically to reduce the population to manageable level by first attaining zero population growth (ZPG) and then reducing the population to save important natural resources for future generation. The rich have to cut down their consumption of the earth natural resources while the poor should cut down their birth rate.

Another problem with the housing shortage is that even with long-term payments, many still find it hard to complete the amortization. This is the main cause of the financial problem facing the world when many subprime borrowers cannot keep up with the mortgage payments. Others find the housing projects located in far flung places where there is little employment or their employment is way off, forcing them to rent units near their work area during the working days.

Unemployment and Underemployment

Many of the ills of the country have been caused by poverty, easy money and greed. Unemployment, underemployment and low wages are some of the prime causes of poverty in the country. Many are so desperate about economic situation in the country that they willing travel abroad for greener pasture in jobs such as domestic helpers, seamen, caregivers, carpenters, etc. Others less fortunate end up as entertainers, prostitutes or worse drug traffickers or couriers. These couriers, called drug mules, sometimes allowed their bodies to be used as reservoirs for swallowed drugs stored in condoms. At their destination, they are given laxatives to retrieve them from their bowels. As much as two kilos can be smuggled across borders.[73] There are those who resorted to heinous criminal activities such as kidnapping for ransom and bank robbery. Some of these criminals are so desperate they will kill without fear or remorse. This is abetted by the revocation of the death penalty law.

Greed and easy money also play an important in some people who are already well-to-do and wanted more. Kidnappers and bank robbers prefer to do their short dirty works to enrich themselves. Drug traffickers can find easy money preying on drug addicts who cannot survive without the drugs for long. A spate of crimes and the controversial case of the "Alabang Boys" where three kids from Alabang were caught selling prohibited drugs by the Philippine Drug Enforcement Agency (PDEA) and the move to release them from custody by prosecutors from the Department of Justice with an allegation of P50 million bribery has infuriated some lawmakers into filing more bills reviving the capital punishment in the wake of increasing heinous crimes in the country. So far, there are two bills in the House of Representative filed by Rep. Rozzano Rufino Biazon of Muntinlupa and Manila Rep. Bienvenido Abante while in the Senate, Majority Floor Leader Juan Miguel Zubiri had filed a similar bill. (*PDI*, January 13, 2009)

The death penalty law is necessary to deter and punish those convicted of the most heinous, violent crimes who have demonstrated their absolute disregard for human life, killing without remorse or hesitation. No society should ask its citizens to risk allowing such criminals to wreak havoc again. Premeditated murder, guns for hire, mass murders, kidnapping with rape or torture or resulting in death should fall under the category of heinous crimes. The law should also

---

[73] http://www.news24.com/News24/Archive/0,,2-1659_1226116,00.html

be applied consistently to prove that society is intolerant for these kinds of crimes. Our criminal justice system is designed around the common sense notion that the more certain the punishment, the less likely the crime; the more severe the crime, the greater the retribution. The death penalty serves both these goals. As one study estimated that each execution in the U.S. deters approximately eighteen murders. Police files and convict's own statements indicated that their decisions to use toy guns during felonies rather than real firearms, and not to kill hostages, were motivated by fear of the death penalty. (LaPierre, 149)

There is no room for leniency when it comes to protecting innocent human lives. Part of the reasons for revoking the law was as a gesture to the Catholic Church, especially Pope John Paul II who was very vocal against the death penalty. But throughout history, the Catholic Church was the prime motivator of the death penalty coupled with torture to force confessions out of their victims. Victims, especially of a different faith have been tortured and dismembered simply for being disrespectful to the Church. The great philosopher Voltaire fought hard against the intolerance of the Catholic Church once wrote to the King of Prussia, Frederick the Great after witnessing victims being tortured by the Church that he wish he had not been born. He could not stomach how supposedly God-fearing Christian Church with a loving God could be so cruel to other God's creatures. Probably God is not as loving as He portrays himself to be after creating people in His image and am ready to send them to hell for sinning and refusing to repent, especially when they are predestined before the creation of the world to go to hell.

Probably the main reason why the Catholic Church is against the death penalty law is because criminally-minded Catholics have little regard for human lives. Of the government which made available homicide data for the 1990 *Demographic Yearbook* published by the United Nations, Columbia had the highest murder and non-negligent homicide rate in the world – forty-nine per 100,000 population each year. Next came El Salvador with forty, then Mexico with twenty. The U.S. came seventh with nine such homicides per 100,000 people. The high crime rates may be due to the drug war in Columbia and the civil war in El Salvador, but that is not the case with Mexico. (LaPierre, 172) An updated 1996 *Demographic Yearbook* had Columbia with 80.0 homicides per 100,000 population, El Salvador, 27.4, Mexico 17.2, U.S. 9.4 and the Philippines with 11.5.[74] The Philippines has the distinction of having the most murders in 2004 with 3,515 victims,

---

[74] www.hacientdapub.com/stolinsky.html

according to the United Nations and quoted in the Guinness World Records 2009. Senator Richard Gordon was lamenting this fact and other headline news that are tarnishing the country's image such as one of the most corrupt countries in the world and the second most dangerous place for journalists, after war-torn Iraq. (PS, January 25, 2009) The daily news of innocent people senselessly getting killed in this country seems to numb the senses that many feel it as a way of life.

Unless an employee is fully compensated with more than just the mandated minimum wage, there is little likelihood for improving their standard of living. There is also the problem of too few jobs available for too many jobseekers. This allows the businessmen to stifle the salary for the jobseekers. The numbers of unemployed stood at about 3 million and growing while an even greater number are underemployed. [(The official preliminary figures from the National Statistics Office (NSO) claimed that the number of unemployed person in October 2008 stood at 2.55 million or 160,000 less than the previous year. (*PS*, December 17, 2008) These figures are disputable because of the economic downturn and retrenchment abroad that is expected to hit our OFWs and the annually increase in labor force entering the market.] The surging underemployment problem has been deteriorating since April 2005. Total underemployment went up from 9% in 2004 to 12% in 2005 and 14% in the first half of 2006.[75] With the current global financial crisis, more unemployment and underemployment can be expected.

In particular, visible underemployment, the proportion of part-time workers wanting additional work hours, has hit a 20-year high. One reason for the underemployment is that there are too many jobseekers forcing management to undercut the number of working hours just to accommodate more workers. There are also those employed part-time because their parents cannot afford to finance their studies forcing them to seek work while studying. The following article is reprinted with permission from the August 2, 2008 issue of *Bulatlat* and written by Marya Salamat of Labor Watch

Low Wages Show the Sorry State of the Nation

---

[75] http://www.malaya.com.ph/dec23/news5.htm

If there is one thing that draws intense reactions from both employers and workers, it is a wage hike. Every time the regional wage boards releases its decisions regarding a wage hike, employers and workers would cry out loudly in bitter complaint, but for opposing reasons. "We'll likely lose (our profits)," cry the employers. The labor organizations, meanwhile, would cry out in disgust, "a pittance!" or, an "insult!"

But considering that the Department of Labor and Employment (DOLE) itself is admitting that the minimum wage is only half of the "living wage", the workers' disgust at the amount of wage hikes emanating from the wage boards is patently more understandable. A pittance won't do when large companies such as San Miguel Corporation are reporting a 200% jump in profits this early in 2008.

In an era of double-digit inflation and weekly oil price increases, a yearly wage increase of measly amounts (that cannot even buy a kilo of NFA rice) will simply never do, said KMU (Kilusang Mayo Uno or May 1st Movement). Year on year, the minimum wage rate hardly creeps near to touching distance with living wage levels.

Worse, according to Elmer Labog, chairman of KMU, data from the DOLE itself show that from the late eighties up to now, the real value of Filipino workers' wage levels has been dropping precipitously and consistently. This, Labog explained, has prompted the KMU to reject the regional wage boards for being "inutile." But of course Labog is representing a labor organization. The regional wage boards' almost two-decade record of handing out paltry wage hikes despite runaway prices of goods and increased profit-taking by companies will likely be evaluated differently by employers.

Wage rationalization: lowering what's already low, limiting what's already limited

Exactly how many employed workers have benefited from the fourteen wage orders granted by the Regional Tripartite Wages and Productivity Board over the years? The answer is as hard to determine as substantial wage hikes are hard to wrestle from the wage boards. But what is certain is that not all employees get to enjoy it in the end.

According to Attorney Remigio Saladero, lawyer from PLACE (Pro-Labor Assistance Center) and columnist of *Pinoy Weekly*, wage orders come down to expectant workers peppered with exemptions and loopholes. From his discussion of labor laws and regulations pertaining to wages, the paltry amounts of wage hikes being granted by regional wage boards is just one of the many problems barring ordinary workers from catching a trickle of the wage hikes.

First, most increases granted by wage boards benefit only minimum wage earners. This shuts out employees who are getting above minimum wage rates, even if they're in establishments that are most likely in a position to grant wage increases, and even if they're also in dire need of wage adjustments. The excuse given by DOLE (and the wage boards) is that unions can demand for increases via collective bargaining agreements (CBA). But only about 10% of the employed are unionized, said Elmer Labog, and of this, not all have managed to hammer out a good CBA with their employers. Intensified trade union repression plays a huge role in pushing back the number of organized and cutting back the organized workers' gains, but that's for another story.

According to Saladero, another reason that can explain why wage rates fail to take off meaningfully with wage orders is that there are numerous low minimum wage levels in the country. This means that the minimum you think of as the definitive lowest of all wages is actually being lowered further to another minimum level in different settings (say, regions or even municipalities) or in different job types (agricultural or non-agricultural).

Now, considering that the wage orders have shut out the non-minimum wage earners (who usually come from large, profitable companies), how do lower paid workers fare? Employers used to cry their hearts out for the small and medium establishments (SMEs) every time a wage hike is demanded.

In 2002, the Philippine government decided to forgo altogether the minimum wage law compliance among selected establishments, namely the SMEs. They exempted the establishments registered as barangay micro-businesses (BMBEs) from complying with the minimum wage law, thus allowing for the further free-fall of what's supposed to be already the minimum. Furthermore, the DOLE issued an order stating that if wage boards decide on a wage hike for SMEs, those registered as BMBE's will not be obliged to implement it.

What constitute the BMBEs and SMEs? Reports said they comprise 99% of the registered establishments in the Philippines. Some of them may indeed be legitimate Filipino small businesses that rightly need incentives, but unfortunately some are not. The National Federation of

Labor Unions or NAFLU-KMU for instance had encountered an export-oriented enterprise in Rizal that is not paying its 300 employees the mandated minimum wages. They filed a case in behalf of the workers but lost because the enterprise was registered as a BMBE. How this exporting enterprise with a 300-strong workforce was able to register as a BMBE speaks a lot about how companies are able to circumvent labor and wage laws.

Militant labor unions whose members frequently receive higher than minimum wages (as a result of past collective actions and because their employers can easily afford it) usually press their employers to apply the increases granted by wage boards to their salaries. At times, it also means bargaining with their employers as the latter slice the paltry amount further to avoid wage distortions. (Wage distortion happens when a relatively new employee who is receiving the minimum wage suddenly gets an equivalent or even higher wage rate compared to co-employees who have been with the company for a longer period when wage increases granted by wage boards or through legislation is applied.)

Thus, for the paltry wage orders to take effect on non-minimum wage earners, workers have to fight for it first. Unorganized workers such as the increasing number of contractual workers, agency-hired and other flexibly hired workers are at a disadvantage. Either they depend on their employers' "social responsibility," or risk their jobs by collectively demanding for the wage order's implementation on them.

The simplest way to give workers some kind of relief from years of eroded wages and rising prices is to legislate a nationwide, across-the-board P125 ($2.826 at an exchange rate of $1-P44.23) wage increase, said Elmer Labog. This will cover everybody, he explained, and would not result in wage distortions.

But for a nationwide wage hike to be legislated, Labog says, hundreds of thousands of workers and employees from all unions regardless of affiliation should take part in campaigning for it. "Obviously, wage rationalization exists not for the workers' benefit but for the employers. If we want to junk the regional wage boards once and for all and to compel the Arroyo administration to see the obvious that a substantial wage hike offers a slightly better relief than band-aid dole-outs, then we have to work together," said Labog. He enjoins all employees to join or form Unions for P125 in their respective towns and barangays.

There must be over ten million Filipinos working overseas with some eight millions considered non-professional oversea foreign workers and need to be registered. Of these, 1.62 millions are irregular migrants who are unlicensed or victims of trafficking or smuggling, according to Senator Loren Legarda. (*PDI*, December 14, 2008). The professionals need not undergo strict government regulation. Those who do face a lot of problems that could greatly reduce their take home pay. The following article written by Angie de Lara is reprinted with permission from the August 2, 2008 newsmagazine *Bulatlat*

Windfall Earnings for Minimal Services: As government bleeds OFWs dry

The Arroyo government fleeces them of their savings before they could work abroad. From the 76 documents required of them, OFWs are charged P17,665 ($399) each, netting for the government around P2.92 billion ($66,018,539) a year. While working abroad, the government charges them for documentary stamps 15% for every remittance transaction. Thus, with the $14.45 billion in remittances coursed through the banking system last year, the government earned $2.1675 billion. Remittances of OFWs prop up the dollar reserves of the country, and are being used as guarantee for loans by the government. But what kind of service do OFWs get in return?

Overseas Filipino workers (OFWs) are being dried out before they can start to work abroad. According to Migrante International, 76 signatures are needed for 76 documents before they can get their passport. These include Community Tax Certificate (CTC), barangay clearance, birth certificate, National Bureau of Investigation and police Clearance, among others. Each document cost from P50 to P100 ($1.13 to $2.26 at an exchange rate of $1=P44.23) or more. An OFW shells out around P17,665 ($399 at an exchange rate of $1=P44.23) in government fees alone before being able to leave for abroad. The following table shows the breakdown.

76 Signatures (100.00/signature (CTC, Brgy. Clearance, Baptismal Cert. NBI & Police Clearance Etc.)	Ps. 7,600.00
Passport	550.00
POEA Fee (Equivalent to 1 month salary)	7,500.00

OWWA Fees	1,115.00
(US$25 per contract/Ps44.60)	
Medicare (Annual charges)	900.00
Total	Ps. 17,665.00
P17,665.00 x 3,400 OFWs = P60,061,000 daily revenues x 365 days =	
P 21.92 billion per year	
Source: Migrante International	

Migrante International said that 3,400 Filipinos are leaving the country every day to work abroad. From these OFWs, the government earns more than P60 million ($1,356,545) a day or P2.92 billion ($66,018,539) per year. Filipinos hoping to work abroad will also have to pay additional charges for recruitment agencies.

Profit from remittances

The Philippine government also charges a 15% documentary stamp tax from every remittance transaction of OFWs. With the unprecedented oil price hikes and increases in prices of basic commodities, there has been a surge in OFW remittances. OFW remittances reached US$6.8 billion from January 2008 to May 2008. It is projected to surpass last year's total remittances of US$14.45 billion to US15.65 billion this year.

John Leonard Monterona of Migrante Middle East said that the Arroyo administration, the banks, money transfer and telecommunications companies are earning a lot out of OFW remittances due to the fees they collect from transactions. "The total yearly remittance is bread-and-butter for the Arroyo administration," he said.

Banks	Remittance Charge	Service Fee
Philippine National Bank	US$15 for every US$500 and below	US$7
MetroBank	US$20 for every US$3,000 and below	US$8
Bank of the Philippine	US$20 for every US$2,000	US$8

Islands	and below	
Allied Bank	US$3.50 – US$5	P30 – P55

Source: BSP

Data from the Bangko Sentral ng Pilipinas (BSP) show that overseas Filipinos remitted $14.45 billion through the banking system last year. "That amounts to more than US$30 million in remittances daily," said Monterona. In documentary stamps alone, this amounts to $2.1675 billion collected by the Arroyo government.

Year	Annual remittances: coursed through banks
1984	US$659 million
1989	US$973 million
1994	US$2.9 billion
1999	US$6.97 billion
2002	US$6.9 billion
2003	US$7.6 billion
2004	US$8.6 billion
2005	US$10.7 billion
2006	US$12.8 billion
2007	US$14.4 billion
2008(Jan-May)	US$6.8 billion

Source: Central Bank

Monterona added that in 2006, OFW remittances are more than double the total allotment for the government's external debt service, five times more than foreign direct investments (FDI), 22 times higher than the total Overseas Development Aid (ODA) and even more than half of the gross international reserves. He said that like previous administrations, the Arroyo regime is making OFW remittances a guarantee for more loans from international banks and financial institutions. Migrante International said that despite the revenues earned by the Philippine government from the sweat of OFWs, Filipino workers remain neglected.

Death row, deportees

There are 34 OFWs on death row, including six women, largely in the Middle East. Migrante said that their cases differ from one another but they are all Filipinos who are forced to work abroad to give a better life to their loved ones only to end up with shattered dreams. According to Migrante International, five OFWs have already been executed in Saudi Arabia since 2001. They are Antonio Alvesa, Sergio Aldana, Miguel Fernandez, Wilfredo Bautista and Reynaldo Cortez. Had the migrants rights advocacy groups not intervened, Marilou Ranario from Kuwait could have been dead by now. Moreover, the crackdown on OFWs continues.

Data from the Department of Social Welfare and Development revealed that from 2001, there were 10,000 Filipinos deported from Sabah, Malaysia. However, Migrante said that for this year alone, there were 450,000 deportees from Malaysia.

As new laws on migration are being implemented in many countries, especially the European Union, Migrante International fears that the human rights of migrants will be violated.

Connie Bragas-Regalado, chairperson of Migrante International, said that the Arroyo government has been a model for other countries when it comes to labor export management. She said though that for OFWs, this means a systematic exploitation and outright neglect. (End of Article)

One of the saddest repercussions of unemployment is the proliferation of prostitution, child labor and child prostitution. In 1999, the Coalition Against Trafficking in Women reported that there were about 300,000 to half a million prostitutes in the country, and the estimated number of prostituted children, numbered about 100,000. We have become the 4th largest source of trafficked women and children in the world.[76] Their numbers may have increased after all these years. The main reasons behind the proliferation of prostitutes are the exploding population coupled with unemployment, underemployment and poverty. There are those who would prefer to work as prostitutes because of easy money to be made. Most of them came are poor, uneducated, sexually molested by the father or relatives, neglected, abandoned with by husband or boyfriend after impregnated and those forced to work because the family expected

---

[76] http://www.ncrfw.gov.ph/inside_pages/legislative_advocacy/anti_prostitution_bill.html

them to care for them. The underemployed try to augment their income by part-time prostitution. Some have been deceptively trafficked into prostitution because of their desperate situation or allowed to become one through their boyfriend who willingly sell them for money. The sad thing is that many of these girls are uneducated and may easily fall prey to sexually transmitted diseases (STDs).

News of abuses of our women folks working abroad is so common, we have become inure to them. If the fates of these women who are legally exported to work, what do you think will happen to those who were trafficked? Some of their fates may never be known. But domestic trafficking of women is even worst. Many women have been forced into slavery and prostitution. Some have suffered from unwanted pregnancies, psychological and physical abuses by their predators under subhuman working conditions. Sometimes the girls are forced to take daily bathe with bleaches to whiten their skin before they are sold to brothels.

The hard and difficult lives of people in other parts of the country, especially in the Visayas and Mindanao have forced many to migrate to the metropolitan areas such as Metro Manila and Metro Cebu. Most of them end up as victims of human trafficking. They are usually 15 to 19 years old or younger. The younger are prime choice of traffic recruiters because they are more docile, easy to intimidate and manipulate. Civil disturbances in Mindanao between the Muslims and Christians have forced many to seek shelter elsewhere. It is in times of difficulties and crisis that human trafficking proliferates. Predators are on hand and ready to prey on them when opportunity arises.

The country is basically an agricultural country with more than 30% of the work force employed in the industry. Most of the farmers cannot afford to hire outsiders to work in the field used their own children as child workers. There are more than four million child workers in the country. Some 20% of them work away from home and have almost no contact with their families. Away from home with no money, they easily fall prey to illegal traffickers. Their desire to earn money for themselves and help their parents and siblings back home often motivated them to look and high-paying jobs only to fall victims to human traffickers who promised them anything. They often end up as prostitutes or entertainers in foreign countries. With too many children and women out of work, the chances of pursuing these routes of least resistance to a better life of wealth and glamour may just be what the traffickers needed to entice so many into prostitution. For those interested on the subject, I have devoted two whole chapters on child labor and child prostitution in my book *Child Abuse*.

The following article is reprinted with the permission of *Bulatlat* magazine:[77]

SPECIAL REPORT
"Scavenging by Day, Prostitution by Night" (Concluding Part)

Gone were the days when vendors and porters of the Port of Batangas could give a decent life to their family and send their children to college. Losing their main source of livelihood after being ejected from their homes because of the privatization of the Port, they turned to sex trade to earn a living - making this a "family business."

BY DABET CASTAÑEDA

BATANGAS CITY - Prostitution, known to be the world's oldest profession, is new to the people who once lived along the shores of the old Batangas Port in this city, some 111 kms. south of Manila.
Amanda (note her real name), 48, a *mamasan* (pimp) born and raised in Barangay Sta. Clara, a village just beside the old Port of Batangas (part of this village has been turned into the port's expansion area completed in 1999). Her parents were port vendors, she said, and life near the port then was strenuous yet profitable. "*Dati, basta mauido ka, kikita ka*" (Before, if you were aggressive in thinking of things to sell, you would earn.), she recalls.
    As a teenager, Amanda helped her parents earn a living by selling pork barbecue after school. This was her family's source of income when she started to raise a family of her own. She said she used to earn at least P400 ($8.28 at today's exchange rate of $1=P48.305) a day then.

Following then President Corazon Aquino's Executive Order No. 431, a part of Barangay Sta. Clara was demolished on June 27, 1994 to give way to the expansion, modernization and privatization of the Batangas Port.
    The Philippine Ports Authority (PPA) opened two relocation centers: Barangay Balete (about seven kilometers from the Batangas

---

[77] http://www.bulatlat.com/news/7-2/7-2-port2_printer.html

Port) and Barangay Sico (about 15 kilometers from the Batangas Port). A study made by Dr. Emma Porio for the JBIC (Japan Bank for International Cooperation) in 2000, "Demolition and Resettlement of Sta. Clara Residents: Policy, Politics, and Personalities in the Batangas Port Development Project," revealed that Balete had an unemployment rate of 53% while Sico had 43%.

Amanda's family was one of 192 families relocated in Sico, a vast and hilly relocation center near a dump, overlooking the Batangas city jail. A trip to this area takes at least an hour from the port. There are no factories or commercial centers in the area. The row houses looked dilapidated and dim. It was deafeningly quiet when Bulatlat visited the area on Jan. 18.

Dark days

Resettling at Sico spelled doom for Amanda's family. With no jobs available, Amanda said, her family set up a small convenience store. In a year's time, their small business went bankrupt because of unpaid debts from neighbors and relatives.

With no other means of income, Amanda started trading girls for sex. "*Bumaba uli ako sa pier. Dun ako humawak ng mga babae,*" (I went back to the pier and peddled prostitutes.), she said.

She said she gets a cut of P50 ($1.035) from a girl who, in turn, gets P300 to P500 ($6.21 to $10.35) for every (trick). When the port turned from an inter-island, domestic port to an international cargo port, they began to cater to foreign seamen.

At first, she said, the girls she handled came from the provinces of Samar, Cavite, Iloilo, Cebu and even Manila. But as poverty spread among the former port dwellers relocated in Balete and Sico, Amanda said girls from the relocation sites started working as prostitutes as well.

Family business

One of those lured into prostitution is Sandy (not her real name), Amanda's niece. A former barbecue and *balut* (boiled duck eggs) vendor, Sandy, now 42, started "going out" with her patrons barely a year after their community was demolished. "*Bata pa ako nun, may itsura, kaya ayun*" (I was still young then and pretty.), she kidded.

She said she only catered to foreign patrons, "*kasi hindi sila maarte kausap.*" (Because it is not difficult to deal with them) Sandy said she earns $50 to $100 for every customer but would only get half of it because she had to give a cut to her *mamasan*, to the ship operator, and to Customs officials. *"Naku, ligal na ligal ang pagho-hostess dito. Biruin mo, pati Customs nakikinabang,"* (Prostitution is legal here. Even Customs officials benefit from it.), she said.

On peak seasons such as Christmas and Holy Week, she would have three to four patrons a night. *"Hanggat merun, sige lang ng sige,"* she said, *"hindi ko naman ginagawa ito para magpasarap lang."* (While there is a customer, I go on and on. I am not doing this to enjoy.)

Sandy has three children to feed, she said, and her husband has left them for good. She spends P500 ($10.35) every month for rent because she sold the rights to her lot at the relocation center.

"Gusto ko sana mamasukan kasi madami din naman akong alam bukod sa humilata sa kama kaya lang walang mapasukang trabaho dito," (I would have wanted to work because I have a lot of skills aside from lying in bed, but there is no work here.), she added.

Sandy said she has now turned into being a *mamasan* (pimp) to earn a living, a job she shares with her 68-year-old mother, Belinda (not her real name). *"Syempre, tumatanda na ako, nababawasan na ng customer. Pero minsan, pag may nago-offer sinusunggaban ko na rin para mas malaki ang kita"* (Of course, I am getting old so my customers are fewer now. But sometimes if there is an offer I still take it to earn more.), she explains.

Days when there are no customers, Sandy said, her mother would scavenge scrap materials at the nearby dump and sell these to the nearest junkshop. The small earnings from junk could at least provide them a meal, Sandy said. *"Pwede na rin pantawid gutom,"* (Just to tide us over the hunger.), she said as she shrugs her shoulders. Bulatlat

Educational Crisis

Under the Constitution, the public education up to the secondary high school is free. Despite this, many students continue to miss proper education because the parents cannot afford to furnish them the incidental expenses such as transportation, supplies, food, allowance, uniforms, and other miscellaneous expenses. The uniform requirement for students in public schools has been dispensed by the President recently (August 2008). Free breakfasts have been made available to induce students to study, but the sheer number of students and limited budget would not be able to feed everyone. Only students in some selected schools were fed for 120 school days with biscuits, fortified noodles and milk. More help from the private sectors are needed.

A recent study by the National Statistical Coordination Board (NSCB) came out with glooming statistics that showed enrollment in primary school dropped from 90% five years ago to 83% last year. The figure for high school students is even worst, with only 59% enrolled last year (2007). This is expected to deteriorate as food and oil prices continue to soar without letup. Even with the dropping oil prices in late 2008, the outlook is still bleak because of the recession. Education of school children have to give way to food and other priorities such as water, electricity, and other necessities. Many parents have shifted their children's education from private schools to the poorer quality of education offer by the public schools. (*The Philippine Star*, July 15, 2008)

Another report by the Department of Education (DepEd) had more than 1.2 million six-year-olds not attending Grade One while up to 3.8 million children of school age have not received any formal education. The NSO reported that 11.6 million did not attend school in 2003. Studies have identified various factors that contribute to high dropout rates despite free public education. These include poverty, the need to help out in household chores, parents being school dropouts themselves, poor health, and high cost of going to school (daily transportation and food, clothing/uniform, supplies, projects), among others. On top of these, rapid population growth and a fast-increasing number of school-age children strains the government's capacity to provide needed classrooms, teachers, books and science equipment. Put more plainly, there are far more Filipino children than the country can afford to educate.[78]

The budget for education has not kept pace with the growing number of students. In trying to balance the national budget, sacrifices has to be made. According to the Alliance of Concerned Teachers (ACT), the real public spending on education has been "limited or zero growth" as recommended by the World Bank and ADB in the wake of the 1997 Asian financial crisis as a means of taming the budget deficit and

---

[78] http://209.85.175.104/search?q=cache:w3NX9YtgehIJ:www.pcpd.ph/
publications/PMS%2520Issue5-2003.pdf+prostitution+
OVERPOPULATION&hl=en&ct=clnk&cd=10&gl=ph

ensuring continued debt payments. According to the Congressional Budget and Planning Office, "the average annual growth rate of the DepEd's budget in real terms from 2001-2006 has been negative 3.5%." Furthermore, it points out that "in terms of share of the national budget, (the 2007) DepEd budget represents one of the lowest at 11.96% since 1995." Education could have been a solution to uplift the lives of the poor except that there are few opportunities for those who have finished their tertiary education. There are just too many graduates for too few jobs. This has forced many to go abroad looking for other jobs, causing a brain drain on the human resources.[79]

Public education is one of the worst institutions run by the government. Lack of schoolrooms, chairs, teachers, school atmosphere, and books are just some of the problems. In the 2005-2006 schoolyear, the shortages in classrooms stand at 57,930, chairs at 3.48 million, and teachers at 49,699. Even with increased budget allocation, the number of school chairs lacking is expected at 3 million, teachers at 29,762, classrooms at 4,215, textbooks and other instructional materials at least 33 million, and principals at 6,000 plus. The lack of classrooms has dwindled considerably due to the donations made by the Federation of Filipino-Chinese Chambers of Commerce and Industry. The cost of each school building of comparable size is only half that compared to those build through the government efforts. According to Senator Franklin Drilon, the reasons are there are no commissions and kickbacks involved and the building materials were bought at very low cost from members of the federation. (*PS*, September 13, 2008)

However, many of the classrooms, especially in the rural areas are not conducive to learning. In some instances, students have nothing to sit on and sometimes the lectures have to be undertaken under the trees. No wonder the rural students have a hard time passing the comprehensive exams given by the DepEd annually. The large shortages in teachers and classrooms have also resulted in a dramatic increase in the average class size in public schools, as reflected in the DepEd's changing policies regarding the official "maximum" class size. Under Sec. Raul Roco (2001), the maximum number of students

---

[79]

http://209.85.175.104/search?q=cache:BGqqEG7HFPoJ:www.arkibongbayan

.

org/2008-07July18-YouthRally/doc2/ACT%2520YearEnd%25202007%2520 press%2520statement.doc+STUDENT+DROPOUTS&hl=en&ct=clnk&cd=3 &gl=ph

per class was set at 54. Secretary de Jesus raised this to 60, Abad raised it to 65, while the present Secretary of Education Jesli Lapus lowered it back to 60. Actual class sizes, particularly in highly urbanized areas, often exceed 60 students per class. Needless to say, larger class sizes in basic education result in the further deterioration of the quality of education provided by public schools.

It is worsen by the many corruptions going on because of the huge outlay of public funds as mandated by the Constitution, so much so that many politicians want a piece of the pie. A large portion of the money allocated for books and school supplies, school buildings, teacher's salaries, etc. have been siphoned to the pockets of corrupt officials and private suppliers. It is common knowledge to insiders for years the mechanics of how the standard of operation of kickbacks is implemented. It is amazing how seemingly honest politicians can tolerate the practice. Even if they do not expose the practice, they are just as guilty as the culprits.

The lack of basic school supplies is easily attributed to the failure to stabilize the population. As long as more students are getting enrolled, there will be no end to the crisis. If the student bodies have been kept constant with a stabilized population, the number of schoolrooms and other needs should stabilized in the near future. Just like the population momentum, there is also the momentum for school supplies as well as housing and other needs especially when the backlogs have not been complied.

Home schooling would be one solution to the education problem. But it is not for everyone. Nothing beats a formal education in school. Getting students to attend regularly may be next to impossible. There are also many more things that could be learned in school than could be learned at home. Nevertheless there are also many expenses that must be met. If computers are going to be used, they must be accessible and can be very expensive for most poor families. In the rural areas, computers may not be available. Periodic reporting to school authorities is still a must to see how the student is progressing.

Corruption is not the main cause of poverty in the country but only part of the manifestation of overpopulation. The competitive of each professional jobs, the lack of opportunity and the low paying job in government offices, have caused many to become corrupt to get ahead. When a person feels he/she is not getting paid enough for his/her efforts, the tendency is to be lousy in their jobs. Even the Education Department, supposedly tasked to educate the children has been visited by corrupt public officials. This may partly explain why many of the school children cannot pass the entrance exams to move up the education levels. As a result of poor education, few ever succeeded to improve their living standards.

Ghost teachers on the payroll are nothing new. In fact, we have all kinds of ghosts around the country taking salaries and pensions without their presence. There are those who report for work during payday or ghost voters voting during election. Investigation into the Autonomous Region in Muslim Mindanao (ARMM) found many tons of forged paperwork at all levels. There is also a serious lack of teachers who qualified and many of them have left the country for greener pastures abroad. Corruption in the DepEd has also derailed many teachers from working. Some of those employed had bribed their way to the teaching jobs only to "subcontract" the jobs to others. The practice of education officials demanding from the prospective teachers their first two months' salaries is common occurrences. There have been reports of long hours of workloads, delayed payments of salaries and benefits that were missing. Some teachers died waiting and never receiving their retirement pays. Many teachers' contributions to GSIS were unremitted that the institution refused to process their loans and benefits from 1997 to 2003. (*PS*, May 16, 2008)

Juvenile Delinquency

Juvenile delinquency is defined under the Child and Youth Welfare Code (PD 603) as a person over 9 years old but below 18 who had committed an offense. This is a rather restrictive definition. Most psychologists would broaden the definition to include many of the anti-social activities committed by them. These would include crimes such as vagrancy, prostitution, alcoholic drinking, acts of vandalism, etc. Although these are crimes under the statue, they are seldom enforced against juvenile unless there have been some complaints or were caught red-handed. There are also two other laws dealing with youth offenders. The Juvenile Justice Law or Republic Act 9344 provides that children 15 years old and below will not be criminally liable while youth offenders aged 15 to 18 can be criminally charged only if they acted out the crime with discernment.

A country with high birth rates has a tendency to have a higher population of children and juveniles. They are supposed to be hope of the fatherland, but not when they cannot get the best society has to offer. They need quality sanitation and health services, education, nutritious food, employment, shelter, etc. that makes life comfortable. That is not the case with most of the youth of today. Many have become more of a burden to society or a victim of child abuse. More than half country's populations are below the age of 25. Most of these youngsters are curious, ambitious, and reckless about life. Teenagers are always willing to try anything that they are warned against such as smoking, gambling, drinking, drug use, premarital sex that often leads to abortion, and other vices that they would later regret. Once they have compromised their future, many became a menace to society by not attending schools, and forced to walk the streets to commit petty crimes such as snatching, holdups, drug addiction, prostitution, and even homicides in some cases. Many have no home to return to and have to sleep on the streets.

Statistics shows that most smokers start off at an early age and that more males do so that female while the number of female smokers are growing. Social drinkers also make up most of the males and out of school children are more likely to be drinkers. Of the 3.4 million Filipino drug users reported by the Dangerous Drugs Board and the Philippine Drug Enforcement Agency, more than half or 1.8 million are adolescents. Suicide attempts are also on the rise among the young. An alarming 12% of them admitted to having tried to commit suicide at least once. The girls appear to be more prone to it than the boys.

Adolescents are now more prone to take risks. They are willing to experiment with their life such as engaged in premarital sex. In this case 23% or almost 5 million young Filipinos have at one time or another experimented with premarital sex. It is also well known that babies born to children below 19 years have a higher mortality than those over 20 because their bodies are not fully developed. Similarly, young mothers have two to four times higher rates of mortality. A small percentage of about 5% of the adolescents resorts to abortion to get rid of the unwanted babies. This is a grim reminder that Christianity has been a big failure for most families when it comes to teaching sexual morality. The Bible is very emphatic about fornication, but it has been relegated to the background in many Christian homes.

Adolescents are often reckless when it comes to sexual behavior. Many are probably not aware that there is a proliferation of sexually transmitted diseases and they need to be protected by using condoms. The UPPI report states that 6% of young females have had discharges and another 19% have had painful urination. For males, 3% have had discharges, 23% experienced painful urination, and 3% had warts or ulcers in their penis. All of the above are indications of some forms of sexually transmitted diseases.

The children from the poor families have additional problems not found among the rich families. By virtue of their special wants and needs and their more numerous numbers, they are often neglected by their parents, one of both of them are seldom at home to rear the children. The children are easily swayed by other street children into joining gangs to commit crimes. Many have become drug addicts.

Years ago, there is an article in the *Reader's Digest* by a judge who claimed to have the solution to juvenile delinquency. His article, *Nine words to stop juvenile delinquency* states: Put-the-father-back-as-head–of the–family. Unfortunately, many fathers have failed to do their duty because they are too busy earning a living or having fun themselves most of the time. Instead of instilling discipline, the children are neglected and have to fend for themselves. As teenage grows up, the mother is often powerless to enforce discipline on the children. Rebellious children can almost be found in every home.

The poor children in the Philippines are often victims of their own government neglect and uncompassionate treatment. Many of them are jailed for minor offenses such as petty theft, playing cards on sidewalks, sniffing solvents, and vagrancy. Unless they are bribed to be released, they are incarcerated until the parents came across. Most of them were detained for months without charges or legal counsel nor are warrants issued at the time of their arrest. According to Amnesty International, over 50,000 children have been arrested and detained since 1995. One estimate put as many as 20,000 children in jail at any one year. Children as young as eight years old are being held in prisons in contravention of international statues and the country's own law. Torture, rape and other forms of cruel and inhumane treatment by adult inmates are part of everyday life for those children while incarcerated.

The jails arc often overcrowded with eighty to a hundred prisoners squat for 24 hours taking turns at lying down on their small cells. The heat and stench is overpowering, the food is only a few cents a day and disease, malnutrition and tuberculosis are the daily hazard suffered by the children. They are also at risk of sickness and death from contagious diseases such as TB, HIV/AIDS and hepatitis. Social workers visited them less than once a month.[80] Convicted felons sent to the National Penitentiary in Muntinglupa fared a lot better than those who are awaiting trials. Many languished for years before their case are heard by the courts. Suspects should be accorded better living standard than convicted felons. UNICEF came out with a situational report in 2003 with these findings.[81]

---

[80] http://en.wikipedia.org/wiki/Children_in_jail_in_Philippines

- In the Philippines, from 1995 to 2000, a total of 52,576 children were monitored as having been deprived of their liberty in detention placement, under custodial setting through suspended sentence. This comes to an average of one child every hour. Most of them were boys as expected.
- As of the end of 2003, there were seven children in Death Row, and 200 children in the Medium Security Unit of the National Bilibid Prisons in Muntinglupa City.
- More than half of every 10 juvenile delinquents in Southern Mindanao suffer from sexual advances and psychological harm while in the custody of government authorities, according to a study conducted from April to December 2002 by the Save the Children Foundation. Most of those abused while in custody were females.
- At the Molave Youth Home in Quezon City, 84 per cent of 159 children (or over 8 in every 10) are first-time offenders. Only 26 are recidivists, or who had been accused once or twice before of committing crime.
- Poverty has driven most children detained at the Molave Youth Home to commit crime, case reports as of September 2003 show. Nearly half or 74 children are facing trial for crimes against property (39 are accused of theft and 34 of robbery). Only 17 per cent or 27 children are named in major crimes, including 14 for rapes, 6 for homicides, and 7 for murders. Another 32 are being detained for using or pushing drugs. The other 33 children are in Molave for alleged violation of city ordinances against carrying deadly weapons or brandishing tattoos on their bodies or both.
- Data from the Social Services Development Department (SSDD) of the Quezon City government show that 77 per cent jailed at the Molave Youth Home in 2002 belonged to families with low monthly income of 2,000 to 4,000 pesos, according to the Coalition to Stop Child Detention Through Restorative Justice.
- In 2001, of the 538 children detained at Molave, 75 per cent or 402 children came from the same income groups. Records dating back to 1990 compiled by the Quezon City government reveal the same pattern - poverty is the common origin of a great majority of children in jail.

---

[81] http://pressinstitute.ph/archives/jds.html

The Presidential Anti-Organized Crime Commission (PAOCC) is taking steps to curtail youth gangs committing drug-related crimes in and around Metro Manila. It called upon mayors in Metro Manila to deal with at least 233 "destructive" gangs that committed 79 serious crimes ranging from robbery, physical injury, murder, auto theft and payroll heists in the last quarter of 2008. The PAOCC is also pursuing the review of the Juvenile Justice Law that proved to be a boon in the proliferation of youth gangs. These gangs even had chapters in other cities. To become a member, the new recruits, mostly out-of-school youth and even some students are required to commit robbery and physical violence as part of their initiation rites. Youth gangs with international ties are the most bold and daring in committing crimes, taking advantage of the lax Juvenile Justice Law, according to PAOCC commissioner Butch Belgica.

The Philippine National Police attributed the proliferation of youth crime gangs to the law that prohibits minors from being prosecuted for their crimes, the proliferation of illegal drugs, offender's tendency to commit crimes, parental neglect and other domestic factors. (*PS*, January 16, 2009)

Child Abuse

Many children from the large, poor families are often unwanted and neglected mostly because the parents cannot provide them with a decent standard of living. The following information are taken from my book, *Child Abuse* to give the readers an idea of how children are being treated around the world. Unless the children are well taken care and not abandoned by their parents because of poverty, they may just end up as victims like some of the fates of the victims below.

- Children in conflict in Asia have been found in countries such as Burma, Sri Lanka, India, Indonesia, Nepal and the Philippines. According to the Anti-Slavery Society, in 2002, some 300,000 children have been recruited worldwide in 36 armed conflicts. As many as 40% of them are girls. They are often raped or given to military commanders as sex slaves. Robbed of their childhood and education, they are often left psychological scarred or physically disabled.
- Children have been recruited as spies and saboteurs because they can move around in enemy territories covertly and unsuspectingly. They are either abducted or recruited from their poor parents who were given incentives such as regular salary for the child's service. These promises are seldom kept.

- Children are often the first victims when fighting erupted because they are placed at the front lines while the adults retreated. Sometimes they are drugged to overcome their fear or reluctance to fight. They are also the first to be ordered to the field to check for landmines.
- Children are often victims of landmines and unexploded ordnance. Many of them look like toys and come in different shapes, sizes and colors and are picked up by children accidentally while working in the field.
- More than one billion children are denied a healthy and protected upbringing as promised by the 1989's Convention on the Rights of the Child.
- Child abuse at home is more rampant than perceived and comes in many forms. It accounts for 89% of the child abuse cases, according to one study.
- Many of the child sex workers interviewed claimed that relatives introduced them to prostitution while others said they were recruited by friends who are already in the business.
- In 2003 in the Philippines, 3,397 children were reportedly raped compared to 1,117 women.
- During the seven-year economic sanctions inflicted on Iraq in the 1990s, about 1.4 million Iraqi died of starvation including over half a million babies and children under the age of 5.
- The Anti-Slavery International describes how children are piled 20 to 30 deep into tiny fishing boats, sometimes without food or water, on a journey that would last for weeks to work on farm in a foreign country. Those who died are simply tossed overboard.
- Some babies born to drug addicted mothers exposed to opiates or cocaine "in utero" are more likely to be born prematurely or be developmentally retarded.
- Sometimes the lowly government officials are no better than criminals in their midst. Children have been used as runners, barkers, lookouts, repackers, etc. by barangay officials in some places in Cebu City
- Children are often victims of tobacco smoke at home, especially if they are living in congested homes. They are also likely to develop into smokers.
- Even in the wombs, babies have been subjected to abuse by their mothers who engaged in alcohol and substance abuse while they are pregnant.

- The money set aside for the improvement of the Education Department has invited a swarm of corrupt government officials, who in connivance with unscrupulous businessmen have deprived the students of their future. As much as 65% of the funds for textbooks have been lost to corruption
- Innocent children have been put in jail because their guardian/single parent has been confined in jail with no one to take care of them.
- The mental disorder of a pedophile is incurable and he will not stop on his own, nor will he turn himself in for treatment because he does not take responsibility for his own behavior and denies that he is doing anything harmful to a child. He will continue to abuse until he is caught.
- The most dangerous aspect of the Internet is when pedophiles gain access to children through the Internet chat rooms where they posed as youngsters themselves.
- Some parents are too poor that they are willing to sell their babies for adoption. Some of them end up as victims of traffickers for transplant organs. Children have also become victims for other children needing their organs.
- Children have been used in satanic ritual sacrifices. Some males are deliberately bred by members of the cult for that purpose because of their innocence and intelligence. Some have to undergo torture and sexual abuse before the actual sacrifice.
- There are 27 million people enslaved worldwide at any given moment, according to Kevin Bates, author of the book *Disposable People: New Slavery in the Global Economy*. The actual count could only increase with the increasing population.
- Poverty has been the driving force behind most of the child slavery going on in Africa and elsewhere. In West and Central Africa, more than 200,000 children were trafficked annually to work as laborers in homes, factories and farms.
- There are 15 million bonded children laborers in India alone. Many suffer from eyestrain from working long hours and lung ailments from inhaling tobacco dust and chemical fumes. Many of them are sent to work to repay the loan incurred by their parents or guardians, with or without their consent. In many cases, bondage is intergenerational, with children becoming bonded workers when their parents became too old or too weak to work.

- Babies have been served as food for adults in times of famine. Some of the babies have been roasted or boiled and kept in bottles for sale to the public. Cannibalism is common in the past that no child is safe whenever famine strikes.
- Children have been kidnapped and used as transporters of drugs placed inside their bodies.
- A 2003 report by the Ending Child Prostitution, Pornography and Trafficking claimed that an international sex tourist destination of 300,000 Japanese visited the country every year. The same report cited the UN International Children's Education Fund estimated 100,000 prostituted children in the country, 10% of whom are males. (*PS*, December 29, 2008)

Garbage Crisis

As a country, we have a poor record for disposing our wastes. Toxic chemicals and recyclables are often disposed along with food wastes. Laws requiring separating recyclables are often ignored. Only the few materials having monetary value are ever recycled and most of them are done by scavengers. The only recyclable done at home are the newsprints, bottles and aluminum cans. Everyday, we produce more than 8,000 tons of garbage in Metro Manila, at half a kilo each person, as we have become a throwaway society. The problem is expected to grow as the population size increases and compounded by people who have not yet learned to segregate their wastes to reduce the garbage disposal problem. The sheer size of our garbage has filled up most of the nearby garbage dumps and new dumpsites can only be found in far off places.

Sanitary landfills, the modern term for garbage dumps, do not hide the fact that they are undesirable and unwanted by the communities where they are located. Most of the household and industrial wastes contain therein can be harmful in the long run. They are also home to rats and other vermin that are often carriers of diseases and their presence alone could make life miserable to the neighborhood inhabitants.

One of the few sanitary landfills left for the Metro Manila garbage is located in Rodriquez, Rizal. It was in a controversy for a while because the mayor threatened to shut it down if the tipping fee is not increase from P600 to P800 per cubic meter of garbage. The 14 hectares site was started in 2002 and can accommodate 1,200 tons of garbage every day. It is only a matter of time before a new dumpsite is needed and it will not be nearby.

Not-in-my-backyard syndrome is the prevailing trend toward the disposal of garbage. This is what happened to the 73-hectare landfill in San Mateo, Rizal, which was closed down two years earlier due to stiff opposition from residents. Aside from the Rodriguez dump, Metro Manila also uses the Payatas open dump and part of the offshore landfill in Tanza, Navotas.[82]

If there is any new disposal site to be found, it will be in faraway place that could cost more for trucking the garbage and tipping fee charged by the owner before they allow their land to be used as dumping ground for outsiders. Even then, it could be a political and sanitary issue in the community where this garbage site is located before it is opened to the Metro Manilans' garbage.

In the meantime, our waterway systems have become one big dumping ground. Some of the human and household generated wastes end up in Manila Bay. Efforts to clean up the Manila Bay has proved futile, especially with many squatters living along the esteros dumping their wastes directly to the rivers leading to the Manila Bay. One picture on page A_3 of the September 14, 2008 issue of the *Philippine Daily Inquirer* says it all. A mother and her child are slogging through the garbage-filled Manila Bay looking for anything recyclable to sell to the garbage collector. The boy, probably less than ten years old, was holding a big plastic bag and kept afloat through an inflated auto interior tube. This is how difficult life for many poor people in this country that can only be blamed on overpopulation that made it difficult for many to be gainfully employed. There are just not enough decent jobs for the poor who desperately wanted to be employed, even taking hazardous, perilous and dirty jobs just to survive.

It took the Supreme Court nine years to come to a decision ordering eight government agencies to clean up Manila Bay. The petition was filed by an environmental lawyer Antonio Oposa, president of the Law of Nature Foundation. (*PDI*, December 20, 2008) The MMDA under the very competent Chairman Bayani Fernando has been chosen as a lead agency to implement the ruling. His first order of business is to remove and relocate all illegal settlers in Metro Manila especially those living near the rivers surrounding the metropolis. It will start off with those from the Marikina River where he used to be the mayor of the city. The DENR has ordered the two water concessioners, Maynila and Manila Water to install sewage plants that would process household and industrial waste before they are discharged to the rivers and ultimately into the Manila Bay.

---

[82] http://www.manilastandardtoday.com/?page=police01_oct24_2005

From the moment of birth until we end up in graves, we are polluters of the environment. Take the example of the disposal diapers. If every baby born in the country were to use them, the two million babies will need at least four million diapers daily, if used sparingly. At 365 days a year, that would mean over a billion pieces of disposal diapers. This is a conservative estimate since babies soiled their skin about ten times a day. It is fortunate that the poor cannot afford to use disposable diapers or it would have compounded the garbage problem.

In the U.S. alone, an estimated 27.4 billion disposable diapers are used annually, adding 3.4 million tons to the landfill. This alone presents big waste disposal problem. Many who are not aware that before disposing to the garbage bins, the diapers should first be rinsed in the toilet bowl to remove the feces. Otherwise, the feces may just end up contaminating the groundwater. Some of the ingredients, like plastics used in the making of the diapers take centuries to decompose unlike the cloth diaper which decomposes within six months. In practice, the cloth can have other uses such as rags.

In one cradle-to-grave study sponsored by the National Association of Diaper Services, it found that disposable diapers produce seven times more solid waste when discarded and three times more waste in the manufacturing process. In addition, effluents from the plastic, pulp, and paper industries are far more hazardous than those from the cotton-growing and -manufacturing processes. According to industry data from Franklin Associates and the American Petroleum Institute, 3.5 billion gallons of oil are used to produce the 18 billion throwaway diapers that end up in landfills each year. Washing cloth diapers at home uses 50 to 70 gallons of water every three days, which is roughly equivalent to flushing the toilet five times a day, unless the user has a high-efficiency washing machine.[83]

Reusable cloth diapers are usually made of cotton. It has its own disadvantages. In the U.S. conventional cotton is one of the most chemically-dependent crops, sucking up 10% of all agricultural chemicals and 25% of insecticides on 3% of arable land. But its advantages still outweigh the disadvantages compare to disposables.

Disposing of human excrement is another problem to resolve. A survey in 2002 shows that around 80% of the urban population had access to sanitary toilets compared to 61% in the rural communities, and overall nearly one quarter of households did not have access to sanitary facilities. While the Metropolitan Waterworks and Sewerage

---

[83] http://en.wikipedia.org/wiki/Diapers

System (MWSS) through its two (2) private concessionaires operates four (4) sanitary sewerage systems, it covers only 11.5% of the population, the remainder depended mostly on defective and poorly maintained septic tank systems. The way septic tanks are setup, the liquid excrement is allowed to penetrate the ground only end up contaminating the groundwater.

Human activities to create a convenient society generate a lot of pollutions. Agricultural and industrial activities such as food processing plants, pulp and paper mills, textiles, animal husbandry, sugar mills, refineries and distilleries, chemical plants, smelters, tanneries, poultry farms, abattoirs and processing plants contribute to the high levels of pollution to the environment.

In many squatter areas bordering the esteros, the convenient way of disposing the garbage is throwing them down the estero. The same is true for many factories bordering the esteros leading to the rivers. The Pasig River is one good example of how indiscriminate dumping of our garbage, raw sewage and factory's chemical wastes has destroyed the river. The river is so dead that one cynic claimed that the poison in the river can be used for lethal injection for convicted criminals. The same is true with the Laguna de Bay, the largest freshwater lake in the country. The proliferation of the human species along with their economic activities has rendered large centers of this country in dire environmental degradation. Half of the waterways in the country are polluted. Even in the rural areas, the water are polluted with pesticides and fertilizers runoff.

Health Problems

Diseases often strike those who are in poor health due to malnutrition, poor sanitation, uninformed and uneducated, mismanaged and unreliable health services. It is also natural that health care for the rich is always given priority. Money can always buy the best health care but the poor have to wait their time for government to serve them. Many are so poor that getting to health center can be a daunting task. Some children have paid with their lives because their parents are too poor to spend money for the care.

According to the latest WHO report, the high cost of health care is pushing more than 100 million people below the poverty line each year. It is due to the way health care is organized, financed, and delivered in rich and poor countries around the world, according to the report. For some 5.6 billion people in low and middle-income countries, the people have to use their own money to pay for their own health care without government help. As a result, the difference in life expectancy between the poor in developing countries and the rich in developed countries is more than 40 years while 58 million women out of the 136 million women giving birth this year will not get any medical assistance. (*PS*, October 15, 2008)

While the developed world has conquered many diseases that strike the children, these diseases still hound the lives of children before they reach the age of five in many developing countries. Their mothers are not spared. Women who experienced frequent pregnancies and childbirth are taking a dreadful toll on their lives.

When too many children are born close together, they are often not given proper maternal and child care at a time when they needed most. They often end up with poor health, malnourished, poor IQ that could not help them cope with life in the competitive world.

While the mortality rate of children below five years old has dropped in many developed countries, it continues to take its toll on children in the Third World. In 1983, 14 to 15 million under five were dying each year, 93.3% of them lived in the developing world. In some countries, 25% of them never lived to reach their fifth birthday. All these deaths can be trace back to poverty. The infants never had a chance to survive for long because of poor health, poor sanitation, and poor quality of food that made them easily succumbed to diseases.

Diseases are caused either by viruses, bacteria and parasites such as malaria. Many of the childhood diseases that have been under controlled in developed countries still take their tolls in the Third World. Vaccinations are available for most of these diseases but in many developing countries they may not always be accessible to the poor and uneducated, especially in the rural areas. Poor sanitation and poor hygiene allow the pathogens to thrive and are often associated with childhood death. Coupled with poor nutrition, children often succumbed to diseases with their poor immune system. The correlation between malnutrition, childhood mortality and infection has been discovered a few decades ago, but little can be done as long as most of the families are too poor to get the necessary health services.

Research by Sir Ian MacGregor of Britain's Medical Research Council in West Arica in 1949 and thereafter discovered the relationship between nutrition and parasitic disease. Babies who are breast-fed are heavier and protected by antibodies during the first three months of life. After the second three months, when infections started to set in the child actually lose weight because the protection offered by the mother's antibodies faded allowing the child to succumb to multiple infections. Their immune system is constantly challenged to defend the body against a series of onslaughts. Some of the highly endemic infections, such as measles and malaria, actually suppressed the immune defenses even further until finally a child's immunity was so weakened that he could succumb even to a common cold. (Goodfield, 12-13) This is why children should be protected through nutrition.

Malnutrition reduces resistance to infection and infection precipitates malnutrition. This vicious cycle of repeated infection, dehydration, malnutrition and immune suppression follow each other. This is compounded if the mother is uneducated, ignorant of the reason for the child's illness, exhausted or apathetic, contributing conditions of dirty water, inadequate sanitation, and poverty that could easily lead to the child's demise. (Ibid)

There is also the danger for mother giving childbirth in underdeveloped countries. Nearly half a million women died every year leaving behind them one million motherless children. In addition five million babies are stillborn or die within their first week of life. There are basically two causes for this mortality: some affect the mothers, others the children. To sum it up, the phrase "too young, too old, too many or too close" is what made mortality so high. Mothers who are under eighteen, or over thirty-five, has already had four children or is giving birth within two years of the previous child are at great risk. If these types of pregnancy were avoided, deaths of both mothers and babies could be halved. Further studies in Asia show that if a mother dies in childbirth, 95% of her young infants will not survive beyond the first twelve months. (Ibid, 14)

The health of people in this country has steadily improved through the years. Life expectancy for men and women has improved considerably from 1960 to 1990, from 51 to 69 years old for women and 63 for men. Infant mortality has also improved from 101 per 1,000 in 1950 to 51.6 per 1,000 in 1989. Babies stillborn or die soon after birth stand at 24 out of 1,000 babies, according to one recent family planning survey. (*PS*, December 1, 2008) Death caused by communicable diseases has also been on the declined for the past decades.

The number of doctors in the country has increased in the past but they are now on the decline due to the migration of physicians and nurses abroad for higher paying jobs. In fact, many doctors have opted to become nurses so that they can go abroad. According to the Professional Regulation Commission (PRC), 10,000 doctors have become nurses and 99% passed the licensure examination for which 6,000 of them have already left the country. Those who stayed behind are mostly concentrated in urban areas where they can afford to recoup their investments for the long years of study. Nevertheless, there are still 120 municipalities nationwide without doctors, down from 271. As a result, some 70% of the sick died untreated due to the lack of doctors, not only in the rural areas, but also in urban areas. (*PS*, August 11, 2008)

Only a few modern medical facilities are available and they are concentration in the urban cities. The ADB estimated that there is only one doctor for every 9,689 people and only one hospital for every 809 patients. Government hospitals are teeming with patients who cannot afford to pay the high doctors' fee in private sectors. More cannot even stay as in-patients where they can get the proper care. (*PDI*, July 29, 2008)

The government and private sectors effort to save children from many childhood diseases have improved a lot today. Still, many are left out because of misinformation, poverty and lack of medicine especially for those living in rural areas. The DOH has been making efforts to provide every child with a minimum health need but they can be expensive and daunting task especially in remote places. The tremendous success of immunization has minimized death of children that the poor workers no longer see the need for big families as a security precaution to take care of them in old age. The dwindling size of farmlands also alleviates the need for more hands to cultivate the land thus allowing smaller families. Even with the dwindling family size, the sheer number of poor families means that the number of babies is bound to increase into the future due to population momentum.

AIDS

Asia, which has 60% of the world's population, is showing the steepest infection curve and could fast become the region with the most HIV infections. By the end of 20th century, HIV infections had reached 25 million in India and 15 million in China, according to the National Intelligence Council, an adviser to the CIA. In 2007, India had already surpassed South Africa as the most heavily afflicted country. Yet, out of an estimated 8.6 million people living with HIV/AIDS in June 2006, only 16% of this total received antiretroviral therapy. (UNAIDS/WHO AIDS Epidemic Update: December 2006)

The number of victims is expected to increase as more people get infected annually. There is no known cure except for medication that can prolong the life of the victims. Unlike other infectious diseases, this disease can lay dormant for years without symptoms, thus contributing to more infection.

The Philippines may have only small registered cases of infected Filipinos, but the figures can be deceiving. Many who are infected may not be aware of it. Their numbers is expected to grow after the passage of the Philippines' AIDS Prevention and Control Act of 1998 that prohibits the mandatory testing of suspected HIV carriers in the Philippines. Any voluntary testing requires written informed consent, guarantees the right to confidentiality, protection against discrimination in the workplace. The law also mandated HIV/AIDS information to all including travelers and migrants and access to treatment. Unfortunately such legislation is ineffective in stopping the AIDS epidemics. At the least, mandatory testing should be given before marriage licenses are issued.

Diarrhea

Even with great advances in health care, a common disease called diarrhea is the number one killer of children in the country due to poor sanitation and access to potable water. A study undertaken by the World Bank and the U. S. Agency for International Development showed that every day, an average of 31 Filipinos died of diarrhea resulting from poor sanitation. The study also showed that 27.5 million Filipinos do not have sanitary toilets at home. Millions of them live as squatters with makeshift homes. Only 3.3% of urban households are connected to sewers that lead to treatment facilities. The cost to the economy is tremendous. The World Bank and United States Agency for International Development (USAID) estimate that the country is losing about P77.8 billion a year in terms of health care costs, lost wages and premature deaths arising from poor sanitation.

The treatment for the common diarrhea is not as easy as it seems for millions of Filipinos who cannot afford even cheap generic medicine for ordinary illnesses. The long-term solution is the installation of proper sanitation and safe water facilities. Health officials hope local governments will give priority to such projects. Lawmakers should set aside part of their pork barrel allocations for the installation of sanitary toilets and safe water facilities for their constituents.

A tropical archipelago rich in fresh water sources, safe water should not be a problem. But poor sanitation and industrial pollution are contaminating fresh water sources. The pesticides used to increase food production have been responsible for contamination of the fresh water as they accumulate and flow to the river system of the country. Some percolate to the groundwater where they became sources of our polluted groundwater. The waters used in many suburban areas coming from the groundwater are not potable are only used for other household chores. Water have to be trucked to them and they are not cheap. There are many contaminants presence in water that cannot be monitored. Even Metro Manila residents drink water straight from the tap at their own risk.

Cholera

Across the country, cholera cases are still being reported due to contaminated water. It will take a lot of funding and political will to solve the problem. Unfortunately, the funding may not be available or fully utilized due to corruption.

Infants and even children have difficulties describing their symptoms. It is therefore imperative that they be immunized against some of the killer diseases while early in life. Unfortunately, this is not a disease that can be immunized. Cholera is an acute diarrheal illness caused by the organism *Vibrio cholerae* that can be transmitted through contaminated food and water or through fecal-oral contamination. The cholera bacterium may also live in the environment in brackish rivers and coastal waters. Shellfish can be a source of cholera, and a few persons in the United States have contracted cholera after eating raw or undercooked shellfish from the Gulf of Mexico. The disease is not likely to spread directly from one person to another; therefore, casual contact with an infected person is not a risk factor.[84] In the most severe forms, it is one of the most rapidly fatal illnesses known. A healthy person may become hypotensive within an hour of the onset of symptoms and may die within three hours if not treated immediately. In most cases, the disease can progress from a loose stool to shock in 4 to 12 hours, and death in 18 hours to several days unless treated with oral rehydration therapy. Vomiting is also one of its common symptoms. Even while patients are being hydrated continuously, they are also getting dehydrated due to the continuous defecating stools that look like rice-water. And when hydration cannot keep up with dehydration, patient succumbs and dies. The oral rehydration solution is a prepackaged mixture of sugar and salts to be mixed with water and drunk in large amounts. This solution is used throughout the world to treat diarrhea. Severe cases also require intravenous fluid replacement. With prompt rehydration, less than 1% of cholera patients die. Antibiotics shorten

---

[84] http://www.medicinenet.com/cholera/article.htm

the course and diminish the severity of the illness, but they are not as important as rehydration. Persons who develop severe diarrhea and vomiting during cholera outbreak should seek medical attention promptly.[85]

Highly populated areas have a perchance for epidemics during natural disasters and we are no exception. The Philippines experienced one of the worst epidemics during the 1902-1904 cholera epidemics that claimed the lives of more than 200,000 people including more than 66,000 children. The original source of the disease was traced to the slums of Tondo and soon spread to the provinces. With so many cases of new infections, the health authorities were overwhelmed. People began burying dead bodies in shallow graves while others were simply tossed to the Pasig River, further worsening the epidemic by contaminating a common water source. It also didn't help that Filipinos were distrustful of the Americans governing them.

As reported in *The New York Times* of August 26, 1902, "The number of deaths in the provinces ranges from 350 to 450 daily. The beginning of the rainy season makes the danger greater, as the streams carry the cholera germs everywhere, and spread the disease. There are on an average from fifty to seventy new cases daily in Manila, and nearly as many deaths. There are many cases on the ships in the bay, and this is an increased case of danger, as the quarantine authority cannot get at them, and violations of the health regulations are constantly occurring. The worst occurrence is the deaths of natives who have crawled off uncared for, and have died in out-of-the-way places. It is a common thing to find bodies of victims of cholera floating in Pasig River, and in one day recently six such bodies were fished out. This disease has in a number of cases broken out on ships that have been in close quarantine for several days. It is said this is due to using the water of the bay, which is very impure. The shops have condenser, but few distil the water to remove all danger of infection."

Neonatal Tetanus

Tetanus is acquired when the spores of the bacterium *Clostridium Tetani* infect a wound or the umbilical stump. Spores are universally present in the soil. People of all ages can get tetanus but the disease is particularly common and serious in newborn babies ("neonatal tetanus"). The disease is caused by the action of a potent neurotoxin

---

[85] Ibid

produced during the growth of the bacteria in dead tissues, e.g. in dirty wounds or in the umbilicus following non-sterile delivery. Tetanus is not transmitted from person to person. Tetanus germs are likely to grow in deep puncture wounds caused by nails, knives, tools, wood splinters, and animal bites.

Neonatal tetanus can be fatal and is particularly common in rural areas where deliveries are made at home without adequate sterile procedures. Many mothers in the rural areas also do not have the benefit of medical attention that only a licensed medical doctor can offer. WHO estimated that neonatal tetanus killed about 180 000 babies worldwide in 2002.

Tetanus can be prevented through immunization with tetanus-toxoid (TT) vaccines on women of childbearing age or during pregnancy. This protects the mother and the fetus through the transfer of tetanus antibodies. Additionally, sanitary practices during the delivery of a baby are also important to prevent neonatal and maternal tetanus. To be protected throughout life, an individual should receive 3 doses of DTP in infancy, followed by a TT-containing booster at school-entry age (4-7 years), in adolescence (12-15 years), and in early adulthood.

Worldwide, all countries are committed to the elimination of maternal and neonatal tetanus (MNT), i.e. a reduction of neonatal tetanus incidence to below one case per 1000 live births per year in every district. As of December 2007, 47 countries around the world have not eliminated MNT.

Diphtheria

Diphtheria is an acute respiratory infection caused by the diphtheria bacterium, *Corynebacterium diphtheriae* and its toxin. The bacteria may be found anywhere, but especially in poor or densely populated areas, where some people have not been vaccinated against diphtheria, encouraging the disease to spread. It affects mostly children.

Mortality in poorer countries is high, up to 30 to 40 per cent, while in Western countries it is between 5 and 10%, partly because the disease may be confused in the early stages with other infections, which results in delayed treatment.

Children are given the diphtheria vaccine together with vaccines against tetanus, whooping cough, polio and Hib as one combination vaccine (Pediacel), at the ages of two, three and four months. A child is given a diphtheria, tetanus, whooping cough and polio booster vaccine (Repevax) when he or she is five years old. The child is given a further booster vaccine before leaving school (Revaxis) and is then considered to be protected for a further 10 years.

Unless vaccinated, it is a serious infection with a high mortality rate, even in Western Europe. The bacteria multiply on the lining (mucous membrane) of the throat, nose or larynx, where they divide and excrete a poisonous substance or toxin. The bacteria and the toxin destroy the mucous membrane, so that a thick coating is formed and the patient develops a serious inflammation of the throat. The membranous coating in the throat can become detached and obstruct the airways, making breathing difficult and sometimes causing asphyxiation. The bacterial toxin penetrates the body and can lead to damage of the cardiac muscle and the nervous system.

The disease is mainly transmitted by droplets from the nose or throat of infected person and passed from person to person through coughing or sneezing and skin contract. The incubation period is usually two to five days. Local symptoms consist of a sore_throat, coughing and breathing difficulties. When the disease infects the skin it causes crusty scabs, similar to impetigo.

General symptoms manifest themselves as a slight rise in temperature, limpness and fatigue. In two to six weeks of the illness, damage to the heart and nervous system may be observed in the form of irregularities of the heart beat and paralysis. In the worst cases, this may cause serious disturbances in cardiac rhythm, and possibly cardiac arrest.

Pertussis (Whooping Cough)

The following article is taken from the WHO website.

Pertussis or whooping cough is one of the diseases covered by the Expanded Program on Immunization, with vaccinations given in routine immunization service in the Western Pacific Region. The disease is caused by bacteria that live in the mouth, nose, and throat. Many children who contract pertussis have coughing spells that last four to eight weeks. The disease is most dangerous in infants. In 2000, an estimated 39 million cases and 297,000 deaths occurred worldwide.

Pertussis spreads very easily from child to child in droplets produced by coughing or sneezing. Children exposed to the germs become infected. In many countries the disease occurs in regular epidemic cycles of three to five years.

The incubation period is five to 10 days. At first, the infected child appears to have a common cold with runny nose, watery eyes, sneezing, fever, and a mild cough. The cough gradually worsens and involves many bursts of rapid coughing. At the end of these bursts the child takes in air with a high-pitched whoop, from where it got its name. The child may turn blue because he or she does not get enough oxygen during a long burst of coughing. Vomiting and exhaustion often follow the coughing attacks, which are particularly frequent at night. During recovery, coughing gradually becomes less intense. Children usually do not have a high fever during any stage of the illness.

Complications are most likely in young infants. The most common and deadly complication is bacterial pneumonia. Children may also experience complications such as convulsions and seizures due to fever or reduction in oxygen supply to the brain. This is caused either by coughing attacks or by toxins released by the pertussis bacteria. They may also experience loss of appetite, inflammation of the middle ear, and dehydration.

Treatment with an antibiotic, usually erythromycin, may make the illness less severe. Because the medication kills bacteria in the nose and throat, the use of antibiotics also reduces the ability of infected people to spread pertussis to others. Infected children should get plenty of fluids to prevent dehydration.

Prevention involves immunization with pertussis vaccine, which is usually given in combination with diphtheria and tetanus vaccines (DTP). More recently, some countries have been using a combination vaccine that includes vaccines for diphtheria, tetanus, pertussis, vitamin A (HepB), and sometimes *Haemophilus influenzae* type b (Hib).

Poliomyelitis

Poliomyelitis is caused by infection of the poliovirus (PV) of the genus *Enterovirus*. This group of RNA viruses prefers to inhabit the gastrointestinal tract and infects only human beings. Three serotypes of poliovirus have been identified -poliovirus type 1 (PV1), type 2 (PV2), and type 3 (PV3) - each with a slightly different capsid protein. All three are extremely virulent and produce the same disease symptoms. PV1 is the most commonly encountered form, and the one most closely associated with paralysis.

Poliomyelitis is highly contagious and spreads easily between human contacts. In endemic areas, wild polioviruses can infect virtually the entire human population. It is seasonal in temperate climates, with peak transmission occurring in summer and autumn. These seasonal differences are far less pronounced in tropical areas.

The incubation period is usually 6 to 20 days, with a maximum range of 30 to 35 days. Virus particles are excreted in the feces for several weeks following initial infection. The disease is transmitted primarily via the fecal-oral route and ingesting contaminated food or water. It is occasionally transmitted via the oral-oral route, a mode especially visible in areas with good sanitation and hygiene. Polio is most infectious as long as the virus remains in the saliva or feces.

Factors that increase the risk of polio infection or affect the severity of the disease include immune deficiency, malnutrition, tonsillectomy, physical activity immediately following the onset of paralysis, skeletal muscle injury due to injection of vaccines or therapeutic agents, and pregnancy. Although the virus can cross the placenta during pregnancy, the fetus does not appear to be affected by either maternal infection or polio vaccination. Maternal antibodies also cross the placenta, providing passive immunity that protects the infant from polio infection during the first few months of life. Therefore it would be more prudent for the mothers to be vaccinated.

Two vaccines are used throughout the world to combat polio. The first polio vaccine was developed in 1952 by Jonas Salk, of the University of Pittsburgh, and announced to the world on April 12, 1955. The Salk vaccine uses inactivated poliovirus vaccine (IPV), is based on poliovirus grown in a type of monkey kidney tissue culture (Vero cell line), which is chemically inactivated with formalin. After two doses of IPV (given by injection), 90% or more of individuals develop protective antibody to all three serotypes of poliovirus, and at least 99% are immune to poliovirus following three doses. Incidentally, the development of the Salk vaccine claimed at least five million rhesus monkeys before it was ready for human use. Even today, millions of rhesus monkeys, mostly imported from India are needed to manufacture the vaccine first by inoculating the monkey and killing them to examine their organs for possible infection.[86]

Subsequently, Albert Sabin developed an oral polio vaccine (OPV) using live but weakened (attenuated) virus, produced by the repeated passage of the virus through non-human cells at sub-physiological temperatures. Human trials of Sabin's vaccine began in 1957 and it was licensed in 1962. The attenuated poliovirus in the Sabin vaccine replicates very efficiently in the gut, the primary site of wild poliovirus infection and replication, but the vaccine strain is unable to replicate efficiently within the tissue of the nervous system.

---

[86] http://www.whale.to/vaccine/bayly.html#HUMAN-TISSUEVIRUS

A single dose of oral polio vaccine produces immunity to all three poliovirus serotypes in approximately 50% of recipients while three doses protect them in more than 95% of the time.

Because OPV is inexpensive, easy to administer, and produces excellent immunity in the intestine, (which helps prevent infection with wild virus in areas where it is endemic) it has been the vaccine of choice for controlling poliomyelitis in many countries. On very rare occasions (about 1 case per 750,000 vaccine recipients) the attenuated virus in OPV reverts into a form that can cause paralysis. Most industrialized countries have switched to IPV, which cannot revert, either as the sole vaccine against poliomyelitis or in combination with oral polio vaccine.

Tuberculosis

Tuberculosis is probably the single greatest plague in the world, claiming as many of one billion lives since ancient time up to the end of the 20th century. It was almost eradicated in the Western world until a resurgence caused by those afflicted with HIV/AIDS got out of hand.

The emergence of drug-resistant strains has also contributed to this new epidemic with, from 2000 to 2004, 20% of TB cases being resistant to standard treatments and 2% resistant to second-line drugs. The rate at which new TB cases occur varies widely, even in neighboring countries, apparently because of differences in health care systems.

There are a number of known factors that make people more susceptible to TB infection. Smoking more than 20 cigarettes a day also increases the risk of TB by two to four times. Diabetes mellitus is also an important risk factor that is growing in importance in developing countries. In fact, data from the CDC states that secondhand smoke causes an estimated 46,000 heart disease deaths and about 3,000 lung cancer deaths among nonsmokers in the U.S. each year. Cigarette smoke damages the lining of the blood vessels and increases the risk for blood clotting, leading to heart attack or stroke. A smoking ban can greatly reduce these incidents as one smoking ban in a Colorado city proved. Since the smoking ban was put in place on July 1, 2003, hospitalization due to secondhand smoke dropped by 41% in three years. (*PS*, January 23, 2009)

It is true around the world as it is in the Philippines. Heart diseases are the number one cause of death. In the Philippines 254 people die of heart attack each day, according to the DOH. The risk factors include smoking, high blood pressure and diabetes, it added.

Although smoking is preventable and known to cause cancers, still 47% of Filipino males, 16% of females are current or ex-smokers, making us one of the highest numbers of smokers worldwide. Thirty-three percent of the minors are also smokers before they are 14 years old. (Ibid)

Tuberculosis remains a major disease afflicting children throughout the world. Although the exact number of annual cases of childhood tuberculosis is unknown, WHO has estimated approximately 1 million new cases and 400,000 deaths per year in children due to tuberculosis. Many of these cases go undiagnosed and untreated and many of these children could be saved if there were improvements in diagnosis and treatment available for them.

Tuberculosis is spread through the air, when people who have the disease cough, sneeze or spit. One third of the world's current population has been infected with *M. tuberculosis*, and new infections occur at a rate of one person per second. However, most of these cases will not develop the full-blown disease. About one in ten of these latent infections will eventually progress to active disease, which, if left untreated, kills more than half of its victims. In 2004, mortality and morbidity statistics around the world included 14.6 million chronic active cases, 8.9 million new cases, and 1.6 million deaths, mostly in developing countries. In addition, the rising number of people in the developed world are contracting tuberculosis because their immune systems are compromised by immunosuppressive drugs, substance abuse, or AIDS.

Many experts in childhood tuberculosis feel that children have been neglected in the worldwide effort to control tuberculosis. There are many reasons for this including the fact that most children with tuberculosis are not infectious and therefore not considered as important as adults with contagious tuberculosis. The frustration at the difficulty in establishing a microbiological diagnosis of tuberculosis in children, and the relative neglect of pediatricians and researchers in studying childhood tuberculosis also contribute to the problem.

The typical symptoms of tuberculosis are chronic cough with blood-tinged sputum, fever, night sweats and weight loss. Infection of other organs causes a wide range of symptoms. The diagnosis relies on radiology (chest X-rays), a tuberculin skin test, blood tests, as well as microscopic examination and microbiological culture of bodily fluids. Tuberculosis treatment is difficult and requires long courses of multiple antibiotics. Contacts are also screened and treated if necessary. Antibiotic resistance caused by the misuse of it, is a growing problem in (extensively) multi-drug-resistant tuberculosis.

Prevention relies on screening programs and vaccination, usually with Bacillus Calmette-Guérin (BCG vaccine).

Treatment for TB uses antibiotics to kill the bacteria. The two most commonly used antibiotics are rifampicin and isoniazid. However, instead of the short course of antibiotics typically used to cure other bacterial infections, TB requires much longer periods of treatment (around 6 to 12 months) to cure the disease. For latent TB, the treatment usually uses a single antibiotic, while active TB disease is best treated with combinations of several antibiotics, to reduce the risk of the bacteria developing antibiotic resistance. People with latent infections are treated to prevent them from progressing to active TB later in life. However, treatment using Rifampin and Pyrazinamide is not risk-free. The Centers for Disease Control and Prevention (CDC) notified healthcare professionals of revised recommendations against the use of rifampin plus pyrazinamide for treatment of latent tuberculosis infection, due to high rates of hospitalization and death from liver injury associated with the combined use of these drugs.

Drug resistant tuberculosis is becoming common. Primary resistance occurs in persons who are infected with a resistant strain of TB. Secondary resistance is acquired during TB therapy because of inadequate treatment, not taking the prescribed regimen appropriately, or using low quality medication. Drug-resistant TB is a public health issue in many developing countries, as treatment is longer and requires more expensive drugs. Multi-drug resistant TB (**MDR-TB**) is defined as resistance to the two most effective first line TB drugs: rifampicin and isoniazid. Extensively drug-resistant TB (**XDR-TB**) is also resistant to three or more of the six classes of second-line drugs.

Many countries use Bacillus Calmette-Guérin (BCG) vaccine as part of their TB control programs, especially for infants. According to WHO, this is the most often used vaccine worldwide, with 85% of infants in 172 countries immunized in 1993. This was the first vaccine for TB and developed at the Pasteur Institute in France between 1905 and 1921. However, mass vaccination with BCG did not start until after World War II. The protective efficacy of BCG for preventing serious forms of TB (e.g. meningitis) in children is greater than 80%; its protective efficacy for preventing pulmonary TB in adolescents and adults is variable, ranging from 0 to 80%.

Several new vaccines to prevent TB infection are being developed. The first recombinant tuberculosis vaccine entered clinical trials in the United States in 2004, sponsored by the National Institute of Allergy and Infectious Diseases (NIAID). A 2005 study showed that a DNA TB vaccine given with conventional chemotherapy can accelerate the disappearance of bacteria as well as protect against re-infection in mice; it may take four to five years to be available for humans. A very promising TB vaccine, MVA85A, is currently in phase II trials in South Africa by a group led by researchers at the Oxford University, and is based on a genetically modified vaccinia virus. Many strategies are also being used to develop novel vaccines. In order to encourage further discovery, researchers and policymakers are promoting new economic models of vaccine development including prizes, tax incentives and advance market commitments.

The Bill and Melinda Gates Foundation has been a strong supporter of new TB vaccine development. Most recently, they announced a $200 million grant to the Aeras Global TB Vaccine Foundation for clinical trials on up to six different TB vaccine candidates currently in the pipeline.

Malaria

Malaria is a common disease in the tropical and subtropical countries and one of the leading causes of death in the developing world even though it is largely preventable. It is the eighth leading cause of morbidity nationwide, affecting 59 of the country's 81 provinces. Pregnant women, children and indigenous population groups are the most vulnerable. (*PS,* December 23, 2008) But how many poor and unemployed upland dwellers can afford the preventive medicine? According to WHO, malaria may be responsible for up 500 million new cases each year and kills 1.5 to 2.7 million people, mainly children in the sub-Saharan countries. The disease is caused by a group of parasites called plasmodia. Like other forms of parasites, plasmodia are organisms that need to feed on other organisms in order to survive. There are four different parasites that cause human malaria: *Plasmodium vivax, Plasmodium falciparum, Plasmodium malariae* and *Plasmodium ovale*. They are transmitted by mosquito bites, specifically female mosquitoes of the group *Anopheles*, which need a supply of blood to produce eggs. Worldwide, some 400 different mosquitoes belong to this group, and approximately 60 of these transmit the malaria disease. Mosquitoes breed in standing water, especially after floods. In colder climates the malaria mosquitoes are not as common, because the low temperatures will kill them. The disease can passed from one person to another through the bites of the mosquito.

Symptoms of malaria include fever, shivering or chill, flu-like illness, anemia, pain in the joints, headache, repeated vomiting, generalized convulsions and coma. If not treated, the most serious kind caused by the *P. falciparum* parasite, can become deadly within two days. The other malaria parasites cause less serious symptoms, but can weaken a person's immune system, making a person vulnerable to other infectious, life-threatening diseases.[87]

The disease is commonly connected to poverty and has been a hindrance to economic development. It is also being exacerbated by global warming because the malaria-causing mosquitoes cannot survive in cool weather but can feed and reproduce more quickly in warm weather. As temperature increases, scientists expect to see more people living under warmer areas within the malarial zone. This could jump to 60% of the world's population from the present 45%. The same is true with dengue fever. Like the malaria parasite, the dengue virus is also carried out by a mosquito, usually Aedes aegypti that thrives also in warm conditions. Even the high-altitude areas are not spared from these parasites. (Brown and Ayres, 41)

Although medicines for the disease have been under development, no vaccine is currently available that can completely cure the disease. Preventative drugs must be taken continuously to reduce the risk of infection. These prophylactic drug treatments are often too expensive for most people living in endemic areas. Most adults from endemic areas have a degree of long-term infection, which tends to recur and also possess partial immunity (resistance). The resistance reduces with time. Malaria infections are treated through the use of anti-malaria drugs, such as quinine or artemisinin derivatives, although drug resistance is increasingly common.[88] The best defense against getting infect in endemic areas is to use bed net treated with insecticides. This effective preventive measure is being promoted by WHO and other health agencies.

Currently, the Roll Back Malaria project is in place to help reduce the malaria infection in 16 provinces in Mindanao, in Luzon's province of Rizal and in the Visayas. It is implemented by the WHO in partnership with the DOH and the support of the Australia Agency for International Development with a new grant of an additional P144 million given recently. The goal is to eliminate malaria totally by 2020. Since 2000, the project has claimed to reduce malaria cases by

---

[87] http://nobelprize.org/educational_games/medicine/malaria/readmore/index.html
[88] http://en.wikipedia.org/wiki/Malaria

32% and malaria deaths by 86% in 12 provinces in Mindanao, and benefiting an estimated six million people.

The Australian support for the program in Agusan del Sur since 1995 has made it possible to reduce the malaria incidence to less than 1% and no recorded deaths in the province from 2004-2007. For the year 2008-2009, the Australian Government will provide an estimated P4.4 billion in development assistance to the Philippines, focusing of equitable economic growth, education, national stability, and human security.

Measles

Measles is a disease caused by the paramyxovirus of the genus *Morbillivirus*. "German measles" is an unrelated condition caused by the rubella virus. The disease is spread through coughing and respiration (contact with fluids from an infected person's nose and mouth, either directly or through aerosol transmission), and is highly contagious - 90% of people without immunity sharing a house with an infected person will catch it. Airborne precautions should be taken for all suspected cases of measles. This is a tall order since highly populated areas with many people living in poor standard of living and not enough doctors and medical supplies make it difficult to stop the diseases from spreading.

The incubation period usually lasts for 4 to 12 days (during which there are no symptoms). Infected people remain contagious from the appearance of the first symptoms until 3 to 5 days after the rash appears.

Reports of measles go as far back to at least 600 B.C. However, the first scientific description of the disease and its distinction from smallpox is attributed to the Persian physician Ibn Razi (Rhazes; 860-932) who published a book entitled *The Book of Smallpox and Measles* (in Arabic: *Kitab fi al-jadari wa-al-hasbah*). In roughly the last 150 years, measles has been estimated to have killed about 200 million people worldwide. In 1954, the virus causing the disease was isolated from an 11-year old boy from the US, David Edmonston, adapted and propagated on chick embryo tissue culture for the development of a vaccine. To date, 21 strains of the measles virus have been identified. Licensed vaccines to prevent the disease became available in 1963.

Once transmission occurs, the virus infects and replicates in the lymphatic system, urinary tract, conjunctivae, blood vessels and central nervous system of its host. The role of epithelial cells is uncertain, but the virus must infect them to spread to a new individual. Patients with the measles should be placed on droplet precautions. Humans are the only known natural hosts of measles, although the virus can infect some non-human primate species.

Complications with measles are relatively common, ranging from relatively mild and less serious diarrhea, to pneumonia and encephalitis (subacute sclerosing panencephalitis), corneal ulceration leading to corneal scarring. Complications are usually more severe amongst adults who catch the virus.

The fatality rate from measles for otherwise healthy people in developed countries is low: approximately 1 death per thousand cases. In underdeveloped nations with high rates of malnutrition and poor healthcare, fatality rates of 10% are common. In immunity compromised patients, the fatality rate is approximately 30%.

Vaccination is the best defense against measles. In developed countries, most children are immunized against measles by the age of 18 months, generally as part of a three-part MMR vaccine (measles, mumps, and rubella). The vaccination is generally not given earlier than this because children younger than 18 months usually retain anti-measles immunoglobulins (antibodies) transmitted from the mother during pregnancy. A booster vaccine is then given between the ages of four and five. Vaccination rates have been high enough to make measles relatively uncommon.

Unvaccinated populations are at risk for the disease. After vaccination rates dropped in northern Nigeria in the early 2000s due to religious and political objections, the number of cases rose significantly, and hundreds of children died. A 2005 measles outbreak in Indiana was attributed to children whose parents refused vaccination. In the early 2000s the MMR vaccine controversy in the United Kingdom regarding a potential link between the combined MMR vaccine and autism prompted a measles comeback after parents deliberately infect the child with weakened measles to build up the child's immunity. This practice poses many health risks to the child, and has been discouraged by the public health authorities. Scientific evidence provides no support that MMR plays a role in causing autism. However, the MMR scare in Britain caused vaccination to drop and measles cases surge. In 2007, 971 cases in England and Wales were reported, the biggest rise since records began in 1995.

According WHO, measles is a leading preventable childhood disease. Worldwide, the fatality rate has been significantly reduced by vaccination with the help of many government and private NGOs. Globally, measles deaths are down 60%, from an estimated 873,000 deaths in 1999 to 345,000 in 2005. Africa has seen the most success, with annual measles deaths falling by 75% in just 5 years, from an estimated 506,000 to 126,000.

The joint press release by members of the Measles Initiative brings to light another benefit of the fight against measles: "Measles vaccination campaigns are contributing to the reduction of child deaths from other causes. They have become a channel for the delivery of other life-saving interventions, such as bed nets to protect against malaria, de-worming medicine and vitamin A supplements. Combining measles immunization with other health interventions is a contribution to the achievement of Millennium Development Goal Number 4: a two-thirds reduction in child deaths between 1990 and 2015."

Pneumonia

One life-threatening illness that causes a disturbing number of infant deaths in the Philippines is invasive pneumococcal disease (IPD), an acute bacterial infection caused by *Steptococcus pneumoniae*. Aside from being the leading cause of pneumonia, the bacterium causes meningitis and sepsis or bacteremia. Pneumonia is characterized by the inflammation of the lungs; meningitis is a condition where the fluid-filled membranes that cover the brain and spinal cord become inflamed, and sepsis/bacteremia is the presence of bacteria in the blood. Young infants below 24 months old whose immune systems are not yet fully developed are particularly susceptible to infection. Without early and adequate medication, IPD is a potentially fatal affliction. "Streptococcus pneumonia is a killer disease that is neglected and forgotten by many. But if you look at the number of children killed every day because of pneumococcal disease, there are staggering statistics," says Dr. Lulu Bravo. "The burden of the disease on the very young cannot be overemphasized."

WHO pegs IPD deaths at 1.6 million people annually. Of these, 700,000 to one million are children under five years old and over 90% of these deaths occur in developing countries. Pneumonia is a top killer in India, China, Nigeria, Pakistan, Bangladesh, Indonesia, and Brazil. The Philippines is 10th in the list and 35% of the patients succumbs to the disease. However, the real figures may still rise significantly. This is because pneumonia is not a reported disease, with any standard surveillance for it. Consequently, the actual statistics for pneumonia mortality may be considerably higher, especially since the disease is easily spread through droplet infection.

The symptoms of IPD are common enough, beginning with a severe chill followed by high fever, cough, and shortness of breath, rapid breathing, and chest pains. Certain patients may complain of nausea, vomiting, headache, tiredness, and muscle pain. Infants and young children may exhibit either increased irritability or lethargy and disinterest or difficulty in feeding. Although antibiotics are employed to treat infection, these are often expensive. In addition, resistant strains would require a longer hospitalization period or could even be fatal.

The good news is that there are vaccines that can prevent the disease. Currently, two vaccines are available commercially. These are the 23-valent unconjugated polysaccharide vaccine and the 7-valent pneumococcal conjugate vaccine (PCV-7). While both were shown to be effective, PCV-7 is licensed for use in children and infants below five years old, an age group that is greatly at risk for life-threatening pneumococcal disease. The downside is that not many children are immunized despite the availability of the vaccine. "Although the disease is vaccine-preventable, PCV-7 is not included in the national immunization program of many countries, including the Philippines," says Dr. Lulu Bravo. The vaccines included in the Philippine expanded program of immunization of the DOH are BCG (against tuberculosis), DPT (diphtheria, pertussis, and tetanus), OPV (oral polio vaccine), measles, and hepatitis B vaccine. Although the Philippine Pediatric Society, the Pediatric Infectious Disease Society of the Philippines and the Philippine Foundation for Vaccination recommends immunization with pneumococcal conjugate vaccine (PCV-7) to children six weeks to five years old, most mothers are unaware that the IPD vaccine is also important.

Poverty and Crimes

There is a simple correlation between poverty and crimes. Crimes are often committed on persons and properties because of the need of the poor and his family to be fed. The jobless cannot afford to see himself and his family starved. That is why most of the inmates are poor, sometimes too poor to engage the services of good lawyers. There is also the greediness in the heart of many people who would resort to illegal means to enrich themselves.

This seems to be borne out by the police report crime incidents that the "non-index crimes" has rose by 7.92% from January to June 2008, citing the rising prices of basic commodities as the culprit. "Criminality is related to poverty. Because of the crisis that we are experiencing today, crimes against property (street crimes) have slightly increased," said Supt. Dionardo Carlos, PNP Deputy Chief Public Information Officer, during a Kapihan forum.[89]

It is normal for crime against properties to shoot up during a crisis. Citing data from the National Capital Region Police Office (NCRPO), GMA News' Marisol Abdurahman reported on QTV's *Balitanghali* that more than 250 incidences of crime against property in Metro Manila have been recorded for the first half of July 2008 alone, with snatching as one of the most rampant.

The more serious crime such as bank robberies in Metro Manila rose from 34 during the first half of 2007 to 41 during the same period this year. Carnapping incidents for the first quarter rose from 375 during the first quarter of 2007 to 392 this quarter. NCRPO chief Director Geary Barias attributed the increase in crimes to the hike in prices of basic commodities, particularly fuel. The number of unemployed is pegged at 3 million, according to the National Statistics Center.[90]

Criminals seem to be much more vicious and fearless in taking human lives. This is augmented by the incompetence of our law enforcement agencies. One of the latest armed robberies resulted in the death of six civilians including a seaman and his 8-year-old daughter in a shootout on December 5, 2008 at Parañaque City. Ten robbers were also killed. The father and daughter were in their vehicle when the shooting started. Their Isuzu Crosswind suffered more than 80 bullet holes for no apparent reason except to be at the wrong place and at the wrong time. (*PDI*, December 23, 2008) The seaman could not have been a suspect while driving along with his daughter. In the past, police officers have been trigger-happy to use their guns even while the victims were still in harm's way.

A grimmer picture of our crime situation is the number of homicides being committed in our predominantly Christian society. Crimes have also been committed against legislators within the confined of the Catholic Church. It is partly the failure of the churches, especially the Catholic Church for not instilling discipline among their flocks. No doubt, most of these crimes are committed by Catholics. Even in the U.S. which has only 25% Catholics, prison records bear out the fact that there are just as many professed Catholic criminals as

---

[89] http://www.gov.ph/news/printerfriendly.asp?i=21694
[90] http://tsikot.yehey.com/forums/showthread.php?t=51948

there are non-Catholics. With only a fourth of the population, that would make them four times as many. In contrast, in the State of Utah, homicides or other crimes for that matter is so far and in between because the Mormons have more value for human lives than any other religious organizations.

In the Philippines, in 2005, the numbers of people slain as compiled by the PNP was 6,334 for murder and 3,240 for homicide; in 2006, 6,196 cases of murder and 3,299 for homicide; and the first five months of 2007, 2,459 murder and 1,241 cases for homicide.[91] A comparative study of our crime index for 2006, the 9,400 plus cases would be projected to around 31,000 plus (300M/90M population ratio) against the 17,000 plus in the U.S. even though the U.S. has many more firearms than we have. What is more worrisome is that most of the homicides are cases of murder. Maybe it is time to revive the death penalty for murder.

Families and relatives of victims of crimes often suffer traumatic events due to the crime. The rich often experience financial problems to catch the criminal/s and bring them to justice and time is often lost from work to handle the legal, insurance, estate taxes and other personal problems associated with the victim. The trauma associated with any crime often makes it hard for victims and their relatives to cope with normal daily routines. Those who try to find justice in our court system find the system elusive and sometimes very expensive. There are so many corrupt and lazy judges who seldom lift a finger unless they are greased. Only the sensational cases are ever decided without much delay. The poor seldom find justice in our courts because they have nothing to offer the corrupt judges to speed up the cases or find good lawyers to handle the cases for them.

More people can only mean more untoward contacts resulting in civil and criminal cases brought to the courts. As of 2006, there are about 800,000 cases lodged in our courts, for which more than 353,000 are pending in the regional trial courts, more than 100,000 in the metropolitan trials courts, and 130,000 in the municipal trials. The long delay in the resolution of cases is due principally to the large number of vacancies in the judiciary, the laziness of some judges and the dilatory tactics of lawyers. (*PDI*, July 14, 2008) Most of these cases involved money matters such as the violation of the Bouncing Check Law, forcible entry and illegal detainer and incidents of crime

---

[91] *www.pnp.gov.ph/stat/content/stat.html*

involving money. Instead of speedy justice, the courts have become a tool to delay justice and even a way of rendering injustice by corrupt judges. The Supreme Court, without a time limit to render decisions can be an unwilling tool used to delay justice. It is for this reason why lawyers often threatened to appeal their cause or their lost cases to the Supreme Court. It is time the SC punished the lawyers for filing frivolous and dilatory appeal cases on pain of substantial fine and even suspension of practice.

Move to declog court cases through the barangay courts have settled more than four million cases from 1980 to 2005 and resulted in the government savings of more than P24 billion. This just goes to show that overcrowded population can cause more incidents of antagonism among people, especially when they live so closely together.

Another reason for the piling up of cases in the judiciary is the indiscriminate filing of cases. Instead of out-of-court settlements, litigants are often coached by their lawyers into battling the cases in courts. With more than 40,000 lawyers, many of them idle professionals, no wonder they need to keep the case from finality. But then, there are those who plainly refused to pay their dues and expect to delay the payments knowing that it will take years for the case to be resolved.

A country that is poor and overpopulated has less opportunity for the poor to enrich themselves with little opportunity available for them. For every rag-to-riches saga, there are tens of thousands who failed to uplift their lives. However, the Church and prolifers do not see it that way. Instead they blame injustice and inequality in the distribution of wealth as the main source of why there are many poor and hungry people. It should have known by now that there is just not enough for everything to go around for everyone. Not everyone can have good food all year round. It is only through hard work and good business acumen and opportunity that they were able to achieve a better life. If we were able to distribute the nation's wealth equally like in communist states, then we will all end up poor. This is why communism has been discredited.

With the population increasing at about 1.8 million annually, there are not enough jobs to absorb the unemployed. How else are these unemployed going to fill their stomachs and that of their family members? The sad fact is that some resort to criminal acts with total disregard for human lives. These are the killers for hire who would kill for a few thousand pesos without any remorse. Cases of fearless murderers in motorcycle are on a rampage. Part of the reason may be the lifting of the death penalty law. The death penalty law was a good law that is seldom applied but served as a sword of Damocles for would-be heinous crime offenders. It no longer instills fear in the hearts of criminals after it was abrogated to appease the Catholic Church. As a result, offenders are becoming bolder in taking lives as a way of settling disputes. Every year thousands are being killed for minor disputes among neighbors to heinous crimes such as bank robberies and even murder of investigative reporters.

The Church's stand against the death penalty is not motivated by its sincere belief in the teaching of the Bible. Anyone who is aware of its past history will know that in time past when it control the central part of what is today's Italy, she is a theocratic state run by popes with dictatorial power. Millions have been killed for deviating from her interpretation of the Bible. More millions had been killed during the reign of terror of the Inquisition and the witch hunt. It was only when the governments had gotten off the religious yoke of the Church and the loss of the Papal States did the people breathe a sigh of relief from being dominated by the Church in their lives. It is the secularization of the states that brought down the Church from enforcing its own brand of justice which is often cruel and unusual punishments such as torture including the imposition of death penalty for crimes against the Holy Church.

Then there is the problem of insurgents trying to take over the rein of government and the separatist movements trying to dismember the country. The Communist Party of the Philippines' military arm, the New People's Army (NPA) has been fighting the government for almost 40 years in trying to turn the country into a communist state. Sporadic fighting has been going on for years, killing thousands of innocent civilians, rebels and military personnel. The NPAs have been attacking isolated military outposts to amass weapons in many provinces. They have recruited and indoctrinated amazons and even children to their ranks. Most of these recruits probably have no meaningful jobs, have been victims of government abuses or victims of injustices by some of our corrupt judges in dispensing justice. Today, there are about 5,000-6,000 active members, according to military estimates, and their presence is felt wherever and whenever they are around. Victims who cannot get justice from our courts often turned to them for instant justice. That is why they are sometimes given the moniker "Nice People Around."

A more serious problem has to do with the Moro Islamic Liberation Front (MILF). This is the latest breakaway group that has been fighting for their ancestral land. Before the coming of the

Spaniards, the Philippines was an Islamic state like her southern neighbors of Malaysia and Indonesia. The country was mostly run by Moro's chieftains before they were gradually displaced and forced to evacuate to the south. Even in their southern stronghold, peace had not come as many Catholics have been transmigrated to the south starting with the presidency of President Elpidio Quirino. The result is more land disputes that often favored the Christians over the Muslims as most of the judges assigned there were Catholics.

The latest controversy has to do with the Memorandum of Agreement (MOA) on Ancestral Domain signed by the government and the MILF. Since then, it has caused widespread chaos in many provinces in southern Mindanao. It stems from the issuance of the temporary restraining order, later made permanent, by the Supreme Court on the signing of the MOA after North Cotabato officials filed a petition against it. As a result of the abrogated agreement, the MILF rebels occupied several villages in some towns in North Cotabato and fighting ensues after they were forcibly moved out. More than 160,000 people were misplaced as the fighting between the rebels and government soldiers took place in one section of a province. Again, the victims were mostly children and women. Some so-called sub-commanders were said to continue the fighting. All it takes is a few rebels to displace thousands of people from their homes because the place was overpopulated. This is what happened in many places in Africa where small scale fighting have displaced whole cities, forcing many to evacuate and face hunger and starvation.

Massive Debts

In our government quest to improve the living standard of the people through industrialization, huge amount have been borrowed from other governments and their financial institutions. Corollary to this noble aim is the possibility of some high government officials to dip into the loans as many of the scams seem to imply.

With unhindered population growth, more money are needed and borrowed if domestic taxes are not enough. Despite the huge borrowings, nothing concrete by way of alleviating poverty and uplifting the standard of living of people had taken place. Neither is country moving toward reducing poverty or becoming self sufficient in basic commodities such as rice. Most of the money earmarked for improving the country ended up in the pockets of corrupt government officials and their cahoots in the private sectors. Many of these massive loans guaranteed by the government have end up as white elephant projects and left the citizenry to pay for them.

There is little doubt that the reason for needing so much foreign exchange is that the taxes collected is never enough to help lift up the standard of living of the poor. We have to resort to foreign borrowings to help alleviate poverty, but as long as the poor people are increasing in number, the debt problem is here to stay. The government has also been selling off some of the lucrative businesses that generate billions for the government annually. Once gone, so are the annual profits that help defrayed some of the government expenses.

Our foreign debts now stood at $54.6 billion as of the end of March 2008. By August, 2008, the government debt stood at P4.024 trillion due to the weakening of the peso against the dollar and the continuing deficit in government spending. (*PS*, November 10, 2008) In terms of per capita, we are theoretically in debt in the tune of P44,711 each. To pay for this huge amount, higher taxes have been imposed on the people, further burdening the middle class and the poor alike. The continuing deficit in government spending is bound to increase this debt. One-third of the taxes paid by the citizenry go into servicing the debt payment. The foreign debts were incurred at a time when it was thought it will hasten the development of the country. Instead most of the foreign exchange dollars were stolen by a dictator and his cronies and other corrupt officials. The sad fact is that corruption is still continuing despite the dire status of the country, no matter who governs the country. The maxim that blood is thicker than water and the thickest of them all is money holds true since time immemorial. Corrupt officials are willing to sell the country down the drain just to enrich themselves. This sad fact is happening to our country in the midst of so many problems plaguing the country.

Now, we end up paying the debts of about P1 billion everyday for the interest alone, money which would have been used to uplift the living standard of the poor. Imagine what a billion pesos a day would have done for the poor members of our society. It would be able to subsidize the roughly three million unemployed Filipinos with P333 daily each for as long as they live. The P1 billion could be spent daily for social services or building homes for homeless people or schoolrooms until the mission is accomplished. The annual budget for debt payments is more than the proposed budgets for the four biggest government departments combined.

Aside from the interest payments, an allocation of a little over P1 billion (P1.045 billion in the proposed 2006 budget) daily is used for paying the principal.

The newly released proposed budget for fiscal year beginning 2009 is P1.415 trillion pesos. Out of this amount, P681.516 billion has been programmed for debt service payment, 7.1% higher than the 2008 allocation of P636.075 billion. This is equivalent to P1.85 billion a day, including Sundays and holidays that we have to work hard to repay the lenders. The proposed budget cannot be covered by domestic taxes and the government is expected to incur a deficit of P40 billion. Unfortunately, the budget deficit has ballooned to P102 billion, thereby incurring additional debt servicing to the tune of P700.6 billion (P384.8 for principal obligation and P315.8 billion for interest payments) from the original P681.516. (*PDI*, November 18, 2008) It is high time for belt-tightening and that we spend within our budget if we want to solve our debt problem. There are actually many rooms for savings especially in the departments known for their corruption. A cap placed on the corrupt departments should be more than enough to solve the expected deficits for years to come until they clean up their departments. Most of the money allocated to them just went to the pocket of the corrupt officials and their cahoots in the private sectors.

The annual budget has been increasing yearly because there are still many essential services that have to be coped with and not enough revenues internally from all sources to satisfy the need. The taxpayers are already burdened with too many taxes, yet new taxes are being imposed only to be stolen in the light of many multimillion scams going on. All these annual increasing budgets could be avoided if only we could maintain our population until such time that we could balance our budget without imposing new taxes. This will not happen in the foreseeable future, but it helps if we could slow down our population growth.

We are always at the mercy of the foreign institutions where we borrowed the money. They can dictate our economic, financial and even political policies. Some of these policies often add more burdens to the poor more than the rich.[92]

We have lost most of our forest resource with nothing to show by way of improving the lives of the upland dwellers and paying off our huge public debts. Now we are opening up our other natural resources of mineral and metals coveted by most of the industrialized countries. Following the declaration of the Supreme Court on the constitutionality of the Mining Act of 2005, the government hoped to capitalize on our mineral resources to pay off our debts and turn our little kingdom into a roaring tiger. Based on defined resources and past

---

92 http://philippinepolitics.net/boards/archive/index.php?t-587.html

production patterns, the Philippines is considered to be the fifth most mineralized country in the world. It has nine million hectares of mineralized land, with established reserves of 13 known metallic and 29 non-metallic minerals spread around the country. Most of the country's 81 provinces have yielded minerals at one time or another. When translated in monetary terms, the country's potential for mineral development is even more astounding. The National Economic and Development Authority (NEDA) has estimated that the country has US$840 billion (PhP47.08 trillion) worth of mineral wealth waiting to be extracted from the ground, almost 10 times the country's annual GDP and 15 times its total foreign debt. At present, only 5% of the country's mineralized areas are being utilized.[93]

Under the Mining Act, mining firms can be 100% foreign-owned and it allows them complete repatriation of all profits back home. It also allocates Filipino tax money to reimburse the corporations for their contributions to the community.[94] The only benefits for the government are the numerous taxes they have to pay the government for the privileges of exploiting our natural resources.

Being the world's second largest producer of gold, copper, and other metals, investors from within and without are busy investing in mining our resources. Unfortunately, mining is one of the most pollutive industries in the world. Many studies have been made about the ill-effects of mining not just in this country but around the world. Investor are only willing to invest if there have little liabilities.

In the case of Lepanto Consolidated and Mining Company (LCMC), water samples in rivers around the plant were reported acidic and contain elevated amounts of suspended solids. The chemical used in gold processing is cyanide. Cyanide is considered the most cost-effective way to retrieve bits of "invisible gold." Along with chromium, lead and mercury, they have been found to be elevated in areas where sample have been taken. The residents of those who lived near the mine site were found to have elevated cyanide, copper and lead in their blood. The more time spent immersed in the mine

---

93

http://209.85.175.104/search?q=cache:Wj291SMxQf4J:www.senate.gov.ph/publications/PI%25202005-11%2520%2520Extracting%2520Growth%2520from%2520Mining.pdf+mining+poverty&hl=en&ct=clnk&cd=4&gl=ph

94

http://ibon.be/index.php?option=com_content&task=view&id=44&Itemid=2

drainages, the higher is the blood contents of these toxic metals and chemicals.[95]

In many areas in Mindanao, the gold miners use mercury for processing has contaminated many rivers and even wells of people living there. Deep wells and reservoirs near the Agusan River, used for drinking water, have been contaminated with mercury. Even the marine resources of the river such as fish, crabs and lobsters have been contaminated.[96]

There are many disadvantages to opening our minerals to foreign exploitation. As per agreement with the government, most of the investors will be using the easiest and cheapest method of open-pit (strip) mining to extract most of the minerals, especially gold and copper. The practice of open-pit mining has already been banned in several industrialized countries including the United States and Canada because of its negative impact on the environment. The mineral are usually located near the surface, and the overburden is removed and the rocks are trucked to the processing area. Only about 1 to 2 ppt (grams per ton) are recoverable. Once the ore are processed, the waste, known as tailings is generally slurry and is pumped to a tailings or settling dam as a storage tank. These tailings dams are often toxic due to the presence of unextracted sulfide mineral and the cyanide used to extract gold. Waste materials and smelters are also known to cause sulfurous dust clouds that result in acid rain.

After years of strip mining, the abandoned mines are nothing but large holes that have no other uses than as landfills for garbage or hazardous wastes. As in all garbage dumps, they contain contaminants that can leach out and contaminate groundwater. It has been estimated that 160,000 tons of mine tailings find their way into rivers, lakes, and irrigation systems across the country everyday.

There have been several documented cases of river poisonings across the country but all of them pale in comparison to the infamous Marcopper tragedy in 1996, considered to be one of the biggest environmental disasters ever to hit the Philippines. Up until today, the effects of the breach of the tailings dam which spilled some three million tons of toxic tailings are still being felt. It has resulted in the biological death of the Boac and Makulapnit rivers, and inundated an

---

[95] http://sunstar.com.ph/static/bag/2005/08/25/news/scientific.studies.on. effect.of.abra.river.pollution.shown.html
[96] http://www.sunstar.com.ph/static/cag/2005/11/29/news/gold.panning. blamed.on.mercury.pollution.html

additional 823 hectares of once productive farmland. It has likewise adversely affected the physical well-being and livelihood opportunities of more than 20,000 families living in 42 communities adjacent to the Boac River. The fact that there has been no clear resolution to the tragedy further erodes the confidence of the public on the capacity of the government to regulate the industry. Subsequent inspections by engineers revealed that the spill was caused by a faulty plugging system due to reckless oversight on the part of government inspectors and private operators. To this day, Marcopper and its former majority shareholder, Canadian mining firm, Placer Dome Inc., continue to deny responsibility for most of the damages caused by mining activities in Marinduque. Placer Dome Inc., the second largest mining firm in Canada, has since divested its share in Marcopper but continues to operate mines around the globe. When the firm was about to be charged in court by the Marinduque Council for Environmental Concern, they were astonished to find that the firm was no longer in existence having sold their shares, change names and ultimately cover their tracks. (Bello, 226) Marinduqueños, on the other hand, continue to contend with the adverse effects of the tailings dam breach.[97] This is also the case with Australia-based BHP Billiton. It sold its profitable Ok Tedi mine in Papua New Guinea in 2001 after having destroyed more than 2,400 acres of rainforest. The company said the mine was not compatible with environmental values.[98]

The World Bank, mostly financed by the rich countries, in her zeal to help the poor countries uplift their standard of living has financed some of the mining companies. Its other aim is to allow the rich nations to get a foothold on the natural resources of the recipient countries. It has helped mining companies bring investment to many remote corners of the globe with investment that hope to bring in roads, schools and jobs. However, these mining companies have jeopardized the environment. A mine in Guyana insured by the bank spilled more than 790,000 gallons of cyanide-laced mine waste into a tributary of the Essequibo River.[99]

Cyanide decomposes in sunlight and is not dangerous if greatly diluted. But a study said that cyanide can convert to other toxic forms and persist, particularly in cold climates. From 1985 to 2000, more than a dozen reservoirs containing cyanide-laden mine waste collapsed. The most severe disaster occurred in Romania in 2000,

---

[97] Ibid
[98] http://overpopulation.org/solutions.html
[99] Ibid

when mine waste spilled into a tributary of the Danube, killing tons of fish and issuing a plume of cyanide that reached 1,600 miles to the Black Sea. A new code sets standards for transporting and storing cyanide and calls on companies to submit to inspections by a new industry body. But the code is voluntary and not enforced.[100]

Some of the areas being exploited are ancestral domain of the indigenous people or infested with rebels. To appease the local residents, the mining firms often promised to pour millions of pesos to help them by constructing schools, set up health care centers and other community projects to strengthen working relationships with the local governments and residents. As often happened in the past, money can buy a lot to appease them to get the leaders to support the project for as long as they are operating. Once the exploitation is completed, the tribal people are left to fend for themselves. As for the rebels, it is against the law to contribute "revolutionary tax" to stop them from harassing the operations. Nevertheless some companies do pay while those refused often found their equipments and buildings torched and personnel abducted for ransom. Move to tighten security could result in more killings instead rather than giving in to their demands.

Another shortcoming of today's operation is that most of the companies employ more efficient technologies and machineries instead of manpower. This greatly reduces the number of people hired that would have alleviated some families from poverty. If past experience is any indication, mining operations have contributed little to alleviating the poverty in the provinces where the operated. In the provinces of Masbate, Camarines Norte and Agusan, where some of the country's biggest gold and copper mines are situated, poverty levels are one of the highest in the country. In Region IV, where the contribution of mining to regional output is the highest at 17%, poverty levels have remained at 39.7%, well above the national average of 24.7% at the time of the survey. While it is true that poverty levels are determined by many other economic and social variables, the contribution of mining in alleviating poverty levels in mining dependent provinces is not obvious. Unlike the developed countries, mining has been a blessing to the industrialization of the country, but not in our country. This is probably due to the fact that only a few elites in the country benefited from the mining operations.

Were it not for the sorry state of our country with its significant number of poor people, there is no compelling reason to

---

[100] Ibid

open up our country to exploitation. The readers may be surprised to find many similarities in the lives of people abroad to those living here after reading the following article written by Lyn V. Ramo, taken from the August 2, 2008 edition of *Bulatlat*

Asia-Pacific Women Bear the Brunt of Mining

A recently-concluded seminar found that mining's adverse impacts fall hardest on women, especially those among the world's poorest populations.

BAGUIO CITY - Participants to the Seminar on Women and Mining at the Asian Institute of Management (AIM) at Camp John Hay here, concluded that mining's adverse impacts fall hardest on women among the world's poorest populations. Khushi Kabir of the Bantey Srei, a women's organization in Bangladesh, said poor women bear the burden of threatened food security due to mining operations.

"It is the poor women who have to scamper for food, face military atrocities and secure the whole family from environmental threats due to mining," Khushi told the Baguio press, shortly after the seminar which gathered more than 30 women from seven countries.

In her native Bangladesh, mining for coal, oil and gas has left communities with large craters and damaged fertile agricultural lands, leaving Bengali farmers in extreme poverty and hunger.

In Thailand, where there is a potash mine, health authorities found cyanide in the blood of residents, and in the river system. Potash is a mineral used to manufacture glass and soap. The Thai mining code, enacted some ten years ago, left landowners only 50 meters from the surface, the resources beyond which include minerals, belong to the Thai government. This is similar to the Regalian Doctrine, adopted in Philippine laws, which states that all minerals belonged to the state. Suntaree, a participant from Thailand said, "People could not get anything from their own lands because the government owns the minerals 50 meters underground."

Sponsored by an all-women development group Asia-Pacific Forum on Women, Law and Development (APWLD), the four-day seminar on mining included tours to Benguet mine sites where participants interacted with local folk in mining communities.

Foreign interests in mining

Mines in all the countries represented are foreign-owned and controlled, with their respective mining laws amended to accommodate foreign ownership. In Indonesia, for instance, the 1965 mining law was amended to suit the interests of foreign investors.

One of the participants said she "did not expect the magnitude of environmental devastation after the minerals have been extracted from the bosom of the earth," describing an abandoned mine site.

Similarly, in the Philippines, the Mining Act of 1995 provides for a financial and technical assistance agreement (FTAA) that allows foreign-owned corporations into mining ventures and grants foreign investors certain rights normally denied aliens.

Newmont, an international mining company with applications for FTAA in the Cordillera, is also in Indonesia. It is being accused of polluting the Indonesian Senunu Bay with heavy metals and other toxic wastes that might be detrimental to the ocean's ecosystem.

Human rights and the Asian women

With mining in their midst, Asian women face security problems due to military presence in their communities. As it turned out during the seminar, extra-judicial killings occur in many mining communities in the Asia-Pacific region. Bangladesh women saw the bitter realities of genocide with the mines at the Thai border displacing many communities before 1979. "When people returned, there was massive landlessness, conflict and poverty," Kushi told the media Monday.

The gathering provided the women a forum to identify their common situations and came up with doable resolutions, according to Vernie Yocogan-Diano, chairperson of Innabuyog-Gabriela, among APWLD conveners and host of the seminar.

APWLD's programs and activities are focused in promoting women's rights as human rights as an analytical and strategic framework of engaging with the legal system to empower women.

APWLD has engaged primarily in policy advocacy, education, training and other activities to address issues and concerns of poor and marginalized women in the region. It has lobbied at regional and international levels for the implementation of government commitments in international conventions and the integration of gender issues at regional and international fora. (End of Article)

Urbanization

In 1800, only 3% of the world's population lived in cities. By the close of the 20th century, 47% did so. In 1950, there were 83 cities with populations exceeding one million; by 2007, this had risen to 468 cities. If the trend continues, the world's urban populations will double every 38 years, say researchers. The UN forecasts that today's urban population of 3.2 billion will rise to nearly 5 billion by 2030, when three out of five people will live in cities.

The increase will be most dramatic in the poorest undeveloped countries with high birth rates and least-urbanized continents: Asia and Africa. Surveys and projections indicate that all urban growth over the next 25 years will be in developing countries. One billion people, one-sixth of the world's population, or one-third of urban population, now live in shanty towns, which are seen as "breeding grounds" for social problems such as crime, drug addiction, alcoholism, poverty and unemployment. In many poor countries slums exhibit high rates of diseases due to unsanitary conditions, malnutrition, and lack of basic health care. By 2030, over 2 billion people in the world will be living in slums.

In 2000, there were 18 megacities – conurbations such as Tokyo, Mexico City, Mumbai (Bombay), Sao Paulo, Shanghai, and New York City – that have populations in excess of 10 million inhabitants. Greater Tokyo already has 35 million, more than the entire population of Canada.

Europe will continue to lag well behind the urbanization seen elsewhere, the UN reported. Of the 19 megacities today, the only European metropolises are Moscow and Istanbul. By 2025 there will be 27 megacities and Europe will only add Paris to the list. It will have an estimated 10 million people, making it number 27 on the list.

The Middle East currently has only one megacity in the capital city of Cairo. In Africa, by 2025, Kinshasa in the Democratic Republic of Congo and Lagos, Nigeria will be added.[101] The Philippines has one megacity which is Metro Manila with about 10.1 million people.

Another report by the *Far Eastern Economic Review*, claimed that by 2025, Asia alone will have at least 10 hypercities, those with 20 million or more, including Jakarta (24.9 million), Dhaka (25 million), Karachi (26.5 million), Shanghai (27 million) and Mumbai (with a staggering 33 million). Lagos has grown from 300,000 in 1950 to an estimated 15 million today, and the Nigerian government estimates that city will have expanded to 25 million residents by 2015.

---

[101] http://www.malaya.com.ph/Mar01/envi1.htm

Chinese experts forecast that Chinese cities will contain 800 million people by 2020.

The latest report coming from the United Nations is that by the end of the year 2008, half the world's population will be living in urban areas or roughly 3.3 billion from the current world's population of 6.7 billion. By 2050 there will be around 6.4 billion living in cities from a total of 9.2 billion. With intense urbanization, the world is expecting eight new megacities (10 million or more inhabitants) by 2025. Tokyo is projected to remain the most populous city in the world with 35.7 million people in its urban agglomeration at last count and should rise to 36.4 million by 2025. India, which is home to two of the world's biggest metropolises, Mumbai and Delhi has 19 and 18.8 million people respectively in 2007. Two new megacities to be added are Calcutta, with an estimated 20.6 million people, and Madras with 10.1 million.

Some people claimed that the country is not overpopulated because of the huge land available in the rural areas. For one thing, this is not true because all alienable lands have been distributed and all inalienable lands are reserves for the common good. The size of the farmlands distributed to the farmers, whatever their sizes are expected to dwindle with each generation as they are subdivided among the children. As a result, many children of farmers are forced to seek their fortune elsewhere. It is also the glittering gold in the urban areas that attract people to them.

It is in the cities where the future lies for most people because it is here where the government concentrates on providing the basic needs and where the standards of living is highest. The basic needs of human for shelter, food, health, education, recreation and employment can be found mostly in cities because here is where most of the wealth are concentrated. Most of the good life can be found in urban areas while people in the rural areas have little opportunity to spend their fortunes. They are often tied to the land they tilled with little hope of improvement. Once their children are grown up, there is also little chance for them to improve and the vicious cycle continues. Those who want to live a different lifestyle have to migrate to urban areas.

The urban population is expected to more than double in the next 30 years with a population growth of over 2%. Many of the urban areas are already congested and can ill-afford to take in more people. Part of the solution is to build high-rise buildings to accommodate the growing population. If the trend continues, more efforts will be necessary to deliver the basic needs such as health services, water supplies, public transportation, public education, peace and order, etc. Most of these will not be forthcoming with our present economic situation and budget deficit. There will just too much problems and priorities and too few resources.

There are many problems associated with urbanization. Urban development has been responsible for encroaching on agricultural land and foreshores to accommodate more people. More roads are needed because of the need for more transport systems such as car that is responsible for the traffic congestion and pollution in many cities. The population of squatters is expected to increase because of the lack of access to adequate housing and services thereby increasing social problems such as crimes, poverty and unemployment. Then there is the perennial problem of solid waste management that has yet to be resolved satisfactorily.

Urbanization has been blamed for the outbreak of many infectious diseases. One example cited by the Secretary of Health Francisco Duque III is dengue. He believes that global warming and rapid urbanization are the two major causes of dengue. He said that warm temperatures make the virus-carrying mosquitoes more active. He went on to cite countries like Vietnam, Thailand, Mexico, and Brazil reporting increases of dengue cases in their country and that even those that did not have dengue before have new cases reported. He added that before, the dengue cases would peak every three years. However, starting 2005 and 2006, there has been a continuous increase in the number of cases of dengue in the country annually. Based on the statistics provided by DOH, from January until May 3, the number of dengue cases in the country reached 10,841. This is 35.6% higher than the figures for 2007's 7,992 cases for the same period, most of them in the slums of the National Capital Region (NCR).[102]

Decentralization or back to the provinces would be a solution to overcrowded cities. But the rate rural dwellers are coming into the urban areas the prospect of a positive decentralization is remote. Plants and factories need to be created in the rural areas to get people to stay put or return home. Few businessmen are willing to move their factories to remote areas unless there is the infrastructure and easy access to the needed raw materials. It is not easy to create new cities in rural areas with all the basic services people hope to enjoy like those in the big cities.

---

[102] http://newsinfo.inquirer.net/breakingnews/nation/view/20080602-140254/Global-warming-rapid-urbanization-blamed-for-dengue-surge

Traffic Congestion

The burning of fossil fuel in the internal combustion engines is the cause of much of our air pollution in the metropolitan areas. With each passing year, the situation seems to be getting worse instead of better in many Third World countries. This is mainly due to the increasing numbers of new vehicles on the road. As of the end of 2007, there are 806 million motor vehicles plying the streets around the world. The U.S, alone has 232 million registered vehicles, accounting for 30% of the world's total.

Each vehicle can consume an average of 600 gallons annually, emitting 12,000 pounds of carbon dioxide in the process. It would take 240 trees to absorb the carbon emitted by each vehicle. Because of the large distances traveled by vehicles in the U.S. - 2.7 trillion miles in 2004, the U.S. share of carbon dioxide emissions stood at 45%.[103] Besides carbon dioxide, there are more noxious gases emitted from burning fossil fuels. These are the hydrocarbons, sulfur dioxide, nitrous oxide, and particulates. Car companies in the U.S. are under pressure to improve mileage or shift to motors using alternative form of energy. They have been trying to produce with less emission. The individuals should also do their share by driving less and taking environmentally promising alternatives.

The need for transportation is very basic to our modern life. As of the end of 2008, there were 5.5 million vehicles registered in this country and increasing by roughly 4.5% annually.[104] At present there is a serious lack of vehicles on a per capita basis, and the increasing affluence of the middle classes and the growing population is expected to keep the demand going. Most of these vehicles are concentrated in the metropolitan areas increasing the traffic congestion. At the same time, there is little room for improvement to accommodate the growing vehicles. Pollution is abetted by the slow flow of traffic causing more unburned pollutants to be spewed to the atmosphere. The same is true whenever the internal combustion engine is idling.

---

[103] http://constantinopal.wordpress.com/2007/04/24/statistics-on-automobiles-and-their-global-warming-contribution/

[104]

http://209.85.175.104/search?q=cache:wDwB3tVAGcwJ:www.lto.gov.ph/Stats2007/

no_of_mv_registered_byMVType_2.pdf+registered+motor+vehicles&hl=en&ct=clnk&cd=5&gl=ph

Motor vehicles are like members of the family. They are well taken care by the rich and poor alike. For the poor which has no parking space at home, the vehicles are forced to squat on public roads, thereby increasing the congestion problem. Many of them are too old to be running, but still they are kept going instead of salvaging the parts for other uses. A vehicle in poor condition is a good candidate for more pollution.

Traffic decongestion need to be addressed to reduce pollution and wasted money. The staggering economic loss has been variously estimated. One NGO, Citizens' Traffic Watch put the loss at more than P15 billion annually. Professors Ricardo Sigua and Noriel Tiglao of U.P. put the economic cost at P100 billion annually while the Department of Transportation and Communication (DOTC), counting direct and indirect economic losses due to traffic congestion at P140 billion.[105] Still another report from The San Francisco-based *Filipinas Magazine* reported that traffic congestion costs the Philippine economy some US$3.6 billion annually. Citing a government study, the magazine said the traffic problem, particularly in Metro Manila, results in a US$1 billion loss to wasted gasoline and electricity, man-hours and hiring of traffic aides; and US$2.6 billion to missed business opportunities, reduced sales and investment disincentives. The study added that total loss would exceed US$36 billion in ten years. It noted that the average speed of a vehicle has slowed to 12.6 kilometers per hour today from 18 kilometers per hour ten years ago.[106] The loss is expected to increase in the coming years as more vehicles hit the roads without the corresponding increase in road networks and the poor driving habits of the motorists.

Not only does traffic congestion reduces average speed and increases emissions, it is also wasting precious time. A U.N. study in 2000 shows that by increasing the average speed from 10 km/h to 20 km/hr could cut CO_2 emissions by nearly 40%. Increasing vehicle speed from 12-15 km/hr to 30 km/hr would be equivalent to fitting a three-way catalytic converter. Studies have shown that measures to decrease traffic congestion by providing more road space eventually increase the volume of traffic.[107] More drastic actions are needed to solve the traffic and pollution problems. Increase the color coding to odd/even would remove half the vehicles off the road during weekdays. The high cost of gasoline through taxation should dampen

---

[105] http://pinoy-business.com/content/view/286/59/
[106] http://philippinepolitics.net/boards/showthread.php?t=254
[107] http://www.klima.ph/cth/solutions/traffic_management/index.php

the use of the motor vehicles. Higher taxes on ownership of vehicles will reduce the buying for motor vehicles. Getting rid of dilapidated vehicles will also reduce the number of vehicles running in the streets.

There are actually a thousand and one ways to save energy for vehicles and clean the environment. Stop corruption in the streets is one way of getting motorists to behave and follow traffic rules and regulations. Traffic lanes should be delineated clearly along the roads and drivers are expected to tow the lines instead of creating new lanes. This should smooth the flow of traffic without the drivers having to worrying about being cut in by other drivers. This often results in road rage and ending with shootout. The traffic intersection should be kept clear at all times to allow traffic flow even during times of congestion. Whether the presence of yellow box is of no consequence and violators should be apprehended and heavily fined. How else do you discipline motorists where it hurts? In Hong Kong, where drivers are well disciplined, there are no traffic aides manning the streets, even in the marketplace.

One of the most frustrating is the lack of road names or too small lettering in many streets. Street names should be visible at a far distance to aid the flow of traffic. The names should also be conspicuous to avoid mistakes. Whenever a driver has to make a choice whether to take a left or right turn, arrow signs with the expected destination should be placed immediate in front. This is what I encountered at the intersection of South Super Highway and the Andrew Blvd. near Magallanes. At the T-intersection, there is no sign indicating which way the left and right turn will lead to. In the case of intersection or junction, the signs should be placed high above the lanes for visibility, or right at the junction and not after the lane as in the Villamor Circle where the lane going to Tramo is placed when the vehicle is already inside the lane. The placement of DO NOT ENTER or restricted signs should be large enough and placed before the motorists have inadvertently entered the lane.

Another sorely lacking are the painted road lanes, many of them have faded to oblivion. How can drivers keep to the proper lanes when there are no delineated lanes to follow? These lanes should be equally spaces, even for the outer most lanes. Vehicles not complying with proper lane procedure should be apprehended for possible drunken driving. The same goes for drivers who have a bad habit of creating new lanes out of nowhere.

Traffic lights are also important, especially in heavy traffic intersections. Many of the traffic lights have busted lights that should be replaced to avoid confusion among drivers.

By far the greatest effort in helping to decongest traffic while reducing the emission of greenhouse gases is to stay and work at home through teleconference or telemarketing and if traveling is necessary, use the public mass transport system. In one survey, if only 1% of the cars in Great Britain is left at home by the owners, once a week, it could save 14 million gallons of petrol a year and cut pollutants about 200 million pounds of carbon dioxide out of the atmosphere. If 2% of the commuters use public transport to work in downtown central London, it will save a million hours of stop-go pollution and gain a million hours of productive work time every years.(Earthworks, 33)

Biking has been the mainstay of travel in many places before the advent of the automobiles. Bicycles are space saving transportation, occupying ten of them in place of one automobile and therefore help in traffic decongestion. It can travel 1,600 miles with the equivalent of one gallon of petrol with the food supplied energy. If just 1% of the people in Great Britain use bicycles instead of car, it could save 400,000 tons of CO_2 from being emitted every year and take 140,000 cars off the road during the same period. (Ibid, 67)

The digital age has made it possible for people from different places and different time zone to work together without so much as a telephone line. The convenience of teleconference not only save traveling time, it also reduces the cost of traveling while giving employee more flexibility. It is healthier than going out and working in buildings that could cause the Sick Building Syndrome. (Ibid, 131)

Chapter 4

ENVIRONMENTAL DEGRADATION

People are the main polluters of the planet. Once the environment has reached its carrying capacity to handle the pollutants, it will start to deteriorate leading to degradation. There are already many signs of degradation in many overpopulated countries including ours. There was a time when people are few and the resilient Earth was able to cope with the situation. Since the Industrial Revolution of the 18th century, things began to turn for the worse for the environment. The demand of people for a better life led to the invention of many conveniences of life at the expense of the environment. As businessmen start to extract more resources from the earth, their wanton destruction leads to much environmental degradation we are facing today. With this in mind, 1500 scientists from around the world, 99 of them Nobel laureates, signed a statement in 1992 claiming that human beings and the natural world are on a collision course that may alter the living world that it will be unable to sustain life in the manner that we know. (Robinson, 13)

Jared Diamond had dire warning about environmental degradation in his book *Collapse* (2005). He argues that many earlier civilizations have collapsed due to environmental problems, and warns of current environmental problems. However, he also notes many situations in which humans have managed their natural resources well. I feel that fifty years from now, with the dwindling natural resources and environmental problems as people try to squeeze out all they needed from this planet, the population may not be able to cope with these problems.

Acid Rain

Acid rain (pH below 5.6) is the common name given to acidic precipitation in the form of rain, snow, sleet, fog, dew, etc. as it falls down to the earth. It is usually caused by the burning of fossil fuels producing the compounds of nitrogen oxides and sulfur dioxide in combination with oxygen. Nitric oxide (NO) is a mixture of one nitrogen atom and one oxygen atom and has been implicated in a host of environmental problems such as smog, acid rain, and water pollution. The other form of nitrous oxide has two atoms of nitrogen and one atom of oxygen is responsible for the greenhouse effect. It is 250 times more powerful than carbon dioxide and can last for 125 years in the atmosphere. These gases are the by-products of firing processes of extreme high temperatures utilized in several industries such as the automobiles manufacturing, utility plants, and in chemical industries (fertilizer production). Natural processes such as bacterial action in soil, forest fires, volcanic action, and lightning make up 5% of nitrogen oxide emission. Transportation makes up 43%, and 32% belongs to industrial combustion.

Sulfur dioxide comes from many sources. It is emitted from coal-burning power plants to produce heat and electricity. It is a colorless, prudent gas released as a by-product of combusted fossil fuels containing sulfur. A variety of industrial processes, such as the production of iron and steel, utility factories, and crude oil processing produced this gas. The smelting of metal sulfate ore to produce iron and steel also releases sulfur dioxide. Metals such as zinc, nickel, and copper are commonly obtained by this process. Sulfur dioxide can also be emitted into the atmosphere by natural means. Another 10% of all sulfur dioxide emission comes from volcanic eruption, sea spray, plankton, and rotting vegetation. Overall, 69.4% of sulfur dioxide is produced by industrial combustion. Only 3.7% is caused by transportation sector.[108] In the air, the sulfur dioxide is oxidized by reaction with the hydroxyl radical via an intermolecular reaction to form sulfur trioxide. Once in contact with moisture it is converted to sulfuric acid leading to acid rain. It has harmful effects on plants, aquatic animals, and infrastructure such as statues. It has also been shown to cause illness and premature deaths such as cancer and other diseases. Some of the effects of acid rain are listed below.

- Building and monuments damaged by acid rain can be quite costly to repair. In Westminster, England, up to ten million pounds has been spent to repair them. In 1990, the United States spent thirty-five billion dollars to repaint damage buildings.
- In 1985, the Cologne Cathedral cost the Germans approximately twenty million dollars in repairs while the Roman monuments cost the Romans about two hundred million dollars so far.
- In areas like the Northeastern United States, where soil-buffering capacity is poor, some lakes have a pH value of less than 5. One of the most acidic lakes reported is Little Echo Pond in Franklin, New York with a pH of 4.2.
- Acid rain reduces fish population numbers and even completely eliminates fish species from a water body. As acid rain flows through soils in a watershed, aluminum is released from soils into the lakes and streams located in that watershed. As pH in a lake or stream decreases, aluminum levels increase. Both low pH and increased aluminum levels are directly toxic to fish. If the fish are not killed, they can suffer chronic stress leading to lower body weight and smaller size and makes fish less able to compete for food and survival. At pH 5, most fish eggs cannot hatch. At even lower pH levels, no fish can survive for long.

---

[108] http://www.geocities.com/capecanaveral/hall/9111/DOC.HTML

- Nitrogen is an important factor in causing eutrophication of water bodies. The symptoms of eutrophication include blooms of algae (both toxic and non-toxic), declines in the health of fish and shellfish, loss of seagrass beds and coral reefs, and ecological changes in food chains in the ocean.
- Acid rain does not usually kill trees directly. Instead, it is more likely to weaken trees by damaging their leaves, limiting the nutrients available to them, or exposing them to toxic substances that are slowly released from the soil. Quite often, injury or death of trees is a result of the effects of acid rain in combination with one or more additional threats.
- The results of laboratory experiments and at least one field study have demonstrated that acid rain can scar automotive coatings. Furthermore, chemical analyses of the damaged areas of some exposed test panels indicate elevated levels of sulfate that directly implicates acid rain.
- The pollutants that cause acid rain - sulfur dioxide (SO_2) and nitrogen oxides (NO_x) - can damage human health. These gases interact in the atmosphere to form fine sulfate and nitrate particles that can be transported long distances by winds and inhaled deep into people's lungs. Fine particles can also penetrate indoors. Many scientific studies have identified a relationship between elevated levels of fine particles and increased illness and premature death from heart and lung disorders, such as asthma and bronchitis.
- High altitude forests are especially vulnerable to acidic air as they are often surrounded by clouds and fog which are more acidic than the precipitation.
- Food crops can also be damaged by acid rain but can be minimized by the application of lime and fertilizers to replace lost nutrients. In cultivated areas, limestone may also be added to increase the ability of the soil to keep the pH stable, but this tactic is largely unusable in the case of wilderness lands. When calcium is leached from the needles of red spruce, these trees become less cold tolerant and exhibit winter injury and even death.[109]
- Tropical trees are less vulnerable to acid rain and there are far fewer coal-fired power plants in the country to cause too much problem from acid rain.

---

[109] http://en.wikipedia.org/wiki/Acid_rain

Solutions lie in minimizing the emission of sulfur dioxide (SO_2) and nitrogen oxide (NOx) to the atmosphere. In the industrial West, many coal-burning power plants use flue gas desulfurization (FGD) to remove sulfur-containing gases from their stack gases. FGD is very expensive to build and operate. An example of FGD is the wet scrubber which is commonly used in the U.S. and many other countries. A wet scrubber is basically a reaction tower equipped with a fan that extracts hot smoke stack gases from a power plant into the tower. Lime or limestone in slurry form is injected into the tower to mix to react with the stack gases containing sulfur dioxide. The calcium carbonate of the limestone produces pH-neutral calcium sulfate that is physically removed from the scrubber. That is, the scrubber turns sulfur pollution into industrial sulfates that can be made in gypsum.

In some areas the sulfates are sold to chemical companies as gypsum when the purity of calcium sulfate is high. In others, they are placed in landfill. However, the effects of acid rain can last for generations, as the effects of pH level change can stimulate the continued leaching of undesirable chemicals into otherwise pristine water sources, killing off vulnerable insect and fish species and blocking efforts to restore native life.

Scientists at U.S. National Aeronautic and Space Administration (NASA) seem to have found some use for acid rain in controlling methane that is causing global warming. Acid rain contains low levels of sulfur and they found that over the years, these seemingly low doses of sulfur reduced methane production in marshlands by at least 30%. Climate experts believe that sulfur in acid rain can prevent methane emissions from increasing. The researchers remain optimistic in the fact that by the year 2030, methane emissions will actually be reduced to levels that existed in pre-industrial levels. However they do not want to emphasize that acid rain is a good thing in general. It still damages forest and grasslands and pollutes rivers and lakes. It is just an effective suppressor of methane gas emissions.[110]

Deforestation

---

[110] http://biologicalresearch.biz/biological-research/scientists-find-acid-rain-an-unlikely-ally-in-the-battle-against-greenhouse-gas/

The earth's surface was once covered with more than 12% forests and is now down to about 5% and continues to diminish at a rate of about 15.5 million km². At this rate of destruction, the forest of the world will be wiped out in half a century. As human population increases, the need for more timber and more room to shelter the increasing population is bound to further put pressure on the forests.

Forests are one of the most important resources of any country. Trees have more than a thousand uses and are the precursor of fossil fuels. With increasing population, the demand for wood will continue for as long as the population is increasing. It is a source of cheap construction materials as there is no cheap substitute that came close to replacing the trees. It is also the only source of energy for forest dwellers. The loss of trees is a good indicator of how a country is faring.

The forest has also served as a sink for carbon for millions of years. By cutting down the trees, or burning the forests, it has released billions of tons of carbon into the atmosphere in the form of greenhouse gases that is the cause of 18 to 20% of the greenhouse gases emitted to atmosphere annually.

The forest is also home to millions of species of plants and animals, some of which may shelter the solutions to many human problems such as medical cures for diseases. Upland farmers sometimes resort to burning down the forest to get the nutrients for the slash-and-burn farming method in the absence of fertilizers. This is one cause of forest destruction, especially in timber rich countries like Indonesia and Brazil. Burning wood has always been a source of warmth, light, and cooking since time immemorial.

Forest burning is sometimes resorted to make room for cattle ranching in South America, for plantation clearing in Malaysia and Indonesia and to make room for new habitation for the teeming urban population. It is a most wasteful solution because the trees could have been harvested and turned into furniture for carbon safekeeping instead of releasing to the atmosphere.

For a time, timber export was the main foreign exchange earner in the country. Despite the loss of great forestland, the country never benefited from the export of this important natural resource. Only a few wealthy individuals in the country benefited while leaving the country devastated from natural calamities. Even the people living in these devastated bald land once covered with trees never benefited. They remained just as poor if not poorer than when the trees were around.

Massive deforestation is the onset of soil erosion leading to desertification. This is the experience of Madagascar's once biologically productive lands. The high population growth has forced people to cut down the forest in trying to subsist. The country is currently unable to provide adequate food, fresh water and sanitation for its population. Madagascar does not have secure property rights that would have encourage the people to protect their lands. When demand outstrips the regenerating power of the trees to meet it, deforestation is sure to follow. The only way to stabilize the demand and supply of a renewable resource is to stabilize the population.

Madagascar's long isolation from the neighboring continents (it is the oldest island in the world, isolated for at least 65 million years) has resulted in a unique mix of plants and Malagasy fauna, many found nowhere else in the world; some ecologists refer to Madagascar as the "eighth continent." Unfortunately, Madagascar has lost 95% of its rainforests during the last 50 years.

Its environmental problems are caused especially by rapid population growth. Extensive deforestation through slash-and-burn farming has taken place in many parts of the country. Slash-and-burn is a method used by shifting cultivators to create short-term yields from marginal soils. The nutrients from the burned trees are used as fertilizers for farming. When practiced repeatedly or without intervening fallow periods, the nutrient-poor soils may be exhausted or eroded to an unproductive state. The resulting increased surface runoff from burned lands has caused significant erosion resulting in high sedimentation to rivers. It has also reduced the forest habitat for many endangered biological species, some unique to the world.

The Philippines is also home to a lot of mineral resources found mostly in the forested areas. In a bid to help the country pay off some of huge debts, the government has been granting licenses to multinational companies to mine these minerals for export to earn dollars from the taxes paid. To mine these minerals, forests stand in the way and have to be destroyed. Mining and road constructions have led to forest destruction and mine tailing have been responsible for pollution in the areas where they operate.

There are roughly 20 million indigenous people scattered throughout the country. Except for those who were well educated and left for the urban areas, most of those left behind live below the poverty level. The upland without the fruits of the forest cover has nothing to offer them except farming and some handicrafts. The government's allocation for the protection and management of their ancestral domains remains bogged down in the face of many vested interests exploiting them. The indigenous people have little hope of taking over the ancestral land due to the inability of the government to grant their wishes with titles to these lands. Instead the government has priority over their ancestral lands should minerals be found underneath the land. As a result, many indigenous people have been driven out of their ancestral land.

There are many other problems confronting the indigenous people. They have to content with militarization of their land because many areas have been invaded by rebels and lawless elements. Then, there are the big-time loggers and mining explorers who often leave nothing behind after they went through their ventures. With the government push to pay off the foreign debts, more than 10.6 million hectares of upland have been allocated to mining firms, most of which are ancestral lands.[111] That was in the year 2000 and more lands have been signed over with other foreign corporations to explore our mineral resources. Even if the indigenous people have the title to the land, the government still has priority over the mineral rights under the law. During the Marcos regime, the government has been sacrificing the rights of the indigenous community who live around the mine sites in order to meet the demands or preferences of the prospectors as it is today. (Bello, 224)

According to the Key Indicators 2005 of the Asian Development Bank (ADB), the Philippines had the worst record of preserving its forests among the Asian countries. This has lead to numerous disasters involving flood and landslides that have been blamed on deforestation. It also claims that the Philippines has been destroying its forests at the rate of 1.4% annually from 1990 to 2000. The result is that the Philippines forest cover now stands at 19.4% from 22.4% a decade ago.

The appetite of the greedy loggers in the country knows no limit even while the country is suffering from natural calamities brought by devastating typhoons on upland and lowland dwellers. Even with only a small intact forest cover left, illegal and legal loggings go on unabated. They are often abetted by unscrupulous government officials while those law-abiding enforcers are threatened or salvaged for their non-cooperation.

Compared to our meager forest cover, our nearest log-exporting countries neighbors such as Malaysia has 58.7% forest

---

[111] http://gina.ph/CyberDyaryo/features/f2000_0531_02.htm

cover; Taiwan, 58.1%; Indonesia, 58%; Laos, 54.4%; Cambodia, 52.9%; Myanmar, 52.3%; and Thailand, 28.9%.

Another problem with deforestation is due to the huge number of forest dwellers upland. With no place for them in the rural areas, they are forced to survive in the forest. Most of them are indigenous tribes that have live this kind of existence for centuries. They survive by gathering their food from the forest or practice slash-and-burn farming. The latter has been responsible for the destruction of forest trees. Forests have been destroyed when fire gets out of hand.

There is almost complete lack of economic activities in the upland except for a few barter among the dwellers. Employment opportunity is unheard of and there is completely no infrastructure to speak of except the logging roads that allow new access for the forest dwellers to colonize deeper into the forest.

What aid coming to the forest dwellers are donations coming from foreign countries or United Nations agencies. There are little incentives from the government except for projects that has to do with forest management to protect the forest from further destruction. Otherwise, these dwellers are often left to fend for themselves.

Most of our forests found in the lower mountains have been denuded and converted into other uses such as farming and subdivisions. In time, some of these farmlands will be converted into industrial, commercial, and residential uses because of the proliferation of landless people seeking their own land. Our millions of homeless people have not yet been accommodated with homes and we are still increasing these landless people without letup.

Water Scarcity and Pollution

The World Economic Forum held in Davos, Switzerland last January 2008 was focus on the growing water crisis around the world. The U.N. Secretary General, in his opening address has this to say, "A shortage of water resources could spell increased conflicts in the future. Population growth will make the problem worse. So will climate change. As the global economy grows, so will its thirst. Many more conflicts lie just over the horizon." Anders Berntell, executive director of the Stockholm International Water Institute told the IPS that there is the lack of safe drinking water for over one billion people worldwide, and the lack of safe sanitation for over 2.5 billion and that is an acute and devastating humanitarian crisis.[112]

Another report by a U.N. study released on the eve of World Water Day on March 22, 2008 claimed the lack of safe drinking water is not confined to the world's poorer nations; it also threatens over 100 million Europeans. The result: nearly 40 children in Europe, mostly in Eastern Europe, die every day due to diarrhea caused by contaminated water. In Eastern Europe, about 16% of the population still does not have access to drinking water in their homes while in rural areas, over half of all people suffer from the lack of safe water and inadequate sanitation. Poor management and lack of funding have been blamed for the water crisis. Then there is an added dimension to the crisis caused by global warming.

The expected warming of the atmosphere may raise the sea level several meters in the long run. This is expected to inundate many coastal areas and seawater is expected to intrude into the aquifers where many people, especially in the rural areas have their sources of fresh water. As if this is not enough, the polluted water that runs throughout the waterways of the country can also contaminate of aquifers during flooding.

In a report by the International Union for Conservation of Nature (IUCN), it claimed that many rivers in developing countries and emerging economies are now polluted to the brink of collapse. The main culprits are due to untreated agriculture and industrial wastes. Not only do we need to stem the pollution of our water supplies, we can do much by conserving the badly needed water, even in time of plenty so as to be prepared for the time when water will be scarce.

Water scarcity is becoming a big problem for many countries with big population. Because it is finite while the population kept growing and demand for better standard of living is forcing the use of water to unsustainable levels. One of the greatest demands for water is in the agriculture sector. Huge amount of money has been invested in building dams to store water and irrigation canals to bring the water to the arid areas for growing food. Today, some 70% of all the water abstracted from rivers and aquifers is being spread onto the 270 million hectares of irrigated land that grows a third of the world's food. This demand was able to keep the world supplied with grain but at great cost to the world's supply of fresh water. Most of the water abstracted from aquifers and rivers are used in many countries to

---

[112] http://www.globalpolicy.org/socecon/envronmt/climate/2008/0319deepwater.htm

increase food for their teeming population. This insatiable appetite for water is only possible by diverting water for from irrigation or draining the water from rivers and lakes.

Irrigation is made possible due to the construction of dams and embankments to collect water from upstream and rainfall. These waters often carry along with them salt that is deposited in the irrigated field that in due time will be poisoning the soil and destroying the crops. This is what is happening in many parts of Pakistan. One estimated that the Indus River in Pakistan delivers 22 million tones of salt onto the plain each year while removing only 11 million tones to the Arabian Sea. As a result, each hectare of irrigated land gets to retain almost a tonne of salt a year. To remove the salt, more water is needed and soon led to short supply. In recent years, Pakistan's farmers have been abandoning farm land at the rate of 40,000 hectares a year. (Pearce, 43)

Another problem with irrigation is waterlogged. A waterlogged field usually produces lesser crops and need to be drained which can be very expensive. It has a tendency to accumulate salt, making the field doubly unproductive.

Mexico, which prided itself as the home to the green revolution with the use of high-yielding wheat varieties during the 1950s has run out of water for irrigating the land that once planted to the wheat. Reservoirs on the Yaqui River in the Sonora desert of northwest Mexico have dried up since the 1990s as demand for water exceed supply in the rivers. Today, the fields are being abandoned and the farmers leaving the valley. Egypt has to import most of its food because there is not enough water to irrigate the land. Likewise, in India, China, the U.S. and many others have to rely on underground water to irrigate the land. Most of these aquifers will not be replaced by the rainfall. Some of the underground water contains salt that contaminate the soil ends up creating desert in a few years. (Pearce, 38-39)

Saudi Arabia has virtually no water and rainfall, but one source of water was found beneath the desert. It spent $40 billion to pump the water to irrigate a million hectares of devoted for wheat farming. The water was given free of charge. Most of the water wasted growing wheat because it takes 3,000 m^3 to produce a ton of wheat, which is three times the global norm. Most of the water was lost to evaporation in the hot desert. In the 1990s, farmers shifted to growing alfalfa to fill the feedlots for a national obsession with dairy cattle. The initial content of the aquifer was estimated to be around 500 km^3 and is now down to 200 km^3 before conservation measures were undertaken. Jordan, which share its border with Saudi Arabia on the aquifer issue is too poor to set up desalinization plant to augment their water need is building a pipe 300 kilometers to the capital in Amman. (Pearce, 83-84)

Ocean, sea and coastal pollution has become big problems for most countries. The ocean, once the dumping ground for all kinds of human generated wastes from sewage to plastics may have lost its ability to digest them without affecting the lives of sea creatures. Instead of swallowing up our wastes, the ocean has periodically coughed up the filth onto the beaches around the world. Fish, birds, and mammals are dying by the thousands as they inadvertently swallowed some pollutants such as plastics and chemicals into their digestive systems leading to their death. Plastics, the most common pollutant found in the sea is posing ever greater danger to sea creatures as the increasing human population continues to discharge this pollutant to the sea. The six-pack plastic rings and lost fishing gears such as nets have been responsible for killing mammals and birds caught in them. Drifting plastic bags and fishing nets often look like food for the birds and the mammals. The plastic looks like jellyfish to sea turtles while plastic pellets are like fish eggs to seabirds.

The coastal areas are particularly vulnerable because 90% of all marine creatures reside. It is also here where many people around the world depend on their livelihood for survival. As the number of sea creatures decline, the poor fishermen are forced to go further into the high sea to catch their share of seafood in competition with large fleet of well financed fish trawlers with their modern methods of harvesting fish. Fish is a valuable source of animal protein for nearly one billion people, most of them poor, according to the Population Action International.

Pollution in the ocean directly affects ocean organisms as well as human who consumed animals that feed on them. These pollutants include oil spills, toxic wastes and other harmful materials discharged from human activities. Toxic waste is the most harmful form of pollution to sea life and humans. They are easily passed along the food chain through the seafood we consumed.

Toxic wastes get into the sea and ocean from mine tailings, leaking dumpsites and landfills, heavy metals from factories, fertilizers and pesticides used in farms to increase food production, discharge from ships and leisure boats, and littering on land that ends up in the seas.

Heavy metals such as mercury, chromium, lead, etc. have been found in the ocean of the world. Lead has been found in many products and they can cause many health problems. It can damage the brain, especially of children, kidneys and reproductive system. It has been known to cause birth defects, lower the IQ, slow down the growth of small children and cause hearing problems.

Medical wastes containing viruses and bacteria and other pathogens indiscriminately disposed can end up in the ocean. They can be ingested by sea creatures and later consumed by people. Leisure boats discharge gasoline and chemicals that could be fatal to sea creatures and the boats are known to kill mammals plying around them.

Liquid and solid human wastes from septic tanks are common pollutants discharge to the sea. The sewage discharge is commonly connected to storm water drains located in the streets which flows out to the esteros leading to the rivers and eventually into the seas. These untreated sewages contain all kinds of viruses, parasites, pathogens, and bacteria that can be harmful to sea life and eventually human beings. They can also deplete the oxygen needed by sea plants and animals.

Many human activities we do daily end up as pollutants. Even the cars we drove daily can be polluting our oceans indirectly such as acidifying the ocean with the too much carbon dioxide as explained earlier. Chemical soaps and detergents, batteries, improper disposal of wastes and plastics often end up in the ocean. It is estimated that the ocean contains about 100 million tons of plastics, accounting for about 80% of the pollutants. Since it is difficult to biodegrade especially when wet, the debris are expected to accumulate as times pass. Toxic ingredients used in the manufacturing process can leak out and kill plants and animals.

There are many things an individual can do to help conserve water. Low-flow shower and faucet can save water during washing. Shutting down the water flow during rinsing and brushing teeth is another way. Making full use of the maximum capacity of appliances utilizing water such as washing machine, etc. can minimize wastage.

Water conservation laws can be effective in ensuring compliance. Law requiring huge consumers to install conservation measures is one way. In Tucson, Arizona, the city government passed an ordinance in 1991 prohibiting new housing developments from devoting more than 10% of their landscaping to laws. (Dolan, 96). They could have added another feature by requiring most of the plants to be xerophytes such as cacti, succulents and Xeriscape plants that could flourish with even less water.

Laws against water pollution can be very effective. The International Convention for the Prevention of Pollution of the Sea by Oil (OILPOL) adopted in 1954 has prevented the indiscriminate dumping of oil wastes into the ocean and forced national ports to provide storage tanks for storing used oil from ships calling on their ports. It was followed up with a more extensive coverage in 1972 with the Convention on the Prevention of Marine Pollution by Dumping Wastes and Other Matter. More contaminants were added to include hydrocarbons, mercury and its compounds, and radioactive materials. A year later, it was followed by the Prevention of Pollution from Ships (MARPOL) barring the dumping of sewage, noxious liquids and solids and even contains regulations against land dumping that would eventually work their way into the sea. Plastic items and garbage consisting of paper, rags, metal, glass, crockery, dunnage and food when sailing within three miles from shore are also prohibited. All these measures are toothless unless full cooperation among the operators of the ships and the ships' captains are realized. (Dolan, 84-87)

Land Degradation

Most of the land degradations point to human activities as the culprit by exploiting the land to feed our runaway population. It is estimated that 40% of the world's agricultural land have been seriously degraded. We have chopped down the forest that was once a bulwark against typhoon and fresh water supply in order to use the wood for our shelter or for export. As a result, the upland soil has been eroded to silt the downstream rivers. Even the use of irrigated water for agriculture has caused serious land degradation as topsoil are often carried by the water as it flows out of the agricultural land. The same is true with the grazing land that cattle have devoured the grass and other vegetation that kept the soil from erosion. Overgrazing can only lead to eroded soil leading to siltation of streams, rivers and reservoirs. Little can be done to stop this kind of soil erosion.

In arid, semi-arid and dry places, coupled with global warming of the planet, the degradation of the land can lead to serious problem such as desertification. Poor farming practices in the past and even today have depleted the soil of badly nutrients. Without the crops and even grass to hold the soil, it is a matter of time before the land is degraded to the point that nothing can grow to hold the soil together.

Once the protective cover of the topsoil is gone, it will not be long for rain and wind to blow away the topsoil. It takes at least a thousand years to produce one inch of topsoil and only in condition conducive to formation. The lost of topsoil is only replenished by using fertilizers in the production of food badly needed by the people.

In many countries in the Third World, the trees that once covered the land have been chopped down to provide the needed fuel for cooking and keeping warm during the cold months. Once the trees are gone, the land can easily be degraded and turned into desert as what happened to the deserts around the world.

Conversion of agricultural lands to other uses is a form of land degradation on a wide scale. This is a serious problem due to the unending population growth that has been responsible for the loss of prime agricultural land. Newly converted land also needs roads for transport that only add to further land degradation. Uphill and forested areas have to be leveled, and the topsoil lost as a result, to make room for new agricultural land that cannot sustain crops for long without additional input of fertilizers.

Land used as sanitary landfills is another high form of land degradation. While it is true that once they are filled up, they can be converted to other uses such as housing as in the case of the Smokey Mountain in Tondo, Manila, or as park and playground, they are not exactly conducive to healthy living. The putrefactive action underneath will continue to emit toxic gases for years.

The seriousness of land degradation cannot be overemphasized. In the worst scenario, it has led to famine and starvation on a wide scale. This is what happened to many parts of the world where crops cannot be grown without special inputs. Land degradation not only affects soil fertility, but the integrity of water courses such as rivers, wetlands and lakes, since soil, along with nutrients and contaminants associated with soil are delivered in large quantities to environments that respond detrimentally to their input. Land degradation therefore has potentially disastrous effects on lakes and reservoirs that are designed to alleviate flooding, provide irrigation and generate hydroelectricity.[113]

One effect of fertilizer runoff is the algal bloom in the seas surrounding the coastal areas commonly called red tide. It is caused by the excess of nutrients, particularly phosphorus. When phosphates are introduced into water systems, it tends to cause increased growth of algae and plants. Algae tend to out-compete other plants under these conditions, and many plant species begin to die. This dead organic matter becomes food for bacteria that decomposes it. With more food available, the bacteria increase in number and use up the dissolved

---

[113] http://en.wikipedia.org/wiki/Land_degradation

oxygen in the water. With declining dissolved oxygen, many fish and aquatic insects cannot survive.

Algal blooms may also be of concern as some species of algae produce neurotoxins. These toxins may have severe biological impacts on wildlife.[114] Shellfish are known to accumulate these neurotoxins in their bodies. Those unfortunate to consume them can experience dizziness, vomiting and numbness which are symptoms of paralytic shellfish poisoning. It has periodically hit parts of the Philippines and can be fatal to some consumers.

Global Warming

The "greenhouse effect" refers to the natural phenomenon that made it possible for the Earth to sustain life at certain temperature ranges. The sun's enormous energy warms the Earth's surface and its atmosphere. As this energy radiates back toward space as heat, a portion is absorbed by a delicate balance of heat-trapping gases in the atmosphere, predominantly carbon dioxide which creates an insulation layer. With the temperature control of the greenhouse effect, the Earth has an average surface temperature of 59°F. Without it, the average surface temperature would be 0°F, a temperature so low that the Earth would be frozen and could not sustain life.[115] The excessive introduction of greenhouse gases is causing further global warming. These chemicals block the heat from dissipating to the outer space. The excess greenhouse gases can raise the temperature of a planet to lethal levels, as what happened in the planet Venus where carbon dioxide contributes to a surface temperature of about 467°C (872 °F). Greenhouse gases are also produced by many natural and industrial processes.[116] Most emissions are directly or indirectly caused by human activities. As long as there are humans on earth there will be some form of emissions of greenhouse gases to the atmosphere. The more people the more emissions can be expected. The needs of the human species for food and energy are chiefly responsible for the emission of greenhouse gases. Everyone from cradle to the grave made utilized materials that are responsible for greenhouse gas.

The naturally occurring and most abundant greenhouse gas is the water vapor. It is responsible for 36%-70% of the warming because of

---

[114] http://en.wikipedia.org/wiki/Algal_bloom
[115] http://www.ucsusa.org/global_warming/science/global-warming-faq.html?print=t
[116] http://en.wikipedia.org/wiki/Greenhouse_gas

its constant fluctuation. Greenhouse gases help heat up the Earth's liquid surface leading to more evaporation and therefore more water vapor. However, the water vapor soon dissipates as rainfall. The role of water vapor has been going on for millennia.

UN scientists warned that greenhouse gases must level off within the next 10 to 15 years and then start to dramatically decline to avoid a rise in average temperatures that could have catastrophic consequences such as severe droughts and flooding. (*Manila Bulletin*, November 27, 2008)

The next most abundant and chiefly responsible by human beings is carbon dioxide, which accounts for 9% to 26% of the global warming. Deforestation and the burning of fossil fuels such as coal, gasoline, natural gas, etc. are the main source of this gas. The tropical countries have been responsible for deforestation as they cut down more trees than they reforest in trying to support the country's industrialization, export to earn foreign currencies, for cattle ranching, clearing for agriculture and for habitation as a result of population pressure. In many poor countries, the trees are a source of burning fuel. Because trees are made up of 50% carbon, it is contributing a fairly large amount of CO_2 into the atmosphere if no corresponding afforestation and reforestation are undertaken. For each tree burn or cut, it would take about a 100 years for the young sapling to grow up to completely replace the carbon. Harvesting the trees as furniture and other wood products can serve as carbon sink.

CO_2 has a variable atmospheric lifetime of thousands of years, if left alone. The only effective way of reabsorbing them is through reforestation as trees need the carbon dioxide from the atmosphere for growing. Crops are also loaded with organic carbon. Even the ordinary grass are made of carbon.

Only a rise of another 3 degrees in temperature, as much as 250 billion tons of stored carbon from the soil may be released either as methane due to the action of the bacteria or as naturally as carbon, further accelerating the process. (Asimov, 51)

Prior to the start of the Industrial Revolution, the level of carbon dioxide in the atmosphere was about 280 parts per million by volume (ppmv). The latest level registered in 2007 stands at 383.1, according to the World Meteorological Organization. The other two main greenhouse gases, nitrous oxide and methane rose slightly, nitrous oxide increased by 0.25 over the 2006 record to 320.9 ppb (parts per billion) while methane increased to 1,789 ppb or a 0.34% increase from 2006. (*Manila Bulletin*, November 27, 2008) The concentration of carbon dioxide and other key greenhouse gases in our atmosphere today is higher than at any time in the past 650,000 years, and probably higher than in the past 20 million years.

Methane contributes a small amount, about 4-9% of the heat absorptive power but it is 25-30 times more efficient at trapping solar heat making them just as dangerous. Natural forms of methane come from bacteria in swamps, septic tanks, and similar places, from the digestive tracks of animals such as cattle, termites in rice paddies, organic matter in rice paddies as they rot under water, the rotting of organic matter in garbage dumps, coal mining that releases the trapped methane and carbon, etc. Methane is becoming more dangerous as greenhouse gases as the earth warms up.

One issue that is often overlooked is the role of the ruminants such as cattle, sheep, goats and buffalo played in global warming through the emission of methane. Because of their special digestive systems, they can convert otherwise unusable plant materials into nutritious food and fiber. This same helpful digestive system, however, produces methane, a potent greenhouse gas that can contribute to global warming. Livestock production systems can also emit other greenhouse gases such as nitrous oxide and carbon dioxide.

Globally, ruminant livestock produce about 80 million metric tons of methane annually, accounting for about 28% of global methane emissions from human-related activities. An adult cow may be a very small source by itself, each cattle is capable of producing as much as 500 to 600 liters of methane daily.[117] With about 100 million cattle in the U.S. and 1.3 billion ruminants worldwide, making them one of the largest methane sources. In the U.S., cattle emit about 5.5 million metric tons of methane per year into the atmosphere, accounting for 20% of U.S. methane emissions.[118]

Cattle are the ruminants we should limit their numbers due to their poor feed conversion. Cattle also contribute to deforestation in some South American countries and occupy important pasture that could be used for planting food crops. The U. S. Department of Agriculture (USDA) reports that animals in the U.S. meat industry produce 61 million tons of waste each year, which is 130 times the volume produced by human waste produced. In addition to its impact on climate, hog, chicken and cow waste has polluted some 35,000 miles of rivers in 22 states and contaminated groundwater in 17 states, according to the U.S. EPA. The cattle industry also consumed a lot of

---

[117] http://news.bbc.co.uk/1/hi/scotland/4582174.stm
[118] http://www.epa.gov/rlep/faq.html

water and more than half of the grain in the U.S., enough to feed 800 million people.[119]

The seriousness of cattle belching has prompted scientists to find ways of reducing cow's belching by adding additives such as urea, a form of ammonia, to their food. The methane in cow's manure can be harness for cooking as some of the people in the poor developing are doing.[120] Feeding the cattle with oil from the shell of cashew nuts can reduce the methane gas production by as much as 90%, according to Japanese scientists.[121] The scientists at New Zealand's agricultural research institute, AgResearch Grasslands, also found that the legume lotus in natural condensed tannin compounds in some grasslands can reduce the methane emissions from ruminant animals by as much as 16%. Other animals that produce methane are sheep, goat, and moose.

Each cattle is capable of producing as much as 500 to 600 liters of methane daily.[122]

At present, most of the methane is harmlessly stored underneath the surface of the Earth. This "fossil methane" is buried organic matter contains about 14% of all the organic carbon in the world. Most of them are found in the tundra in Siberia and the Canada. Once the warming reaches a high enough level bacteria will start turning that carbon into methane. (Asimov, 50-51)

There is also the methane trapped at the bottom of the oceans that contains even more carbon than all the coal reserves on the planet. If that undersea warms up enough, the gas will come bubbling up in "methane plumes" as is happening in the Sea of Okhotsk that started a few years ago. (Ibid)

Methane has an atmospheric lifetime of 9 to 15 years. It is degraded to water and CO_2 by chemical reactions in the atmosphere. Another potentially important indirect effect of methane aside from its direct radiative impact is its contribution to the formation of troposphere ozone.

Other greenhouse gases include, but are not limited to, nitrous oxide which mostly came from the use of fertilizers and in the manufacture of nylon stockings and pantyhose. Nitrous oxide absorbs

---

[119] http://www.foodreference.com/html/a-cows-methane-815.html
[120] http://timesofindia.indiatimes.com/Earth/Cattle_linked_to_warming/articleshow/3564260.cms
[121] http://www.reuters.com/article/environmentNews/idUST34833520080611
[122] http://news.bbc.co.uk/1/hi/scotland/4582174.stm

270 times more heat per molecule than carbon dioxide and has an atmospheric lifetime of 120 years. Man-made greenhouse gases include sulfur hexafluoride, hydrofluorocarbons, perfluorocarbons and chlorofluorocarbons (CFCs). A potentially significant greenhouse gas not yet addressed by the Intergovernmental Panel on Climate change (IPCC) or the Kyoto Protocol is nitrogen trifluoride. Most of this gas came from industrial processes.

Although CFCs are greenhouse gases and regulated by the Montreal Protocol, it was motivated by CFCs' contribution to ozone depletion rather than by their contribution to global warming. CFCs were manufactured for use in the refrigeration, spray cans, electronic manufacturing, etc. before it was stopped. The CFC molecules can survive for about a century while destroying 100,000 molecules of ozone. The depletion of the ozone in the stratosphere has only a minor role in greenhouse warming. The use of CFC-12 (except some essential uses) has been phased out due to its ozone depleting properties. The phasing-out of less active HCFC-compounds will be completed by 2030.

Carbon monoxide is another greenhouse gas and has an indirect radiative effect by elevating concentrations of methane and troposphere ozone through scavenging of atmospheric constituents (e.g., the hydroxyl radical, OH) that would otherwise destroy them. Carbon monoxide is created when carbon-containing fuels are not burned completely. Through natural processes in the atmosphere, it is eventually oxidized to carbon dioxide. Carbon monoxide has an atmospheric lifetime of only a few months.

Carbon dioxide, methane, nitrous oxide and three groups of fluorinated gases (sulfur hexafluoride, HFCs, and PFCs) are the major greenhouse gases and the subject of the Kyoto Protocol, which came into force in 2005. Individuals can do a lot to reduce their emissions. Conservation measures such as improving home building insulations to reduce the use of natural gas for heating, using compact fluorescent lamps and energy-efficient machineries such motor vehicles, refrigerators, and other appliances.

Motor vehicles represent one of the greatest sources of carbon dioxide. By driving less and using less energy from coal-fired power plants, or heating our homes with oil or natural gas, we release carbon dioxide and other heat-trapping gases into the atmosphere. Less demand on forest products is another significant way of reducing greenhouse gas. Trees have a thousand and other uses, and minimizing these products should cut down the demand for wood.

Global warming increases the trapped heat leading to changes in the climate such as aggravating the El Niño effect and altering weather patterns may hasten species extinction, influence the length of seasons, causes the seas to rise and inundate low-lying islands and coastal areas. It is expected to lead to more frequent and severe storms. The breaking up the icebergs in the Arctic and Antarctic zones is just one of the consequences of global warming.

In 1987, one of the biggest icebergs ever to break up came from the Ross Ice Shelf. The size of the iceberg was nearly 6,400 km². The National Science Foundation estimated that the volume of fresh water is enough to supply Los Angeles for 675 years. (Robinsons, 246) In 2000, three enormous icebergs in the Antarctica's Ronne Ice Shelf have broken up, floating free and posed hazard to navigational vessels. The combined size of the three icebergs is slightly smaller than the state of Connecticut and is believed to have broken loose sometime between May 4 and May 6, 2000. The Ronne Shelf is located in the Weddell Sea, the portion of nearest to the continent of South America. The past several years have seen an unusually rapid calving of icebergs from the Ronne Ice Shelf and from the Ross Ice Shelf. Some scientists believe that the increased activity could be an early sign of global warming.[123]

The latest report had it that the average warming of the Antarctica is about 0.22°F per decade. This is a serious problem considering that Antarctica holds enough ice to raise global sea levels by 57 meters. (*PDI*, January 22, 2009) Global warming and the billions of tons of sedimentation caused by soil erosion ending up in the ocean makes the sea level rising a catastrophe in the making.

The latest news from Canada is that a huge 55 km² ice shelf in Canada's northern Arctic broke away in August 2008. The Markham Ice Shelf, one of just five remaining ice shelves, split away from Ellesmere Island while two large chunks totaling 76 km² had broken off the nearby Serson Ice Shelf, reducing its size by 60%. Experts blamed the new development to global warming. Ellesmere Island was once home to a single enormous ice shelf totaling around 5,633 km² and is now down to 483 km². (*PS*, September 4, 2008)

According to marine geophysicists Robin Bell of Columbia University's Earth Institute, sea levels rise by about 1/16" for every 150 mi³ of ice that melts from the poles. If the West Antarctica ice sheets were to disappear, sea level would rise about 19 feet, Greenland

---

[123] http://edition.cnn.com/2000/NATURE/05/10/icebergs.02/index.html

ice sheets could add 24 feet, and the East Antarctica ice sheets could add 170 feet or a total of 213 feet.[124]

The rise in sea level has dire consequences not only on small island nations and atolls, but even large continents can be affected. This is because most of the cities around the world are concentrated on coastal areas and many of them are not elevated high enough to escape the rise of the sea level. The UN environment Program predicts that by 2010, some 80% of the people will live within 62 miles of the coast, with about 40% living within 37 miles of a coastline.

Even a degree increase, the atolls around New Zealand like the Tuvalu have been experiencing regular flooding. With her sister atolls, they are expected to disappear in the near future and the inhabitants cannot expect much help from the big emitters/nations responsible for their disappearance. (Lynas, 46) The islanders on Tuvalu are scrambling to find new homes as salt water intrusion has made their groundwater undrinkable while increasingly strong hurricanes and ocean swells have devastated shoreline structures. In Samoa, thousands of islanders have moved to higher ground as shorelines have retreated by as much as 160 feet, according to the World Wildlife fund.[125]

The latest report from NASA's Grace Satellite is that more than two trillion tons of land ice from Greenland, Antarctica and Alaska has melted since 2003. More than half of the ice came from Greenland which is to be expected because of is lower latitude in the hemisphere. Alaska has lost about 400 billion tons. Although the melting of land ice is not as critical as sea ice, contributing to about one-fifth of an inch in the past five years, the warming of the water can rise further as it expands, scientists warned. (*PDI*, December 17, 2008)

Global warming is not only threatening the inundation of the world, but it is causing health problems to the people affected. According to a team of health and climate scientists at WHO and the University of Wisconsin at Madison, it is already contributing to the death of 150,000 people and 5 million illnesses annually and the number could double by 2030. This is happening through the speeding up of the spread of infectious diseases such as malaria and dengue fever, creating conditions that lead to potentially fatal malnutrition and diarrhea, and the increasing likelihood of heat waves and floods. Most of these deaths will occur in poor countries although they contributed

---

[124] http://environment.about.com/od/greenhouseeffect/a/rising_sea_leve.htm
[125] Ibid

the least to the global warming. They include those residing near coastlines along the Pacific and Indian oceans and sub-Saharan Africa.[126]

The lists below are some examples of the consequences of global warming that is happening to the planet. Some of them are serious enough to call the attention of governments around the world.

- There is an average increase in global average surface temperature of about 1°F in the 20th century. In Europe, the average increase in temperature was 2.3°F above normal. More areas are expected to experience hotter weathers.
- There has been decrease of snow cover and sea ice extent and the retreat of mountain glaciers in the latter half of the 20th century.
- The increase in ocean water temperatures is likely to affect sea life of many ocean animals and destroy some food chain for higher forms of life.
- There is a likelihood of erratic temperature such as increase in the frequency of extreme precipitation and extreme droughts in some regions of the world. Extreme heat caused more evaporation that falls back to earth causing extreme flooding.
- The length of heat waves on the Continental Europe has doubled. During the summer of 2003, temperature in Great Britain rose to 100°F for the first time. Other places in Europe also experience high temperature especially in France. At temperature of 104°F, it could be fatal for some people without emergency services. More than 10,000 Parisians died of heatstroke. Across Europe, as many as 35,000 may have died. (Lynas, 58)
- Some 24% of the land masses in the Northern Hemisphere are permafrost – perennially frozen ground, and they are fast disappearing. The thawing of permafrost can lead to rockslides in mountainous areas and melting of glaciers.
- The landscapes in many temperate and arctic zones are changing due to global warming. Antoni Lewkowicz of the University of Ottawa has studied several northern landslides and rockslides that he says can be at least partially attributed to thinning and weakening of ice or permafrost caused by

---

[126]

http://environment.about.com/od/globalwarmingandhealth/a/gw_deaths.htm

climate warming. In one case, an earthquake broke off a weakening glacier in the Yukon. About 500,000 tons of ice raced down a mountain.[127]

- Railroad tracks built atop permafrost are likely to deform with the thawing of the permafrost underneath making them useless.
- A study in 2005 found 125 large lakes in the Arctic have vanished while others have shrunk as temperatures rose over the past two decades. These lakes once sat atop permanently frozen soil called permafrost. Other studies have shown permafrost is melting around the world, causing low-lying ground to slump and rock to fall from mountains.[128]
- Warming of the atmosphere tends to lengthen the growing season of crops in middle and high latitudes. Some plants and animals have to shift toward the Poles to survive. There will be a decline of some plant and animal species as they cannot adapt to the new environmental makeup.
- Plants and trees are likely to bloom earlier than expected. Seed yields are particularly sensitive to brief episodes of hot temperatures if these coincide with critical stages of crop development. Hot temperatures at the time of flowering can reduce the potential number of seeds or grains that subsequently contribute to the crop yield.
- Global warming is expected to put more severe stress on many forests, wetlands, alpine regions, and other natural ecosystems as they try to readjust.
- The disruption of agriculture will affect some parts of the world due to increased temperature, water stress, and sea-level rise in low-lying areas such as Bangladesh and the Mississippi River delta.
- A 2003 research study published in the journal *Nature*, analyzed numerous studies involving wild plant and animals for changes due to global warming. Out of the nearly 1,500 species examined, the researchers found that about 1,200 exhibited temperature-related changes consistent with what scientists would expect if they were being affected by global warming.
- Earlier egg-laying in birds can be expected

---

[127] http://www.livescience.com/environment/041222_permafrost.html
[128] http://www.livescience.com/environment/050603_lakes_gone.html

The IPCC's Third Assessment Report projects that the Earth's average surface temperature will increase between 2.5°F and 10.4°F (1.4°-5.8°C) between 1990 and 2100 under the "business-as-usual" scenario. This is significantly higher than what the Panel predicted in 1995 (1.8°-6.3°F, or 1.0°-3.5°C), mostly because scientists expect a reduced cooling effect from tiny particles (aerosols) in the atmosphere.[129]

Scientists also predict that even if we stopped emitting heat-trapping gases immediately, the climate would not stabilize for many decades because the gases we have already released into the atmosphere will stay there for years or even centuries. So while the warming may increase at a slower pace if we reduce emissions significantly, global temperatures cannot quickly return to today's averages. The faster the Earth warms, the greater is the chance that it may be irreversible.

One important aspect of global warming caused by carbon dioxide is the possibility of the destroying the seafood chain of the oceans around the world. The oceans have served as the largest natural sinks for CO_2 since time immemorial. This role is driven by two processes, the solubility pump and the biological pump. The former is primarily a function of differential CO_2 solubility in seawater and the thermohaline circulation, while the latter is the sum of a series of biological processes that transport carbon (in organic and inorganic forms) from the surface euphotic zone to the bottom of the ocean. A small fraction of the organic carbon transported by the biological pump to the seafloor is buried in anoxic conditions under sediments and ultimately forms fossil fuels such as oil and natural gas.[130]

At the present time, approximately one-third to one-half of anthropogenic emissions is estimated to be entering the ocean. The natural slight alkalinity of the ocean is being altered with too much carbon dioxide as it dissolved in the ocean in the form of carbonic acid. This is going to affect the many plants and animals that need the alkali state to build calcium carbonate shells. So far, the pH of the ocean has drop 0.1 pH unit and may reduce further the alkalinity at the present rate of carbon dioxide emission from pH 8.2 to about 7.7 in about 100 years. As a result, the lowered alkalinity of the ocean may not support calcareous marine life. (Lynas, 53, Friedman, 121)

---

[129] http://www.ucsusa.org/global_warming/science/global-warming-faq.html?print=t

[130] http://en.wikipedia.org/wiki/Carbon_dioxide_sink

Climate change affecting the biological pump may reduce the food supply by limiting nutrients to surface waters and cause the destruction of one of the most important food chains: planktons. There are actually several types of planktons depending on their genetic origin such as plant, animal, bacteria and archaea. Some calcifying organisms such as coccolithophores, foraminiferans and pteropods cannot survive in an acidic state. This has been verified by scientists when they artificially pumped dissolved CO_2 into a Norwegian fjord and watched in dismay as coccolithophore structures first corroded and then began to disintegrate altogether. The same effect can happen to other shellfish such as crabs, sea urchins, mussels, oysters and other crustaceans that depended on them to survive. Even the corals can be corroded by acidification of the ocean. (Lynas, 55) The planktons, being the lowest food chain for most of the mammals in the ocean from the whales to the mackerel can spell the doom for these mammals.

Phytoplankton (plant plankton) has also an important role in removing carbon dioxide from the atmosphere by producing calcium carbonate in their limestone shells that settle on the ocean floor as they died. They are capable of absorbing half of all the carbon dioxide emitted to the atmosphere. Phytoplankton fixes carbon in sunlit surface water via photosynthesis. Through the primarily zooplankton (animal plankton) grazing, this carbon enters the planktonic foodweb, where it is either respired to provide metabolic energy or accumulates as biomass or detritus. Organic material is typically denser than seawater and tends to sink, transporting the carbon from surface waters to the deep. This process is known as the biological pump, and is one of the reasons that the oceans constitute the largest (active) pool of carbon on Earth.[131]

Each year, the ocean takes in about 90 billion tons of carbon dioxide in the air and released about 88 billion tons back to the atmosphere for a net reservation of two billion tons. The ocean absorbed carbon dioxide in the forms of dissolved carbon dioxide, bicarbonate and carbonate ions. The carbonate ions act as link between carbon dioxide and bicarbonate. The increase concentration of carbon dioxide limits the supply of carbonate ions that make the ocean less able to take up carbon dioxide from the atmosphere. Furthermore, the increasing water temperature reduces the solubility of carbon dioxide leading to an overall reduction in oceanic carbon dioxide uptake.[132] In

---

[131] http://en.wikipedia.org/wiki/Plankton
[132] http://www.ghgonline.org/co2sinkocean.htm

due time, the ocean may no longer serve as ocean sink for carbon dioxide, especially with the reduction of planktons that made it possible for the carbon to sink to the ocean floor.

Planktons also play an important role in providing food for the world. They are the lowest food chain in the ocean and served as food for many sea animals that provide protein for many poor coastal people and even inland dwellers. With global warming, the supply of nutrients needed by the planktons for growth and survival may be hampered. Scientists have reported in 2006 a decline in plankton productivity of 190 megatons a year as a result of the current warming trend and the acidification (actually reduced alkalinity). With the reduced planktons, its synergetic effect would accelerate global warming and further reduce food supply for sea creatures. (Ibid, 56)

Global warming is expected to increase the population of the insect kingdom. This is because insects have high metabolic rates during warm seasons and can reproduce more of their kind faster. If the insects relied on plants, fruits, and crops for survival, they may just eat into our food supplies. To control them, we may have to resort to more pesticides with their high cost and other dangerous overtones.

Taking cue from records of past geological times, scientists have found that insects are likely to eat more leaves in warmer temperature than during colder period. Currano and her colleagues found that during the comparatively cooler end of the Paleocene epoch, 15 to 38% of leaves showed insect damage. The same is true at the beginning of the Eocene when temperatures had dropped after the thermal maximum, 33% of leaves were damaged. But during the warmth of the Paleocene-Eocene Thermal Maximum (PETM), insect damage was found on 57% of leaves. Currano and her colleagues think these more voracious insect appetites were a result of a concurrent rise in carbon dioxide levels during the PETM that would have made plant leaves less nutritious. It has been shown by several studies that some plants produce fewer nutrients in elevated carbon dioxide levels and therefore need to consume more to obtain the necessary nutrients.[133]

Some disease-bearing insects are likely to increase health problems with their increasing numbers. They include malaria and Lyme disease that are carried by insect vectors. Scientists have observed malaria in areas that never experienced malaria cases before. Scientist blamed the change to global warming and the expansion of

---

[133] http://www.msnbc.msn.com/id/23117270/

their habitat.[134] The same holds true for other disease bearing vectors such as rats and rodents. Rat and rodents infestation have always been very costly to agricultural crops around the world.

Flooding of low-lying and densely inhabited areas by people and wild animals is another problem that could lead to extinction of endangered species. One good example is the tigers roaming their small and shrinking world in India. Because of habitat loss due to dwindling prey caused by climate change, tiger attacks on people in India's Sundarban islands is growing. Wildlife experts say that the endangered tigers in the world's largest reserve are turning on humans as food as their natural swamp habitat is shrinking due to rising sea levels and coastal erosion. The tigers have already lost 28% of its habitat in the last 40 years. Two islands have disappeared and the others are vulnerable. Many plants have lost their red and green colors and are more like bare twigs, exposing tigers to poachers for their body parts. Their common prey such as crocodiles, fish and big crabs is dwindling due to the destruction of the mangroves. Their population is now down to 1,411 from a high of about 40,000 a century ago and 3,642 in 2002. (*PDI*, October 21, 2008) Once these animals start to attack people, they could be at the mercy of the local inhabitants.

Ozone Depletion

Ozone or trioxygen (O_3) is like a double edged sword. It is a useful chemical in the stratosphere where it blocks our ultraviolet rays from reaching the earth by filtering our photons with shorter wavelengths from the Sun. However, it is toxic to humans and animals on the troposphere. Ozone in the stratosphere (10-50 km) above the earth is produced by the reaction of ultraviolet rays with oxygen. On the troposphere, it is formed by the reaction of sunlight on air containing hydrocarbons, nitrogen oxides, carbon monoxide, and volatile organic compounds (VOCs). Most of these came from the motor vehicles.[135] Other sources include industrial emissions, and chemical solvents, fumes paint shops, dry cleaning equipment, aerosol deodorant, and gas ovens. (Asimov, 51) Others include photocopiers, laser printers, ionic air purifiers, arc welders, and electric motors that use brushes. It is the chief ingredient in smog and is corrosive to living and non-living things that it is used to kill bacteria and viruses in sewage and water treatment.

---

[134] http://www.livescience.com/animals/061104_gb_insects.html
[135] http://en.wikipedia.org/wiki/Ozone;

Ozone causes respiratory problems such as chest pains, headaches, triggers more asthma cases, pulmonary congestion, burning sensation in the eyes and nose, and sore throats. (Weiner, 156)

There is a great deal of evidence to show that high concentrations of ozone, created by high concentrations of pollution and daylight UV rays at the earth's surface, can harm lung function and irritate the respiratory system. A connection has also been shown to exist between increased ozone caused by thunderstorms and hospital admissions of asthma sufferers. Exposure to ozone and the pollutants has been linked to premature death, bronchitis, heart attack and other cardiovascular problems. According to scientists with the U.S. EPA, susceptible people can be adversely affected by ozone levels as low as 40 ppb.[136]

Ozone is a poisonous gas for human to breathe but in its proper place at the stratosphere it acts as an invisible shield protecting the earth from too much ultraviolet rays, especially UVB. Without the ozone layer, ultraviolet rays from the Sun would damage the DNA molecules in birds, bees, green leaves and human skin on the ground. The UVB is also implicated in the proliferation of cortical cataract, but not nuclear or posterior subcapsular cataract. By 2050, 830,000 additional cases are expected in the U.S. alone. The medical expense for removing these cataracts is around $2.8 billion.[137] UVB has been implicated in sun blindness, sunburn, and weakened immune system.

UVB causes several types of skin cancer, including basal cell carcinomas and squamous cell carcinomas, and is strongly suspected as the cause of malignant melanomas. Carcinomas of the skin grow slowly and are rarely fatal while melanomas grow rapidly and often spread to other organs and in 40% of the cases are fatal. Persons with fair skin are susceptible to skin diseases cause by UV-B because they lack the dark pigments that block the radiation. (Weiner, 154)

The depleted ozone layer can damage the food chain in the ocean and food crops on land. Laboratory tests show that UVB can damage fish, shrimp and crab larvae, copepods, krill, and the zooplankton and phytoplankton at the base of the food chains in the sea. Phytoplanktons are the grass of the sea and they take solar energy and the minerals afloat in the water that include the phosphates, nitrates and silicates and convert them into a form that other creatures can use as food.

---

[136] Ibid
[137] http://www.bmj.com/cgi/content/full/331/7528/1292-d

They are consumed by krills which in turn are the main source of food for many mammals including the whales, seals, and the penguins. Without the krill, the whole ecosystem of the ocean will collapse. (Weiner, 158-159)

According to the U.S. Department of Agriculture, ozone depletion is costing the farmers about $2 billion worth of damaged crops annually. It also stunts the growth of young poplars and cottonwoods. (Ibid, 159)

Living plants, by its very nature are exposed to the sunlight will simply be scorched to death. The cyanobacteria that are valuable to farmers for fixing some 35 million tons of nitrogen annually for the rice paddies will be killed by the UV-B. The result is that we need nitrogen fertilizer and without it, there will be crop failures and possibly famines. (Asimov, 121)

Human activities have done a lot of damage to the ozone layer before it was discovered. Fortunately, something is being done to reverse the trend by reducing if not totally removing the ozone depleting substances (ODS). ODS are man-made compounds containing chlorine and bromine, particularly chlorofluorocarbons (CFCs), halons used in fire extinguisher, and methyl bromide that can react with ozone, thereby destroying them.

CFCs in particularly are the main culprit because of the large volume manufactured and released to the environment before it was discovered to be harmful to the ozone layer. CFCs had all the qualities of an ideal chemical with a lot of uses. Because, it is inert, they have been used as coolants in refrigerator, freezer and air conditioner, as propellant in aerosol cans, metered-dose inhaler, as foaming agents in polyurethane, and solvents in computer and electronic circuits and other industrial applications. CFC accounted for 89.86% of total ODS consumption in the U.S, according to a 2003 report.[138] Once released to the atmosphere, CFCs inertness allowed it to diffuse through the atmosphere until it reaches the stratosphere. There, ultraviolet radiation would do what nothing on the ground could do, break them apart into its basic component. The one common denominator is the chlorine. It is the chlorine in the stratosphere that interacts with one ozone atom, thereby turning it into oxygen molecule. The chlorine molecule will keep on reacting with ozone until it bumps and reacts with nitrogen. Each chlorine atom can destroy as many as 100,000 ozone. (Weiner, 139-140)

---

[138] http://www.emb.gov.ph/philozone/template/ozone%20trivia_2.htm

Loss of Biodiversity

According to the 2008 ICNU report, hundreds of animals have been added to the "Red List" and threatened with extinction, while hundreds of others have moved up the scale to endangerment status leading to extinction. Overall, 38% of 44,838 species cataloged to date are listed as "threatened" with extinction include a quarter of all mammals, one out of eight birds, one out of three amphibians, and 70% of plants.[139] The main cause of this dilemma is human encroachment on their habitats.

Overpopulation, deforestation, and loss of biodiversity are interconnected. People need land and the wood from trees with their multiple uses. All of these trees have to be taken from the forest, home for most of the animal and plant species. Only a halt to deforestation can the world hope to stop the loss of biodiversity. The Philippines, together with Malaysia and Indonesia are considered three of the 17 megadiversity countries in the world. With less than 3% in land areas, together they harbored more than 20% of the world biodiversity species.

There have been moves by the United Nations Convention on Biological Diversity (UNCBD) to stop the deforestation in the hope of preventing further loss of the rich biodiversity in the Asean countries by 2010. According to the UNCBD Executive Secretary Ahmed Djoghlaf, an Algerian biodiversity expert, about 20 million hectares of forestland in the world is lost because of deforestation. He was on an Asean tour to discuss with governments on how to protect and conserve the highly threatened biodiversity by 2010.

The importance of conserving biodiversity is because they affect food production. Many types of plants that could help solve the food crisis that existed before were no longer around. Biodiversity can help prevent the proliferation of pests to keep the ecosystem in balance. Half a billion people living in the region are at risk if the destruction of diversity is destroyed along with the destruction of the forests.

Biodiversity is not confined to land. The sea, once of the source of protein for the poor is also at risk. Whales have been hunted to almost extinction by seafarers despite protests from many environmentalists. The Japanese refused to stop these wanton killings by conveniently

---

[139] http://www.terradaily.com/reports/Hanging_on_for_dear_life_ animals_from_biodiversity_Red_List_999.html

hiding behind the name of scientific research. After decades of research, these idiots have not learned enough to stop the killings or more probably hiding behind their greed. The whales other cousins, the sharks have been maimed for their fins and their cartilage touted as cancer cure. Without the fins, the sharks will have difficulty swimming and absorbing the oxygen from the water through their gills. Baby seals have been killed for their white fur. Many food fish have been harvested to unsustainable level that will take decades to replenish. Too many people depended on the ocean resources have upset the delicate balance causing depletion and making replenishment difficult to achieve for decades.

Most of the coral reefs in Southeast Asia have experienced some form of destructive fishing leading to the death of corals and bleaching. All these destruction have been caused by too many mouths to feed and few food resources to gather the needed protein for the teeming population. A more thorough treatment can be found in my book *Saving the Animals*.

At our present population of more than 6 billion people, we are already losing about 70,000 species a year. This is expected to increase as our population increase to somewhere between 10 to 12 billion people sometime in the 2050s.

Dwindling Natural Resources

Many Third World countries are nothing but repository of important natural resources needed by the world. They are often at the mercy of companies from the developed world out to extract these resources. Natural resources located in the developing countries are at the heart of many wars and civil strife. Most of these resources are being mined by huge mining and logging companies with the blessing of the powerful dictators or leaders. Some of these companies include well respected names in financial circle such as Exxon Mobil and Anglo American/DeBeers. They would not hesitate to use force in pursuit of their corporate interests. There are many other players involved such as smugglers, corrupt local officials, arms dealers, transport operators and mercenary companies. Increasing scarcity of resources, driven by rising world population and the spread of unsustainable consumption, further sharpen such conflicts. NGOs, investigative journalists and UN expert panels have revealed some of the players in these clandestine networks and spotlighted governments that give them comfort, in the North as well as the South.

Africa, which is the number one producer of diamonds in the world, has been torn by civil strife in many countries. In countries such as Angola, the Democratic Republic of Congo, Sierra Leone and Liberia, rebels have used the proceeds of illegal diamond sales to purchase weapons, pay for the soldiers, and even importing mercenaries.[140] A movie was even made starring Leonard DiCaprio entitled *Blood Diamond.*

Since the early years of the 20th century, when Cecil Rhodes sowed tribal strife in South Africa to gain control of rich diamond deposits, diamonds have often been associated with violence and misery for the inhabitants. The connection between diamonds and conflicts goes far beyond rebel groups seizing control of diamond-rich areas and selling the precious gems for arms and war supplies. Large diamond companies are involved in this deadly game, along with traders, transport companies, arms smugglers and financial firms.

The worst of the diamond wars commenced in 1975 when the Portuguese colonial government of Angola abandoned the country because it cannot subdue. Half a million white colonists fled Angola leaving the country in a civil war. The main protagonists were the Popular Movement for the Liberation of Angola (MPLA) and the National Union for the Total Independence of Angola (UNITA). The war raged on for years with Cuban troops helping the MPLA while South African troops sided with UNITA. (Hart, 189) After the war ended in 1994, an estimated 1.5 million people may have been killed. As external support waned, illegal sale of diamonds, mined in UNITA-controlled areas, helped to fund the group's military campaign.[141] In 1999, the UN Security Council acted to enforce sanctions on diamond sales by the UNITA rebel group and the

---

[140] http://www.globalpolicy.org/security/docs/minindx.htm
[141] http://www.globalpolicy.org/security/sanction/indexang.htm

conflict finally ended a short time later. But since then, further diamond-related conflicts have raged in Sierra Leone, Liberia, Ivory Coast and the Democratic Republic of Congo.[142]

In addition to diamonds, the mining of cobalt, coltan, copper, and gold has fueled civil and interstate conflict. Like diamonds, mineral resources also promote conflict by providing rebel groups with money to purchase arms, and by providing governments with the incentive and the resources to establish a repressive military presence in mineral producing regions.

Africa, being a contiguous continent, what is happening in one country often affects the other neighboring countries. One example is the 14-year long conflict in Liberia. Move to control the natural resources is one cause of the conflict. The UN recognized the integral role natural resources played in the conflict by first sanctioning the export of Liberian diamonds in 2001, and later sanctioning the Liberian logging industry in May 2003. Much like with diamonds, revenue from the logging industry supported violent armed groups helped by the timber traders in facilitating the importation of weapons, delivering to rebel strongholds and violating the sanctions imposed. The two western Ivorian rebel groups, the MPIGOa and MJPb, were launched from timber areas in eastern Liberia and some fighters were housed in logging company bush camps along the border with Côte d'Ivoire. Ongoing unrest in Côte d'Ivoire, where conflict timber also funds the warring parties, will likely lead to increased exports of timber into Côte d'Ivoire in violation of UN sanctions, and further undermine Liberia' security.

The situation in Liberia is highly unstable, made worse by the government's continued lack of control over its natural resources, interior and borders, and the continued threat posed by the uncontrolled Liberian timber industry to regional peace and security, particularly in neighboring Côte d'Ivoire. There are continuous reports of sanctions-violating exports. Moreover, the Liberian government has yet to implement Kimberley Process requirements for the control of its diamond industry. Until Liberia's timber and diamond industries are reformed so that they no longer contribute to conflict, they will pose a threat to Liberia's security and must be sanctioned accordingly.[143]

---

[142] http://www.globalpolicy.org/security/issues/diamond/index.htm
[143] http://www.globalpolicy.org/security/issues/liberia/2004/1208dliaisons.pdf

There are consistent reports of timber crossing the border into Guinea and Côte d'Ivoire. There is also concern about the possibility of timber being trafficked via containers at Monrovia Freeport. The escalating violence in Côte d'Ivoire is likely to increase the illegal export of timber from Liberia, as timber traffickers exploit the Ivorian government and Forces Nouvelles' use of timber revenue to fund the war there.

The rise of the new middle class will only aggravate the demand for elements from the natural resources. At present, the middle class in the poor countries is the fastest-growing segment of the world's population, swelling to 1.8 billion by 2020. A third of them will come from China alone.[144]

Homi Kharas, a researcher at the Brookings Institution, estimates that by 2020, the world's middle class will grow to include a staggering 52% of the total population, up from 30% now. The middle class will almost double in the poor countries where sustained economic growth is fast lifting people above the poverty line. This is expected to increase the demand for quality and high value food, shelter, basic services, energy, and natural resources.

With globalization, what is happening in one country is expected to affect others in another country. The new middle class are expected to want to live the standard enjoy by those from the developed countries. They are expected to buy more clothes, appliances, toys, automobiles, computers, mobile phones, almost anything to make their lives as comfortable as the Westerners. The huge number of people around the world is expected to consume more natural resources such as oil, coal, iron, steel, gold, silver and other metals. China and India, with nearly 40% of the world's population - most of it still very poor - already consume more than half of the global supply of coal, iron ore and steel. Other developing countries are expected to follow.

Moreover, a middle-class lifestyle in these developing countries, even if more frugal than those in rich nations, is expected to increase the demand for energy. In 2006, China added as much electricity as France's current total supply. Yet millions in China lack reliable access to electricity; in India, more than 400 million don't have power. The demand in India is expected to grow fivefold in the next 25 years.[145]

---

[144] http://www.latimes.com/news/opinion/la-oe-naim8feb08,0,3322827.story
[145] Ibid

The demand for oil has set an unprecedented record high price of more than $140 per barrel that partially helps trigger the financial crisis due to the subprime mortgage meltdown in the U.S. As a result, the whole world is feeling the brunt of an expected recession in the U.S. that has slowed down the demand for oil causing the price of oil to plummet. This is only a temporary setback for the oil industry. The planet has gotten a breathing space temporarily.

The rise of the new middle class and the dwindling natural resources coupled with their high prices should awaken us to the problems created by overpopulation. Even the poor, with their sheer number can consume more than their share of the dwindling resources. The emergence of China and India with their 2.5 billion people is expected to present a big challenge to the world's resources. The world cannot forever consume the natural resources on a "business as usual" basis if we are going to survive to the next millennia. There is a need to readjust our lifestyle and start reducing the population worldwide if the welfare of the future generations is not to be sacrificed.

The U.S. uses 25% of the world's total output of oil and is using 10 times more than the individual Chinese and 20 times than an Indian. The use of oil has doubled in India since 1992 while China has become the 2nd largest importer since 2004. Each U.S. citizen requires about 9.7 hectares to provide resources and space for waste, 205% of what the country can provide. That figure is only 1.6 hectares for the average Chinese or 201% of the country's capacity, and 0.8 hectares for the average Indian, or 210% of the country's capacity.[146]

The Earth does not contain enough resources to indefinitely sustain the current demand along with the ever increasing population growth and standard of living. Many of the Earth's resources are limited such as land and fresh water. We have managed to increase land use through high-rise buildings and water through desalinization and diversion of water resources from other areas. The latter has caused international conflicts among nations in the Middle East and even within municipalities. The idea of towing icebergs from the Poles is one solution but will create new problem such as increasing sea level. The demand for food has placed many people in the hungry category worldwide because of the twin effect of grain shortages and rising prices. At present, about 40,000 children die from malnutrition and its related disease. Another 150 million children in the world suffer from poor health due to food shortages.[147]

---

[146] http://overpopulation.org/solutions.html

Air Pollution

Air pollution is one problem few countries were able to tackle satisfactorily. In their rush to industrialized, many developing countries use all kinds of dirty fuels without much regard to the environment. They need to promote their goods with lower price to stimulate growth and compete economically. It is only when a country has industrialized that a combination of government regulations and technological innovation are instituted to address the environmental issues. Even with these measures, the poor air quality remains while the population continues to grow.

China is a good example of how economic growth is abetting environmental problems such as air pollution that posed grave threat to the people. Its annual growth of about 9% for years has caused air pollutants to claim the lives of about 590,000 deaths annually. The burning of its coals and increasing demand for oil consumption is spewing more carbon dioxide to the atmosphere, emitting 47% more carbon dioxide in 2005 than in 1990 and is projected to keep on increasing.[148] It now ranks second to the U.S. in emission of carbon dioxide.

The U.S., with many stringent laws against air pollution still faced high levels of air pollution in many parts of the country. According to the *State of the Air 2005* report, published by the American Lung Association (ALA), millions of Americans still face dangerous levels of air pollution. ALA report that despite pro-environmental sentiment and strong regulations, more than half of the U.S. population lives in counties with unsafe levels of either smog or particle pollution.

Smog is a mixture of air pollutants including nitrogen oxides and volatile organic compounds that combine with sunlight to form ozone. It is a very harmful to living things on the ground level and is often directly responsible for cases of decreased lung function, respiratory infection, burning eyes, lung inflammation and aggravation of respiratory illness. The December 1952 London smog killed an estimated 12,000 people in a span of four days. Although not as serious as the London smog, some 142.7 million Americans live in counties rated with failing grades by the ALA for this airborne pollutant.[149]

---

[147] http://www.sixpak.org/vince/overpopulation.html (1995)
[148] http://overpopulation.org/solutions.html

Children who are active outdoor are likely to suffer from smog because of their smaller lungs. They are prone to asthma, the most common ailment induced by smog. Even healthy adults who exercise or work outdoors are also a risk. Those who are suffering from respiratory diseases or sensitive to smog are likely to suffer further damage to their respiratory system. Elderly people are often warned to stay indoors on heavy smog days. Like any other adults, however, elderly people will be at higher risk from exposure to smog and other pollutants in the smog if they suffer from respiratory diseases, are active outdoors, or are unusually susceptible to ozone.

Another 76.5 million Americans live in areas where they are exposed to unhealthy short-term levels of particle pollution. Children and the elderly are especially at risk. Short-term, or acute, exposure to particle pollution has been linked to increase heart attacks, strokes, and emergency-room visits for asthma and cardiovascular disease. Particle pollution is most dangerous to those already suffering from asthma, heart disease, bronchitis and emphysema. If a highly developed country like the U.S. with their stringent environmental protection laws in force can suffer so many problems, what can be expected for the developing countries?

The main source of air pollution comes from the burning of fossil fuels such as oil and coal. Before the advent of oil, coal is the main source of fossil fuel used in generating electricity then as it is now in many countries. Coal is one of the cheapest sources of generating electricity, although the power plant is very expensive to build. It is also the number one source of carbon dioxide, accounting for three-quarters of all CO_2 emissions. Coal is abundant and much cheaper that other fossil fuel. It takes about two cents to generate one kilowatt of electricity compared to four cents for gas-fired power plants. On the other hand, burning coal produces twice much carbon dioxide as much as gas-fired power plant. Investors are not about to give their profitable investments soon. The lifetime of each coal-fired plant can last for three to four decades and it also takes that time to recoup the investment. Therefore, despite its dirty emission and inefficiency, governments around the world, including the U.S. have tolerated the dirty emissions by exempting them from the Clean Air Act against pollutants. This is one reason why the UN's Kyoto Protocol has not been ratified by the U.S. government. China and India are exempted from the limit imposed by the protocol until they have reached a

---

[149] http://environment.about.com/od/healthenvironment/a/stateofair.htm

certain degree of industrialization. More than 70% of the coal's energy went up in smoke through the smokestack. Investment in scrubbers to clean the coal would have been prohibitive, especially for old power plants. (Roberts, 266)

The U.S. has nearly 900 coal-fired plants and harbored more coal reserves than any country in the world. In the 1980s, the U.S. coal fleet burned 500 million tons of coal annually. By 2000, even though few new coal-fired plants were built, the use of coal nearly doubled to 900 million tons, generating 320,000 MW of power, or a little more than half of all energy produced in the U.S., two-thirds of these plants have no scrubbers to clean up the coal. Besides, scrubbers cannot remove carbon dioxide which accounts for more than half of all the U.S. emissions of it and roughly one-eighth of the world's total. Scrubbers can only remove conventional pollutants such as sulfur, nitrous oxide and mercury. There is as yet no economical way of removing CO_2 from the existing plants. The only way is to refine the coal into a synthetic gas by the so-called Integrated Gasification Combined Code while the extracted carbon is sequestered underground. This method is so expensive that producing electricity this way would be more expensive than gas-fired power plants. It is for this reason why utility firms are opposed to any climate change legislation especially with regard to the carbon emissions. (Ibid, 267-269)

In the metropolitan areas, it is the burning of gasoline and diesel coupled with the release of toxic fumes and particulate matters. Because of their minute size, they are easily lodged in the lungs and respiratory system of the body. According to one report released in 2007, there is an average of about 5,000 deaths in the Metro Manila area alone annually.

Other sources come from the emissions from power plants, smelters, garbage burning, etc. The serious implication on the health of the people forced the Philippine Congress to pass the Clean Air Act to tackle the air pollution besieging the country in 1999. One of the provisions of the law is the phasing out of the lead in the gasoline. This should have been done decades ago. It was hailed as a breakthrough but long delayed considering that the U.S. had longed outlawed leaded gasoline decades ago after it was found that they can destroy the normal growing of the children's brain resulting in lower IQ, stunted growth and impaired hearing. Except for this accomplishment, not much has come out of the law partly because there is little fund for implemented clean air from other sources.

The anti-smoke belching law was implemented only sporadically by civic minded citizens with a little help from the government agents.

Even the monitoring of vehicles requiring the exhaust emission test has become a scam by operators to profit from government corruption and ineptitude. Many simply issue the clearance without even having the vehicles undergone the test.

Many industrialized countries alarmed by the air pollution caused by motor vehicles were forced to install catalytic converter to reduce some pollutants. The converter can only be used with unleaded gas and therefore the catalytic converter would not have been used before 1999. It took years before it was adopted here in the Philippines. The only vehicle I know that had one on it is the new Honda motor vehicles that only came out in 2007.

A catalytic converter is a device installed in automobiles that is designed to reduce harmful emissions released from the vehicle's exhaust. In the United States, all vehicles produced after 1975 are required to have a catalytic converter. Without a catalytic converter, the noxious gases such as carbon monoxide, hydrocarbons and nitrogen oxide are emitted to the atmosphere. They are the largest source of ground level ozone that is responsible for the formation of smog causing myriad respiratory problems and damage to plant life. A catalytic converter uses metallic catalysts, usually platinum, rhodium or palladium to react with the noxious gases, converting them into less harmful gases.

The catalytic converter can reduce the emission of noxious gases by at least 75% when it was first introduced in 1975 in the U.S. It is constantly being improved upon and is now more efficient than ever. In the US, these improvements are in accordance with the EPA more stringent amendments to the Clean Air Act.

Although the catalytic converter has been very successful in reducing the dangerous pollutants released by automobiles, particularly ground level ozone, it has fallen under criticism. The catalytic converter may help to solve one serious environmental problem, but its use is a trade-off at the expense of increasing global warming. The catalytic converter creates and releases into the atmosphere gases that are responsible for global warming. Carbon dioxide, which is released along with the noxious gases from the vehicle's exhaust system, is increased by the catalytic converter. Carbon monoxide, which is transformed into carbon dioxide, is harmless to humans and plant life, but it is responsible for absorbing the sun's infrared waves and causing the planet to warm up.[150]

---

[150] http://www.wisegeek.com/what-is-a-catalytic-converter.htm

Gasoline is one of the major fuels consumed in the United States and the main product refined from crude oil. Consumption in 2007 in the U.S. was about 142 billion gallons, an average about 390 million gallons per day and the equivalent of about 61% of all the energy used for transportation, 44% of all petroleum consumption, and 17% of total U.S. energy consumption. About 47 barrels of gasoline are produced in U.S. refineries from every 100 barrels of oil refined to make numerous petroleum products. Most gasoline is used in cars and light trucks. It also fuels boats, recreational vehicles, and farm, construction, and landscaping equipment. While gasoline is produced year-round, extra volumes are made and imported to meet higher demand in the summer. Gasoline is delivered from oil refineries mainly through pipelines to an extensive distribution chain serving about 167,500 retail gasoline stations in the United States.[151]

The fuel used to drive our motor vehicles are either gasoline or diesel fuel. Both have their problems in relation to the environment and human health. Gasoline has several problems when they are burned in the car engines. One problem is the carbon dioxide produced from the exhaust and emitted to the atmosphere. It is one of the main causes of the greenhouse effect. Another problem has to do with smog and ozone in big cities that is causing some health problems among the inhabitants. Smog came from the nitrogen oxides while ozone came from the unburned hydrocarbons. Another gas that is poisonous to humans is carbon monoxide.

The staggering health cost from air pollution is due to the particulate matters. These are solids or liquids from smoke, soot, rubber, small bits of metal, fly ash, and condensing vapors that can remain suspended in the air for a long time. They affect breathing and respiratory systems of an individual by causing increased respiratory and lung damage, coughing and throat irritations. Some particulates can carry cancer-causing organic compounds and heavy metals into the lungs, especially threatening for small children and older people. A study made in 2001 by the World Bank-sponsor project shows the total health cost for victims in Metro Manila, Cebu City and Davao City at $430 million with 2,000 premature death, 9,000 chronic bronchitis cases and 51 million suffering from respiratory symptoms.

Other important pollutants are carbon monoxide and hydrocarbons. Carbon monoxide (CO) is a colorless, odorless, and

---

[151] http://www.eia.doe.gov/bookshelf/brochures/gasolinepricesprimer/

tasteless gas. Carbon monoxide is produced from the partial combustion of carbon-containing compounds, notably in internal combustion engines. Carbon monoxide forms in preference to the more usual carbon dioxide when there is a reduced availability of oxygen present during the combustion process. It has significant fuel value, burning in air with a characteristic blue flame, producing carbon dioxide. Despite its serious toxicity, CO plays a highly useful role in modern technology, being a precursor to myriad products.

Carbon monoxide is a poisonous gas emitted from the exhaust system of motor engines. Symptoms of mild poisoning include headaches, fatigue, vertigo, and flu-like effects. Prolong exposures can lead to significant toxicity of the central nervous system, heart failure and even death. Following poisoning, long-term sequelae often occur. Carbon monoxide can reduce the ability of the blood to absorb oxygen in body cells and tissue. It can impair vision and judgment, slow reflexes and can lead to unconsciousness and death at high concentrations. It can worsen heart and lung conditions. Pregnant women inhaling CO may cause physical and mental damage to developing babies.

The mechanisms by which carbon monoxide produces toxic effects are not yet fully understood, but hemoglobin, myoglobin, and mitochondrial cytochrome oxidase are thought to be compromised.[152] Carbon monoxide has a significant affinity to the iron sites in hemoglobin, the principal oxygen-carrying compound in blood. The affinity between carbon monoxide and hemoglobin is 240 times stronger than the affinity between hemoglobin and oxygen. CO binds to hemoglobin, producing carboxyhemoglobin (COHb) - which decreases the oxygen-carrying capacity of the blood. This inhibits the transport, delivery, and utilization of oxygen, resulting in asphyxiation.

It has been estimated that more than 40,000 people per year seek medical attention for carbon monoxide poisoning in the United States. In many industrialized countries, carbon monoxide may be the cause of greater than 50% of fatal poisonings. In the U.S., about 200 people die each year from carbon monoxide poisoning associated with home fuel-burning heating equipment. The Center for Disease Control (CDC) reported that each year, more than 500 Americans die from unintentional CO poisoning, and more than 2,000 commit suicide by intentionally poisoning themselves.

---

[152] http://en.wikipedia.org/wiki/Carbon_monoxide_poisoning

Suicide has often been committed by inhaling the exhaust fumes of a running car engine, particularly in an enclosed space such as a garage. In the past, automotive exhaust may have contained up to 25% carbon monoxide; but newer cars are fitted with catalytic converters which can eliminate over 99% of carbon monoxide produced. However, even cars with catalytic converters can produce substantial carbon monoxide if left idling in an enclosed space.

Hydrocarbons (HC) are primarily composed of hydrogen and carbon, with trace elements of nitrogen, sulfur, chlorine, fluoride and oxygen. They are known to cause headaches, eye irritations, respiratory infections, bronchitis, throat problems and coughing. Long-term exposure to relatively high levels of benzene, a kind of hydrocarbon, can cause cancer.[153] Benzene can be found in many solvents, inks, paints, plastics, and rubber. It is also used in making detergents, explosives, drugs, and dyes. Not only does it cause cancer, it damages the nervous system and brain. It is inhaled and absorbed through the skin and eyes. (Steinman and Wisner, 186)

Nuclear power stands the best option for generating electricity without air pollution. Nuclear provides about 18% of the energy produce worldwide, but many problems still persist that made them unviable in many places. Our own Bataan Nuclear Power Plant, with a capacity of 619 MW was mothballed because of fear that the site may be visited by earthquake. It is located at the foot of a potentially active volcano, Mount Natib and near geological fault lines. The high cost of constructing the plant, originally contracted out for $500 million soon ballooned to $2.3 billion due to changes and kickbacks. (*PDI*, January 9, 2009) After spending this much and years of planning and construction, the mothballed nuclear power plant, completed in 1984 never generated any electricity while the government has to pay off the debt incurred, which took 21 years. There is also the problem of where to store the spent the nuclear waste that can last for centuries. Only a few de developed countries have any plan to use nuclear energy as part of their strategy. One reason for this fear is the accidents at the Three Mile Island in the U.S. and the 1986 Chernobyl nuclear accident in the old Soviet Empire. But not in Asia where several countries such as Thailand, Vietnam, and Indonesia have been planning to put up nuclear power plants.

---

[153] Ibid

Postscript

There are only 16 landfills in the country to serve the 90 million polluters. Two of the two landfills under construction in Rodriquez, Rizal and in Norzagaray, Bulacan are being questioned by an environmental group called Kalikasan-People's Network for the Environment for being "defective." Its national coordinator, Clemente Bautista claimed that the technical aspect of the project was not studied carefully because of various flaws and irregularities which range from technical feasibility, environmental and health safety to kickbacks and corruption. There are also no plan for materials recovery facilities. On the other hand, Engineer Darrow Lucenario, an environmental and sanitary engineer, claimed that the projects are located in areas covered by the La Mesa and Ipo dam watershed, which is against an administrative order disallowing projects like that to be located near sources of deep wells, rivers, and other bodies of water. (*PDI*, January 29, 2009)

Chapter 5

ROLE OF THE CATHOLIC CHURCH

There is an underlying reason why the Catholic Church continues to turn a blind eye to the overpopulation problem. It is her desires to have the world populated by Catholics just as the Muslims do. The Church needs the Catholics to contribute to her coffer and defend her if the need arises. Her primary concern is the welfare of the Mother Church while that of her followers are secondary. It is also her desires to dominate the world as she once did in the past. Only through the use of

Catholics around the world in command of the countries can she hopes to accomplish this goal. The U.S., a predominantly Protestant country is her prime target for domination. One good example is the intrusion of many Catholics into the Republican Party with cabinet ranks during the Reagan and Bush eras and making pro-Catholic policies and decisions.

Another example is when the U.S. decided to crack down on overstaying and illegal aliens, the Catholic Church was overwhelming opposed to the idea, even openly calling on the prelates to open the door to the churches to all illegal aliens, to hide and feed them if necessary. An overwhelming majority of them are Catholics from the south.

In the Philippines, the Church is embroiled in many political issues and even issues of reproductive health and the use of contraceptives. Her role in the overpopulation problem seems to be much maligned not so much for her stand but more so for her insistence that the use of contraceptives is sinful and morally wrong. People of other faith are being maligned by her pronouncements even though their own faith does not view all form of contraceptives as evil and morally wrong. Who are the Catholic prelates to tell them that they are sinning against the laws of God and are bound for hell? There is nothing more disgusting than being self-righteous especially to those who were well aware of the reason behind her decision on contraceptives.

Historical Background

There is a need to adopt a reproductive health bill to put to rest the problems arising from overpopulation and the dictates of the Catholic Church. As long as there is no law authorizing the use of contraceptives, parents will be at the mercy of whoever is in charge of the population problem. All efforts in the past to try to control the runaway population had proved futile. During the time of Marcos, when he perceived the coming population problem, the criticisms of the Catholic Church forced the government to shift its emphasis to family welfare and development instead of population control. Little was accomplished even with the creation of the Population Commission which were mostly headed by Catholics who are indoctrinated by the Church teachings.

By the time President Aquino took over, the Popcom budget of P120 million in 1983 was down to P56.8 million. Most of the budget went to operating expenses and nothing much was left for birth control. When President Ramos took over, he appointed Dr. Juan

Flavier who had much experienced with the rural people and was a firm family planning crusader. He sets about purchasing birth control pills and other contraceptives and even advocated condom use in an anti-AIDS campaign. The Catholic Church was vehemently against him so much so that when he ran for a Senate seat, the Church continues to vilify him. President Fidel Ramos, a Protestant, refused to join the fray, probably thinking there is no point in a quarreling with the powerful Church that could only tear the country apart. Even President Joseph Estrada took a "hands-off" policy, refused to antagonize the powerful Church which has no respect for the separation of the Church and State.

Like a maverick, the Estrada administration tried to continue with the policy of giving the women a choice in the use of contraceptives by committing to purchase P70 million worth after the USAID decided to stop donating contraceptives. It would probably put a big dent on the population explosion if the country were saturated with contraceptives as in Thailand. In the past four decades, Thailand was able to reduce its population by 20 million in comparison to ours. Today, they have a better standard of living than we have.

Under the present administration, any hope of getting the government to purchase contraceptives may be gone. The population policy has been devoluted to local government units. Only donations and purchases by heads of the local government units who advocated the use of artificial methods are made available to the mothers. As a result, the women do not have a freedom of choice. The president, a staunch Catholic, refused to antagonize the Church, refused to endorse artificial contraceptives together with natural family planning.

The result is that in some government clinics the health workers have their own convictions and therefore their own agenda when they are consulted by prospective mothers. Women who went to health centers were given runaround while others were put to shame and ridiculed. Furthermore, there are not enough health workers to monitor the women or even to make house calls for those who are too ashamed to visit the clinics. To add to the problem, the donation from the USAID has been dwindling and the women have to buy whatever they needed and it could be expensive.

To be fair to the women, they should be given the choice because it is their bodies and health that are involved. No one should be able to dictate on what they can and cannot do to their own health, especially those unrelated people who have no experience raising a family. Also, it is almost impossible for every male Catholics to abstain from sex as advocated by the Church whenever they wanted to.

During period of fertility, they should be allowed to use other alternatives.

Then there is the issue of adolescent sexuality which is more prevalent than most parents are willing to admit. The East West Center study says about 87% of Filipinos ages 15-24 had their first sexual experience outside of marriage. National data also show that 36% of young Filipino women ages 15 to 24 conceive before marriage. Young mothers account for 17% of induced abortion cases; 6% of spontaneous abortions and 74% of illegitimate births. (*PCIJ*, 2003)

Teenage pregnancies have become a major social problem in the country. Once impregnated and given birth, teenagers, whether male or female have been forced by circumstances to stop education in order to care for the baby while the father may be forced to work to support the new family. Teenage girls are often unaware of the many problems connected with their health and rearing a family. The teenage girl is even in a dilemma whether to have the baby, be a single mother, or whether the male will be responsible for supporting the child, etc.

Some teenagers may not be aware of the implication of unprotected sex. Earlier age at initiation of sexual activity which oftentimes takes place without adequate protection are detrimental to young people since it poses heightened risk of unintended pregnancy which, in turn, precipitates either a hasty marriage or in many cases, end in abortion. There are also limited employment opportunities as well as greater financial difficulties and marital conflict. Young unmarried mothers also face social stigmas that can have harmful psychological and social impact.[154] The reproductive health bill provides for sex education partly to address teenage pregnancies and problems and what teenagers may expect from premarital sex.

Unprotected sex and sex with either casual partners, commercial sex workers or multiple partners are risk markers for exposure and transmission of sexually transmitted diseases (STDs) including HIV/AIDS. Sex outside marriage, specifically premarital sex, is generally viewed as socially unacceptable and undermines traditional moral values which may be psychologically damaging to young people

---

[154]

http://209.85.175.104/search?q=cache:Nio1IaKOooEJ:web.kssp.upd.edu.ph/talastasan/papers/marquez_icophil_paper_revised.pdf+east+west+center+abortion&hl=en&ct=clnk&cd=4&gl=ph

especially in a Catholic country such as the Philippines. Needless to say, the risks associated with these activities are magnified by their interconnectedness or what Jessor, Donovan and Costa (1991, as cited in Arnett, 1998) refer to as the "interrelated syndrome of risk behaviors." Youth whose sexual debut comes early in life are more likely to have multiple sex partners, to practice unprotected sex and to turn to selling sex to make a living (Mateo, 2003; Smith, 1997; Alan Guttmacher Institute, 1994; Coker, Valois and Mckeown, 1994 and Klitsch, 1993). For instance, Klitsch (1993) documented that American women whose first intercourse happened before age 15 are much more likely than those who initiated sex at later ages to have had recent multiple partners, to have had sex with a risky partner (either bisexual, an intravenous drug user or an HIV-infected man) and to have had a sexually-transmitted disease. Among Filipino adolescents, the strong linkage of premarital sex experience with drug use, smoking, drinking, contemplation of suicide, involvement in physical violence and suspension from school has also been established (Raymundo and Cruz, 2004).

In the country, what makes adolescent sexual risk-taking doubly problematic and enormously challenging is due to the sheer size of the Filipino adolescent population. Constituting about 20% of the total population, the number of Filipino youth in the ages 15-24 has ballooned from 12.4 million in 1990 to 15.1 million a decade later (Ericta, 2003). In recent years, policymakers and the general public have demonstrated a growing concern about issues pertaining to adolescent wellbeing. The fact that the Commission on Population, the agency mandated to serve as the central coordinating and policymaking body of the government in the field of population, devoted its most recent edition of the *State of the Philippine Population Report* (Commission on Population, 2003) on adolescent reproductive health with prominent attention accorded to youth sexual risk-taking is a testimony to the urgency and seriousness of this issue.

Responsible parenthood like its earlier counterpart family planning has been used by the Church and their advocates as if it is the solution to overpopulation. It is precisely because by allowing the parents the option to plan the size of the family is what makes responsible parenthood even more acceptable to many but it will not solve the problem of overpopulation. What is needed it honest to goodness control of the family size especially for the poor members of society because it is from their ranks that most of the poor babies are coming from. It is for this reason why the bill was being endorsed by many lawmakers and interested groups for passage into law.

A recent study by the 27 economic professors of the U.P. School of Economics endorses the passage of the reproductive health bill now pending in Congress. One glaring finding was that only 10% had only one child, while 57% had nine or more children. Although the poor families want smaller families except that they were not able because of the unmet need for family planning services by the government. They found that among the poorest 10% of women of reproductive age, 44% of their pregnancies are unwanted. The weak population control policy only aggravates the poverty leading to higher rate of material mortality and ill health of the mother. They also found that for every 100,000 births, 162 mothers died during delivery. (*PDI*, August 14, 2008)

Papal Infallibility

"*And Judah said unto Onan, Go in unto thy brother's wife, and marry her, and raise up seed to thy brother. And Onan knew that the seed should not be his; and it came to pass, when he went in unto this brother's wife, that he spilled it on the ground, lest that he should give seed to his brother. And the thing which he did displeased the Lord: wherefore he slew him also*" (**Genesis 38:8-10**). The sin committed by Onan before God was not *coitus interruptus* that is gravely looked down upon by the Church. His sin was disobedience to the law of God for refusing to bear children who will bear his dead brother's name (**Deuteronomy 25:5-7**). It is a form of contraception and a sin worse than incest in the eyes of the Church as taught by Thomas Aquinas. (Wills, 76) This was the basis of the Church's law for a long time that all forms of contraception including the rhythm method is sinful until Pope Pius XI came out with his encyclical allowing the use of the rhythm method as the only natural form of contraception beside abstinence. He wrote in his encyclical *Casti connubii*, citing St. Augustine "Marital intercourse, even with one's legitimate spouse, is forbidden and immoral, if the awakening of new life is prevented. This is what Onan, the son of Judah did, and on account of that God killed him." (Ranke, 85) This has no biblical foundation even according to Jewish Scripture of the Old Testament and their extensive and detailed laws on the matter. Even some theologians who helped wrote the *Humanae Vitae* agreed on the ban on contraception but not with the natural law justifying its ban. (Wills, 76-77) The original draft even had the term "with our infallible authority" until it was dropped at the last minute. (Berry, 181)

The real issue besieging the Catholic Church in the Philippines was once played out in the United States. It is not so much an issue of morality, but an issue of papal authority over the political power of the state to dictate what is moral and good for the country. This is why the much maligned *Humane Vitae* is still in the limelight whenever papal infallibility is discussed.

According to Cardinal Joseph Ratzinger (Pope Benedict XVI), then head of the Congregation for the Doctrine of the Faith before becoming Pope, the possibility of invoking "papal infallibility," was discussed but had been rejected as unnecessary because, as it is, the Pope's language on abortion invokes the full power of church doctrine, even if the word "infallible" is not there. This is true of all of the pope's pronouncements, and for this reason, for the believer, all of the pope's pronouncements are de facto accepted as infallible.[155]

At the heart of the issue of the reproductive health bill is the use of contraceptives and sex education, but the Church made it a point to include abortion because the issue against the use of contraceptives, even among Catholics have long been discredited. The Vatican had failed to halt legalized abortion and contraception in the U.S. and many predominantly Catholic countries in Europe and South America. The Philippines should not be intimated into submitting to the will of the Church. Just because at one time the Church played a decisive role in the downfall of a dictator does not give her the prerogative to dictate on the wishes of the people. The country can ill afford to allow the Church to dictate the fate of the country just because the Vatican demands supremacy over civil governments in matters of faith and morals. While the Church is saying that family planning and abortion are evil and grave sins, the U.S. government is saying they may be good and should be used. Obviously, most American Catholics are accepting morality as defined by the government and rejecting morality as defined by the pope. As a result, Papal authority is undermined.[156]

There are a number of Catholic countries in Latin America with abortion rates two to four times as high as the U.S. rate. But the bishops ignore abortions there. Why? Because they are illegal abortions, not legal ones. They do not threaten Papal authority. Only legal abortions do, because their legalization establishes their morality. Thus, the bishops take no significant actions to halt abortions in Latin America.

---

[155] http://www.population-security.org/14-CH6.html#4
[156] Ibid

In *Papal Power: A Study of Vatican Control Over Lay Catholic Elites*, published by The University of California Press in 1980, Jean-Guy Vaillancourt, Associate Professor of Sociology at the University of Montreal, closely examines the sources of papal power and how it evolved. He found that papal authority is vital to the maintenance of papal power. This power is derived in significant part from papal authority. If the Pope's authority is diminished, papal power is diminished and vice versa. Less authority means less power which means even less authority. With diminishing power, survival of the institution of the Roman Catholic Church in its present hierarchical form is gravely threatened. Thus, the very survival of the Vatican is threatened by programs of population growth control.

In his book, *Persistent Prejudice: Anti-Catholicism in America*, published by *Our Sunday Visitor* in 1984, Michael Schwartz summarized the position of Catholic conservatives on the abortion issue: "The abortion issue is the great crisis of Catholicism in the United States, of far greater import than the election of a Catholic president or the winning of tax support for Catholic education. In the unlikely event that the Church's resistance to abortion collapses and the Catholic community decides to seek an accommodation with the institutionalized killing of innocent human beings would signal the utter failure of Catholicism in America. It would mean that U.S. Catholicism will have been defeated and denatured by the anti-Catholic host culture."

The strong stand of the Catholic Church against abortion is reiterated in April 1992, in a rare public admission by Cardinal John O'Connor of New York when he delivered a major address to the Franciscan University of Steubenville, Ohio, acknowledging, "The fact is that attacks on the Catholic Church's stance on abortion, unless they are rebutted, effectively erode Church authority on all matters, indeed on the authority of God himself." What better to instill fear in God-fearing people than by invoking the name of God? In our case, the reproductive health bill is still vehemently against abortion and does not undermine the papal power over Catholics on this issue.

According to Father Andrew Greeley, the Vatican is against the use of contraceptives has nothing to do with religious fervor but with its vast worldwide political power. This is because having more communicants or faithful followers gives the hierarchy more power. The Church is willing to place the religious dimension at risk in order to prevail politically.[157] This is becoming a serious problem as

Muslims are becoming more numerous than Catholics around the world. From the biblical point of view, having more people may not be in the best interest of the people around the world. The Bible is very emphatic that many are called into the world but only a few are chosen to go to heaven.

It would do anything to undermine any nation from restricting the population of Catholics around the world. The U.S. National Security Council in 1979 and 1980 determined that the population problem threatens the security of the world. This puts it in conflict with the Vatican. This forced the Vatican to act decisively in helping elect an American president using the infrastructure created by the Catholic Bishops' 1975 Pastoral Plan for Pro-Life Activities, to combat legalized abortion. Ronald Reagan was elected and his administration became the most Catholics in American history and his agenda often run parallel to that of the Vatican.[158]

The Vatican was fortunate to have Ronald Reagan as president of the United States because his father and a brother were Irish Roman Catholic. The president has also appointed Irish Catholics to important positions that affect the population growth-security in the persons of Richard Allen, William Clark, and James McFarland. His two Secretaries of State were Alexander Haig, an Irish Catholic and George Schultz, a Catholic of German extraction. His CIA director was William Casey, another Irish Catholic as his Attorney General William French Smith. His Health and Human Services was Margaret Heckler, another Irish Catholic.[159]

In 1979, August Bernhard Hasler published his book, *How the Pope Became Infallible*, that the world was given the text of the minority report which persuaded Pope Paul VI to reject the majority position. Hasler was a Catholic theologian and historian who served for five years in the Vatican secretariat for Christian unity. During this period, he was given access to the Vatican Archives where he discovered numerous documents, never studied before, that revealed the story of Vatican Council I. Dr. Hasler died suddenly at age 43, four days after writing a critical open letter to Pope John Paul II and six months after completing the second edition of his book.

---

[157] Dr. Stephen Mumford, "American Democracy & the Vatican: Population Growth & National Democracy," ww.mosquitonet.com/~pewett/amdempreface.html
[158] Ibid
[159] Ibid

The declaration of papal infallibility was a product of Vatican Council I when Pope Pius IX declared himself infallible on issue of moral and faith in an *ex cathedral* setting, i.e. as a shepherd of the Church. The reason and the timing for this declaration was the loss or impending loss of the Papal States. Without the Papal States, the only way to hold the Church and the faithful together under the Vatican was this papal infallibility dogma. The Vatican has lost much of her glorious days and she needed this power to continue her empire. The stress on the absolute authority of the pope in questions of faith and morals helped turn the Church into a unified and powerful bureaucratic organization, and paved the way for the establishment of the Papacy-laity relationship as we know it today.

Pope Paul VI was faced with the prospect of personally destroying the concept of papal infallibility, a concept vital to the continuation of papal power. Personally, I think he was forced to accept the minority report or be damned to hell by his cardinals and others who are capable of murder. His decision cause a firestorm in the Catholic world that many priests resigned from their posts. There were insinuations that he was later drugged and replaced by an impostor. (see *The Dark Side of Catholicism*),

A survey made by the National Survey of Family Growth in 1995 found that 95% of Catholic women used contraception at one time or another while less than 3% used the rhythm method faithfully. On the issue of abortion, the number of Catholics and non-Catholics who went through abortion was almost identical. (Wills, *Catholic*, 272-273) The reason for so many abortions is the untimely and unwanted pregnancies. Many Catholics are just like non-Christians when it comes to sexual escapade. Being faithful is not a trait among the machos of the world. Man is a polygamous creature since Biblical times. This is the greatest failure of the Catholic Church. Her moral teaching is not being followed by most Catholics. How else do you explain why half of the families in this country are broken? The truth is that Catholicism as an institution is a failure because many cannot live up to the high moral standard imposed by the Church.

The proliferation of abortions can partly be blamed on the prohibition against the use of contraceptives. The pill is used to delay fertility such that conception is impossible to achieve. Sometimes they fail but that does not means it is ineffective unlike the rhythm method which is hard to put into practice effectively. The use of the condom has additional advantages of protection against most sexually transmitted diseases. Other mechanical methods can also be employed. These methods could have helped prevent many unwanted births and therefore reduce the rate of abortions. But the infallible pope had other ideas that soon led to widespread disenfranchisement of many of the faithful. Since the issuance of his encyclical *Humane Vitae*, Pope Paul VI never issued another encyclical nor travelled outside the Vatican during the last ten years of his papacy. (Timothy McCarthy, 325) No "doctrine" bordering on dogma has been violated or ignored by the faithful than this encyclical.

The papacy refused to acknowledge it but every time she made a pronouncement on issues of morals and faith, and expects the faithful to follow her teaching especially under pain of automatic excommunication for disobedience, it is tantamount to an *ex cathedra* declaration. This is especially true in cases of sexual morality such as the use of contraceptives and issues regarding abortion, divorce and remarriage. The Ordinary Magisterium that includes the Pope and the bishops of local churches is considered to be infallible in their teachings on matters of faith and morals such as *Humanae Vitae* and as such their teachings are considered infallible. (Flannery, Vol. 11, 420)

The debate on contraception has boiled down to only one acceptable method of natural contraception, the "rhythm method." After centuries of debate, the issue was finally settled with Pope Pius XI's encyclical *Casti Connubis* of 1930 and reiterated by Pope Paul VI with his even more controversial encyclical *Humanae Vitae*. It was a decision based more on papal authority and infallibility than reason or logic. Any change would mean her previous teachings were wrong even with the advances in the medical field. Here again is a shade of her war on science and medicine. His decision was made despite the contrary decision of the majority of the committee members he called to help him formulate the decision. The theologians called to help him voted fifteen to four against the claim that contraception is intrinsically evil. Another larger group including laymen also voted overwhelmingly for new teachings on contraception. (Timothy, McCarthy, 324) The sixteen bishops of the commission voted nine to three with three abstentions for a new Church position on contraception. With the centuries of Church's policy against contraception and the encyclical of Pius XI, there is no way for Pope Paul VI to reverse the doctrine as it would be tantamount to admitting papal fallibility.

One of the authors of the minority report was none other than Archbishop of Krakow, Karol Wojtyla who would later become Pope John Paul II. In his report he states, "If it should be declared that contraception is not evil in itself, then we should have to concede frankly that the Holy Spirit had been on the side of the Protestant churches in 1930, in 1951 and in 1958. It should likewise have to be admitted that for a half century the (Holy) Spirit failed to protect Pius XI, Pius XII, and a large part of the Catholic hierarchy from a very serious error. This would mean that the leaders of the Church, acting with extreme imprudence, had condemned thousands of innocent human acts, forbidding, under pain of eternal damnation, a practice which would now be sanctioned. The fact can neither be denied nor ignored that these same acts would now be declared licit on the grounds of principles cited by the Protestants, which popes and bishops have either condemned or at least not approved."[160] The rest is history. Contraception became a serious threat to the principle of infallibility and to backtrack on the issue of contraception would be to admit error and destroy infallibility.

During the International Conference on Population and Development held in Cairo in 1994, the Vatican was able to shut down the meeting for the first six days that stunned everyone. Unlike the 1984 International Population Conference in Mexico City, the Vatican was able to impose her stance on abortion and family planning. All her actions have been grounded on papal infallibility that made her difficult to change her teaching.[161] The extent of what the Vatican will do to anyone who tried to undermine this authority can be fatal.

When Pope John Paul I succeeded Pope Paul VI, he had planned to move the Church away or totally reverse her stand against other forms of contraception. He gave away his thoughts on the matter when he congratulated the parents of the first test tube baby despite the condemnation of intro *fertilization* found in *Humanae Vitae.* (Wills, 97) This may be one of the reasons why some Churchmen think he had planned to reverse the Church's old stand on contraception and was "murdered." This is not surprising when as bishop of Vittorio Veneto, he advocated the use of contraception and even endorsed a specific anovulant pill. (Berry, 181) Or he could have been killed for trying to cleanup the Vatican Bank under the controversial Archbishop Marcinkus. In a desperate move, someone had him poisoned, according to David Yallop's research into the untimely death of Pope John Paul I (1978) in his book *In God's Name.* The official report however is that he suffered a heart attack. (Green, 37-38) My personal

---

[160] www.prochoiceactionnetwork-canada.org/articles/vatican.shtml
[161] "The Vatican's Role in the World Population Crisis: the untold story," www.population-security.org/phil95/htm

opinion, which many who had read the book by Yallop is that his Secretary of State Cardinal Jean Villot may be the instigator of his murder by the many acts he had done after his death and his being one of the few who has access to his room on the night of his death. The author gave a convincing account of that fateful night that point in that direction.

Pope John Paul II's stand on contraception is well known. Before becoming a pope, he wrote *Love and Responsibility* that was used by Pope Paul VI as a reference when he wrote *Humane Vitae*. (Bernstein, 133) It was said that when he was yet a cardinal, he convinced Pope Paul VI not to change the Church's doctrine on artificial birth control. (Hutchinson, *Kingdom*, 322) He reiterated the teaching of *Humanae Vitae* and even went on to emphasize sex as God's gift of life while condemning contraception as anti-life in his encyclical *Familiaris Consortia.* (Wills, 99) But this does not deter Catholics from rejecting the teaching outright. A number of theologians such as Charles Curran of the U.S. emphasized that contraception should be permissible in some circumstances. He also batted for a more liberal interpretation on sexual matters such as masturbation and premarital sex. (Bokenkotter, 374, 396)

Not all Catholics believed in the infallibility of the Church on issue of contraceptives and even on abortion. Catholic women have their fair share of abortion. This is not surprising to Catholic theologians. Bernard Haring lamented the fact that Catholics have lost their concern about abortion because the Church has made so much of contraception as another form of "baby killing." (Wills, 189) Women are forced to appeal to their conscience for their decisions as some priests have repeatedly advised.

There is also the issue of whose life to save when there is a mortal conflict between the life of a mother and her unborn child. Who is authorized to make the decision in this case? It is well known that Roman Catholic teaching prohibits direct abortion as a means of saving the mother's life. But it is also a form of killing the mother if the child is not aborted. This puts the Church in a dilemma as to which life is to be saved. It is fair to say that the decision should be up to the mother and to some extent the husband. Likewise, the issue of a woman with damaged uterus needing hysterectomy should be left to the mother to decide even if she has been impregnated. The Church is not the best judge of the woman's health and should refrain from voicing her opinion on matters that properly belong to the family to decide.

One auxiliary bishop of Brazil, Rafael Llano Cifuentes was so exasperated he told his congregation in a sermon that "the Church is against condom use. Sexual relations between a man and a woman have to be natural. I have never seen a little dog using a condom during sexual intercourse with another dog." Cardinal Wamala has even opined that women who died of AIDS rather than employ latex protection should be considered martyrs. (Hitchens, 45-46)

The theology of the Vatican regarding contraceptive condom in connection to AIDS is very complicated, not so much on the issue of life and death but on her dogma of infallibility. She is afraid that people will question or even ridicule her reversal on the issue as tantamount to a fallible doctrine. The idea that using condom is of the "lesser evil" than infecting one's spouse without using condom may not sit well with the Church hierarchy. The Church would rather have the spouses get infected than have them using condom. This illogical logic has been responsible for the proliferation infectious diseases in Africa and elsewhere.

Encouraging sexual abstinence has long been a staple of HIV prevention approach by the Vatican and the U.S. Agency for International Development (USAID). The introduction of abstinence-only to the developing world has caused considerable anxiety among AIDS service providers, particularly those associated with family planning. The USAID seems to have shifted to the Vatican's viewpoint when it cancelled multimillion dollars contract for condom social marketing in Brazil and cancellation or reduction in condom shipments or funding to twenty-nine developing countries. There is growing fear of a shift in USAID policy away from condom promotion and toward strategies based on sexual abstinence.[162]

If the Vatican continues its stand against the use of condom for the infected spouse, it could be committing the cardinal commandment of God against killing a person. This is what will happen to the innocent spouse getting infected that could prove to be fatal. How is a woman to react when she cannot refuse her HIV-positive husband's sexual advances if she cannot defend her own life with the use of condom?

Besides the scientific evidences that condoms can prevent HIV/AIDS infection, surveys in Thailand and Cambodia have proven that condoms worked. WHO has taken the initiative to stem the

---

[162] "The global condom gap,"
http://hrw.org/reports/2004/philippines0504/5.htm

growing HIV/AIDS problem by aggressively promoting sex workers in Asia to adopt this uncompromising stand when facing clients. It is implementing 100% condom use in commercial sex establishment in HIV/AIDS devastated countries of China, Myanmar, Mongolia, Vietnam, Laos, Thailand, Cambodia and the Philippines. In Thailand and Cambodia, it is most successful where new infections have nose-dived by more than 80% since the peak in the last decade. Only 16% of cases in Thailand and 21% in Cambodia developed from the sex industry compared with 80 to 90% in the previous decade.[163]

Church Teachings on Population

The Church prelates have a bad habit of talking in ambiguity to hide their true intention. They talk of immorality when using contraceptives of any kind without justifying how some contraceptives that do not even cause the death of a fertilized egg could be immoral. When the issue of the sin of Onan was explained away by the exegetes, they have stopped using the issue of the sin of Onan to justify the practice of *coitus interruptus* or withdrawal method. Yet for a time, it was considered more sinful that committing incest. For centuries they have advocated unlimited children until the world is now filled with people and they have come out with natural family planning allowing parents to be responsible parents. While they tell faithful parents the natural right to determine the size of their families, they refused to sanction other means of more effective ways of controlling the family size, insisting on natural family planning which does not work well with parents. They claimed that parents are allowed to determine the size of their family on the basis of spiritual, economic, and social responsibilities, but how come most Catholic families around the world in the Third World are poor? They never wanted them to have small families. The poor Catholics are like soldiers they needed to protect the Church in some future event. Today, the Church is on a move to saturate the world with Catholics against all religion, especially the more numerous Muslims. Not to be outvoted, the Muslims are also one in promoting more children to the world.

The Philippines is at the center of a firestorm on the non-issue of abortion. There is presently no serious effort to allow the use of abortion in any of the law being presently in Congress. Yet, the

---

[163] P. Parameswaran, "WHO-Asia-condoms: AIDS battle reaches new climax in Asia with aggressive condom policy," www.aegis.com/news/afp/2003/AF030861.html, 8/15/2003

Church is barking at the wrong tree in her insistence that the reproductive health law will lead to legalized abortion. In most of Europe where she once supreme, there are laws allowing abortion for the first trimetric period. She has lost out also in most part of South America. We are probably the only country where the Church still claims sexual moral power over the people. As long as most Filipinos remain poor, the Church can find support among them because they are easier to manipulate. That is why she is allowing the poor to continue procreating for the benefit of the Mother Church. Some of the latest proclamations of the Popes are listed below:

Pope John XXIII's 1961 social encyclical Mater et magistra:

188. Now to tell the truth, the interrelationships on a global scale between the number of births and available resources are such that we can infer that serious difficulties in this matter do not arise at the present, nor will they in the immediate future. The arguments advanced in this connection are so inconclusive and controversial that nothing certain can be drawn from them. (Author's note: The encyclical was written 47 years ago and by today's standard outdated. The overpopulation problem has been compounded by more serious problems facing the world and the Philippines in particular such as food and energy shortages leading to high prices, pollution, crimes, squatters, lack of schoolrooms, education, etc. to name a few.)

191. But whatever be the situation, we clearly affirm these problems should be posed and resolved in such a way that man does not have recourse to methods and means contrary to his dignity which are proposed by those persons who think of man and his life solely in material terms. (Author's note: Words are always easier said than done. Most people on earth are motivated by material good and good life and that those who have less or nothing will often resort to criminal activities to get what they need. Statistics have shown that most crimes have been committed against persons and properties for reason for covetousness. Even the local Church is not completely innocent of material wealth as she amasses wealth from her numerous enterprises and schools for the benefit of those at the Vatican.)

192. We judge that this question can be resolved only if economic and social advances preserve and augment the genuine welfare of individual citizens and of human society as a whole. Indeed, in a matter of this kind, first place must be accorded everything that

pertains to the dignity of man as such, or to the life of individual men, than which nothing can be more precious. Moreover, in this matter, international cooperation is necessary, so that, conformably with the welfare of all, information, capital, and men themselves may move about among the peoples in orderly fashion. (Author's note: The world we live in is a cutthroat society where each one tries to outwit the others. There is a serious problem of unemployment and underemployment leading to greater poverty in our midst. When a person or members of his family are hungry, morality and even spiritualism is out. We should never expect free dole outs like beggars from others to solve problems of our own doing. With the sheer number of poor in the country, the Church should be promoting birth control by legal means instead of hindering it. It is the only easy way of promoting genuine welfare for each individual.)

Pope John Paul II's Sollicitudo rei socialis:

25. One cannot deny the existence, especially in the southern hemisphere of a demographic problem which creates difficulties for development. One must immediately add that in the northern hemisphere the nature of this problem is reversed: here, the cause for concern is the drop in the birthrate with repercussions on the aging of the population, unable even to renew itself biologically. In itself, this is a phenomenon capable of hindering development.... (Author's note: The graying of the population is not a serious as the problem we are now encountering, which is lack of quality of life for most of the people. We need to tackle the present problems related to overpo16:1pulation before we should worry about depopulation which is a very farfetched problem for us. The point may not be reached anytime in the future because by then, most of the earth's carrying capacity may have been breached. A smaller population is what we need to solve most of the social ills plaguing the nation now and into the future.)

Pope John Paul II's Evangelium vitae

16. "Today...the powerful of the earth...are haunted by the current demographic growth and fear that the most prolific and poorest peoples represent a threat for the well-being and peace of their own countries." (Author's note: The Pope must be misinformed. I do not think the powerful nations of the world are fearful of the poor countries. Most of them have actually been contributing to help the poor countries of the world. They prefer to help the people of the poor

countries improve their living standard by limiting their population instead of allowing tragedies to occur such as famine and looking up to them for help.)

17. "We are in fact faced by an objective 'conspiracy against life' involving even international institutions, engaged in encouraging and carrying out actual campaigns to make contraception, sterilization and abortion widely available. Nor can it be denied that the mass media are often implicated in this conspiracy, by lending credit to that culture which presents recourse to contraception, sterilization, abortion and even euthanasia as a mark of progress and a victory for freedom, while depicting as enemies of freedom and progress those positions which are unreservedly pro-life." (Author's note: Their good intention to help us from overpopulation is being maligned, especially when some of the methods of contraception are also legalized in their own countries. They are more honest than the Church could ever be.)

20. "To claim the right to abortion, infanticide and euthanasia, and to recognize that right in law, means to attribute to human freedom a perverse and evil significance: that of an absolute power over others and against others. This is the death of true freedom." (Author's note: Most countries allowing abortion has been forced upon them because there are many unwanted pregnancies arising from the Church stands against contraception. On the issue of infanticides and euthanasia, I know of no known nation that has such as law. The few cases of euthanasia have been sanctioned by the law due to incurable diseases or comatose victims.)

62. "I declare that direct abortion, that is, abortion willed as an end or a means, always constitutes a grave moral disorder, since it is the deliberate killing of an innocent human being. This doctrine is based upon the natural law and upon the written Word of God, is transmitted by the church's tradition and taught by the ordinary and universal Magisterium....No circumstance, no purpose, no law whatsoever can ever make licit an act which is intrinsically illicit, since it is contrary to the law of God which is written in every human heart, knowable by reason itself, and proclaimed by the church." (Author's note: The Pope should have addressed this encyclical to his prelates first before the general public. Furthermore, the Church teaching on morality is being ignored by the Church's followers more than the followers of other religions in the country. It is the perception of most people that the

Church has failed in her role as messenger of morality because of her many "sins" such as child abuse cases and immorality of her priests.)

70. "Democracy cannot be idolized to the point of making it a substitute for morality or a panacea for immorality. Fundamentally, democracy is a 'system' and as such is a means and not an end. Its 'moral' value is not automatic but depends on conformity to the moral law." (Author's note: Democracy is still the best form of government; it is the people who have abused the system for their selfish ends. Whatever form of government has nothing to do with immorality.)

72. "Laws which legitimize the direct killing of innocent human beings through abortion or euthanasia are in complete opposition to the inviolable right to life proper to every individual...Laws which authorize and promote abortion and euthanasia are therefore radically opposed not only to the good of the individual but also to the common good; as such they are completely lacking in authentic juridical validity." (Author's note: While I do not condone abortion or euthanasia, they are acceptable as long as they are done within the law. Who are we to question the legitimacy of the acts?)

73. "Abortion and euthanasia are thus crimes which no human law can claim to legitimize. There is no obligation in conscience to obey such laws; instead there is a grave and clear obligation to oppose them by conscientious objection.....It is precisely from obedience to God - to whom alone is due that fear which is acknowledgment of his absolute sovereignty - that the strength and the courage to resist unjust human laws are born. It is the strength and the courage of those prepared even to be imprisoned or put to the sword, in the certainty that this is what makes for the endurance and faith of the saints.....In the case of an intrinsically unjust law, such as a law permitting abortion or euthanasia, it is therefore never licit to obey it, or to take part in a propaganda campaign in favor of such a law or to vote for it." (Author's note: It is unfortunate for many Catholic countries whose lawmakers are also Catholics to pass laws that do not conform to the teaching of their Church. The Church infallible right to teach issues over morality and faith has been ignored.)

81. "The consequences of this gospel (the gospel of life)....can be summed up as follows: Human life, as a gift of God, is sacred and inviolable. For this reason procured abortion and euthanasia are absolutely unacceptable." (Author's note: In time past, the Church has destroyed the lives of millions who refused to bow down to her

religious teachings. It is only with the ascension of the secular governments that the yoke of religious intolerance have been destroyed forever.)

82. "In the proclamation of this gospel, we must not fear hostility or unpopularity, and we must refuse any compromise or ambiguity which might conform us to the world's way of thinking. We must be in the world but not of the world." (Author's note: These words could have been spoken by those pro-choice advocators. It is this uncompromising stand of the Church on the use of some form of contraception that is not intrinsically evil that has caused so many unwanted pregnancies that many Catholics were forced to commit abortions.)

91. "[On]...the issue of population growth...It is...morally unacceptable to encourage, let alone impose, the use of methods such as contraception, sterilization and abortion in order to regulate births.....Service of the Gospel of life is...a valuable and fruitful area for positive cooperation with our brothers and sisters of other Churches and ecclesial communities....." (Author's note: The self-righteous Church should not expect other religious organization to accept her moral teaching especially when she has repeatedly distorted the Bible to suit her wishes with infallible doctrines and dogmas.)

In Italy, *Evangelium Vitae* was strongly criticized in the press, according to the National Catholic Register. The Italian press takes the Vatican much less seriously than does its American counterpart. In an article by Jeffrey Donovan, *At Home the Pope's Encyclical Takes Beating*, the negative reactions were widespread and strongly worded. For example, the Rome daily *Il Manifesto* termed the encyclical "fundamentalist and desperate" and offers: "The Pope multiples his condemnations, repeats his classic arguments and searches for new ones, too, but fails to consider the realities of modern life, which contradict everything he says." According to the Register, "Many commentators accused the Pope and the Church of interfering with the political process."

On the other hand, in the United States there was not one critical report of *Evangelium Vitae*. *The New York Times* devoted nearly two full pages of text to it. Not one American journalist or publisher declared that this encyclical calls for anarchy in this country to destroy the principles of our government that threaten the Papacy. This is a most serious attack on American democracy since Pope Pius IX's *Syllabus of Errors*.

In his contribution, Catholic *New York Times* writer, Peter Steinfels quoted only the responses of four other Catholics - Rev. Richard A. McCormick, Pamela J. Maraldo, Francis Kissling, and Richard Doerflinger - and their quoted criticisms were remarkably mild. No reactions of Protestants, Jews or secularists were cited in any of the *New York Times* articles. Pope John Paul II has obviously dismissed the idea that American Protestants, Jews and secularists, who are in the majority among our democratic law makers, are capable of determining what is moral. Only he and other popes, as God's representative on earth, can make this determination. When the pope ruled that peace and the well-being of the people of the world are insufficient justification for the use of contraception, sterilization and abortion in this encyclical, it appears that he was referring to the NSSM 200 report.[164]

One thing that stands out in the encyclical is that abortion is always lumped together with contraceptive and sterilization. The latter two are made out to be just as evil when it fact it is the prerogative of every individual to resort to them in their family planning and the control of their livelihood. Abortion is evil in the eyes of many, even non-Christians, but the Church has no stool to stand in her war against contraceptives and have to lump the use of contraceptives as if it were abortion. The government has been powerless to help uplift the poor from poverty while the Church, with its billions has not taken concrete steps to help the poor in their midst.

Some prolifers think there is an alarming trend when foreign governments in the West are launching campaigns for birth control here. They are actually here to help our overpopulated poor families reduce their suffering. It is out of pity that they are calling us to act now and not the lack of respect for our sovereignty since they have been extending aids in helping us cope with the population problem. A lot of our poor mothers who wanted to birth control cannot afford to pay for the contraceptives is the reason for the contribution of these contraceptives by foreign organizations. They could actually spend the money elsewhere instead of reprimanded for interfering with our affairs.

There are actually only a few of them that seem to be "dictating" our population policy. From their experience and the help extended to us, they are only helping us with our population problem, knowing that we are hardly equipped to tackle the problem on our own. These

---

[164] http://www.population-security.org/14-CH6.html#4

friendly countries are not motivated by selfish ends but only as a gesture to advice us on the runaway population that has continue to stifle our quality of life. They know firsthand how it is difficult to have a population that is mired in poverty.

Because of the grave problems encountered by the friendly developing countries, the U.S. has poured millions of dollars to help stem unwanted births in the country. They could have spent the taxpayers' money for other purposes at home rather than spending them on foreign countries. We are not compelled to accept the aids if we do not need them.

The prolifers often made unfounded charges that sex education or making condoms available in supermarket will lead to promiscuous sex. It is always better to be formally informed than having children and young adults learn the facts of life from unsavory sources. Obviously this is a ticklish issue that parents and teachers have to face what is good for the children. I am more incline to think that proper sex education at home and in school is more likely to give young adults the proper and right thing to do about sex. Teaching safe sex is only proper in this age of HIV/AIDS and the use of condoms is so far the best defense against getting infected and there is absolutely nothing wrong unlike what the Church has been publicly lying about condoms being unsafe.

Speaking of the church leaders as shepherds of the flocks on issue of faith and moral, the Protestant pastors are in a better position to give them advices. Unlike the priests, most of the Protestant pastors do not have the stigma of being branded as child abusers. There are few instances of Protestant pastors engaged in extramarital sex or visiting prostitutes because they have no problem with celibacy.

Instead of following the lines of the Catholic Church, the Council of Christian Bishops of the Philippines (CCBP), which is composed of Protestant prelates with 20,000 churches nationwide, took the opposite view of the Catholic Church by endorsing the use of contraceptives and other birth control devices such as injectables, IUD, sterilization or tubal ligation for women and vasectomy for men. This is in complete contrast to the Catholic Church stand on using the unreliable, impractical and difficult to apply natural family planning method. The Catholic Church often claimed that it is the only Church guided by the Holy Spirit since time immemorial, so are the other religious organizations. But history had actually proven her wrong on many occasions.

Role of Pope John Paul II

Pope John Paul II is considered one of the greatest popes of modern times. He could have completely revised the thinking of the Church on the use of condoms in relation to AIDS without repercussions because of his popularity. But since his death, many non-Catholics and even Catholics have branded him as a mass murderer like Adolf Hitler for refusing to condone the use of condoms. One of them is the distinguished expatriate scientists, Lord May of Oxford who blamed the Vatican for the spread of AIDS in the Third World. Lord May is a pioneer in the use of mathematical theory to analyze the spread of disease in populations. He harbors a strong resentment against the Vatican for what he believes is an unforgivable deniable of reality. He said that the Vatican's opposition to the use of condoms was an example of "dogma" leading to the deliberate misrepresentation of facts at great cost of human lives. In a private seminar in the early 1990s, he believes the Pope to be responsible "for more deaths than Hitler" through Vatican's policy of anti-contraception.[165]

In the first decade when HIV/AIDS came into light, John Paul II has condemned "morally illicit" means of HIV prevention as "only a palliative for deep troubles that call upon the responsibility of individuals and society" and "a pretext for a weakening that opens the road to moral degradation." Since then, it has at various times sought to omit references to condoms from U.N. documents. At the June 2001 United Nations General Assembly Special Sessions (UNGASS) on HIV/AIDS, the Holy See representative, Archbishop Javier Lozano Barragan, stated that the Vatican "has in no way changed its moral position" on the "use of condoms as a means of preventing HIV infection. The following year, at the May 2002 UNGASS on Children, the Holy See joined the United States, Iran, Libya, Pakistan and Sudan in endorsing sexual abstinence "both before and during" as the only way to prevent HIV.[166] This would have been an ideal solution except the fact there are many promiscuous people around the world, making it unrealistic and unreliable.

Some Catholics hold that the issue of condoms and AIDS should be left to the discretion of public health officials, pastoral

---

[165] Annabel Crabb, "Scientist blames Vatican dogma for AIDS pandemic," www.theage.com.au/news/world/scientist-blames-vatican......December 4, 2005

[166] "The global condom gap," http://hrw.org/reports/2004/philippines0504/5.htm

health workers, or simply the conscience of individual Catholics. And indeed, at the legal of pastoral practice, many Catholic service providers advise their parishioners to use condoms against HIV. However, Catholic theologians who condone the use of condoms against AIDS risk swift censure from the Vatican. In 1988, Joseph Cardinal Ratzinger, while head of the Congregation for the Doctrine of Faith, criticized the U.S. conference of Bishops for having supported condom use in their document, "The Many Faces of AIDS." When South African Bishop Kevin Dowling urged the use of condoms against HIV, the South African Bishops Conference responded with a statement condemning condom use, except in the case of couples in which only one partner is HIV-positive.[167]

In the U.S. and Western Europe including her own home base, Italy, the Vatican has lost her battle against legal abortion. However, it chose to target the U.S. as leader and the most powerful country in the world to assert its will on the rest of the world. If influential U.S. policy on population control can be made to match papal policy, many other countries relying on the U.S. for financial aid will have little choice but to follow suit. In 1975, American Catholics bishops issued their Pastoral Plan for Pro-Life Activities in response to the legalization of abortion in the U.S. only two years before. This comprehensive blueprint laid out numerous objectives, such as:

1. passing a Human Life Amendment to the Constitution, giving full human rights to fetuses;
2. lobbying for appointment of anti-abortion judges to the Supreme Court to overturn Roe vs Wade, or at least restrict abortion legally as much as possible;
3. lobbying all types of leadership (business, government, professions, academic, labor) and the media to promote public policies against abortion
4. working with non-Catholics press to advocate the anti-abortion view;
5. using the Catholic press and Catholic schools and churches to disseminate political and educational information against abortion.

With the exception of the passing of a Human Life Amendment, the bishops' pastoral plan has been successfully implemented.[168]

---

[167] Ibid
[168] Joyce Arthur, "Mortal Sins of the Vatican,"

In his encyclical *Veritatis Splender* (Splendor of the Truth), Pope John Paul II has this to say about moral truth. He insists that certain acts are intrinsically evil. In the language of Catholic moral theology, this means that certain acts are always wrong, and that there are never circumstances in which they may be permitted if done knowingly and intentionally. Stated another way, this is a strong support for the long-held doctrine of Catholic moral theology that "the ends do not justify the means." Pope John Paul II bases this on the argument that certain acts are so destructive to the human person that there are no extenuating circumstances that would allow them. As an example, Pope John Paul II specifically reaffirms the teaching of Pope Paul VI in the encyclical *Humanae Vitae* concerning contraception that there are no circumstances in which the practice can ever be licit.[169] Put it another way, contraception and abortion are mortally sinful. There are no mitigating circumstances, such as rape in war or the likelihood of a fatal exposure to AIDS that could serve as an exception to mitigate the sin of these actions. (Manning, 67)

The pope should have been more compassionate with his teaching considering that the Church has been wrong in the past with her proclamations. During the 17th century, it is a mortal sin to believe in the heliocentric theory of Copernicus. This teaching was not official repudiated until Galileo was rehabilitated in the 20th century by him. In the 18th century, it was the reading of the Bible without the presence of the priest. Offenders have been damned to hell. In the 19th century, freedom of conscience, freedom of speech and press, and freedom of religious worship other than Catholicism were all condemned as mortal sin by various popes. How much longer do Catholics have to put up with their present Pope before another Pope rose up to repudiate the wrong moral teaching?

Now we are in the midst of the greatest crisis facing the Catholic Church. Many Catholics no longer take her teachings on morality at face value. It has been questioned by many Catholics who view that too many children are hindrance to a good life. The truth is that the Church has been guilty of committing mortal sin when nuns in danger of rape have been issued the contraceptive pill. Many nuns and other women who have been impregnated by priests have been forced to undergo abortions. The priests have not been held responsible and often assigned to other diocese, just as those who have committed

---

www.prochoiceactionnetwork-canada.org/articles/vatican.shtml
[169] http://en.wikipedia.org/wiki/Veritatis_Splendor

grave sins against the children by their sexual abuses. Most of the priests violating its celibacy law have not been punished.

Pope John Paul II even quoted Romans 3:8, "…..Let us do evil, that good may come? whose damnation is just…." The pope has basically equated contraceptive as evil without so much as justifying the evilness on the use of contraceptives. How can it be evil when it can save lives in the face of the prevalence of many STDs and a sure way of avoiding unwanted pregnancies that often led to abortion? The Catholic Church refuses to admit it, but there are more Catholics undergoing abortions that any other Christian sects. Many predominantly Catholic countries have even legalized abortions. At any rate, how can it be evil if the parents cannot give the child a decent upbringing? How can it be evil when women have been raped by an enemy and would not like to bore the baby while in the first trimester term? How can it be evil to abort a baby knowing that he will be deformed or mentally retarded or suffering from incurable disease? These are issues that appeal to individual conscience and no religious organization or priests can dictate on the individual.

The issue of abortion has been a consistently central feature of the Catholic hierarchy's participation in American politics even though 93% of American Catholics do not support the Pope's stance against birth control, abortion, women's ordination, and many other progressive issues. Unfortunately, liberal Catholics have very little political power and influence in their own church.[170]

The Vatican has vast resources at its disposal to force national leaders to do her bidding. Even within the U.S., she has a lot of minions at her disposal. Within the U.S. resides a powerful and conservative Catholic hierarchy of cardinals and bishops who answer only to Rome. In addition, many key players in the American government are devoted Roman Catholics.[171]

Even with the separation of state and church, the Vatican continued to meddle in the politics of governments. The Philippines is no exception. The toppling of the government of President Marcos and President Estrada were greatly abetted by the Catholic Church. In the U.S. President Jimmy Carter actively courted the Catholic vote, and worked to establish a supportive relationship with the bishops. One of the deals Carter made with 15 Catholic leaders was to de-emphasize

---

[170] Joyce Arthur, "Mortal Sins of the Vatican,"
www.prochoiceactionnetwork-canada.org/articles/vatican.shtml
[171] Ibid

federal support for family planning in exchange for Catholic support for his presidential bid. Once elected, Jimmy Carter puts the two federal agencies with family planning programs under Catholic control, effectively rendering them useless.[172]

Similarly, the bishops succeeded in their efforts to elect conservative Republican Presidents Ronald Reagan and George Bush. In both of these administrations, U.S. population policy reflected Vatican policy. In 1982, Reagan struck a deal with Pope John Paul II to cut off funding to U.S. foreign aid programs that promoted population control, in exchange for Vatican funding of the Polish Solidarity movement (Blanchard, 1994). Both Reagan and later George Bush made numerous appointments from the ranks of the Religious Right, who then waged a campaign of bureaucratic harassment and obstruction against the family planning establishments. Bishops were allowed to infiltrate every U.S. government office that had anything to do with population control. Reagan and Bush also appointed five Supreme Justices and 70% of all sitting judges in the federal court system, all of them anti-abortionists. (Mumford, 165)[173]

The Vatican has worked diligently to snuff out sexual and ideological progress in her own ranks and faithful followers. She is willing to let her faithful servants die because the Vatican disapproves the use of latex prophylactics that could have put a big dent on some of the scourges of mankind such as STDs and AIDS. Without sufficient proof, the Vatican has instructed her numerous cardinals in interviews to condemn condom use and even made unfounded claim that condoms do not prevent the transmission of the AIDS virus.

On the 40th anniversary of the encyclical *Humanae Vitae* a group of 50 Catholic lay groups from the U.S. and Europe calling themselves Catholics for Choice and based in Washington, put up a paid advertisement in an Italian newspaper *Corriere della Sera* urged Pope Benedict XVI to lift the ban on artificial contraceptives. It went on to describe the failure of *Humanae Vitae* as a "failure…that has had a catastrophic impact on the poor and powerless around the world, endangering women's lives and leaving millions at risk of HIV." Some diehard lay Catholics came to the defense of the Church even refused to accept the ban on condom use may be responsible for the proliferation of HIV/AIDS. Logic does not support their contention

---

[172] Ibid
[173] Ibid

since scientific tests on the effectiveness of condoms against sexually transmitted diseases including HIV have been very favorable.

It is difficult to argue against people who are closed-minded even if they are shown the folly of their arguments. Many are just blind followers of the Church when they have long been brainwashed into believing that the teaching magisterium of the Church is infallible. The more liberal and open-minded Catholics in the developed countries no longer blindly follow the Church's teachings on moral issues. Conscience should take over when there is doubt about the moral teachings. No one should dictate whatever that is against one's conscience.

Catholic Church and Women

The Catholic Church has always looked down on women. Ever since St. Augustine and St. Thomas Aquinas, the two pillar theologians of the Church wrote about the role of women as good only for reproduction of the human species and doing household chores. It has since governed the treatment of women. It would be interesting to know how women had been treated in the Bible in comparison to how it has been (mis)interpreted by the Popes, and the Church's doctors.

St. Augustine, after his conversion, had a neurotic fear of women. He never spoke with women unless in the presence of other people without exception. Even his elder sisters and two nieces who were all nuns were not exempted. Women were considered the conduit to sin and were to be avoided at all cost. His view was adopted by many synods and councils called to deal with the issue of women and celibate priests. Under the Synod of Elvira of 306, it was decreed that women were forbidden from entering the houses of clergymen unless they were virgins and had vows of chastity. The same synod forbade women from writing or receiving letters in their own name. (Ranke, 122, 130)

St. Augustine considered women as very inferior to men and blamed Eve for the fall of Adam. Instead of approaching Adam directly, the devil turned to the weaker sex for consummating the temptation. Adam was not gullible but only yielded to Eve's mistake. Even the saintly nun, St. Hildegard of Bingen (1098-1179) went on to add that Adam's violent love for Eve caused him to follow Eve into the temptation and sin. (Ibid, 185)

St. Thomas Aquinas view of women is even worse. For him, women are better off remaining virgin all their lives, even repeating what St. Jerome calculated that they would receive 100% reward in heaven against 30% reward for married people. (Ibid, 184) Together with his mentor, Albert the Great, they had nothing good to say about women. They claimed that women contained more liquid than men in their bodies. Because liquid could be easily moved, women were therefore inconstant and curious and what they could not get they obtained by lying and diabolic deception. Both considered the existence of woman a mistake, a slippage in the process of birth. Girl was considered a "misbegotten or defective man." She was to be avoided and treated like a poisonous snake and a horned devil. (Ibid, 185, Wills, 109)

On family affairs, women were also considered inferior in training and in educating the children. The fathers are considered intellectual leaders with stronger virtues and should do the intellectual training of the children. Because of the subordination of women to men, they could not receive Holy Orders and were denied any churchly office. (Ibid, 189) Women were forbidden from the priesthood because of their inferior sex, according to St. Aquinas. St. Bonaventure claimed that only men were made in the image of God and therefore only men are called to the priesthood. John Dun Scotus claimed that Eve caused the fall of mankind and therefore her successors could never act as officers for the
salvation of humanity. St. Chrysostom, one of the earliest anti-Semites, considered woman an enemy of friendship, an inescapable punishment, a necessary devil, a natural temptation, a desirable misfortune, a domestic danger, delectable mischief, a fault in nature painted with beautiful color. For him, women were not smart enough to be priests. Tertullian considered Eve and her descendants as temptresses and served as the gateway through which the Devil comes to tempt mankind. (Wills, 107, 109)

As one Catholic author laments, "A woman's duty as wife and mother has been to give her life in the service of her husband and children. This pattern of domestic submission has been invested with religious sanction that it constitutes women's primary means of achieving salvation. Women's biological gift of birthing has been enlarged into an exclusive role as the nurturers of the human race, as the tamers of the brute nature of men, and as the sacrificial appeasers of the violence inherent in patriarchal culture. When women suffer abuse, violence, death even, at the hands of a partner, they have taught to endure this for the sake of the preservation of the family and of society…..The idea that suffering is redemptive and that the meek suffering of women will save the world is still very much part of papal discourses on women. So unless women are being self-sacrificing, the implication is, they are not good women and the violence that may be inflicted on them to bring them into line is deserved. Not only do these attitudes perpetuated the idea of a masochistic God and encourage passivity in women, but they also prevent women from taking the necessary steps to disengage themselves from dangerous situations."

This is probably why few Catholic Filipinas are taking up arms to defend their rights for more reproductive health care in the face of great opposition from the male-dominated Catholic Church and their pro-life minions. The poor women of this country have almost no say on this issue which affects them the most. Except for a few liberated Filipinas, Catholic women are supposed to be submissive in most issues, even those that affect their health.

Pope John Paul II had missed a great opportunity to right what was wrong in the Church's treatment of the women. His popularity would have done away with centuries of misogynic treatment of women. Instead in 1995, he came out with his apostolic letter *Ordinartio sacerdotalis*, forever barring the debate on the ordination of women into the priesthood. (Wills, 107) Cardinal Joseph Ratzinger even tried to push for the infallible claim which was not realized due to the horde of protests. The ground taken in support of his stand was that Jesus had chosen only male apostles.

This is not true. The Bible has depicted many instances where women played an important role in the history of evangelization of the world. Paul addressed Junia (woman's name) in **Romans 16:7** as one of the apostles but the Church would hear nothing of this sort and had her name changed into Junias (masculine form) in the 19th century. This is to justify the continued suppression of the role of women in Christ's ministry. St. Jerome and St. Chrysostom had taken for granted that she was a woman (Ranke, 127; Wills, 115). There were other women such as Phobe (**Romans 16:1**), Priscilla (**Romans 16:3**), Julia and the sister of Nereus (**Romans 16:15**), Enodias and Syntyche (**Philippians 4:2-3**) and even Peter's mother-in-law.

Even the Virgin Mary, the goddess of the Catholic Church had no match for the position taken by the popes down the ages. According to the Sacred Congregation of the Doctrine of Faith in its decree, *Inter insigniores* of October 15, 1976, "But it must be recognized that we have here a number of convergent indications that make all the more remarkable the fact that Jesus did not entrust the apostolic charge to women. Even his Mother, who was so closely associated with mystery of her Son, and whose incomparable roll is emphasized by the Gospels of Luke and John, was not invested with the apostolic ministry.....as Pope Innocent III repeated later, at the beginning of the 13th century, 'Although the Blessed Virgin Mary surpassed in dignity and in excellence all the Apostles, nevertheless it is not to her but to them (popes and their minions) that the Lord entrusted the keys of the Kingdom of Heaven." (Manning, 43)

With pronouncement such as this, there is no way the Church can renege on her words. Otherwise, the issue of her infallibility will be put into question. The Church cannot afford anyone, especially her faithful, to question her infallibility or it could lead to her downfall.

In these modern times, liberated women have fought hard to win more rights for themselves. Many secular governments have given rights to women, even in some Muslims countries, but not within the Vatican. While the Vatican kept proclaiming the equality of women in dignity and responsibility equal to men allowing them access to public function, she kept emphasizing her maternal role in the family. While the popes often called for justice and make pronouncements against apartheid and racial discrimination, they deliberately refused to give justice to women contrary to what Jesus taught. Pope John Paul II's unprecedented act of asking forgiveness for past errors was well received. But he failed to do justice to the abuse on women by the Church. By refusing to recognize the wrongful teachings of past popes and the Church Fathers on women, the injustice is allowed to continue. As long as women cannot be allowed into the priesthood, they shall forever be treated as an inferior to men.

Pro-life vs. Pro-choice

It is important to differentiate between the stands of prolifers and advocators of pro-choice for a better understanding of their agenda. Pro-choice subscribes to the political and ethical that a woman should have complete control over her fertility and the choice to continue or terminate a pregnancy. As such they should be guarantee reproductive rights and access to sexual education, safe and legal abortion, the use of contraception, fertility treatments, and legal protection from forced abortion. Some of them see abortion as a last resort and focus on a number of situations where they feel abortion is a necessary option. Among these situations are those where the woman was raped, her health or that of the fetus is at grave risk, when contraception was used and failed, or she feels unable to raise a child. Some pro-choice moderates, who would otherwise be willing to accept certain restrictions on abortion, feel that political pragmatism compels them to oppose any such restrictions.[174]

On the other hand, pro-life is the exact opposite of pro-choice. The term represents a variety of perspectives and activist movements in bioethics. It usually refers to opposition to abortion while supporting fetal rights. The term describes the political and ethical view which maintains that fetuses and embryos are human beings, and therefore have a right to live, often with priority over the mother. In some cases, prolifers are also opposed to the practices such as euthanasia, the imposition of death penalty, cloning of human and research involving human embryonic stem cells.[175]

In between the two camps are some gray areas of contention. Some groups that oppose abortion are contented to work at reducing the number of abortions through prevention of unwanted pregnancies such as abstinence, sex education, and the use of contraception. There are also some who support legal abortion within the first two trimesters but oppose late-term abortions. Those who oppose late term abortions usually take the view that once a fetus has reached the point where it could live independently from the pregnant woman, the balance of rights perhaps swings in favor of the fetus. Some oppose most abortions but make exception for cases where the woman's life is in serious risk or the fetus is suffering from severe deformities. Others make exceptions in cases of rape and incest. Some allow for all these exceptions, but stop short of abortion-on-demand.

There are those who oppose abortion unless there is mandatory notification and consent from the concerned parent or guardian in the case of a minor or spouse because of the risks and possible medical complications. In a 2003 Gallup poll in the U.S., 72% of respondents were in favor of spousal notification, with 26% opposed. In many states, such restrictions are mandated by law, though often with the right of judicial oversight.

As a general rule, prolifers consider abortion as infanticide because the mother have the option to put up the child for adoption in a foster home if she is unable or unwilling to raise the child. The other option is to give the child in favor of their relatives or even childless couples.

Public opinion polls in the U.S. in 2007 regarding the issue of abortion are almost evenly split among the pro-life and the pro-choice. The first poll conducted by CNN from May 4 to May 6 shows that 45% are pro-choice and 50% are pro-life. Another poll taken by

---

[174] http://en.wikipedia.org/wiki/Pro-choice
[175] http://en.wikipedia.org/wiki/Pro-life

Gallup a week later found that 49% of the respondents are pro-choice and 45% are pro-life.

Life does not consist of being born into the world. In fact, there are just too many people today compared to what the world can offer the people. Many lived out their lives in squalor and hardship that many wished they were never borne in the first place. There is no dignity in trying to hold body and soul together through begging and handouts. This is on top of the many problems encountered by these poor elements of society. Hunger, malnutrition, poor health, poor intelligence, and the lack of basic necessities of life are some of the problems they encountered throughout their subsistence.

I have consistently claimed that pro-life is a misnomer because those who advocate giving birth without limit are shortsighted for not taking into consideration the kind of existence these children are under. Since most of the children born to the parents in the country are coming from the poorest members of society, what kind of quality of life are they experiencing? No children, if they can decide for themselves would want to live a hellish life or hunger and want, sickness and poor health, with little clothing or wandering the streets as street urchins begging and stealing for their daily food. Some prolifers would even claim that children are happy in big family while they packed themselves like sardines, sleeping on the floor. The truth is that most of these advocators of prolife came from well-to-do families and never experienced the life of the poor and destitute. Most probably never experienced the financial problems plaguing the family or they would have been cursing those having big families. Most of them probably never suffer the traumatic stigma of being hungry during period of plenty or walking kilometers to school.

Some prolifers blamed poverty as the cause of overpopulation instead of vice versa. I do not see the logic of this thinking. No good decent family with well educated parents would want to see their children grow up to become part of the statistics of neglected children. One report had it that there are about five million child laborers in the country, 1.5 million live on the streets, 60,000 have turned themselves or forced into prostitution. If they have their ways, they probably would want to wait for another time and another place to be born.

Some 3.7 million preschool children are malnourished numbered while another 3.8 million suffer from stunted growth and 700,000 are weak or enfeebled.[176] These are the statistics for 2004 and the figures must have increased because of the worsening hardship experienced by most families as result of the food and oil price increases. With the recession going around the world, the number of poor families is expected to increase.

The statistics are even grimmer for those five years or younger. Out of every 100 children who die before reaching the age of five, 38 deaths are due to curable diseases while 49% of the total population of infants and 26% of children one to six years old suffer from iron-deficiency anemia with another third of them deficient in vitamin A. Sixty percent of the children live in poverty and squalor and one in six below age six suffers from neglect, one in three kids is abused, and one in seven does not have access to potable water.[177] These are just grim reminder that there is a need to slow down the population growth of those coming from the ranks of the poor. It is easy to have children but it is not easy to give them the proper love and care if we cannot give them a decent and quality of life. That is the real meaning of life, not one that is neglected and they have to fend for themselves at their young age.

The prolifers have a convenient excuse for poverty. They claimed that poverty is caused by corruption and other factors except the population explosion. They refused to take into account the difference in the technological and agricultural advancement in developed countries in comparison to developing countries that cannot yet cope with their myriad problems of uplifting their standard of living. Only such time that developing countries can attain the same degree of industrialization can they really cope with the population problem. By them, parents will have a different outlook in many children.

The Catholic Church, which prided itself as the chosen one would like nothing better than to be different from other religious organization. When the breakaway Anglicans adopted the use of contraception during the 1930 Lambeth Conference, the Catholic Church, known for her self-righteous moral teaching took an opposite view by outlawing contraception except the natural family planning. Because of her public announcement, it made her hopelessly tied up with her stand without becoming the laughing stock among her faithful followers. She has to continue with the charade until hell freezes over before she can change her stand. One of the old adage describing the Catholic

---

[176] http://www.manilastandardtoday.com/?page=news02_july29_2004
[177] Ibid

Church teaching "once wrong, always wrong" still holds very true today.

In order to support her claim, the Catholic Church and her prolife supporters are in unison over the issue on why there is so much poverty in the country. They refused to acknowledge that part of the reasons is that there are just too many mouths to feed with the limited resources. They prefer to lay the blame on corruption and injustice in the distribution of wealth and almost everything except the population explosion. They blamed the concentration of wealth in a few families around the country, ignoring the fact that being rich is not illegal and it is human nature to accumulate wealth. It is unfortunate that the poor have difficulty getting out of the cycle of poverty precisely because of the large families, making it difficult for them to improve their living standard.

UN Human Development Reports show that countries with higher population growth invariably score lower in human development. The ADB in 2004 also listed a large population as one of the major causes of poverty in the country. The NSO affirms that 57.3% of those mired in poverty came from families with seven children or more while only 23.8% families with two children are poor. Recent studies also show that large family size is a significant factor in keeping families poor across generations. (*PDI*, August 3, 2008)

For those who refused to heed her teaching, the Catholic Church has branded them as "anti-life" and should be refused communion. In reply, the Philippine Legislative Committee on Population and Development (PLCPD) clarified that nowhere in the reproductive health bills now pending does it state that abortion is allowed. The Church conveniently included some objectionable contraceptives such as vasectomy, IUD that are more invasive, along with the non-invasive pills and condoms and branding them together as abortifacient.

The PLCPD was so disgusted with some of the bishops' statement regarding communion that they came out with this statement, "....We are disgusted with how some bishops continue to display irresponsible behavior of spreading disinformation on the bill, refusing to take it for its real intentions and choosing instead to demonize it; to look for ghosts that are not there. We look at bishops as symbols of truth and morality. And yet, they themselves propagate blatant lies to instill fear both among policymakers and the public. This behooves us to wonder, what are the real reasons behind the Church's very antagonistic position towards the bills? Whatever they are, it is certain that saving lives is not among them."[178]

On September 21, 2008, the PLCPD even came out with an ad in major newspapers calling on Congress to pass the Reproductive Health Bill. It added some statistics from the Pulse Asia survey conducted in March 2007 showing that 92% of the Filipinos consider family planning important, 89% (90% of them Catholics) think that government should allocate funds for modern methods of family planning including the pill, condoms, ligation, and vasectomy; 76% say it is important for politicians to include family planning in his/her program of action, that the Church should not meddle in the issue of family planning methods for couples to the tune of 44% vs 33%.

Instead of getting honest and enlightening replies to questions raised, I read that in the July 17 issue of CDN under the headline *Cooperators of Murder*, Cardinal Vidal was quoted as saying that those who push for legislation that favors contraception and abortion are "cooperators of murder of an innocent human life." Coming from the cardinal, these are very strong words. Even calling the use of contraceptives as "evil" is unfounded. What is so evil about avoiding unwanted child or unable to give the child a decent life? No matter how you look at it the purpose of contraceptives is precisely to avoid conception in the first place. The use of contraceptives has the added feature of reducing unwanted abortions.

Prolifers seem to find solace in countries with high density and high standard of living such as Japan to support the issue that overpopulation is not a problem. They conveniently forget that there are only a few countries such as Japan and Singapore that are able to overcome overpopulation problems. In fact, the population of Japan has been declining for the past few years because of the problem posed by their overpopulation. There is nothing wrong with having a high density if it is mitigated by a high standard of living. Even then, people there are living in overcrowded environment. This is happening in congested Japan, Hong Kong and other places where they people live in houses no bigger than most shanties in Metro Manila. In fact, many of the so-called socialized and economic housing in this country are not bigger than 50 m², thereby giving a family of four just 12.5 m² space. This overcrowded atmosphere is not conducive to good health should one member suffers an infectious disease.

The reproductive health of women is a national issue and should not be left to the discretion of the local unit heads, Secretary of Health or

---

[178] http://www.siawi.org/article471.html

even the President. We need a unified stand on the issues that affect almost everyone in the country. It cannot depend on a few vested interested especially when most of those affected are too poor to fend for themselves. Many of the women would want the government to help them out with their reproduction health problems but have nowhere to get all the necessary assistance especially when they are faced with some opposition from those who are tasked with the job.

It is time for us to have a clear and consistent government policy of the issue of our population because of the many problems connected with it. There is also the real issue of the rights of the women to their bodies. The women should be allowed to take care of their bodies the way they see fits as long as they are not illegal and that they should not be discriminated against.

Unless the poor mothers-to-be are well educated on the facts of life, there is little chance for them to get out of the vicious cycle of poverty. They also need to take care of their own health which is not easy especially if they are not educated. Many mothers are still too young to give many births and it is destroying their bodies. They need counseling that can only be offered with the help of the government. Unfortunately, they will have to depend on the local government unit leaders who may not endorse what is needed by the mothers. Mothers need protection provided by the bill instead of being maligned and mistreated.

There are an estimated 350 million women in the poorest countries of the world who either did not want their last child, do not want another child and want to space their pregnancies, but they lack access to information, affordable means and services to determine the size and spacing of their families. In the developing world, some 514,000 women die of complications from pregnancies and abortions annually. Additionally, 8 million infants die due to malnutrition and preventable diseases. In the Philippines, according to one recent survey, 162 out for every 10,000 mothers die during childbirth. (*PS*, December 1, 2008) This is one compelling reason why the reproduction health care bill should be passed into law.

According to the latest United Nations Children's Fund (UNICEF) report, there are about 4,500 Filipinas dying annually from complication related to pregnancy and childbirth every year. The reason it gave was that there is not enough comprehensive health service available that is publicly accessible for them. It noted that too few mothers receive skilled care before, during and after pregnancy and in case of emergency, few have access to quality emergency obstetric care services. Only less than 40% of them deliver either in public or private health facility. This explains why 99% of all maternal deaths, numbering about half a million of them, occurred in the developing countries. (*PS*, September 20, 2008) With grim pictures of women dying from complication during pregnancy, the prolifers and especially the Catholic Church should soften their stand on the use of contraceptives such as condoms and pills. It is only the Catholic Church and some of her followers that are vehemently against contraceptives of all kinds because it is contrary to her teachings. The fact is that even in the developing countries, most Catholics ignored her teaching on contraceptives. Some priests who are their own teaching on contraceptives choose to ignore them, preferring to tell the faithful to follow their conscience. At the time of the promulgation of the encyclical *Humanae vitae* more than 30,000 priests requested to leave the priesthood and more than 20,000 were laicized by the Pope upon their request. Could it be that the Holy Spirit had left them that they can willfully go against the teaching of the Pope?

The United States Agency for International Development (USAID) claimed that 45% of all pregnancies in the Philippines are "unwanted or mistimed." This is manifested, says the USAID, in the country's high abortion rate of more than 400,000 each year or about 16 per 100 pregnancies. Most of these clandestine abortions occur in large, poor households and involves 20- to 29-year-old women.

On the contrary, if the Catholic Church is to be believed, the reason for these abortions is the proliferation contraceptives because it causes moral decay that lead to promiscuity. How do you explain the use of contraceptives can lead to more abortions? The contraceptives are used to stop pregnancies and not the other way around. A better explanation is necessary before the Church loses its credibility before her faithful and blind followers.

The Catholic Church does not have a monopoly of the sanctity of marriage and respect for life. Its insistence on the natural family planning alone made it sound as if the use of contraceptives is against the laws of God. The truth is that most Catholics do not obey her teachings on the sanctity of marriage because of the many broken families in the country. There are probably more broken homes than good families in the country, despite being called Christians.

Natural Family Planning (NFP)

There is no doubt that natural family planning (NFP) methods would be desirable for Catholics but only if they can be effective implemented by the couples. NFP requires a woman to keep track of her fertility period. She does this by recording her body temperature when she wakes up, how long her menstrual cycle lasts and her cervical secretions. For the NFP to work, both partners must follow the recording process religiously and avoid intercourse during the woman's fertile period.

There are several advantages to this method. No chemical agents or physical devices are used and therefore side effects can be expected. Brochures detailed this method is available free of charge in government clinics and NGOs. As to their effectiveness, doubts have been raised because it needs a lot of discipline.

A couple will need to control their sexual urges for as long as 11 straight days in a 23-day cycle. Health experts note as well its other disadvantages, which include the keeping of daily records, the length of time to learn it effectively (three to six cycles), and its inability to protect partners against sexually transmitted diseases.

With so many poor and uneducated women of child-bearing ages, it is a difficult task to communicate and train these prospective mothers. It is also impractical to implement because of the difficulties of reaching these women, especially in the rural and slum areas. Most of them are also irresponsible when it comes to sexual encounters. There are other problems to deal than just monitoring their fertility period. Usually it is only after they have several children before they even thought of limiting the family size. By then there is already a mini-population explosion in the family. Only when the family starts suffering from too many mouths to feed will they be awakened to the reality that they have to limit the family size.

The persistent opposition of the Catholic Church is not helping resolve the overpopulation problem. The poor women are often blind followers of the teaching of the Church and will not adopt other family planning methods because they have been indoctrinated that they are committing mortal sins. Most Catholics do not find it sinful to engage to extra-marital affairs, but not when it comes to natural family planning.

Many prolifers think that a large population is conducive to economic powerhouse may not be always true. It can only be true if there are employment, enough food and social services for everyone. Otherwise, the excess population will only be an albatross on the government that is already burdened by lack of funds and shrinking natural resources. Some countries are richer than others and we are on the lower scale in terms of quality of life and should humble ourselves until we have advanced to the point of improving our quality of life without needing a lending from our friendly neighbors.

Some prolifers think that we have enough arable lands to plant food crops to feed several times the present population by employing American style of food production. Theoretically, this may be true but the cost of harnessing all these lands into productive use would be tremendous. There is also the problem of delivering the needed food from one part of country to another and the local distribution to the needy areas especially in areas undergoing civil wars or famine. Even without any civil disturbances, poverty among the people is one reason why many cannot afford three decent meals.

Many Catholics claimed that more people mean more likelihood of finding great men and women who will help solved the world's problems, particularly the dwindling food, energy and natural resources. Some self proclaimed notables even claimed that the country would have lost a few great men if their parents have limited their number of children. They conveniently forget that their accomplishment would have been done by others, maybe even better. They also conveniently forget to mention that for every great man there are hundreds or thousands ordinary people who will live out their lives in hunger and misery.

There is also the chance that dictators and tyrants would come out of these added people who could destroy lives and properties and ruin and country. Those who advocate that the world is not overpopulated are often the rich who does not experience the miseries encountered by the poor and downtrodden. They have never sleep on concrete or wooden floor in their bare back, never finishing their education, and never miss a meal when they are hungry. If they have known these miseries that the poor have undergone, their outlook on the population may be different.

Most of the prolifers came from the rich families where they never had it so good. Most probably never heard directly from the poor members of society with large families and how difficult they have to cope with life. Some wealthy prolifers would not be a good judge of the problems of overpopulation in place of the poor who have experienced the hardship of being poor. It is true that many places are under populated, but it is only a question of time before it will become overpopulated when the population growth is not stemmed early.

Some who opposed birth control often cite the graying population in the developed countries to justify their stand. This is an idea decades ahead of our time. With the country teeming with young children and high fertility rate, we should worry about how to give them a better life by improving their standard of living by way of limiting their numbers. Their future is now and not in distant future.

There may be some legitimate fear about the graying population. But it is not a problem that we need to worry because it is not going to happen soon. Besides, we have a different culture about respect for the elders. Unlike the West where the elders are often put in homes for the ages, I do not think our elders will be unfortunate to be treated this way in their old age. There will always be some relatives to take care of them.

Fear of what is called a demographic winter or graying of the population is not going to happen for decades. It will only occur when the population growth is reduced to less the replacement rate of 2.1 children per family. The National Statistical Coordinating Board estimates that the rate will come sometime in 2040. At this rate, the population will continue to grow for two generations and stop at around 240 million. (*PDI*, August 3, 2008)

There is also the fear that the graying population cannot sustain the country with enough labor to keep production at optimum level. There is fear that there will come a time when there are not enough trained technicians and blue collar workers to run the industries. There is fear that there will not be enough consumers to buy all the goods being manufactured. With fewer consumers, there will be less employment problem to worry about. Another fear is the need to support and care of the constantly expanding elderly population. Most elderly people live on fixed incomes, and many are retiring at earlier ages. These fears are mostly unfounded and of short duration. The industrialized countries have partly solved the problem by importing laborers from across the world to run their businesses which is good for the developing countries. The taxes collected from them should take care of the elderly population in the long run. With fewer people in the First World, the consumption of the world's non-renewable natural resources would be curtailed.

Here is an interesting anecdote about the problem of declining birth rate in Spain. In 2006, the ruling Socialist Party introduced a bill in parliament legislating that apes be included in the "the category of persons, and that they be given the moral and legal protection that currently are only enjoyed by human beings." The party's argument was that the humans shared 98.4% of their genes with chimpanzees, 97.7% with gorillas, and 96.4% with orangutans. (Steyn, 11)

Some prolifers imagine that the passage of the reproductive health bill will lead to the other more controversial and immoral issues such as abortion, divorce and even gay marriages. These imaginary provisions are not in the bill pending before Congress. The issue of abortion will be taken up later. On the issue of divorce, it was started by the Catholic Church through their annulment processes. Divorce in the name of annulment has become common practices only with the adoption of the Family Code. The rules have been liberalized just as the annulment processes in the Catholic Church has been liberalized. In the civil courts, a person can get an annulment simply by declaring the spouse as psychologically incapacitated while in the ecclesiastic court, a person can get an annulment simply by changing his faith to Catholicism.

Chapter 6

REPRODUCTIVE HEALTH BILL

The health of women in this country has never been given priority partly because of the constraint imposed by the lack of budget and the low regards for women by some of the domineering opposite sex. There is also the problem of too many poor families in this country coupled with too few doctors and health clinics devoted to their welfare. There is also the bias of those who are manning the local and national government-run clinics toward women who were unfortunate to be pregnant out of wedlock or have undergone illegal abortions. Some of them are deeply religious and diehard Catholics who follow the dictates of the Church and willingly ostracize these women. Unless a law is there to protect them, these women are at their mercy.

There is now a consolidated bill in Congress dealing with the reproductive health for mothers. One of the controversial provisions being debated publicly is abortion although there is no provision calling for their use. It is only the Catholic Church prelates voicing its sentiment on a non-issue. To support their contention, they even include the use of IUD and morning after pill (RU-486), an outlawed drug, as a possible means of abortion. IUD is not a means of abortion. It was feared by those who claimed to be pro-life that the bill would involve the use of the pills and intrauterine devices and possibly embrace abortion in a subtle way even if it is specifically outlawed in the bill. Some diehard churchmen even warned those who advocated for the passage of the bill would be denied communion and even be excommunicated. Those who advocated the use of contraceptives are being branded as pro-abortion when in fact, that is not the case and none of the authors of the bill even advocated abortion as a solution to the reproductive health of the mothers. The Catholic Church seems to like the world to believe that any move to protect the health of the women goes against the laws of God when it is the other way around.

House Bill No. 5043

There have been several bills taken up by Congress in the past but none have ever reached the stage where the Congress had taken them seriously. Most of them never get to be debated until now. There are many important features in the bill protecting the health of the womenfolk in the country that need to be debated and approved before the Catholic Church and her pro-life minions forever devastate the country with all the ills of overpopulation.

HOUSE BILL NO. 5043[179]

AN ACT PROVIDING FOR A NATIONAL POLICY ON REPRODUCTIVE HEALTH, RESPONSIBLE PARENTHOOD

---

[179] http://jlp-law.com/blog/full-text-of-house-bill-no-5043-reproductive-health-and-population-development-act-of-2008/

AND POPULATION DEVELOPMENT, AND FOR OTHER PURPOSES

Be it enacted by the Senate and the House of Representatives of the Philippines in Congress assembled:

SECTION 1. **Short Title**. - This Act shall be known as the "**Reproductive Health and Population Development Act of 2008**".

SEC. 2. **Declaration of Policy**. - The State upholds and promotes responsible parenthood, informed choice, birth spacing and respect for life in conformity with internationally recognized human rights standards.

The State shall uphold the right of the people, particularly women and their organizations, to effective and reasonable participation in the formulation and implementation of the declared policy.

This policy is anchored on the rationale that sustainable human development is better assured with a manageable population of healthy, educated and productive citizens.

The State likewise guarantees universal access to medically-safe, legal, affordable and quality reproductive health care services, methods, devices, supplies and relevant information thereon even as it prioritizes the needs of women and children, among other underprivileged sectors.

SEC. 3. **Guiding Principles**. - This Act declares the following as basic guiding principles:

a. In the promotion of reproductive health, there should be no bias for either modern or natural methods of family planning;

b. Reproductive health goes beyond a demographic target because it is principally about health and rights;

c. Gender equality and women empowerment are central elements of reproductive health and population development;

d. Since manpower is the principal asset of every country, effective reproductive health care services must be given primacy to ensure the birth and care of healthy children and to promote responsible parenting;

e. The limited resources of the country cannot be suffered to, be spread so thinly to service a burgeoning multitude that makes the allocations grossly inadequate and effectively meaningless;

f. Freedom of informed choice, which is central to the exercise of any right, must be fully guaranteed by the State like the right itself;

g. While the number and spacing of children are left to the sound judgment of parents and couples based on their personal conviction and religious beliefs, such concerned parents and couples, including unmarried individuals, should be afforded free and full access to relevant, adequate and correct information on reproductive health and human sexuality and should be guided by qualified State workers and professional private practitioners;

h. Reproductive health, including the promotion of breastfeeding, must be the joint concern of the National Government and Local Government Units (LGUs);

i. Protection and promotion of gender equality, women empowerment, responsible parenthood, human rights, including reproductive health rights, are imperative;

j. Development is a multi-faceted process that calls for the coordination and integration of policies, plans, programs and projects that seek to uplift the quality of life of the people, more particularly the poor, the needy and the marginalized;

k. Active participation by and thorough consultation with concerned non-government organizations (NGOs), people's organizations (POs) and communities are imperative to ensure that basic policies, plans, programs and projects address the priority needs of stakeholders;

l. Respect for, protection and fulfillment of reproductive health rights seek to promote not only the rights and welfare of adult individuals and couples but those of adolescents' and children's as well; and

m. While nothing in this Act changes the law on abortion, as abortion remains a crime and is punishable, the government shall ensure that women seeking care for post-abortion complications shall be treated and counseled in a humane, non-judgmental and compassionate manner.

SEC. 4. **Definition of Terms**. - For purposes of this Act, the following terms shall be defined as follows:

a. Responsible Parenthood - refers to the will, ability and commitment of parents to respond to the needs and aspirations of the family and children more particularly through family planning;

b. Family Planning - refers to a program which enables couple, and individuals to decide freely and responsibly the number and spacing of their children and to have the information and means to carry out their decisions, and to have informed choice and access to a full range of safe, legal and effective family planning methods, techniques and devices.

c. Reproductive Health - refers to the state of physical, mental and social well-being and not merely the absence of disease or infirmity, in all matters relating to the reproductive system and to its functions and processes. This implies that people are able to have a satisfying and safe sex life, that they have the capability to reproduce and the freedom to decide if, when and how often to do so, provided that these are not against the law. This further implies that women and men are afforded equal status in matters related to sexual relations and reproduction.

d. Reproductive Health Rights - refers to the rights of individuals and couples do decide freely and responsibly the number, spacing and timing of their children; to make other decisions concerning reproduction free of discrimination, coercion and violence; to have the information and means to carry out their decisions; and to attain the highest standard of sexual and reproductive health.

e. Gender Equality - refers to the absence of discrimination on the basis of a person's sex, in opportunities, allocation of resources and benefits, and access to services.

f. Gender Equity - refers to fairness and justice in the distribution of benefits and responsibilities between women and men, and often requires women-specific projects and programs to eliminate existing inequalities, inequities, policies and practices unfavorable too women.

g. Reproductive Health Care - refers to the availability of and access to a full range of methods, techniques, supplies and services that contribute to reproductive and sexual health and well-being by preventing and solving reproductive health-related problems in order to achieve enhancement of life and personal relations. The elements of reproductive health care include:

1. Maternal, infant and child health and nutrition;
2. Promotion of breastfeeding;
3. Family planning information and services;
4. Prevention of abortion and management of post-abortion

complications;
5. Adolescent and youth health;
6. Prevention and management of reproductive tract infections (RTIs),
HIV/AIDS and other sexually transmittable infections (STIs);
7. Elimination of violence against women;
8. Education and counseling on sexuality and sexual and reproductive
health;
9. Treatment of breast and reproductive tract cancers and other
gynecological conditions;
10. Male involvement and participation in reproductive health;
11. Prevention and treatment of infertility and sexual dysfunction; and
12. Reproductive health education for the youth.

h. Reproductive Health Education - refers to the process of acquiring complete, accurate and relevant information on all matters relating to the reproductive system, its functions and processes and human sexuality; and forming attitudes and beliefs about sex, sexual identity, interpersonal relationships, affection, intimacy and gender roles. It also includes developing the necessary skills do be able to distinguish between facts and myths on sex and sexuality; and critically evaluate and discuss the moral, religious, social and cultural dimensions of related sensitive issues such as contraception and abortion.

i. Male involvement and participation - refers to the involvement, participation, commitment and joint responsibility of men with women in all areas of sexual and reproductive health, as well as reproductive health concerns specific to men.

j. Reproductive tract infection (RTI) - refers do sexually transmitted infections, sexually transmitted diseases and other types of infections affecting the reproductive system.

k. Basic Emergency Obstetric Care - refers to lifesaving services for maternal complication being provided by a health facility or professional which must include the following six signal functions: administration of parenteral antibiotics; administration of parenteral oxyttocic drugs; administration of parenteral anticonvulsants for pre-eclampsia and iampsia; manual removal of placenta; and assisted vaginal delivery.

l. Comprehensive Emergency Obstetric Care - refers to basic emergency obstetric care plus two other signal functions: performance of caesarean section and blood transfusion.

m. Maternal Death Review - refers to a qualitative and in-depth study of the causes of maternal death with the primary purpose of preventing future deaths through changes or additions to programs, plans and policies.

n. Skilled Attendant - refers to an accredited health professional such as a licensed midwife, doctor or nurse who has adequate proficiency and the skills to manage normal (uncomplicated) pregnancies, childbirth and the immediate postnatal period, and in the identification, management and referral of complication in women and newborns.

o. Skilled Attendance - refers to childbirth managed by a skilled attendant under the enabling conditions of a functional emergency obstetric care and referral system.

p. Development - refers to a multi-dimensional process involving major changes in social structures, popular attitudes, and national institutions as well as the acceleration of economic growth, the reduction of inequality and the eradication of widespread poverty.

q. Sustainable Human Development - refers to the totality of the process of expending human choices by enabling people to enjoy long, healthy and productive lives, affording them access to resources needed for a decent standard of living and assuring continuity and acceleration of development by achieving a balance between and among a manageable population, adequate resources and a healthy environment.

r. Population Development - refers to a program that aims to: (1) help couples and parents achieve their desired family size; (2) improve reproductive health of individuals by addressing reproductive health problems; (3) contribute to decreased maternal and infant mortality rates and early child mortality; (4) reduce incidence of teenage pregnancy; and (5) enable government to achieve a balanced population distribution.

SEC. 5. The Commission on Population (POPCOM) - Pursuant to the herein declared policy, the Commission on Population (POPCOM) shall serve as the central planning, coordinating, implementing and monitoring body for the comprehensive and integrated policy on reproductive health and population development. In the implementation of this policy, POPCOM, which shall be an attached agency of the Department of Health (DOH) shall have the following functions:

a. To create an enabling environment for women and couples to make an informed choice regarding the family planning method that is best suited to their needs and personal convictions;

b. To integrate on a continuing basis the interrelated reproductive health and population development agenda into a national policy, taking into account regional and local concerns;

c. To provide the mechanism to ensure active and full participation of the private sector and the citizenry through their organizations in the planning and implementation of reproductive health care and population development programs and projects;

d. To ensure people's access to medically safe, legal, quality and affordable reproductive health goods and services;

e. To facilitate the involvement and participation of non-government organizations and the private sector in reproductive health care service delivery and in the production, distribution and delivery of quality reproductive: health and family planning supplies and commodities to make them accessible and affordable to ordinary citizens;

f. To fully implement the Reproductive Health Care Program with the following components:

> (1) Reproductive health education including but not limited to counseling on the full range of legal and medically-safe family planning methods including surgical methods;
> (2) Maternal, pre-natal and post-natal education, care and services;
> (3) Promotion of breastfeeding;
> (4) Promotion of male involvement, participation and responsibility in
> reproductive health as well as other reproductive health concerns of men;
> (5) Prevention of abortion and management of post-abortion complications; and
> (6) Provision of information and services addressing the reproductive
> health needs of the poor, senior citizens, women in prostitution, differently-disabled persons, and women and children in war and crisis situations.

g. To ensure that reproductive health services are delivered with a full range of supplies, facilities and equipment and that service providers are adequately trained for reproductive health care;

h. To endeavor to furnish local Family Planning Offices with appropriate information and resources to keep the latter updated on current studies and research relating to family planning, responsible parenthood, breastfeeding and infant nutrition;

i. To direct all public hospitals to make available to indigent mothers who deliver their children in these government hospitals, upon the mothers request, the procedure of ligation without cost to her;

j. To recommend the enactment of legislation and adoption of executive measures that will strengthen and enhance the national policy on reproductive health and population development;

k. To ensure a massive and sustained information drive on responsible parenthood and on all methods and techniques to prevent unwanted, unplanned and mistimed pregnancies, it shall release information bulletins on the same for nationwide circulation to all government departments, agencies and instrumentalities, non-government organizations and the private sector, schools, public and private libraries, tri-media outlets, workplaces, hospitals and concerned health institutions;

l. To strengthen the capacities of health regulatory agencies to ensure safe, high-quality, accessible, and affordable reproductive health services and commodities with the concurrent strengthening and enforcement of regulatory mandates and mechanisms;

m. To take active steps to expand the coverage of the National Health Insurance Program (NHIP), especially among poor and marginalized women, to include the full range of reproductive health services and supplies as health insurance benefits; and

n. To perform such other functions necessary to attain the purposes of this Act.

The membership of the Board of Commissioners of POPCOM shall consist of the heads of the following AGENCIES:

> National Economic Development Authority (NEDA)
> Department of Health (DOH)
> Department of Social Welfare and Development (DSWD)
> Department of Labor and Employment (DOLE)
> Department of Agriculture (DA)
> Department of the Interior and Local Government (DILG)
> Department of Education (DepEd)
> Department of Environment and Natural Resources (DENR)
> Commission on Higher Education (CHED)
> University of the Philippines Population Institute (UPPI)
> Union of Local Authorities of the Philippines (ULAP)
> National Anti-Poverty Commission (NAPC)
> National Commission on the Role of Filipino Women (NCRFW)

National Youth Commission (NYC)

In addition to the aforementioned members, there shall be three private sector representatives to the Board of Commissioners of POPCOM who shall come from NGOs. There shall be one (1) representative each from women, youth and health sectors who have a proven track record of involvement in the promotion of reproductive health. These representatives shall be nominated in a process determined by the above-mentioned sectors, and to be appointed by the President for a term of three (3) years.

SEC. 6. **Midwives for Skilled Attendance**. - Every city and municipality shall endeavor to employ adequate number of midwives or other skilled attendants to achieve a minimum ratio of one (1) for every one hundred fifty (150) deliveries per year, to be based on the average annual number of actual deliveries or live births for the past two years.

SEC. 7. **Emergency Obstetric Care**. - Each province and city shall endeavor to ensure the establishment and operation of hospitals with adequate and qualified personnel that provide emergency obstetric care. For every 500,000 population, there shall be at least one (1) hospital for comprehensive emergency obstetric care and four (4) hospitals for basic emergency obstetric care.

SEC. 8. **Maternal Death Review**. - All LGUs, national and local government hospitals, and other public health units shall conduct maternal death review in accordance with the guidelines to be issued by the DOH in consultation with the POPCOM.

SEC. 9. **Hospital-Based Family Planning**. - Tubal ligation, vasectomy, intrauterine device insertion and other family planning methods requiring hospital services shall be available in all national and local government hospitals, except: in specialty hospitals which may render such services on an optional basis. For indigent patients, such services shall be fully covered by PhilHealth insurance and/or government financial assistance.

SEC. 10. **Contraceptives as Essential Medicines**. - Hormonal contraceptives, intrauterine devices, injectables and other allied reproductive health products and supplies shall be considered under the category of essential medicines and supplies which shall form part of the National Drug Formulary and the same shall be included in the regular purchase of essential medicines and supplies of all national and local hospitals and other government health units.

SEC. 11. **Mobile Health Care Service**. - Each Congressional District shall be provided with a van to be known as the Mobile Health Care Service (MHOS) to deliver health care goods and services to its constituents, more particularly to the poor and needy, as well as disseminate knowledge and information on reproductive health: *Provided*, That reproductive health education shall be conducted by competent and adequately trained persons preferably reproductive health care providers: *Provided, further*, That the full range of family planning methods, both natural and modern, shall be promoted.

The acquisition, operation and maintenance of the MRCS shall be funded from the Priority Development Assistance Fund (PDAF) of each Congressional District.

The MHCS shall be adequately equipped with a wide range of reproductive health care materials and information dissemination devices and equipment, the latter including but not limited to, a television set for audio-visual presentation.

SEC. 12. **Mandatory Age - Appropriate Reproductive Health Education**. - Recognizing the importance of reproductive health rights in empowering the youth and developing them into responsible adults, Reproductive Health Education in an age-appropriate manner shall be taught by adequately trained teachers starting from Grade 5 up to Fourth Year High School. In order to assure the prior training of teachers on reproductive health, the implementation of Reproductive Health Education shall commence at the start of the school year one year following the effectivity of this Act. The POPCOM, in coordination with the Department of Education, shall formulate the Reproductive Health Education curriculum, which shall be common to both public and private schools and shall include related population and development concepts in addition to the following subjects and standards:

     a. Reproductive health and sexual rights;
     b. Reproductive health care and services;
     c. Attitudes, beliefs and values on sexual development, sexual behavior
     and sexual health;
     d. Proscription and hazards of abortion and management of post-abortion complications;
     e. Responsible parenthood.
     f. Use and application of natural and modern family planning methods
     to promote reproductive health, achieve desired family size and prevent unwanted, unplanned and mistimed pregnancies;
     g. Abstinence before marriage;
     h. Prevention and treatment of HIV/AIDS and other, STIs/STDs, prostate cancer, breast cancer, cervical cancer and other gynecological disorders;
     i. Responsible sexuality; and

j. Maternal, peri-natal and post-natal education, care and services.

In support of the natural and primary right of parents in the rearing of the youth, the POPCOM shall provide concerned parents with adequate and relevant scientific materials on the age-appropriate topics and manner of teaching reproductive health education to their children.

In the elementary level, reproductive health education shall focus, among others, on values formation.

Non-formal education programs shall likewise include the abovementioned reproductive Health Education.

SEC. 13. **Additional Duty of Family Planning Office**. - Each local Family Planning Office shall furnish for free instructions and information on family planning, responsible parenthood, breastfeeding and infant nutrition to all applicants for marriage license.

SEC. 14. **Certificate of Compliance**. - No marriage license shall be issued by the Local Civil Registrar unless the applicants present a Certificate of Compliance issued for free by the local Family Planning Office certifying that they had duly received adequate instructions and information on family planning, responsible parenthood, breastfeeding and infant nutrition.

SEC. 15. **Capability Building of Community-Based Volunteer Workers**. - Community-based volunteer workers, like but not limited to, Barangay Health Workers, shall undergo additional and updated training on the delivery of reproductive health care services and shall receive not less than 10% increase in honoraria upon successful completion of training. The increase in honoraria shall be funded from the Gender and Development (GAD) budget of the National Economic and Development Authority (NEDA), Department of Health (DOH) and the Department of the Interior and Local Government (DILG).

SEC. 16. **Ideal Family Size**. - The State shall assist couples, parents and individuals to achieve their desired family size within the context of responsible parenthood for sustainable development and encourage them to have two children as the ideal family size. Attaining the ideal family size is neither mandatory nor compulsory. No punitive action shall be imposed on parents having more than two children.

SEC. 17. **Employers' Responsibilities**. - Employers shall respect the reproductive health rights of all their workers. Women shall not be discriminated against in the matter of hiring, regularization of employment status or selection for retrenchment.

All Collective Bargaining Agreements (CBAs) shall provide for the free delivery by the employer of reasonable quantity of reproductive health care services, supplies and devices to all workers, more particularly women workers. In establishments or enterprises where there are no CBAs or where the employees are unorganized, the employer shall have the same obligation.

SEC. 18. **Support of Private and Non-government Health Care Service Providers**. - Pursuant to Section 5(b) hereof, private reproductive health care service providers, including but not limited to gynecologists and obstetricians, are encouraged to join their colleagues in non-government organizations in rendering such services free of charge or at reduced professional fee rates to indigent and low income patients.

SEC. 19. **Multi-Media Campaign**. - POPCOM shall initiate and sustain an intensified nationwide multi-media campaign to raise the level of public awareness on the urgent need to protect and promote reproductive health and rights.

SEC. 20. **Reporting Requirements**. - Before the end of April of each year, the DOH shall submit an annual report to the President of the Philippines, the President of the Senate and the Speaker of the House of Representatives on a definitive and comprehensive assessment of the implementation of this Act and shall make the necessary recommendations for executive and legislative action. The report shall be posted in the website of DOH and printed copies shall be made available to all stakeholders.

SEC. 21. **Prohibited Acts**. - The following acts are prohibited:

a) Any health care service provider, whether public or private, who shall:

> 1. Knowingly withhold information or impede the dissemination thereof, and/or intentionally provide incorrect information regarding programs and services on reproductive health including the right to informed choice and access to a full range of legal, medically-safe and effective family planning methods;
> 2. Refuse to perform voluntary ligation and vasectomy and other legal and medically-safe reproductive health care services on any person of legal age on the ground of lack of spousal consent or authorization.
> 3. Refuse to provide reproductive health care services to an abused minor, whose abused condition is certified by the proper official or personnel of the Department of Social Welfare and Development (DSWD) or to duly DSWD-certified abused pregnant minor on whose case no parental consent is necessary.
> 4. Fail to provide, either deliberately or through gross or inexcusable negligence, reproductive health care services as mandated under this

Act, the Local Government Code of 1991, the Labor Code, and Presidential Decree 79, as amended; and

5. Refuse to extend reproductive health care services and information on account of the patient's civil status, gender or sexual orientation, age, religion, personal circumstances, and nature of work; *Provided,* That all conscientious objections of health care service providers based on religious grounds shall be respected: *Provided, further,* That the conscientious objector shall immediately refer the person seeking such care and services to another health care service provider within the same facility or one which is conveniently accessible: *Provided, finally,* That the patient is not in an emergency or serious case as defined in RA 8344 penalizing the refusal of hospitals and medical clinics to administer appropriate initial medical treatment and support in emergency and serious cases.

b) Any public official who prohibits or restricts personally or through a subordinate the delivery of legal and medically-safe reproductive health care services, including family planning;

c) Any employer who shall fail to comply with his obligation under Section 17 of this Act or an employer who requires a female applicant or employee, as a condition for employment or continued employment, to involuntarily undergo sterilization, tubal ligation or any other form of contraceptive method;

d) Any person who shall falsify a certificate of compliance as required in Section 14 of this Act; and

e) Any person who maliciously engages in disinformation about the intent or provisions of this Act.

SEC. 22. **Penalties.** - The proper city or municipal court shall exercise jurisdiction over violations of this Act and the accused who is found guilty shall be sentenced to an imprisonment ranging from one (1) month to six (6) months or a fine ranging from Ten Thousand Pesos (P10,000.00) to Fifty Thousand Pesos (P50,000.00) or both such fine and imprisonment at the discretion of the court. If the offender is a juridical person, the penalty shall be imposed upon the president, treasurer, secretary or any responsible officer. An offender who is an alien shall, after service of sentence, be deported immediately without further proceedings by the Bureau of Immigration. An offender who is a public officer or employee shall suffer the accessory penalty of dismissal from the government service.

Violators of this Act shall be civilly liable to the offended party in such amount at the discretion of the proper court.

SEC. 23. **Appropriations**. - The amounts appropriated in the current annual General Appropriations Act for reproductive health and family planning under the DOH and POPCOM together with ten percent (10%) of the Gender and Development (GAD) budgets of all government departments, agencies, bureaus, offices and instrumentalities funded in the annual General Appropriations Act in accordance with Republic Act No. 7192 (Women in Development and Nation-building Act) and Executive Order No. 273 (Philippine Plan for Gender Responsive Development 1995-2025) shall be allocated and utilized for the implementation of this Act. Such additional sums as may be necessary for the effective implementation of this Act shall be included in the subsequent years' General Appropriations Acts.

SEC. 24. **Implementing Rules and Regulations**. - Within sixty (60) days from the effectivity of this Act, the Department of Health shall promulgate, after thorough consultation with the Commission on Population (POPCOM), the National Economic Development Authority (NEDA), concerned non-government organizations (NGOs) and known reproductive health advocates, the requisite implementing rules and regulations.

SEC. 25. **Separability Clause**. - If any part, section or provision of this Act is held invalid or unconstitutional, other provisions not affected thereby shall remain in full force and effect.

SEC. 26. **Repealing Clause**. - All laws, decrees, orders, issuances, rules and regulations contrary to or inconsistent with the provisions of this Act are hereby repealed, amended or modified accordingly.

SEC. 27. **Effectivity**. - This Act shall take effect fifteen (15) days after its publication in at least two (2) newspapers of national circulation.

The following is the reproduction of the Fact Sheet and Explanatory notes for the bill. The Explanatory notes were taken from Rep. Edcel Lagman's House Bill No. 17.

REPRODUCTIVE HEALTH AND POPULATION DEVELOPMENT ACT OF 2008

OBJECTIVE/S:

- To uphold and promote respect for life, informed choice, birth spacing and responsible parenthood in conformity with internationally recognized human rights standards.
- To guarantee universal access to medically-safe, legal and quality reproductive health care services and relevant information even as it prioritizes the needs of women and children.

355 *REPRODUCTIVE HEALTH BILL*

KEY PROVISIONS:

- Mandates the Population Commission, to be an attached agency of the Department of Health, to be the central planning, coordinating, implementing and monitoring body for effective implementation of this Act.
- Provides for the creation of an enabling environment for women and couples to make an informed choice regarding the family planning method that is best suited to their needs and personal convictions.
- Provides for a maternal death review in LGUs, national and local government hospitals and other public health units to decrease the incidence of maternal deaths.
- Ensures the availability of hospital-based family planning methods such as tubal ligation, vasectomy and intrauterine device insertion in all national and local government hospitals, except in specialty hospitals.
- Considers hormonal contraceptives, intrauterine devices, injectables and other allied reproductive health products and supplies under the category of essential medicines and supplies to form part of the National Drug Formulary and to be included in the regular purchase of essential medicines and supplies of all national and local hospitals and other government health units.
- Provides for a Mobile Health Care Service in every Congressional District to deliver health care goods and services.
- Provides Mandatory Age-appropriate Reproductive Health Education starting from Grade 5 to Fourth Year High School to develop the youth into responsible adults.
- Mandates the inclusion of the topics on breastfeeding and infant nutrition as essential part of the information given by the City or Municipal Office of the Family Planning to all applicants for marriage license.
- Mandates no less than 10% increase in the honoraria of community-based volunteer workers, such as the barangay health workers, upon successful completion of training on the delivery of reproductive health care services.
- Penalizes the violator of this Act from one month to six months imprisonment or a fine ranging from ten thousand to fifty thousand pesos or both such fine and imprisonment at the discretion of the Court.

Republic of the Philippines
HOUSE OF REPRESENTATIVES
Quezon City, Metro Manila

FOURTEENTH CONGRESS
FIRST REGULAR SESSION

HOUSE BILL NO. 17

Introduced by HONORABLE EDCEL C. LAGMAN

EXPLANATORY NOTE

The present population of the country of 88.7 million has galloped from 60.7 million 17 years ago. This makes the Philippines the 12th most populous nation in the world today. The Filipino women's fertility rate of 3.05% is at the upper bracket of 206 countries. With four babies born every minute, the population is expected to balloon to an alarming 160 million in 2038.

It is worth noting, however, that available studies, data and statistics show that the Filipinos are responsive to having smaller-sized families through free choice of family planning methods:

a. The desired fertility rate of Filipino women is 2.5 children per woman. However, the actual total fertility rate is 3.5 or a difference of one child because of the lack of information and absence of access to family planning. The current unmet need for contraceptives for example is 23.15% for poor women and 13.6% for women who are not poor (2003 National Demographic and Health Survey)

b. 61% of currently married women do not want additional children (2003 National Demographic and Health Survey)

c. 50.6% of the youth want to have only two children (2002 Young Adult Fertility and Sexuality Survey)

d. 97% of all Filipinos believe it is important to have the ability to control one's fertility or to plan one's family. It is significant to note that 87% of the total respondents are Roman Catholic (February 2004 Pulse Asia Survey)

e. Nearly nine in ten Filipinos or 86% say that candidates for elective positions who advocate a program for women's health should be supported while only 2% say they should be rejected and 12% are undecided on the matter;

f. 82% say that candidates in favor of couples' free choice of family planning methods should be supported while only 3% think otherwise and 15% are undecided;

g. 82% of Filipinos consider candidates supporting a law or measure on population issues worthy of their votes while only 3% say such candidates should not be backed at the polls and 15% are undecided;

h. 83% of Filipinos say they are in favor of candidates who support the allocation of government funds for family planning while only 2% say they are not and 15% are undecided; and

i. A mere 8% of Filipinos believe that a candidate's championing of family planning issues will spell that candidate's defeat at the polls.

j. In July 1991, the Social Weather Stations conducted a survey that revealed that 97% of Filipinos want to have the ability to control their fertility and plan their families.

Notwithstanding these findings that favor smaller-sized families, this bill is not a population control measure with the sole objective of limiting population growth. It provides for population development that aims to:

(a) help couples/parents achieve their desired fertility size in the context of responsible parenthood;
(b) improve reproductive health of individuals and contribute to decreased maternal mortality rate, infant mortality and early child mortality;
(c) reduce incidence of teenage pregnancy and other reproductive health problems; and
(d) contribute to policies that will assist government to achieve a favorable balance between population and distribution, economic activities and the environment.

This measure is not coercive. It gives couples the freedom to decide whether or not to plan their families or space or limit their children. Those who decide to plan their families also have the freedom to choose what method of contraception is best suited for them. The so called "two child policy" is voluntary, not compulsory; suggestive, not coercive; and absolutely not punitive. It is not even a policy. It is a suggested ideal or norm.

Accordingly, this bill seeks to provide the enabling environment for couples and individuals to enjoy the basic right to decide freely and responsibly the number and spacing of their children and to have the information, education, and access to safe, effective, affordable and acceptable methods of family planning of their choice.

This proposed law aims to uphold and promote the four pillars of population and development enunciated by no less than President Gloria Macapagal-Arroyo herself in her statement of support for the International Conference on

Population and Development (ICPD) namely: (1) responsible parenthood, (2) informed choice, (3) birth spacing, and (4) respect for life.

It should be clarified, however, that this bill does not only protect the life of the unborn from the moment of implantation but that of the mother as well. Hence, the bill seeks to promote the reproductive health of women basically through massive and sustained information campaign on reproductive health rights, care, services and facilities coupled with universal access to all methods of family planning ranging from the natural to the modern which are medically safe and legally permissible. In the event they fail to prevent pregnancy and resort to abortion, they shall be provided with appropriate health and medical care. Despite the provision for humane and compassionate management of post abortion complications, this bill continues to proscribe and penalize abortion which is a crime under the Revised Penal Code.

To contribute to the empowerment and responsible behavior of the youth, this proposed legislation provides for age-appropriate reproductive health and sexuality education that may be initiated by parents at house, and shall be sustained and complemented by formal education in school.

An effective reproductive health education does not only instill consciousness of freedom of choice but responsible exercise of one's rights. According to the United Nations Population Fund: "It has been, repeatedly shown that reproductive health education leads to responsible behavior, higher levels of abstinence, later initiation of sexuality, higher use of contraception, and fewer sexual partners. These good effects are even greater when parents can talk honestly with their children about sexual and reproductive matters."

To guarantee the right of all persons to a full range of information on family planning methods, services and facilities and to ensure their access to an equally full range of medically safe and effective family planning methods at an appropriate time and by competent and adequately trained persons. The bill mandates the Commission on Population (POPCOM) to be the central planning, coordinating, implementing and monitoring body for the comprehensive and integrated policy on reproductive health and population development. Section 5 of the bill specifies the functions of POPCOM as the lead agency in the implementation of the "Reproductive Health, Responsible Parenthood and Population Development Act of 2007".

This proposed Act doses not only seek to protect and promote reproductive health and rights and to empower couples, individuals, more particularly women, and the youth, but it also aims to improve the quality of life of the people in general. Studies show that rapid population growth exacerbates poverty while poverty spawns rapid population growth. Consider the following:

- The Family Income and Expenditures Surveys by the National Statistics Office (NSO) from 1985-2000 disclose that 57.3% of families having many children are poor but only 15.7% of families having two children are poor.
- Large family size is associated with negative determinant of school participation and poor health and survival rates among children. (Orbeta, Population and the Fight Against Poverty, 2003)
- The prevalence of child labor rises, and school attendance falls, with the number of children in the family (Raymundo, 2004). Moreover, the odds of a child becoming underweight and stunted are greater if he/she belongs to a household with 5 or more members (FNRI 1998). This partly explains why poverty tends to be transmitted and sustained from one generation to the next.
- According to the UN Population Fund 2002 Report, "lower birth rates and slower population growth over the last three decades have contributed faster economic progress in a number of developing countries."
- Moreover, the same Report disclosed that fertility declines accounted for 1/5th of the economic growth in East Asia between 1960 and 1995. Additionally, it showed that countries that invest in health, including reproductive health and family planning, and in education and women's development register slower population growth and faster economic growth.

A consistent and coherent national population policy along with sound monetary and fiscal policies and good governance could propel our people toward sustainable human development.

Accordingly, approval of this measure is earnestly sought.

The proposed consolidated bill authored by several House Representatives seeks to limit the family to two children on a voluntary basis. It also includes a provision for mandatory reproductive health and sexuality education for school children starting from Grade 5 and up high school. The bill also seeks to spend 10% of the allocation for LGU to be used for reproductive health. Instead of learning about the birds and the bees, children will be learning about the facts of life formally based on their growing age instead of learning them from the unsavory sources. This is an area where child psychologists can work to help the children understand the facts of life instead of making sex a dirty subject or taboo. The bill also includes the proposed prevention and management of reproductive tract infections, HIV/AIDS and STDs and treatment of breast and reproductive tract cancers and prevention and treatment of infertility. There is absolutely nothing wrong with all these provisions.

The bill includes some provisions that the Church finds immoral. They include requiring hospitals-based family planning methods like ligation, vasectomy and IUD insertion in all government hospitals. Contraceptives shall be made available for those who want them. One good feature of the bill requires that before a marriage licenses to be issued by the Local Civil Registrar, the prospective couples must underwent adequate instructions and information on family planning, responsible parenthood, breast feeding and infant nutrition as certified by the local Family Planning Office before they are granted.

By promoting information on and access to all kinds of family planning methods that are both medically safe and legally permissible, it will enable women and couples to have the freedom of informed choice on what method they want to use. Their decisions will be based on their personal convictions and religious beliefs.

The bill seeks to support a two-child family to stabilize the population. This is solely needed by the country to limit the population for a more sustainable development of the country. Even if the two-child family was implemented immediately, it will still take two generations to stabilize the population. This is because of population momentum. Essentially, population growth is like a moving vehicle. Even if the brake is gradually applied on the vehicle, it will continue to travel a short distance before the vehicle comes to a complete stop. This also works with population. The father who begets two children will continue to live for at least another generation while their two children will beget two more offspring before the grandparents start dying off. Only after then will the population starts to stabilize.

Like all the other bills pending in Congress before, none of the bill ever advocated the use of abortion in dealing with the population issue. On the other hand, all the bills categorically ban the use of abortion as criminal acts as provided in the Revised Penal Code. Abortion is never part of the family planning methods but those who underwent them should be accorded decent health services should their needs arise.

At times, there are some smear campaigns that the use of contraceptives and the management of post-abortion will eventually lead to the legalization of abortion. In fact many countries have legalized contraceptives use continued to criminalize abortion as all the bills now pending in Congress. According to some studies, correct and regular use of contraceptives reduces abortion rates by as much as 85% and negates the need to legalize abortion. (*PDI*, August 3, 2008)

The complaint of prolifers is that the provision on prevention of abortion and management of post-abortion complications is a sinister plot to legalize abortion. This is not what the proponents intended. Legal and illegal abortion is a fact of life in this country. The intention of the law is not to legalize abortion but to help those who were unfortunate to suffer from post abortion complications after obtaining illegal abortions from some unsanitary fly-by-night clinics. Just because they have violated the law does not warrant them to continue suffering the untoward fate just as criminals who are wounded are given proper care to heal them before they are brought to the court of justice.

If prolifers are concerned about the lives of fetuses and women resorting to abortions, they should start to rethink their stand on contraceptives. The experienced in Europe for attaining depopulation is due mainly to legalized abortion. Either we allow the use contraceptives to avoid unwanted pregnancies or have the women resort to abortions to achieve the same goal.

One survey conducted in Manila in 2006 showed that Filipinos at the lowest sector of society would like to have only two or three children but these destitute families still managed to have six or seven children. The main reason is that there is no strong family planning or reproductive program being implemented in the country. We need unhindered programs that would take care of all the reproductive stages of mothers and child, not diehard prolifers dictating what others should or should not do.

Because of the stringent ban on the use of contraceptives, some would-be mothers have given up their unwanted birth and probably had the fetus killed and left them at the church yards as a sign of their protests. A plastic bag with twin fetuses, about six months old, was found at the back of St, Paul the Apostle Church in Barangay Laging Handa in Quezon City. It was left behind by unknown person.[180] Even more shocking was a report that a fetus inside a jar hidden in a basket of fruits was left at the altar as an offering during Sunday Mass in the Quiapo Church in Manila.[181] Another fetus with a detached head was found in a drainage in Iloilo City. It was the third reported news in the months of July and August 2008.[182] The latest is a reported 7-9 months

---

[180] http://www.journal.com.ph/index.php?issue=2008-07-27&sec=1&aid=68034
[181] http://www.prolife.org.ph/article/articleview/1160/1/84
[182] http://www.sunstar.com.ph/static/ilo/2008/07/18/news/

old fetus placed inside a Tupperware and left inside the compound of the Sta. Cruz Church in Quiapo. (*Tanod*, November 14, 2008) before the end of the year, another fetus was found near the entrance of the Quiapo Church. (*PDI*, December 18, 2008) All these would not have happened had the country passed the reproductive health bill a long time ago.

The Catholic bishops of the Philippines have vehemently opposed the reproductive bill by alluding to them as pro-abortion. All who have carefully studied the bills found them to be unfounded. Some bishops had even declared that authors of these bills would be denied the holy sacraments. But the bishops are fearful of declaring it against the ordinary laymen because they may just leave the church in drove. Many of the Church's teachings on morality elsewhere have been discredited. The Church has even the audacity to voice its intention to campaign against the election of politicians favoring reproductive health and the use of contraceptives with total disregard to the separation of the Church as an institution and States.

To show their dismay on what the Church has been saying, Senator Miriam Santiago said that the "natural-law mentality" of the Church in the Middle Ages, especially the Inquisition of Galileo had prevented many advances in physical and medical science is still prevailing in this country today. She also noted that many Catholic teachings on religious liberty and usury that were banned before are now accepted.

An SWS survey released on October 5, 2008 shows that 68% of Filipinos agree that there should be a law requiring government to distribute legal contraceptives and that half of them disagreed with the oppositors that they are abortifacients. Those who agreed numbered 33% while the rest are undecided.

The survey also showed that 54% do not agree that the youth will become promiscuous because family planning is taught in school, compared to 25% who thinks so with 19% undecided. The survey was conducted where 81% of them are made up of Catholics.[183]

The survey was dismissed by prolifers as not reflective of the true will of the people because some of them have been misled by the questions. This has been a convenient excuse if the results are not favorable. It is often said that the voice of the people is the voice of

---

fetus.found.in.drainage.html

[183] http://www.gmanews.tv/story/127193/Solons-laud-SWS-survey-on-family-planning

God, but the Catholic Church disagrees if it runs counter does not adhere to their teachings. The prelates think they have the high moral ground and should be followed consistently even by those of different faith.

The latest survey conducted from October 14 to 27, 2008 and released by Pulse Asia on January 19, 2009 shows that 63% of the adults here are in favor the reproductive health bill, 8% are against while 29% are undecided on the matter. In addition, the survey shows that 82% not only think but insists that the government should not only educated couples regarding modern methods, both natural and artificial methods of family planning but also provide them with services and materials on these methods. Sixty-nine percent agree with the provision of the bill recognizing the rights of women and couples to choose the family planning method they want. Some 44%, most of them under the Class D and E category even express the opinion that the government should pass a law specifying the number of children couples may have. (*PS*, January 20, 2009)

One of the issues raised by prolifers is that some of the devises are actually abortifacients because they allowed fertilization but destroyed the fertilized ovum from implantation in the uterus. This is not true because fertilization was never intended by the devises in the first place. Fertilization does occur because some of the devises are not foolproof. But they are better than the natural family planning method in preventing conception. Furthermore, the added feature of preventing implantation is only incidental to the development of the devises, when the primary purpose of contraception failed.

Contraceptive

Contraceptive is a devise or substance such as drug that is taken orally or through infection to prevent conception or pregnancy. There are many methods of birth controls or contraceptives that are available in the market. They are generally grouped together into natural family planning or fertility awareness methods such as rhythm method, ovulation method, temperature tracking sympto-thermal techniques, withdrawal or *coitus interruptus*; barrier methods such as male and female condoms, cervical cap, intrauterine devices (IUDs), contraceptive sponge, and diaphragms; hormone-based methods such as oral contraceptives popularly known as the pill, progestine-only minipills, Norplant or under-the-skin contraception, and Depo-Provera. Others include the use of vaginal spermicides, and sterilization such as tubal ligation (occlusion) for women and vasectomy for male. Still other methods include morning-after pill, abortion, breast-feeding, etc. Aside from preventing pregnancy, some even provide protection against sexually transmitted diseases and much more.

Most of the contraceptives in used today are safe and do not have life-threatening side effects. It is even safer than undergoing pregnancy and childbirth in good health services which is 1 in 10,000 compared to using pills at 1:200,000; vasectomy at 1 in one million, IUD at 1 in 10 million and absolute no risk in the use of condom. Condoms have the added feature of preventing sexually transmitted diseases. The DOH has come to realize lately that condoms is not intrinsically evil (any action that ought never to be done no matter how much good might result) because one of its personnel was willing to contradict the Church. This would get the DOH in collision course with the Catholic Church since the Church has hope to find the DOH as an ally in the debate against the pro-choice legislators.

Access to all legal contraceptives would have saved many mothers from unwanted birth that forced them to undergo abortions. Contraceptives are not as abhorrent as the Catholic Church would like her faithful to believe. It does not cause any conception in the first place or kills the unborn baby. In one report by the UN Population Fund, about one-third of the 1.4 million unplanned pregnancies in the Philippines ended up in abortion, accounting for at least 400,000 cases of induced abortions, with more than 90% of them carried out on married women. Almost 60% of them relied on the government to supply them the contraceptives. Most of these women are probably not promiscuous and therefore it would be wrong for the Church to claim that contraceptives promote promiscuity. The reason for their pregnancies is that many are poor and have no access to family planning health services unless they are provided by the government. The actual issue of population management is not so much a moral issue but a social and political issue that need to be addressed by the government as guardian of the welfare of the people. The Church's role as moral guardian of the people is an utter failure considering that there are many broken families among Catholics. Christians are among the worst hypocrites in the world even as they go to church and pray together while they cheat on their fellowmen out of their hard earned money. Nowhere is it more rampant than in the realm of sexuality where the sins of fornication and extramarital affairs are rampant.

The rural women are more prone to commit abortions because they are too poor to spend on contraceptives and even less access to maternal health facilities. Many of them are burdened with unwanted and unplanned pregnancies but have few alternatives without government intervention. Most of them end up with induced abortions carried out by risky practitioners such as *hilots* and unlicensed herbal medicine practitioners to terminate the pregnancies that often lead to complication and health risks.

The Catholic Church has been vehemently against the use of artificial contraception because it runs counter to their teaching. It has not been forthright with her faithful by giving the impression that reproductive health right can lead to abortion. The issue is not so much a moral issue that the Church would like her faithful to believe, but an issue of papal supremacy and papal infallibility. The Church has always been adopting unpopular stance against the wishes of the majority. Since the 1930s, the Church's adoption of the use of natural family planning with all its shortcomings could not be countermanded by any pope without offending its survival.

The government as guardian should not allow the Church to impose her will on others, especially the minority of non-Catholics. The country is not owned by the Church that she can have her ways. This is what happened during the administration of ex-Mayor Lito Atienza of Manila. He issued an executive order banning pills and contraceptives in all public health centers and city hospitals forcing many to go underground. Those who persist in selling them were harassed by City Hall officials. Others have to go to other cities for their health needs. Even the veteran health workers of the city were forced to follow the dictates of the mayor for fear of losing their jobs. This timely reproductive health bill should put the issue to rest once and for all as to the rights of the women not to be dictated by a few religious bigots who think they possessed the only morality in town. Only a law could put an end to dictatorship of the few religious bigots who insist on following their religious conviction to the detriment of others. Knowledge should be open to everybody and it can only be attained when information are allowed to be disseminated without fear.

Some contraceptives have uses beyond birth control which is badly needed in these times of sexual revolution. They can be used as a defense against sexually transmitted diseases (STDs) that can be transmitted to a fetus. Some STDs may lead to pelvic inflammatory disease or PID which has become epidemic in some countries. PID occurs when sexually transmitted bacteria travel upward from the vagina to the uterus and fallopian tubes. It can occur after childbirth or abortion. The infection leaves behind scar tissue that may cause infertility or an ectopic pregnancy. If caught early, PID can be treated with antibiotics. Otherwise, it can lead to chronic pain, major surgery or even death. (Winikoff, 2)

The best defense against STDs beside abstinence and exclusive sex with healthy partner is the condom, but they are not foolproof. Despite knowledge that some Catholics are just as promiscuous as others, the Catholic Church refuses to allow their members the use of condoms to avoid contracting STDs. She would rather see them dying of AIDS instead preventing the spread and contracting it and other diseases for that matter. This is borne by the fact that despite promise to come out with a pronouncement with regard to AIDS-infected spouse in Africa several years back during the reign of Pope John Paul II, the Church has yet to make a decision on an important issue of life and death.

Barrier Methods

Those who use the natural family planning hope to avoid pregnancy by abstaining during the period when the egg is released. The egg can only survive for one day and they try to avoid those days that the egg may probably be released. On the other hand, the sperm can survive from three to seven days in the female reproductive tract. Whatever natural family method is used, the women should attend a seminar on which one is best suited for them but the chances of success is small when using only one of these methods. Many women adopt several techniques in combination to natural family methods that include barrier methods, etc. to achieve more success.

Most people considered withdrawal a form of natural planning method. Most Christian denominations except the Catholic Church do not approve of this method. It has to do with the sin of Onan as explained earlier. At any rate, this is not a very reliable contraception method. Premature ejaculation is the reason because it unreliability and the difficulty of controlling ejaculation.

Both diaphragm and cervical cap are barrier methods that cover the cervix and keep sperm from entering the uterus and fallopian tubes where fertilization can take place. The bowl shape device is also used to hold the spermicide to kill the sperm in case any of them penetrate past the cervix. Spermicide is a chemical compound whose active ingredient is nonoxynol-9. The chemical works by fatally damaging the surface membrane of the sperm cell. It comes in the form of creams, jellies and foams.

Intrauterine devices (IUDs) are devices made with progesterone or copper and inserted in the uterus to prevent pregnancy. It interferes with the sperm's ability to move and makes the egg less easily fertilized in ways that are not entirely understood. The IUD also seems to cause an inflammatory response in the tissue lining of the uterus, similar to what one would see in the case of an infection, although it is not caused by the presence of germs. This appears to make the uterine lining less receptive to the implantation of a fertilize egg. (Pasquale, 171) Some studies have found decreased numbers of sperm or no sperm at all in the fallopian tubes of women using IUDs, leading to speculation that the devices somehow alter either the number of the vitality of sperm. (Winikoff, 123)

These devices are popular with women because they do not cause any hormonal changes in the body. It has no side effects and does not interfere with lovemaking and can be effective against pregnancy and STDs because of the presence of spermicide that can kill organisms that caused some of the diseases such as gonorrhea, general herpes, trichomoniasis and syphilis. The rate of failure is about 2 to 20% during the first year of use and improve gradually through experience, and also depending on how often it is used. (Winikoff, 28, 31)

Oral Contraceptive

Oral contraceptives commonly called pills contain a combination of two hormones, an estrogen and a progestin. Both synthetic hormones are versions of the natural female hormones (estrogen and progesterone) produced by the ovaries every month during the menstrual cycle. The hormones in oral contraceptives stop ovulation by acting on the pituitary gland to suppress follicle-stimulating hormone (FSH) and luteinizing hormone (LH). It works by "mimicking pregnancy" because with the steady hormone input from the pills, the brain never receives the signal to release new eggs. Without the eggs, pregnancy cannot occur. The progestin in the Pill also makes the cervical mucus thicker, making it harder for the sperm to get through and it also makes the lining of the uterus thick and unable to support the growth of a fertilized egg, in the unlikely event that there is one. (Pasquale, 118)

One pill, sometime called the minipill is made up of progestin only. It works very much like the pill except that it is taken daily without break. It works by suppressing ovulation and the release of a mature egg from the ovary approximately half the time. Progestin also makes the cervical mucus very thick and sticky so sperms are unlikely to get to an egg and fertilize it. The minipill also slows the movement of the egg through the tubes by making the lining of the uterus thick and unreceptive. (Ibid 134)

Norplant is like the minipill except that it is embedded just under the skin of the inner, upper arm. It can only be done by a trained doctor or health professional. The active ingredient of the capsules is another man-made progestin. Once in place, the active ingredient is slowly and steadily released for five years. The progestin makes ovulation less frequent, makes the cervical mucus thick and sticky and keeps the uterine lining thick and unreceptive to the implantation of a fertilized egg, in the unlikely event that there is one. (Ibid, 145)

Depo-Provera is an injectable contraceptive made up of synthetic progestin. Each injection is effective protection against pregnancy for three months. It works much like the other progestin products above. It has some unwanted side effects such as menstrual irregularities, bleeding and spotting or darkening of the skin around the eyes and face, amenorrhea or not having any periods, weight gain due to increased appetite, pregnancy-like symptoms such as sore breast, nausea, fatigue, and abdominal discomforts. After a year of taking Depo Provera, 57% of the women are not menstruating and 68% after taking the drug for two years. Those who want to get pregnant will have to wait as long as a year after the last injection. Some may suffer from headaches, dizziness, nervousness, loss of scalp hair but increase in body hair, decrease sex drive, leg cramps and bloating. Young women may have low bone mass density in 18% of the cases while 40% of those with over a year of injection.[184]

Incidentally, the developer of the anovulant pill or chemical contraceptive was a Catholic doctor, John C. Rock (1890-1984) and his associates. He also popularized the pill that helps arrest the ovulation process without hindering the act of sexual intercourse. He and his associates do not see any difference between the pill and the use of the rhythm method. (Timothy McCarthy, 323)

The Church's teaching against the use of contraceptives goes against her own action on the matter. During all the time the encyclical *Humanae Vitae* was being discussed, the Church was profiting from the sale of an oral contraceptive called *Luteolas,* made by one of the many companies she owns, the Instituto Farmacologico Sereno. She was forced to dispose of the company after being exposed to the public. (Manhattan, *Billions*, 203, 302; Yallop, 61) It is interesting to note that the Vatican had always been free to invest in profitable companies even if these products were inconsistent with her teachings. Aside from contraceptives, many companies manufacturing products used for killing people were high in her profit goal. (Ibid, 140-149)

---

[184] www.monheit.com/Depo-Provera/side_effects.asp

One of the latest weapons employed by Vatican against contraceptive pill is that it is polluting the environment and is in part responsible for male infertility. It claimed that for years tons of hormones have been released into nature through the female urine, claimed Pedro Jose Maria Simon Castellvi, president of the International Federation of Catholic Medical Association. No explanation was given as to how it could cause male infertility. On the other hand, several organizations dismissed the charge. "Once metabolized, the hormones contained in oral contraceptives no longer have any of the characteristic effects of feminine hormones, according to Gianbenedetto Melis, vice-president of a contraceptive research organization. The hormones contained in the pill such as oestrogen are present everywhere, in plastic, in disinfectants, in meat that we eat, according to Flavia Franconi, of the Society of Italian Pharmacology. (*South China Morning Post*, January 5, 2009)

Sterilization

Sterilization comes in two forms: one for the female and one for the male. For the female it is called tubal occlusion. Healthy women can be fertile until they are in their late 40's while healthy men can be fertile all their lives. It is a surgery done to permanently close a woman's fallopian tubes, which is connected to an ovary in the uterus, so that sperm and egg can no longer meet and fertilized. It is one of the most popular and effective birth control methods available without side effect but is almost irreversible. The same is true with vasectomy for the male. This involves cutting the vas deferens, the narrow tubes through which sperm travel from the testicles to the penis. Except for the absence of sperm, the semen remains exactly the same and sex plays are not affected in any way. (Pasquale, 194)

All the above methods of contraception are meant to stop the fertilization of the egg and the sperm. Not all of them all fool-proof and accidental conception can happen. Some of them, such as IUD, Norplant, Devo-Provera can failed and caused fertilization, but they have the added feature of preventing implantation in the uterus. This is what some prolifers are vehemently against, the accidental fertilization and prevention of implantation in the uterus. These cases rarely happen compared to their effectiveness. At any rate, there is no reason to generalize and discard all methods of contraception as totally anti-life when some of these methods have nothing to do with avoiding implantation of the fertilized eggs.

One of the issues that prolifers refused to face up is the issue of unwanted pregnancies and their unwanted babies. Some of these babies have been aborted as fetus, some left behind by their parents because they cannot afford to give them a decent life or put them up in foster homes for adoption. Some of these foster homes run by nuns and priests have been turned into child abuse center by pedophiles. Foster homes are not exactly conducive to child rearing considering that most of these children needed parenting love that is not easily found at foster homes. Adopted children are seldom treated right when there are natural children around. They are often discriminated upon especially during hard times.

There are many reasons for unwanted pregnancies. Some parents have already too many children to feed and cannot afford another one. Others may have been impregnated by their boyfriend who refused to marry them. They end up becoming single mother. Some cannot afford to care for them and unwillingly have them put up for adoption. Still some have them aborted early in the pregnancies while others have been known to slay the babies after giving birth. Most parents of unwed mothers are willing to have the unwanted child by their daughters. There are some government and NGO programs in place to help unwed mothers but they are not well-known.

If an official survey by the government in the U.S. is an indication, most of the unwanted pregnancies happened to women living below the poverty level. The poor are more likely to have unplanned pregnancies than the parents coming from the affluent families.[185] This is the more reason why contraceptives should be made available to the poor. Otherwise, we will only add more poor souls in our midst with little hope for their future.

In the U.S. any pregnant woman has the right to have an abortion within the first three months of pregnancy. In fact, many predominantly Catholic developed and developing countries have similar laws. The Philippines, under the grip of the Catholic Church when it comes to the issue of sexual behavior finds it hard to unburden itself despite the hardship on their lives. After childbirth, neither the government nor the Church, which is very vocal about having more children ever lends a helping hand to give the child a proper upbringing. Almost all the Church-run educational institutions are programmed for the rich with their high tuition. Only very limited poor students with exceptional talents are accepted for scholarship.

---

[185] http://www.washingtonpost.com/wp-dyn/content/article/2006/05/04/AR2006050400820.html

Pregnancies need prenatal care and rest which many unwanted pregnant mothers cannot afford. Some may be just students trying to earn a degree for her future. Unwanted pregnancies can easily derail such ambition. Once a baby is born, it may not end the college career but it makes it more difficult for them to pursue the course, especially when the woman has to work to bring up the child at the same time.

A people that have been burdened by the Catholic Church for more than four hundred years will find it difficult to change the dictates of the Church. Instead of unshackling the moral issue on family planning, many still cling to her teachings as if it were gospel truth. While the women of the First World countries have smaller families, the poor women of the Third World countries continue to breed more people into the world despite the hardship and difficulties to their daily lives.

One contention of the Church is that life is a gift from God and therefore we should continue to breed as many children into the world as possible. That may be true during Biblical times when the world is so sparsely populated. But I doubt whether it is true today. If God really wanted more babies born into this world, why are there so many babies dying before, during and after conception? Why are there so many children being abused? Why are there so many children growing up and never hearing the words of God and ended up in hell? Why are so many people dying before they survive to old age? God may have been frustrated with mankind to allow so much hardships and atrocities to befall mankind. Or have we become such a sinful nation that we have been forsaken by God?

According to the UNICEF's State of the World's Children report for 2009, the Philippines had one of the highest maternal mortality rates in the world, with about 11 mothers dying every day or 4,500 annually. The lifetime risk of maternal death is 1 in 76 compared to 1 in 8,000 for women in developed countries. Newborn babies also remained high with half of the deaths of those 5 years old and under occurring during infancy. It is one of the 68 developing nations where 97% of all maternal, newborn and child deaths worldwide. The causes of deaths are due to severe hemorrhage, hypertensive disorders, sepsis and problems related to obstructed labor and abortion. The report also added that the Millennium Development Goal of improving maternal health was unlikely to be achieved by the Philippines by 2015. (*PDI*, January 16, 2009) Part of the reasons is that those who underwent abortions are looked down and refused health care. Many of them were forced to go into abortion in the first place because of the failure of the government to support them with the use of contraceptives and the kowtowing of many Catholics to the wishes of the Church. The great socialist, Karl Marx said it right when he declared that religion is the opium of the poor.

One writer on the Internet was so exasperated with the Church that he wrote, "Overpopulation is the result of stupidity & greed. Stupidity and greed on the part of the bishops, priests & nuns who have no experience whatsoever in married life and raising a family yet threaten the poor and ignorant with eternal damnation if they attempt family planning techniques in their married life. Maintaining a growing poor population is actually beneficial to these Catholic terrorists. They can always claim being shepherds to the needy masses who breed like rabbits because of their religious stupidity. If poverty is eliminated, the religious clergy will cease to be a significant organization for the masses. They lose their stature & the millions of pesos they generate from taking advantage of the poor & the ignorant."[186]

AIDS and Condom

Acquired Immune Deficiency Syndrome is caused by a virus called the Human Immunodeficiency Virus (HIV). White blood cells are part of the body's immune system, which normally help the body fight off infections and cancers. The HIV attacks and kills a certain type of white blood cells called lymphocyte, destroying an important part of the immune system. As a result, AIDS patients easily develop infections and cancers which normally do not affect healthy people. There is no known cure for AIDS, though medicines called anti-retrovirals can make life bearable and extend the life of victims.[187]

The HIV is transmitted via body fluids such as blood, blood products, sperm, and vaginal secretions. These in turn can occur in three ways. The most common is sexual contact. The second way is through blood and blood products. Kissing with a person with bleeding gum can also be infectious. Intravenous drug users are at risk from using unsterilized hypodermic syringes or from sharing syringes with infected persons. The third way is babies born from infected mothers. The HIV may pass the infection to an infant during pregnancy and even breastfeeding.[188]

Condoms are the single most effective technology to protect against sexual transmission of HIV/AIDS, a disease that killed up to

---

[186] http://www.tipidpc.com/viewtopic.php?tid=142188
[187] "HIV/AIDS: Basic Facts" www.amrc.org.hk/4710.htm
[188] Ibid

3.5 million people in 2003 alone and infected up to 5.8 million others then. (The figures were taken from the UNAIDS and WHO *AIDS Epidemic Update: December 2003*) Unsafe sexual practices remain the dominant mode of HIV transmission in most regions of the world. In Asia, where an estimated 7.2 million adults and children are living with HIV, low condom use among sex workers and their clients accounts for a substantial proportion of new HIV infections. Widespread and consistent condom use has been shown to reduce the number infected with HIV enough to slow the spread of AIDS. Multilateral organizations such as WHO and the Joint United Nations Programme on HIV/AIDS (UNAIDS) recommend condoms as an essential intervention against HIV.[189] But the Church refused to sanction its use. The reason is that the Church considers using a condom more evil than death by AIDS. (Wills, 189)

Relative to their effectiveness at preventing HIV, however, condoms are a scarce and restricted commodity. WHO estimated in August 2003 that billions of condoms were needed to prevent the escalation of the AIDS epidemic in Asia, including more than one billion condoms in China alone. Globally, the gap between the number of condoms needed for HIV prevention and the number available was estimated in 2000 at anywhere from 15 to 18 billion condoms. In developing countries, many of which rely principally on international donors for condom supplies, only 950 million of the estimated 8 billion condoms needed to achieve a "significant reduction" in HIV infection were donated in 2000. The average international price of a male latex condom is US $0.03, including the costs of sampling, testing and shipping.[190]

In Brazil, the government had found a new source of material for making condoms while preserving the Amazon forest and preventing pregnancy and stopping the spread sexually transmitted diseases. On April 7, 2008, the government started producing condoms from rubber trees in the Amazon rainforest by giving the local people an economic alternative to clearing rainforest land for agriculture and cattle grazing while simultaneously reducing Brazil's dependence on imported condoms that the government gives away as part of a national program to fight HIV/AIDS.[191]

---

[189] "The global condom gap,"
http://hrw.org/reports/2004/philippines0504/5.htm
[190] Ibid
191

The government gave away half a billion condoms for free to Brazilians in its fight to prevent the spread of HIV/AIDS. In fact, a new condom factory was set up to use latex drawn from trees in the Chico Mendes Forest Reserve by small-time rubber tappers. The reserve is named for the internationally renowned rainforest conservationist and rubber tapper who was shot and killed by cattle ranchers in December 1988. More than 550 families will earn a total of 2.2 million reais ($1.3 million) every year, either by gathering latex from the rainforest for the factory or working at the new factory. By giving local people an economic stake in keeping the rainforest intact, the government hopes to lessen the pressure for them to fell trees to earn money through timber sales, agriculture and cattle ranching.

The Vatican's obsession against the use of contraceptives is beyond comprehension. She tried to stop NATO from supplying 'morning-after pills' to victims of Serbian rapes during the ethnic cleansing of Kosovo. The pill would have allayed the future anxiety of mothers or parents who never wanted the child in the first place and may have the fetus aborted. The probability of the baby being killed in the future is a distinct possibility especially when there is so much hatred for the ethnic cleansing. In Africa, the spread of HIV/AIDS did not soften the stand of the Vatican to allow the use of condoms.

Even worse, for years, the Vatican has peddled the view that condoms are not the best safeguard to use against contracting the AIDS virus. According to Cardinal Alfonso Lopez Trujillo (November 2003), the Vatican's spokesperson on family affairs, condoms are too permeable to prevent the spread of HIV/AIDS. This is the same stand taken up by other prelates and repeated spread in all the media around the world.[192] He suggested that the AIDS virus is roughly 450 times smaller than the spermatozoa making it easy to pass through the "net" formed by the condom. For this reason, he urged all Catholics not to use condom. Some priests are even more desperate by saying that condoms are laced with HIV/AIDS.[193] Trujillo was citing studies made by an anti-condom and pro-abstinence-only Medical Institute for Sexual Health in Texas. The truth is that condoms are impermeable by

---

http://environment.about.com/od/biodiversityconservation/a/condoms_forest.htm

[192] "Vatican Continues Lies about Condoms,"
www.libchrist.com/std/vaticanlies.html

[193] BBC News, "Vatican in HIV condom row," http://newsvote.bbc.co.uk/ mpapps/pagetools/print/news.bbc.co.uk.......October 9, 2003

the smallest STD pathogens, including HIV, and provide almost 100% protections against HIV when used correctly and consistently. In October 2003, WHO dismissed allegation of condom porosity as "totally wrong."[194]

The WHO immediately reacted to the unfounded pronouncement, saying that AIDS have already killed 20 million people (25 million by the end of the year 2005 with the loss of about 3.1 million lives in 2005; 570,000 of them children; close to 5 million people were newly infected with the virus in 2005)[195] and continuing to spread especially in Africa where Catholics are growing in numbers. Scientific research by groups such as the U.S. National Institutes of Health (NIH) has found "intact condoms are essentially impermeable and highly effective barrier to transmission of HIV. Without the benefit of any scientific research, Cardinal Trujillo responded that they are wrong and that it is an easily recognizable fact.[196]

The comment of Trujillo would have been harmless and ridiculous were it not for the fact that it is being taken seriously to the detriment of many Catholics and non-Catholics alike. Like other Vatican's doctrines, it is being promoted and instructed by its priests all over the world, including those in AIDS-ravaged countries in Africa, where there are more than 25 million HIV/AIDS victims, and Asia with more than seven million victims for the 2005 alone.[197]

The Church is guilty not only of misinformation; it also restricts Catholic doctors from talking about condoms in poor nations. She prohibits AIDS-testing centers operated by Catholics from handling out condoms to those most at risk of the deadly disease. The only solution is for them to abstain from sex as if her priests are all snow white and sinless. Many of her priests have been guilty of child abuse and suffer from AIDS way above the average for the ordinary citizens. In November 2005, Fr. Joseph Fessio, S.J. admitted on American national television that 400 U.S. priests have died of AIDS.[198]

---

[194] "The global condom gap,"
http://hrw.org/reports/2004/philippines0504/5.htm
[195] AIDS epidemic update by UNAIDS and WHO
[196] "Vatican Continues Lies about Condoms,"
www.libchrist.com/std/vaticanlies.html
[197] Mark Morford, "Slap A Condom on the Vatican…" http//sfgate.com/cgi-bin/article.cgi?file=/g/a/2003/10/17/note1017, October 17, 2003
198 "Nothing Extraordinary?"
www.insidethevatican.com/newsflash/2005/newsflash-dec20-05.htm

AIDS in the African continent is spreading like wildfire and will continue to do so unless the Vatican starts to condone the use of condoms especially when many are being converted to the Catholic faith. Entire towns are being depopulated and the demographic balances in half-dozen countries are being destroyed. In Kenya, where an estimated 20% of people have HIV, the Church condemned condoms for promoting promiscuity and repeated the absurd claim about their permeability. Nairobi Archbishop Raphael Ndingi Nzeki made an absurd claim that the availability of condoms is responsible for the spread of the AIDS virus. Promiscuity is common among the male species even among priests. Many Africans think they can be cured of AIDS by having sex with virgins without using condoms thus spreading the disease.[199]

This is one irresponsive lie that has been responsible for the pandemic plague in the continental Africa. With more than 100 million Catholics[200] and growing very fast, it is bound to continue to suffer the ravages of the disease. Not only is the use of condoms being neglected, it is being put in a bad light. There are some important pointers that should be followed in the use of condoms. Use only high quality condoms and store them in a cool place away from heat or sunshine which can damage the rubber. Practicing how to use condom in private can help. Condom should be used only once. Open the packet carefully, so that condom is not damaged. Check that the condom is neither brittle nor sticky, otherwise use another one. When having sex, wait until the penis goes hard, and put them on before the sex act. Check that the condom is the right way up, with the roll on the outside. With one hand, pinch the top of the condom to press out the air bubble. With the other hand, roll the condom right down to the base of the penis. If a lubricant is needed, use a water-based one and not fat or cream which can damage the rubber. After sex, hold the condom in place and withdraw the penis from the vagina. Take the condom off carefully, making sure that no semen is spilled, wrap it up and dispose of it carefully in a toilet or latrine.[201]

Many studies have been undertaken to study the effectiveness of condoms. In one study, none of the 124 healthy Europeans who used

---

[199] Mark Morford, "Slap A Condom on the Vatican…"
[200] Brendan O'Neill, "Did the Pope spread AIDS in Africa?" www.spiked-online-com/Articles/0000000CA993.htm
[201] "How to use a condom," www.bbc.co.uk/worldservice/sci_tech/features/health/...

condoms every time they had sex with an AIDS infected partner became infected over a two year period. Another twelve out of another 121 Europeans (10%) who did not use condoms became infected. The highest risk was when one partner had full-blown AIDS, rather than just HIV infected. This leads researchers to put the risk of infection at 5% with unprotected sex with an AIDS infected partner. Over 300 other studies consistently show clearly the effectiveness of condom use. Another Italian study also confirms that the infection rate was only 9.7 per 100 in the group that did not use condoms, and 1.1 per 100 years in group that used condoms. Most of the transmission was when the male was the infected partner to the female spouse. Withdrawing before ejaculation reduced the risk of spreading HIV from an infected male to his female partner as expected.[202]

Two of Nevada's legal brothels are making national headlines in a study of condom use conducted jointly by Princeton and Emory Universities. The results of the study were made public in the *American Journal of Public Health*. Nevada prostitutes averaging six clients per day showed that when used correctly, few condoms break and they work well in preventing disease when used properly and consistently.[203]

Although users often fear that the condom will break or fall off during intercourse, studies show that these events rarely occur when condoms are used properly. Many studies conducted in economically developed countries have shown that the incidence of condom breakage and slippage during vaginal intercourse is very low. Typical studies indicate that the rate of breakage for good quality condoms is less than 4%, although rates as low as 1% to 2% have been reported in studies from Zambia, Ghana, and Mali.[204]

The hierarchy at the Vatican, unless they are blind, must be well aware of the connection between the proliferation of the AIDS virus and the non-use of the condoms between infected and non-infected people. This has forced Pope Benedict XVI to call a commission of scientific and theological experts to prepare a document on condom use by those couples where one spouse is suffering with AIDS and other infectious diseases. Cardinal Javier Lozano Barragan, head of the Pontifical Council for Health Care Ministry, said on April 23, 2006, during an interview in Rome with the newspaper *La Republica*, the document

---

[202] Ibid
[203] Ibid
[204] Ibid

would focus, at least in part, on condom use by married couples when one spouse is infected. The commission was called in response to a comment of a retired archbishop of Milan, Cardinal Carlo Maria Martini, who during an interview with the Italian magazine *Expresso* said the use of condoms can be the lesser evil in some situations such as an obligation of spouses to protect his or her partner. However, he ruled out anti-AIDS condom campaigns as promoting sexual irresponsibility. This is the same argument most religious leaders adopted saying that chastity and fidelity are the only fail-safe ways to prevent the spread of the disease.[205] This however is not a realistic approach to solving the promiscuity of people. Christians are just as capable of immorality as non-Christians.

The Catholic Church has always been against all types of contraceptives as intrinsically immoral because they prevent the possibility of procreation. But the proliferation of AIDS, especially in Africa has awakened many prelates to speak out for the relaxation of the ban. So as not to anger the married couple, the Church hierarchy is planning to allow the use of condom for married couples as long as the intention is to prevent a deadly disease and not to prevent procreation. This is a thin line of rationalization just so when the Vatican finally allowed the use of condom will not affect its dogma of papal infallibility. Until the Vatican made a definitive pronouncement on the use of condoms in cases where one spouse is affected, the Church itself is guilty of practicing what she refers to others as something intrinsically immoral and evil. While the Vatican continues to dilly-dally on the issue, Catholics, especially in Africa are dying by the millions. What could be intrinsically evil and immoral, disallowing condoms and likely killing the victims or using condoms and saving lives?

The importance of sex education can be found in the case of Uganda and Senegal. When Yoweri Museveni seized power in 1986 in Uganda, half the population was illiterate. Years of chaos and civil had allowed HIV to spread unchecked without the knowledge of the government because most of the doctors have fled the country. When the president found out the problem, he went into high gear to stop the spread by discouraging risky sex through posters erected along busy roads. A rise in literary from 51% in 1980 to 65% in 1998 allowed the people to learn more about the disease. NGOs and foreign-owned

---

[205] John Thavis, "Vatican preparing document on condom use and AIDS, officials says," www.catholicnews/data/stories/cns/0602330.htm

charitable institutions were also given free rein to educate the people about HIV. They published newsletters that teach adolescents and pre-teens about sex in a straightforward, unpreachy way. Rather seeking to scold or scare, they probe the complexities of puberty relationships and sex. The problem with many young people is not that they are ignorant about AIDS but how to deal with romantic situations. They run romantic role-playing sessions in schools. These help girls learn how to insist on condoms and how to persuade their boyfriends that they are not ready for sex. (Guest, 102-103)

The climate of free debate has led young Ugandans to delay losing their virginity, to have fewer partners, and to use more condoms. Among fifteen-year-old girls, the proportion who said they had never had sex rose from 20% in 1989 to 50% in 1995. Between 1994 and 1997, the proportion of teenage girls who reported ever having used a condom tripled. Between 1992 and 2002, HIV prevalence among women attending urban antenatal clinics fell from almost 30% to about 5%.(Ibid)

In the case of Senegal, prostitution had been under government supervision and prostitutes have been encouraged to use condoms. Blood supply has been screened carefully. Vigorous education has allowed the people to read and people have learned to avoid the HIV virus in 95% of the population. The use of condoms has risen from 800,000 in 1988 to 7 million in 1997, allowing infection rate to stabilize at 20% annually for the ten year period surveyed. (Ibid)

On the other hand, South Africa which has been relatively free of the AIDS virus in early 1990s practically did nothing to stem the tide of HIV. Nelson Mandela, the first black president never mention about AIDS. The government in power did nothing to inform the citizenry of the problem that by 2002, South Africa became the most infected people anywhere in the world. Roughly 4.5 million South Africans carried the virus. (Ibid, 105) Public awareness program and sex education would have made a big difference.

Confidential Vatican reports obtained by the National Catholic Reporter, a weekly magazine in America, have revealed that priests have been exploiting their authority to gain sexual favors from nuns, particularly those from the Third World who are more likely to be culturally conditioned to be subservient to men. The favors include getting certification from the priest to work at certain diocese. In some instances, the priests had made nuns pregnant and then encouraged them to have abortions.

The article in the National Catholic Reporter was based on five documents, which senior women from religious orders and priests have presented to the Vatican over the past decade. They describe a particularly bad situation in Africa. In a continent devastated by AIDS, nuns, and early adolescent girls, are perceived by some as safe sexual targets. Countless cases of nuns forced to have sex with priests were cited. Some were obliged to take the Pill; others became pregnant and were encouraged to have abortions. In one case in which an African sister was forced to have an abortion, she died during the operation and her aggressor led the funeral mass. Another case involved 29 sisters from the same congregation who were impregnated by priests in the diocese. The reports said that the church authorities had done little to tackle the problem. Some incidents of sexual abuse allegedly took place almost within the Vatican walls. The Vatican even tried to downplay the problem claiming they were isolated cases in the midst of the overwhelming majority who are doing good works.

One of the most comprehensive documents claimed that priests considered nuns as "safe" targets and in one case in 1991, a community superior was approached by priests requesting that the nuns be made available to them for sexual favors. When she refused, the priests warned they would be obliged to go to the village to find women and might thus get AIDS. In another report, Sister Maura O'Donohue, a medical doctor, reported incidents of sexual abuse in 23 countries including India, Ireland, Italy, the Philippines and the United States. She said she was told about priests encouraging the nuns to take the Pill by telling them that it would prevent HIV. Others were encouraged to take abortion.[206] In November 1998, Sister Marie McDonald of the Missionaries of Our Lady of Africa, presented a paper *The Problem of the Sexual Abuse of African Religious in Africa and Rome* to the Council of 16 delegates from the Union of Superiors General, an association representing men's religious communities based in Rome. Still the rapes continue. When a mother superior reported to her archbishop that 29 nuns in her community had been impregnated by priest, she was publicly removed from her post.[207] There seems to be a conspiracy of silence when it came to treating the inferior sex by the domineering male prelates.

There are actually many ways to discourage parents from having more babies to achieve the goal. Once the governments are willing to realize the problem, resources should be channel to bring the population down. Government propaganda, increase family planning services, sex

---

[206] http://www.ivanfoster.org/article.asp?date=4/1/2001&seq=2
[207] http:www.talkingfive.com/Rome_watches.htm

education and awareness programs, improving women's status, and economic incentives can help a lot. Many of these solutions have been implemented in various ways and in various countries with great success.

The Chinese government has been able to control population by giving economic incentives for families with less than two children. The incentive includes a one-time reward of money and rice. If that child does not live to maturity, the couple is allowed another. The child will also receive a private plot of 70 m^2 of land, compared to 50 m^2 for a child in a larger family.[208] In some part of China, single-child incentives are reinforced with other incentives such as sick leave for birth control surgery, bonus leave for later marriage and delayed pregnancy, nutrition allowance after sterilization and compulsory abortion should the contraceptive failed. Those who have received incentives earlier have to refund the incentives should they failed to limit the number of children in the future. Others are penalized for unauthorized child with a fine of 10% of their wages for seven consecutive years while those with two extra children are fined 20% of the parents' wages for 14 consecutive years. For violation of the birth control policies for workers in government offices, they became ineligible for day-care or hardship subsidies, no pay increase or bonuses for three years, etc.

Another incentive that is widely used is limiting the tax write-off or deduction for more than two children. At present, our tax code allows deductions for up to four minors. This should be reduced to two children while increasing the deduction for one child. Raising the marriage age is one way. Giving incentive for delayed pregnancy for married couple is another.

A little more drastic actions include monetary child penalty for having more than the allowed number of children, elimination of maternity leave or benefits, cash payment for sterilization, end of welfare benefit after having two children, elimination of government-subsidized medical care and scholarship for having more than the allowed children, etc.

Unless we limit our population growth to a more manageable level in the future, more drastic actions would have to be undertaken such as compulsory abortion for excess children, mandatory abortion for out-of-wedlock pregnancies, eugenics for poor and retarded mothers, putting the children up for adoption by childless couples, etc.

---

[208] http://www.sixpak.org/vince/overpopulation.htm

Sometimes it takes innovation to accomplish the goal. A national nonprofit group is offering alcoholics and drug addicts in Tucson, Arizona, $300 if they get permanent or long-term birth control. The organizers of Project Prevent told the press that are will to pay for the tubal ligation, vasectomy, or other birth-control procedure for addicts who cannot afford them. The idea is to reduce the number of fetuses damaged by exposure to drugs or alcohol, and to reduce the number of children born to incompetent, neglectful parents. That is accomplished by preventing conception.[209] The idea in this case is to have quality children instead of quantity. This is what our country needs, more quality children instead of pathetic children with little hope for improving their living standard. Maybe it is time for government to refuse marriage license for alcoholics and drug addicts to encourage them to stop the bad habits for the sake of the fetus.

Abortion

Abortion is not a method of contraception because it does not prevent conception. It is often resorted to for unwanted pregnancies. No woman is her right mind would risk pregnancy only to terminate the fetus through surgery. Unless they are given other options to avoid pregnancy, the risk of getting pregnant is high. According to an Alan Guttmacher Institute survey in the early 1990s, 92% of fertile women in the U.S. use some form of contraception. But 43% of all unintended pregnancies are experienced by couples who practice birth control. A very small percentage of women who do not use contraceptives accounts for the 57% of unintended pregnancies. (Winikoff, 197)

Another study conducted by the Alan Guttmacher Institute and U.P entitled, *The Incidence of Induced Abortion in the Philippines: Current Level and Recent Trends*, conducted from 2002 to 2005 shows the correlation of abortion and natural family planning method. The data were gathered from 1,658 Philippine hospitals to estimate abortion incidents from 1994 to 2000 and projected nationwide. It found that the use of natural planning method in Metro Manila during the term of Mayor Lito Atienza was responsible for the highest number of induced abortions, increasing it by 33.72% from 104,585 in 1994 to 139,853 in 2000. One out of three pregnancies in Metro Manila result in abortion, lamented one congresswoman. While the

---

[209] http://www.azstarnet.com/opinion/272491.php

Visayas experienced a decrease in the use of modern methods, induced abortions increased by 113.6% from 34,375 in 1994 to 73,427 in 2000.

Furthermore, the study noted that Filipinas who resorted to induced abortion could not avail of modern family planning because of the high cost of contraceptives; the social and psychological stigma attached to the methods of service; the devolution of health services to local government, which discourage or punish the use of modern family planning; the prejudice of the husband and misconceptions about modern family planning. It is for these reasons why contraceptives should be widely available for all women who want to avoid pregnancies instead of resorting to abortion in the future.

In an unprecedented act on his third day in office, newly elected U.S. President Barack Obama repealed the rules set down by his predecessor restricting federal money for international organizations that promote or provide abortions overseas. Under the old policy, organizations receiving funding from the USAID cannot use the funds to support safe and even legal abortion.

"For the past eight years, they have undermined efforts to promote safe and effective voluntary family planning in developing countries," Obama said of the restrictions. "For these reasons, it is right for us to rescind this policy and restore critical efforts to protect and empower women and promote global economic development." He planned to restore financial support for the UN Population Fund and promised to reach out to all sides for discussion of how to reduce unintended pregnancies. His action is expected to touch a lot of debates in the coming days. (*PDI*, January 25, 2009)

The news was criticized by the Vatican but was greatly hailed by the women rights and advocators of pro-choice movements. According to Clara Rita Padilla, executive director of EnGendeRights, "The Vatican's position on access to safe and legal abortion is contrary to international human rights law." She added that in August 2006, the Committee on the Elimination of Discrimination against Women (CEDAW) had urged government to consider the problem of unsafe abortion as a matter of high priority and review the laws relating to abortion. CEDAW has noted that the lack of access to contraceptive methods and family planning services, as well as restrictive abortion laws tend to coincide with the prevalence of unsafe abortions that contributes to high rates of maternal mortality. Criminalizing abortion does not eliminate the practice, but only makes it dangerous for women who undergo clandestine and unsafe abortion, she noted. (*PS*, January 27, 2009)

The insistence of the Catholic Church outlawing abortion has been repudiated in her own domain in Europe. Countries predominated by Catholics that have approved abortion include Spain, Belgium, France, Italy, Poland, Hungary, Colombia, and Mexico, to name a few. Even the predominantly Protestant countries such as the U.S. have approved abortion on demand during the first trimester of the pregnancy.

References

Asimov, Isaac and Pohl, Frederick, *Our Angry Earth*, 1991
Bello, Walden, *The Political Economy of Permanent Crisis in the Philippines*, 2004
Benjamin, Daniel and Simon, Steven, *The Age of Sacred Terror*, 2002
Bernstein, Carl and Politi, Marco, *His Holiness*, 1996
Berry, Jason, *Lead Us Not into Temptation*, 2000
Bokenkotter, Thomas, *A Concise History of the Catholic Church*, 1990
Bongiorno, Lori, *Green Greener Greenest*, 2008
Brown, Lester, *Tough Choices*, 1996
Brown, Lester & Ayres, Ed (ed), *The World Watch Reader*, 1998
Coffel, Steve, *The Lifesaving Guide to Good Water*, 1989

Davis, Devra, *When Smoke Ran Like Water*, 2002
Deb, Dr. Swapan C., *Environmental Management*, 2004
Dolan, Edward, *Our Poisoned Waters*, 1997
Earthworks Group, the, *Earth Limited*, 1991
Friedman, Thomas L., *Hot, Flat, and Crowded*, 2008
Goodfield, June, *The Planned Miracle*, 1991
Green, Vivian, *A New History of Christianity*, 1996
Guest, Robert, *The Shacked Continent*, 2004
Hart, Matthew, *Diamond*, 2001
Hatkoff, Amy & Klopp, Karen Kelly, *How to Save the Children*, 1992
Hutchinson, Robert, *Their Kingdom Come*, 1998
Jocano, F. Landa, *Slum as a Way of Life*, 1975
Kungstler, James Howard, *The Long Emergency*, 2005
LaPierre, Wayne, *Guns, Crime, and Freedom*, 1994
Liqueur, Walter, *The New Terrorism*, 1999
Levy, Elinor and Fischetii, Mark, *The New Killer Diseases*, 2004
Lynas, Mark, *Six Degrees*, 2008
MacCarthy, Timothy, *The Catholic Tradition*, 1998
Manning, Joanna, *Take Back the Truth*, 2002
North, Richard D., *Life on a Modern Planet*, 1995
Pasquale, Samuel A, and Cadoff, Jennifer, *The Birth Control Book*, 1996
Pearce, Fred, *When the Rivers Run Dry*, 2006
Pilger, John (ed), Tell Me No Lies, 2005
Pohlman, Edward (editor), *Population: A Clash of Prophets*, 1973
Power, Samantha, *"A Problem From Hell"*, 2002
Reeve, Simon, *One Day in September*, 2000
Ranke-Heinemann, Uta, *Eunuchs for the Kingdom of Heaven*, 1990
Robbins, David, *Heavy Traffic*, 2005
Robbins, Ocean & Solomon, Sol, *Choices for Our Future*, 1994
Roberts, Paul, *The End of Oil*, 2004
Robertson QC, Geoffrey, *Crimes Against Humanity*, 2002
Robinson, Andrew, *Earth Shock*, 2002
Simontacchi, Carol, *The Crazy Makers*, 2007
Spignesi, Stephen J., *Catastrophe!: The 100 Greatest Disasters of All Time*,
        2002
Steinman, David, *Diet for a Poisoned Planet*, 1990
Steinman, David & Wisner, N. Michael, *Living Healthy in a Toxic World*,
1996
Steyn, Mark, *America Alone*, 2006
Weiner, Jonathan, *The Next One Hundred Years*, 1990
Weintraub, Skye, *The Bacteria Menace*, 2002
Wills, Garry, *Papal Sin*, 2000
Winikoff, Beverly, Wymelenberg, and Editors of Consumers Union, *The
        Contraceptive Handbook*, 1992
Yallop, David, *In God's Name*, 1984
Zimmerman, Richard, *What Can I Do to Make a Difference?*, 1991

* 9 7 8 9 7 1 9 2 6 8 8 8 8 *